Global Legal Insights
Merger Control

Second Edition
Contributing Editors: Nigel Parr & Ruth Sander
Published by Global Legal Group

GLOBAL LEGAL INSIGHTS - MERGER CONTROL
SECOND EDITION

Contributing Editors
Nigel Parr & Ruth Sander

Marketing Managers
Suzanne Millar
Andrea Rubino

Sales Support Manager
Toni Wyatt

Production Editor
Andrew Schofield

Senior Editor
Penny Smale

Group Consulting Editor
Alan Falach

Publisher
George Archer

Group Publisher
Richard Firth

We are extremely grateful for all contributions to this edition.
Special thanks are reserved for Nigel Parr & Ruth Sander for all their assistance.

Published by Global Legal Group Ltd.
59 Tanner Street, London SE1 3PL, United Kingdom
Tel: +44 207 367 0720 / URL: www.glgroup.co.uk

ISBN 978-1-908070-55-5
ISSN 2048-1292

Printed and bound by CPI Group (UK) Ltd, Croydon, CR0 4YY
March 2013

CONTENTS

PREFACE

We are pleased to present the second edition of *Global Legal Insights – Merger Control*. This edition contains 35 country chapters, and is designed to provide general counsel, government agencies and private practice lawyers with a comprehensive insight into the realities of merger control, as well as practical, policy and strategic issues. As part of the *Global Legal Insights* series, this book goes beyond an overview of the black letter law, adding important colour and texture to the basics of the merger control regime in each jurisdiction.

In producing this new edition, the publishers have again collected the views and opinions of a group of leading competition law practitioners from around the world. The various authors have been given considerable scope to express their own professional judgment on policy and strategy, and to offer useful practical insights into the more subtle workings of their home regime. They were each asked to offer personal views on the most important recent developments in their own jurisdictions, with a free rein to decide the focus of their own chapter.

As noted in the preface to the first edition, one of the great attractions of comparative analyses is the possibility that what is happening in one jurisdiction may inform understanding or influence developments in another jurisdiction: we hope that this latest edition will go some way towards facilitating these insights.

Nigel Parr and Ruth Sander,
Ashurst LLP

Albania

Shpati Hoxha
Hoxha, Memi & Hoxha

Overview of merger control activity during the last 12 months

In 2012, the Albanian Competition Authority (ACA) reviewed a very small number of concentrations (overall total of 10 transactions).

Such a limited number of filings is naturally correlated with the small size of the Albanian economy, as well as to the generally low understanding and knowledge of domestic investors with respect to the obligations they have under the Competition Law (Law no. 9121 dated 28.07.2003 on Protection of Competition). The number of merger control filings in front of the ACA remains low, notwithstanding the fact that in 2012, Law 10317[1] lowered the turnover thresholds.

If we consider the number of transactions reviewed by the ACA during 2012, the ratio of concentrations related to domestic undertakings and related to off-shore undertakings (undertakings that either have subsidiaries or distribution networks in Albania) was 50-50.

Out of the total five transactions pertaining to domestic undertakings, the ACA applied fines for late filing for two domestic transactions. Late notification fines were imposed for one off-shore transaction.

The average value of fines imposed during 2012 by the ACA was €800 for late notification, in two cases. In one case it applied a symbolic fine of less than €1 (see below).

Potential higher fines for failure to notify may be applied to a fourth transaction reviewed during 2012, which is currently still under investigation.

As a general consideration, the overall value of the fines that the ACA has imposed on undertakings for breach of the Competition Law (overall for all types of infringements) is relevant for the Albanian market[2]. However, the reported fine collection rate for 2011 is very low[3].

In 2010 Parliament approved a new law on Administrative Contraventions with the aim of facilitating the collection of fines and public sanctions. However, as of this date, the new legal provisions on administrative contraventions have not proved to be more effective than the previous ones[4].

Out of 10 transactions reviewed by the ACA during 2012, nine have been cleared and at the time of this update, one transaction is still under investigation.

Based on the statistics of the ACA, the number of reviewed concentrations since its establishment (2004) has been growing on a steady basis[5], and considering the peak of 11 notifications in 2008, the international financial crunch has not impacted the limited amount of files landing on the Albanian Competition Authority's desk.

New developments in jurisdictional assessment or procedure

Due to the limited number of concentrations reviewed by the ACA, as well as the fact that unconditional clearance has usually been granted, there are no significant jurisdictional developments as to assessment or procedure for transaction clearance.

Competition-related court cases in 2012 mainly related to issues of penalties imposed by the ACA and their collection.

In 2010 the Albania Parliament approved Law 10317[6], which provided for significant amendments to the Competition Law.

These amendments extended filing terms of merger control notifications from 7 to 30 days after the conclusion of the concentration agreement, thus providing the parties with the necessary time to prepare the notification form and relevant documentation.

The amending law additionally clarified that the establishment of full-function joint ventures is a notifiable concentration under the Competition Law.

Another significant amendment relates to the reduction of the applicable fines for failure to notify a concentration. Under the new provisions, failure to notify a concentration is deemed to be a minor infringement punishable with a fine of up to 1% of the total turnover in the preceding business year. Under the original text, failure to notify a concentration was deemed to be a serious infringement, and as such punishable with a fine of between 2% and 10% of the total turnover in the preceding business year.

The notification fees for merger control procedures in front of the ACA were amended in 2012, and are now at the level of:

- Obtainment of the notification form – approx. €50 (if the acquiring undertaking has a domestic turnover of approx. €1.4m to 7m) and €100 (if the acquiring undertaking has a domestic turnover higher than approx. €7m).
- Obtainment of temporary authorisation – approx. €1,000 (if the acquiring undertaking has a domestic turnover of approx. €1.4m to 7m) and €2,000 (if the acquiring undertaking has a domestic turnover higher than approx. €7m).
- Obtainment of final authorisation – approx. €1,800 (if the acquiring undertaking has a domestic turnover of approx. €1.4m to 7m), and €3,500 (if the acquiring undertaking has a domestic turnover higher than approx. €7m).

The ACA has further provided for case law with respect to the notification obligations of the parties in the transaction. In one of the cases it reviewed during 2012,[7] the acquiring party failed to submit the notification to the ACA within the requested deadline, based on the argument that the transaction was not effective until it had been approved by the EU merger control authority.

The ACA clarified that the standstill obligations under EU Merger Regulation (or other national laws) do not suspend the obligation to notify a concentration under the Albanian Law. The ACA applied leniency for this case, however, and therefore imposed a symbolic fine of 100 Lek (less than €1).

Key industry sectors reviewed and approach adopted to market definition, barriers to entry, nature of international competition etc.

From an industry standpoint, the concentrations of domestic undertakings were related to the media, real estate, gambling and oil distribution sectors, whilst on the other side, the off-shore concentrations were related to the banking, automotive, food and tobacco industries.

Out of 10 reviewed cases, two concentrations related to transactions between banks, thus making merger control files for banking sector the most numerous ones for 2012. The reviewed transactions related to off-shore concentrations between European banks[8] operating in Albania[9]. Such concentrations were therefore deemed to indirectly affect the Albanian banking market.

In both transactions, the ACA considered the relevant product market as the market of banking services for individuals (retail banking) and corporate banking. Main banking services included in the relevant product market were: the collections of deposits, the granting of loans (retail and corporate) as well as the offering of investment products in treasury bonds.

From a geographical point of view, the relevant market was considered to be the national market for banking services, therefore the Albanian domestic market.

The domestic banking market in Albania is composed of 16 second tier banks, 13 of which are fully owned by international banks.

As such, the ACA considers domestic banking market in Albania as prone to frequent changes with regard to ownership, geographical coverage and product development.

The Competition Authority cleared the mentioned transactions as it considered the off-shore concentrations not to be harmful to the domestic banking market, since the concentrations did not cause a change in the structure and shares of the domestic relevant market.

Key economic appraisal techniques applied e.g. as regards unilateral effects and co-ordinated effects, and the assessment of vertical and conglomerate mergers

The ACA appraises the effects of mergers based on its guidelines (of 2009) on non-horizontal and conglomerate mergers, as well as on horizontal mergers. These guidelines substantially mirror the relevant EU Commission guidelines on the assessment of non-horizontal mergers, and the guidelines on the assessment of horizontal mergers.

Non-horizontal and conglomerate mergers

The ACA guidelines consider non-horizontal mergers as generally less likely, with respect to horizontal mergers, to significantly impede effective competition.

Similarly to the EU guidelines, the ACA non-horizontal merger guidelines envisage settings and behaviours for both coordinated and non-coordinated effects for vertical mergers (i.e. input foreclosure – customer foreclosure, ability to foreclose, incentive to foreclose, existence of deterrent mechanisms, reactions of outsiders, overall likely impact on prices and choice etc.).

Under its non-horizontal merger guidelines, the ACA considers that the following post non-horizontal merger situations are unlikely to cause concern:
* 25% market share; and
* 1,800 – HHI[10].

These market shares and HHI are considered as practical indicators (and not absolute legal presumptions) of the lack of anticompetitive effects of a concentration, and the ACA will not extensively investigate such concentrations, unless:
* it involves companies that are likely to significantly expand in the near future, e.g. because of a recent innovation;
* there are significant cross-shareholdings or cross-directorships;
* one of the merging parties is highly likely to disrupt coordinated conduct; or
* there are indications of past or ongoing coordination, or facilitating practices.

Horizontal mergers

According to the ACA guidelines on horizontal mergers, the market shares and levels of concentration are the main indicators to be considered during the evaluation of a concentration, from both the viewpoint of the participating undertakings as well as for their competitors and the market as a whole.

Normally the ACA should consider the actual market shares, however, possible projections of future changes (i.e. entire market expansion etc.) shall not be disregarded.

With regard to the levels of concentration, as for the non-horizontal merger guidelines, the HHI is taken as a basis for the evaluation.

The guidelines explain that a market share of 50% or more constitutes a serious indicator for a dominant position. However, a firm whose market share remains below 50% after the merger may also raise competition concerns, in view of other factors such as the strength and number of competitors, the presence of capacity constraints, or the extent to which the products of the merging parties are close substitutes.

On the side of the HHI, if its level is below 1,000, the transaction is unlikely to establish competition issues.

The ACA may also identify that there is no particular implication for the horizontal competition if the HHI is between 1,000 and 2,000, and the delta is below 250. The same is envisaged with regard to post-merger HHI above 2,000 and delta below 150. The ACA guidelines list the same special circumstances to be evaluated (i.e. a merger involves a potential entrant or a recent entrant with a small market share; one or more merging parties are important innovators in ways not reflected in market shares, etc.).

Approach to remedies (i) to avoid second stage investigation and (ii) following second stage investigation

The ACA reports to date only one concentration, in relation to which it started second stage investigations.[11] The main remedy adopted in this case was to closely monitor the insurance market in order to guarantee free and effective competition.

Given the lack in number of cases where the ACA has started second stage investigations, practices for the approach and remedies to avoid and/or follow up a second stage investigation have not been developed.

Key policy developments

There have been no key policy developments in Albania over the past year.

In 2012 the ACA approved the Merger Control Instructions, which aim to further explain how the ACA implements provisions of Law no. 9121 dated 28.07.2003 on Protection of Competition, as well as its Merger Control Regulation. In addition, the Merger Control Instructions aim to provide further examinations to undertakings on what the ACA deems to be a modifiable concentration (inducing full function joint ventures), how to calculate turnover, and other matters relevant for merger control procedures.

Reform proposals

There are no currently published key reform proposals in Albania.

* * *

Endnotes

1. The current turnover thresholds are as follows: the parties' combined annual worldwide turnover exceeded €50m (approximately) and the annual turnover of at least one of the parties in Albania exceeded €1.5m (approximately); or the parties' combined turnover in Albania exceeded €2.8m (approximately) and the annual turnover of at least one of the parties in Albania exceeded €1.5m (approximately).
2. Under the 2011 Annual Report the Competition Authority (http://www.caa.gov.al/uploads/publications/Raporti%20Vjetor%20%202011-2012.pdf) states that the total fines it has imposed amount to approximately €7.5m.
3. Pursuant to the ACA 2011 Annual Report, the collection rate is 24%.
4. For more information see also: http://www.internationallawoffice.com/newsletters/Detail.aspx?g=57328918-7c1e-421b-99c4-ae90b7d800e6.
5. Under the 2011 Annual Report, the Competition Authority states to have reviewed a total of 50 transactions, of which in: 2004 – 2; 2005 – 0; 2006 – 4; 2007 – 9; 2008 – 11; 2009 – 8; 2010 – 6; 2011 – 10.
6. For more details see also http://www.internationallawoffice.com/newsletters/Detail.aspx?g=087f380f-a296-4afb-a703-a6a9381f3771 and http://www.internationallawoffice.com/newsletters/Detail.aspx?g=d0952f46-a096-4acd-baa0-2503f2a0809c.
7. Transfer of Emporiki Bank of Greece S.A from Credit Agricole S.A. to Alpha Bank S.A.
8. Transfer of Emporiki Bank of Greece S.A from Credit Agricole S.A. to Alpha Bank S.A., and acquisition of control of Eurobank Ergasias S.A from National Bank of Greece S.A.
9. Credit Agricole, Alpha Bank and NBG have active operations in the Albania banking market.
10. The Herfindal-Hirschmann Index (HHI) is used by ACA as an internationally recognised measure of market concentration.
11. Strengthening of the share of Vienna International Group in the domestic insurance market, following the acquisition of the Intersig Sh.a (clearing decision no. 199 Dated 15.09. 2011).

Shpati Hoxha
Tel: +355 42 274558 / Email: shpati.hoxha@hmh.al

Shpati Hoxha is a founding Partner of Hoxha, Memi & Hoxha. He specialises in Commercial and Corporate Law, Antitrust, IP & IT. He has been involved in a number of privatisations and M&A transactions and has assisted several international investors in corporate governance, antitrust & competition regulations, IP registration and administrative/judicial enforcement matters.

In addition, Shpati has been called to assist in several business law pieces of legislation, such as the commercial registry law, the company law and recently new cross border merger law (effective from 2012). Shpati is a Local Partner for the World Bank's Doing Business project.

Shpati received in 2002 a J.D. in comparative commercial law from the Turin University Law School. He is author and co-author of several publications in corporate and competition law. His native language is Albanian and he is fluent in English and Italian.

Hoxha, Memi & Hoxha

Rr. Nikolla Tupe no. 5, First floor, Tirana, Albania
Tel: +355 42 274558 / Fax: +355 42 244047 / URL: http://www.hmh.al

Australia

Peter Armitage
Ashurst Australia

Overview of merger control activity during the last 12 months

Merger control activity in Australia has been slightly down on previous years because of a general downturn in merger activity, but it continues to be a central aspect of competition law administration and enforcement in Australia.

Unlike many other jurisdictions, Australia's merger control regime is voluntary. The regime derives from the prohibition, in section 50 of the *Competition and Consumer Act* (Cth) *2010* (the **CCA**), on any direct or indirect acquisition of shares or assets which would have the effect, or likely effect, of substantially lessening competition in a market in Australia. This prohibition is enforced by the Australian Competition and Consumer Commission (the **ACCC**). The ACCC has extensive investigative powers and may investigate any transaction to ascertain whether it contravenes the merger prohibition. The ACCC may seek an injunction from the Federal Court of Australia (the **Federal Court**) to block a proposed acquisition. The ACCC (or any other interested person) may, in the case of a completed transaction, apply to the Court for a divestiture order or, if the vendor is involved in the contravention, a declaration that the transaction is void and order that shares or assets be deemed not to have been disposed of by the vendor, and that the vendor refund part or all of the payment made to it. The ACCC may also seek court orders imposing substantial financial penalties on the merger parties in respect of a completed merger.

There is no mandatory pre-merger notification requirement in Australia, but the ability of the ACCC to investigate any transaction, and the serious risks of court action to prevent a transaction from closing, or for divestiture and penalties post-closing, has resulted in merger parties voluntarily seeking "informal clearance" from the ACCC.

The following table contains some key statistics concerning the voluntary informal clearance process.

	2012 financial year (to 30 June)	2011 financial year (to 30 June)	2010 financial year (to 30 June)
Matters assessed – no review required	250	236	153
Reviews undertaken	90	140	168
Not opposed	60	110	131
Finished – no decision (including withdrawn)	17	14	16
Publicly opposed outright	1	3	8
Confidential review – opposed or ACCC concerns expressed	6	4	6

	2012 financial year (to 30 June)	2011 financial year (to 30 June)	2010 financial year (to 30 June)
Resolved through remedies	3	7	4
Variation to remedy accepted	3	2	2
Variation to remedy rejected	0	0	1
Total matters assessed and reviews undertaken	340	376	321

The table indicates that the ACCC is "clearing" an increasing proportion of transactions without undertaking market enquiries (the first phase of the ACCC's informal clearance process). This is quite a marked change and suggests a growing confidence on the ACCC's part concerning its ability to identify potentially contentious transactions. As a corollary, the ACCC is devoting more time and resources to the detailed consideration of those potentially contentious transactions.

Strategic considerations – information sharing between regulators

The ACCC's desire to consult with other regulators concerning multi-jurisdictional transactions, combined with its unusual statutory ability to disclose confidential information, may be of particular significance in some transactions.

The ACCC's practice, when assessing a transaction which is also being assessed by competition regulators in other jurisdictions, is to consult with those jurisdictions.

Unlike many other competition regulators the ACCC does not, however, require a confidentiality waiver in order to disclose confidential information to other regulators. Section 155AAA of the CCA allows the ACCC to disclose information provided to it in confidence to a "foreign government body" (which includes anti-trust authorities), if the ACCC Chairperson is satisfied that particular confidential information will enable or assist the foreign government body to exercise its functions or powers.

The ACCC's ability to disclose confidential information applies not only to confidential information disclosed voluntarily to the ACCC but also to information which it has obtained, from the merger parties or third parties, by exercising its compulsory powers. The ACCC can require, for the purposes of its informal merger clearance process, any person to provide their verified written answers to questions, to produce documents and to answer oral questions on oath. Information obtained in this way (such as strategy documents, competitor analyses and marketing reports), may be relevant to the assessment of the transaction in other jurisdictions as well as in Australia, and may be of considerable interest to regulators in those other jurisdictions.

To date the ACCC's practice has been to request confidentiality waivers from the merger parties, allowing it to exchange and discuss confidential information about a particular transaction with overseas competition regulators. The terms of the confidentiality waiver proposed by the ACCC are, however, frequently more permissive and generous than those required in other jurisdictions, and the negotiation of the terms of the waiver is necessarily affected by the ACCC's statutory powers to disclose confidential information without a waiver.

Key industry sectors reviewed and the significance of international competition

Australia is a relatively isolated island nation with a relatively small population and substantial natural resources. As a consequence its economy has some sectors which are very concentrated and relatively insulated from international competition, and other sectors which are export-focused and subject to intense global competitive pressures. Even though the statutory prohibition requires a focus on markets in Australia, the mixed nature of the economy means that merger reviews in Australia oscillate between the assessment of transactions involving purely domestic considerations, and others which require an understanding of global markets.

Sectors in which domestic considerations predominate include retailing. Retailing, especially in grocery, liquor, hardware/home improvement and petrol, is very concentrated in Australia, with a small number of very large market participants, some very small competitors and suppliers that range from very large to very small. As a consequence, allegations of misuse of market power and cartel conduct in these sectors are frequently made by politicians and commentators. The ACCC is pressured to investigate these allegations and also to scrutinise proposed acquisitions in those sectors very closely. Consequently a disproportionate number of informal merger clearance investigations concern the acquisition of grocery, liquor, hardware or petrol retailing businesses or sites. In many instances the transaction value is small, but the merger parties and the ACCC devote very substantial resources to the informal merger clearance process. The outcome of many of these assessments depends on the state of competition in the relevant retailing activity within a 3-5 kilometre radius of the target business.

By contrast, the assessment in other sectors requires an appreciation of competitive pressures from countries which are thousands of kilometres away from Australia. For example, a merger of two natural gas exploration/production companies cannot be assessed without reference to the international supply of, and demand for, LNG. This is because any analysis of natural gas pricing in Australia following the merger must take into account the role of export markets in setting the domestic price.

Key economic appraisal techniques applied e.g. as regards unilateral effects and co-ordinated effects

The ACCC's approaches to analysing unilateral effects and coordinated effects, as set out in its *Merger Guidelines, 2008,* are uncontroversial and similar to the approaches in many jurisdictions. The ACCC, however, does not always rigorously follow its stated approaches.

For example, the ACCC controversially refused to clear the acquisition of the petrol retail assets of Mobil Oil Australia by Caltex Australia Limited, on the basis that the proposed acquisition would create a greater risk of more stable and more effective coordinated pricing. Petrol retailing in Australian cities is characterised by regular weekly pricing cycles in which a period of discounting is followed by a price-restoration phase. The ACCC considered that Caltex was a leader in the price-restoration phase, and concluded that its proposed acquisition of Mobil's retail outlets would significantly increase the likelihood that the restoration process would be effective. As part of its counterfactual analysis the ACCC assumed that, if the Mobil outlets were purchased by some smaller operators, they would have less incentive to participate promptly in the restoration phase. This view seemed to be based on the dubious presumption that the behaviour of a small participant in a market was a reliable indicator as to how it would behave once it became a much larger participant in the market.

The ACCC's analysis of unilateral and coordinated effects is also informed by the need, if it wishes to prevent a transaction from proceeding, to prove to the satisfaction of the Federal Court that the acquisition would be likely to have the effect of substantially lessening competition in "a market". In other words, in a contentious merger review, the ACCC must prepare for the possibility that it will need to prove, on the balance of probabilities, in court proceedings, the existence of the market in which it contends the anti-competitive effect of the merger would be felt.

Notwithstanding this underpinning need for clarity about market definition, the ACCC has, in recent years, focused increasingly on the closeness of competition between the merging parties, rather than on market definition and market shares. The ACCC will endeavour to ascertain the relative intensity of rivalry between different products and suppliers within the relevant markets. If the merger parties are each other's closest competitors, the ACCC will explore the ability and incentives of other rivals to become close competitors by entering the merged entity's product or geographical space.

This increased focus on closeness of competition might suggest that the ACCC would more routinely utilise economic techniques in its analysis. Natural experiment-type evidence, concerning customer behaviour in circumstances where the product of one of the merging parties was not available, is very likely to be found useful by the ACCC, but other techniques, such as calculations of cross-elasticities of demand for relevant products and diversion ratios, do not appear to enjoy much support from the ACCC. If the ACCC is receptive to such analyses, it does not disclose that in any of the merger assessment documents – Statements of Issues and Public Competition Assessments – which it publishes. The experience of merger parties is that the ACCC appears to prefer anecdotal evidence from market participants on these issues.

There is also no public evidence that the ACCC is receptive to techniques such as the Upward Pricing Pressure theory. At least one Commissioner of the ACCC has expressed considerable doubt about the utility of such analyses, because of the frequent shortcomings in the quality of the data, and the inability to publicly test the data.

Remedies

The ACCC's stated preferences are for structural remedies (i.e. divestitures), which are to be offered on a fix-it-first basis. The ACCC states in its Merger Guidelines that "wherever practicable, divestiture should occur on or before the completion date of the merger, particularly in cases where there are risks in identifying a (suitable) purchaser or asset-deterioration risks".

Despite its preference for fix-it-first remedies, the ACCC continues to accept post-closing divestments. The ACCC's requirements for post-closing divestments are, however, becoming increasingly onerous. Typically the merger parties will be required to agree to: detailed and increasingly onerous hold-separate obligations until the divestment has occurred to an ACCC-approved purchaser; a short period for the sale process to take place; a fire-sale mechanism for sale of the divestment business by a third party agent if it is not sold within the divestment period; and, in some cases, the inclusion of 'crown jewels' in the assets to be sold by fire sale.

The ACCC is also increasingly inserting itself into the divestment process. In the undertakings accepted in relation to a merger of parts of two funeral services businesses, the ACCC required that the parties seek its approval of the following aspects of the divestment:
- any technical assistance or interim supply agreements proposed with the purchaser of the divestiture business;
- the separation and management plan; and
- the marketing and sale plan for the 'fire sale', if required.

Despite the ACCC's preference for structural remedies, it will clear some transactions on the basis of behavioural remedies. The ACCC recently reviewed the acquisition of Austar United Communications Limited by Foxtel Management Pty Limited, which will combine the two market participants in Australia who had substantial customer bases in subscription television. The ACCC concluded that, in the absence of the proposed remedies, the proposed acquisition would, among other things:
- foreclose potential future competition between Foxtel and Austar in the supply of subscription television services; and
- allow the merged entity to leverage its substantial customer base in the national market for retail supply of subscription television services, to acquire IPTV rights on an exclusive basis, and to constrain competitive entry or expansion by other parties.

The ACCC was, however, prepared to clear the transaction on the basis of a suite of behavioural undertakings offered by Foxtel. The core undertaking is that Foxtel will not acquire certain distribution rights to specified categories of independent content on an exclusive basis. The distribution rights include IPTV and some mobile distribution rights, but do not include most satellite and cable distribution rights. There is considerable interest in the ACCC's ability to monitor compliance with these undertakings.

Key policy developments

In 2011 the ACCC failed to obtain a court injunction to prevent the acquisition of approximately 80 Franklins grocery retail stores by Metcash, a wholesaler of groceries to independent retailers. The ACCC had failed at trial and on appeal and, after the appeal, the Chairman of the ACCC stated that the ACCC "agrees that in relation to any acquisition, it must consider the likely effect on competition, based on commercially relevant facts, assessments and evidence, and not speculative possibilities".

This statement appears innocuous but it has meant that the ACCC is more sceptical of economic theories and quantitative economic analysis, unless the key assumptions of those theories and analysis are clearly supported by the facts. It has also meant that the ACCC's investigations of some mergers are more thorough, intrusive and time-consuming.

The ACCC's scrutiny of information supplied by the merger parties, and by third parties in potentially contentious transactions, has intensified. Increasingly the ACCC appears to be operating on the basis that it should be equally sceptical of information and propositions supplied by opponents of a transaction as it is of information supplied by the merger parties. This even-handedness will result in improved decision-making.

The ACCC has also become more willing to exercise its compulsory investigative powers to obtain documents and information from merger parties and third parties. This has, in some transactions, added considerably to the time taken by the ACCC to make its final decision to seek to block a transaction, or permit it to proceed.

Reform proposals

The problem of so-called creeping acquisitions – that is, the acquisition by a substantial market participant of a small business such as an independent grocery retail outlet – continues to vex politicians and some media commentators, but there are currently no reform proposals which would affect merger control in Australia. The coalition parties, which are currently in opposition in the Federal Parliament, have promised a "root and branch" review of competition law if they are elected to government in September 2013. It is unclear whether such a review would result in any material change to the merger control law in Australia.

Peter Armitage
Tel: +61 2 9258 6119 / Email: peter.armitage@ashurst.com
Peter is a senior partner in the Ashurst Australia competition practice. He is consistently ranked as one of Australia's leading competition lawyers by Chambers and APL500. Peter has been involved in numerous merger clearances for a wide range of acquisitions and joint ventures in Australia and has developed innovative merger remedies and successfully defended one of the rare ACCC court challenges to a merger.

Ashurst Australia

Level 36, 225 George Street, Sydney, NSW, Australia
Tel: +61 2 9258 6119 / Fax: +61 2 9258 6999 / URL: http://www.ashurst.com

Austria

Dr Dieter Thalhammer & Judith Feldner
Eisenberger & Herzog

Overview of merger control activity during the last 12 months

Any merger notification falling under the scope of the Austrian Cartel Act 2005 ("ACA") needs to be filed with the Austrian Federal Competition (*Bundeswettbewerbsbehörde;* "FCA"). Phase I begins on the day of receipt of the notification by the FCA. Upon receipt of a notification, the FCA has to forward two of the submitted copies of the notification to the Federal Competition Prosecutor (*Bundeskartellanwalt;* "FCP"). Within the statutory waiting period of four weeks (Phase I), the FCA and the FCP have to carry out a preliminary assessment of the envisaged transaction in order to decide whether to clear the merger in Phase I or to initiate Phase II proceedings at the Cartel Court. If none of the Statutory Parties (FCA/FCP) applies for Phase II within the waiting period of four weeks, the notified concentration is cleared. If the Statutory Parties raise concerns in Phase I, the parties to a concentration may offer remedies in order to have the deal cleared subject to conditions and/or obligations instead of facing a long Phase II proceeding at the Cartel Court.

In 2012, 307 concentrations were notified with the FCA, while only 281 concentrations were notified in 2011. In 2009 and in 2010 there were significantly fewer notifications (2009: 213; 2010: 238).

In 2012, 98% and in 2011, 97% of all notified concentrations were cleared already during Phase I. However, as regards some cases, this high track record could only be achieved by intense negotiations during Phase I and in pre-notification consultations. The Austrian merger control rules do not provide for any formal pre-notification consultation, but informal contact between the notifying party and the FCA are common practice in complex cases. Such informal consultations enable the FCA to review a contemplated acquisition even prior to formal notification, and could enable the parties involved to avoid Phase II proceedings even in difficult cases. Nonetheless, no official figures regarding pre-notification consultations exist.

In 2012, 249 concentrations out of the 307 notifications were cleared due to lapse of time, e.g. the Statutory Parties did not apply for Phase II. Only three out of these 249 concentrations were already cleared in Phase I due to commitments. In cases which will not have a material impact on the Austrian market, it is possible to file a request to the Statutory Parties to reduce the waiting period of four weeks. In practice, the Statutory Parties do not grant a waiver of their right to initiate Phase II proceedings (reducing the statutory waiting period) before around 16 to 18 days after publication of the summary of the notification on the website of the FCA. In 2012, 46 waivers were granted (this is about 15% of the Phase I clearances).

An in-depth review of a notified concentration by the Cartel Court (Phase II) only takes place upon written request filed by one of the two Statutory Parties. In Phase II the waiting period extends to up to five months starting from the day of receipt of the first request for instituting Phase II. In principle, a request to initiate Phase II is filed if a merger raises serious concerns, or if Phase I was too short to review a complex transaction in sufficient detail. The "stop-the-clock" mechanism which will be introduced to the Austrian merger control regime by the current reform entering into force on 1 March 2013 will provide more flexibility in this respect (see below, "Key policy developments").

During Phase II, the Statutory Parties and the notifying parties still have the opportunity to further discuss possible options for a "quick clearance". It is common practice for the Cartel Court to grant the

Statutory Parties and the notifying parties some time prior to the first hearing to continue discussions on possible remedies. If the notifying parties are able to offer remedies that would outweigh the concerns of the Statutory Parties, the Statutory Parties withdraw their requests for Phase II and the merger is cleared subject to the obligations and/or conditions agreed upon.

Within the five months granted to the Cartel Court by the ACA, the Cartel Court must either prohibit or clear the notified concentration. Clearance decisions may be subject to obligations and conditions. If the Statutory Parties have withdrawn their request for the institution of Phase II proceedings, or if the waiting period of five months has elapsed without any formal decision of the Cartel Court, the Cartel Court has to adopt a resolution on the immediate termination of the review proceedings. In both of these cases, the notified concentration is cleared. In 2012 only one final decision in merger control proceedings was adopted by the Cartel Court (without any conditions or obligations). This case, namely *Telekom Austria/Yesss!*, will be summarised in detail below. In the last years, no concentration has been formally prohibited. However, this does not mean that all critical concentrations have been cleared by the Cartel Court. The notifying parties usually withdraw the notification if clearance may not be expected, or if clearance may only be expected subject to unacceptable conditions and/ or obligations. In 2012 seven notifications were withdrawn by the notifying parties. There is no information publicly available as to the reasons for which the notifying parties withdrew them.

Out of the high number of notifications in 2012, only a few cases went to a Phase II in-depth investigation by the Cartel Court. In three cases, both the FCA and the FCP requested an in-depth review before the Cartel Court. In one additional case, only the FCA applied for Phase II proceedings. Many cases subject to a Phase II investigation are cleared shortly after initiation of Phase II, as the reason for a Phase II request often is that the Statutory Parties have been provided with insufficient information for the assessment of the concentration.

Decisions of the Cartel Court are subject to judicial review by the Supreme Cartel Court. If an appeal against the decision of the Cartel Court is lodged, the Supreme Cartel Court has to decide on the appeal within two months. The Supreme Cartel Court may only decide on legal aspects, and not on factual aspects.

Annual reports providing more detailed data on the activities of the FCA are published on the website of the FCA. However, the annual report for 2012 has not yet been published.

In 2012, the acquisition of Yesss! by Telekom Austria was clearly one of the major Austrian merger control cases. Yesss! was Orange Austria's "no-frills" mobile virtual network operator. The divestiture of Yesss! was allegedly carried out as a preparatory step in order to facilitate clearance of the *Hutchison3G/Orange Austria* case by the European Commission. Both transactions were reviewed by the authorities in parallel proceedings and the European Commission, the FCA and the Austrian telecom regulator (*Telekom-Regulierungsbehörde RTR*) cooperated quite closely.

Already during pre-notification consultation the FCA circulated more than 50 information requests to mobile operators, resellers, mobile virtual network operators and fixed network operators. After several months of pre-notification talks and after such market testing, the FCA expressed serious concerns regarding the envisaged concentration for the following reasons: unilateral effects (Yesss! was considered a close competitor to Telekom Austria's "no frills" brand, "bob"); increased likelihood of undertakings coordinating their behaviour (only three competitors would have remained in the market after completion of the concentration); there would have been fewer incentives for the undertakings to compete; and finally, Telekom Austria was considered as already holding a very strong market position pre-merger. Due to these concerns, the Statutory Parties requested the initiation of a Phase II proceeding at the Cartel Court. However, the in-depth investigation in Phase II did not confirm these original concerns and the Cartel Court cleared the concentration without conditions or obligations in November 2012. The Statutory Parties did not appeal.

New developments in jurisdictional assessment or procedure

In 2012, few significant new developments may be reported in terms of jurisdictional assessment or procedure.

Third parties' rights

If a concentration has already been implemented and the "clearance" was based on incorrect or incomplete information, the Cartel Court may upon request order that the undertakings concerned have to take measures to diminish or eliminate the effects of the concentration, if the Statutory Parties or the Cartel Court would have decided differently had the correct and complete information been provided.

In October 2012, the Austrian Supreme Cartel Court adopted an interesting decision in this respect. Thus far, it has been unclear whether a third party may apply for the implementation of such subsequent measures, or whether only the Statutory Parties have the right for such application. In its decision, the Supreme Cartel Court concluded that all undertakings having a legal or economic interest may, in principle, file such applications. Theoretically, this clarification would have constituted a major improvement of third parties' rights in Austrian merger control proceedings. This is particularly true as the Austrian merger control regime only provides for a limited protection of third party rights. In Phase I and Phase II, third parties are only entitled to hand in written complaints. However, third parties making use of such right do not become a party to the proceedings, nor do they have the right to access to the files.

However, due to the lack of information that third parties usually have access to, it is questionable whether a third party is actually in a position to substantiate its application, e.g. how the third party shall substantiate that incorrect or incomplete information has been provided by the notifying party. Ultimately, the improvement of third parties' rights following this decision will only be of "academic interest", as the reform of the Austrian Cartel Act entering into force on 1 March 2013 explicitly states that only the Statutory Parties will be entitled to file such application.

Violation of the Austrian standstill provisions

Companies implementing the concentration before receiving clearance are subject to fines. At the request of one of the Statutory Parties, the Cartel Court may impose on each undertaking that has intentionally or negligently violated the standstill obligation a fine of up to 10 per cent of the total worldwide turnover generated in the last business year. Moreover, agreements infringing the standstill obligation are null and void under civil law, unless the concentration is subsequently cleared. So far the highest fine (€1.5m) for the implementation of a concentration without prior notification has been imposed in *Lenzing/Tencel*. Compared to previous years, more decisions imposing fines for the reason of infringing the standstill obligation were adopted by the Cartel Court in 2012. The fines ranged from €2,500 to €25,000.

International activities of the FCA

The FCA is a member of the European Competition Network ("ECN") and the International Competition Network. Whenever parallel merger filings are handled in several Member States of the EU, the competition authorities involved typically liaise with each other in order to coordinate their proceedings. In November 2011, Best Practices on cooperation between EU National Competition Authorities in merger review were adopted. The Best Practices aim at fostering cooperation and the sharing of information between NCAs in the EU, for mergers that do not qualify for review by the European Commission itself (one-stop-shop review) but require clearance in several Member States. As already set out above, the FCA and the European Commission are also closely cooperating if a certain case requires.

The FCA is also a member of the Marchfeld Competition Forum ("MCF") whose members are – besides the Austrian FCA – the national competition authorities of Bulgaria, Estonia, Hungary, Latvia, Lithuania, Poland, Slovakia, Slovenia, Croatia and Switzerland. In 2010, the MCF launched a platform for information exchange between these national competition authorities on notified concentrations. By using this platform the national competition authorities can retrieve information on the participating countries where a concentration has also been notified.

Practice has shown that the FCA is particularly active in this respect, whenever filings are also made in other countries. For this reason, it is important to coordinate parallel filings well, in order to avoid unnecessary inconsistencies in the various notifications.

Furthermore, in 2012 the FCA signed a joint declaration on the establishment of an Energy Community Competition Network ("ECCN") whose members are – beside the Austrian FCA – the national competition authorities of Albania, Croatia, Macedonia, Moldova, Bosnia-Herzegovina, Montenegro, Serbia, Ukraine, Kosovo and Armenia. The aim of the ECCN is the establishment of a network of national competition authorities in the energy sector.

Key industry sectors reviewed and approach adopted to market definition, barriers to entry, nature of international competition, etc.

As regards media concentrations, three particularities exist under the Austrian merger control regime: Firstly, concentrations between parties in the media market are subject to specific rules for the calculation of the relevant turnover. When assessing the established thresholds, the turnover of media and media service undertakings has to be multiplied by 200, while the turnover of media support undertakings has to be multiplied by 20. As a consequence, apparently small transactions in the media sector can trigger the thresholds. Secondly, in general, if a concentration falls within the scope of the ECMR, the "one-stop-shop" principle applies and no filing is required in Austria. However, if the transaction qualifies as a media concentration, a parallel notification in Austria is required. In such a case the material assessment of the Austrian competition authorities is limited to whether the concentration will have an impact on the plurality of the media. Thirdly, in case of a media concentration, media-specific information needs to be submitted in the notification. The FCA tends to scrutinise media concentrations in detail.

In the last years, the FCA thoroughly assessed numerous concentrations regarding the food (retail) market. In September 2011 the FCA cleared a concentration in the dairy sector already in Phase I (after intensive pre-consultation), since the notifying party committed to ensure access to milk procurement markets. To address the FCA's concerns, the parties committed to introduce an additional distribution channel for raw milk, by committing to procure milk from non-member farmers at the generally available index price for milk exports. Thereby, farmers who were not members of an association and whose contracts of sale to other dairies were discontinued were offered access to the market at market price.

In the last months, the FCA has carried out several dawn raids in the food retail market. Due to the knowledge the FCA might have gained from these inspections, it can be expected that the FCA will scrutinise future concentrations related to the food retail market even more intensely.

In 2012, the FCA continued its efforts regarding the motor fuel sector. The FCA submitted information requests and examined upstream and downstream markets as well as the retail prices for motor fuels at petrol stations.

Key economic appraisal techniques applied

The FCA has set up an organisational department for economic analyses. This department is composed of six members. The FCA joins forces with the regulators in the field of energy, telecommunications and railway (e-control, RTR, Schienen-Control GmbH).

On the website of the FCA, a handbook on market definition and the application of the Herfindahl-Hirschman index composed by external economic experts, has been available since 2006. However, when publishing the handbook, the FCA referred to the fact that the handbook would not be binding for the FCA.

In Phase II the Cartel Court must assess the notified concentration in detail. In order to be in a position to carry out such an in-depth review, usually an external court expert who prepares an expert opinion on the impact of the concentration is appointed by the Cartel Court.

Approach to remedies

The ACA provides that a notified transaction leading to a dominant position may still be cleared if adequate remedies (conditions or obligations) are offered by the undertakings concerned. As the ACA does not specify which types of remedies are acceptable under the Austrian merger control regime, a wide range of structural and behavioural remedies could be offered to clear a concentration. Hence, any behavioural or structural remedy will be accepted if it sufficiently addresses the identified competition concerns.

Behavioural remedies are commitments to follow a certain course of conduct in the future, for example to maintain certain products, not to change prices, not to solicit certain employees, or not to set up interlocking directorships. Structural remedies lead to a direct change in the structure of the market, for example by selling a specific business or shareholding. In Austrian practice, behavioural remedies are more common than structural remedies.

The undertakings concerned may offer remedies during Phase I and Phase II. If specific competition concerns are discussed during Phase I, the undertakings concerned may, in the course of Phase I, submit proposals for remedies in order to convince the Statutory Parties that an in-depth review by the Cartel Court is not necessary. In Phase II, if the notifying parties are able to offer remedies that would outweigh the concerns of the Statutory Parties, the merger is cleared by the Cartel Court subject to the obligations and/or conditions agreed upon.

In 2012, three concentrations were cleared in Phase I subject to commitments:

Fresenius/Fenwal (BWB/Z-1815) concerned the market for blood products for transfusion. Fresenius committed to abstain from selling certain products in Austria, which Fresenius and the target already offered outside of Austria, for a period of five years. Moreover, Fresenius committed to inform the FCA every six months about its participation in tenders and its other activities on certain markets.

In *SPB Beteiligunsverwaltung GmbH/Dr Anna Bauthen Gesellschaft m.b.H.* (BWB/Z-1850) the notifying party intended to acquire the entire share capital of the target "step by step" over the upcoming years by 2015/2017. It appears that the Statutory Parties took the view that one single notification covering all steps in the upcoming years would not allow a proper assessment, as it would not be foreseeable which market conditions would exist in 2017. In order to prevent a Phase II proceeding, the notifying party limited the merger notification to the acquisition of only 25.1% of the shares of the target ("the first step"). Further increase of the shareholding qualifying as a concentration (particularly reaching 50% of the shares) will have to be notified at a later stage.

In *Valida Holding/Siemens Pensionskasse* (BWB/Z-1890) the notifying party intended to acquire 100% of the shares of a pension fund, and all shares in an employees' severance pay fund (*Mitarbeitervorsorgekasse*). The Statutory Parties expressed competition concerns as regards the management of certain investment and risk associations by a consortium. Consequently, the notifying party committed not to conclude a consortium agreement for the next three years. However, if customers ask for such services, the notifying party may refer to the Statutory Parties and ask for an exemption to the commitment. The notifying party also committed to grant the FCA access to certain business documentation regarding the investment and risk associations.

In two cases the FCA withdrew its request for a Phase II proceeding after the notifying party had offered commitments:

In *Knauf/USG* (BWB/Z-1831) the FCA expressed concerns regarding the building and auxiliary materials sector, as the acquirer offered a product (ceiling panels) which in the future could be sold bundled with a certain product of the target's portfolio (subconstructions) and requested a Phase II proceeding. After committing not to sell its ceiling panels only bundled with subconstructions but also separately, the FCA withdrew its request and the concentration was cleared.

Ankünder/Progress Außenwerbung/PSG Poster Service/ISPA Werbung (BWB/Z-1818) concerned outdoor advertising activities. In the view of the FCA, the acquirer Ankünder held already pre-merger a strong market position on a certain regional outdoor advertising market. This position would have been strengthened due to the intended transaction. As regards scrollers (rolling boards and poster lights), the transaction would have increased Ankünder's market share from around 50% to 100%. The FCA and Ankünder agreed on several commitments. *Inter alia* Ankünder committed to allocate a certain amount of poster lights to competitors on the basis of predefined and advantageous conditions. Consequently, the FCA withdrew its request and the concentration was cleared.

Key policy developments

After a broad public consultation, an amendment to the ACA was adopted in December 2012. This reform will enter into force on 1 March 2013.

The major amendment regarding merger control relates to the introduction of "stop the clock" provisions in Phase I and II. In Phase I the notifying party may apply for a two-week prolongation of the four-week period. Phase II may respectively be extended from five to six months upon request of the notifying party. These new provisions will grant more flexibility. Under the current regime, the FCA or the FCP have sometimes applied for a Phase II proceeding only because the information needed (e.g. replies to information requests addressed to competitors and customers) for a proper assessment of the case could not be made available within the four-week period.

Furthermore, the supervision of dominant undertakings will be extended by means of lower market share thresholds for the statutory presumption of collective dominance ("oligopoly presumption") being in force from 1 March 2013 onwards; accordingly, a group of undertakings will be deemed to be dominant if it holds: (i) a market share of at least 50% and consists of three or fewer undertakings; or (ii) a market share of at least 66.6% and consists of five or fewer undertakings. The statutory presumption of collective dominance must be rebutted by the undertaking(s) concerned, providing evidence that there is still effective competition between them.

So far, decisions of the Cartel Court are not publicly available. Only short summaries of such decisions can be retrieved from the FCA's website. For this reason, if a decision of the Cartel Court is not challenged before the Supreme Cartel Court, only very little information is available. This practice so far has led to a lack of transparency as, in particular, aspects of market definition are not covered in the mentioned summaries. Following the reform, non-confidential versions of the decisions adopted by the Cartel Court as of 1 March 2013 will be publicly available.

Reform proposals

In 2010, the Austrian Social Partners including the Austrian Trade Union Federation, the Austrian Economic Chamber, the Austrian Federal Chamber of Labour and the Austrian Chamber of Agriculture presented the study, "Future of Competition Policy in Austria". In this study, the Austrian Social Partners proposed *inter alia* amendments to the Austrian merger control regime. Some of these proposals are covered by the recent reform of the ACA. Currently, a follow-up to this study is carried out and the following topics regarding Austrian merger control are on the agenda:

According to the EU Merger Regulation, a merger will be prohibited if it would significantly impede effective competition ("SIEC"-test). The creation or strengthening of a dominant position is a primary form of such competitive harm. The SIEC-test is not applied in Austria yet. In Austria, the competent authorities (mainly the Statutory Parties in Phase I and the Cartel Court in Phase II) have to review a notified concentration in order to assess whether the contemplated transaction creates or strengthens a dominant position in the relevant market(s). In any further reform, such inconsistency might be eliminated.

Other issues probably dealt with in the next reform are (i) whether "step acquisitions" (successive increase of shares), and (ii) whether parallel transactions only partially qualifying as notifiable concentrations, shall be regarded and assessed jointly as "one single transaction".

Dr Dieter Thalhammer
Tel: +43 1 606 36 47 / Email: d.thalhammer@ehlaw.at
Dieter Thalhammer is head of the Competition Law Practice Group of Eisenberger &
Herzog. Dieter is a renowned expert on European and national competition law and
he represents clients in a broad range of industries including transport, automotive,
energy, telecommunication, banking and finance, consumer goods and postal services.
He has a strong focus on merger control cases as well as on cartel and abuse-of-
dominance cases. Moreover, Dieter has advised a number of clients regarding the
implementation of their competition law-related compliance programmes.
Dieter holds a *doctor iuris* degree from the University of Vienna and an LL.M. from the
University of Saarbrücken (LL.M. Eur.). After six years with Freshfields Bruckhaus
Deringer, Dieter joined Eisenberger & Herzog in 2005. Dieter is the author of several
articles on competition law and lectures at the University of Graz. He speaks German
and English.

Judith Feldner
Tel: +43 1 606 36 47 / Email: j.feldner@ehlaw.at
Judith Feldner is an associate with Eisenberger & Herzog in Vienna, where she is a
member of the Competition Law Practice Group. Her focus is on merger control as
well as on cartel cases. Moreover, she advises clients regarding the implementation of
their competition compliance programmes. She studied law at the University of Graz
and the Universitat Autònoma de Barcelona. Before joining Eisenberger & Herzog
she used to work as research assistant at the Department of European Law at the
University of Graz where she is still lecturing.

Eisenberger & Herzog

Vienna Twin Tower, Wienerbergstraße 11, 1100 Vienna, Austria
Tel: +43 1 606 36 47 / Fax: +43 1 606 36 47 58 / URL: http://www.ehlaw.at

Bulgaria

Peter Petrov & Meglena Konstantinova
Boyanov & Co.

Overview of merger control activity during the last 12 months

In 2012, the Bulgarian Commission for the Protection of Competition (the "CPC" or the "Commission") initiated **24** proceedings relating to the control of concentrations, and adopted 28 decisions on merger control. The number of merger control decisions was remarkably lower than that achieved in previous years. By comparison, in 2010 the CPC initiated 37 proceedings; in 2009 – 54; in 2008 – 81; and in 2007 – 74.

The significant decrease was the result of two factors: firstly, the major contributing factor was the global economic slowdown which resulted in Bulgaria, as in other parts of the world, in a significant decrease of merger activity, which has not been significantly overcome since. Secondly, the new jurisdictional thresholds for Bulgarian merger control almost doubled the turnover threshold at the end of 2008, and introduced a second cumulative turnover threshold as regards the different parties to the transaction or the target. This, coupled with decreased turnovers, contributed to fewer mergers being caught by merger control.

It should be noted that the decreased workload from regular merger cases has allowed the CPC recently to step up its enforcement practice in respect of cases which were not notified to it in previous years, even though the respective transaction did constitute a notifiable concentration. While in each of 2007 and 2008 only three sanctioning decisions were issued for failure to notify a merger, in 2009, 12 sanctioning decisions were imposed for breaching the notification obligation. In 2010, five sanctioning decisions were issued, and in 2012, one.

Recent years saw another notable change – an increasing number of merger decisions are being appealed by third parties (not only by competitors and other undertakings, but also by consumers). This was made possible by the expansion of the range of interested parties who may appeal a merger control decision, outside the range of competitors and organisations of competitors, by the 2008 Protection of Competition Act (PCA). Now any person or entity who can demonstrate sufficient legal interest to appeal against a merger control decision can do so. The track record of the Supreme Administrative Court shows that the court has never annulled a decision by which a concentration was cleared, outside the context of a sanctioning proceeding. The court has, however, annulled partly some of the decisions of the CPC by which it imposed sanctions for failure to notify a concentration.

New developments in jurisdictional assessment or procedure

Throughout the years the Commission has continually expanded its case-law on the range of transactions which may be considered to fall within the definition of a concentration and therefore be subject to assessment under merger control rules.

Thus, by its Decision No. 45/29.01.2009, *Case KZK-744/2008, Maxima Bulgaria*, the CPC imposed a sanction on a daily consumer goods retailer because it considered that the entry into four long-term rent agreements for supermarkets constituted a notifiable concentration, and the respondent had failed in its obligation to receive prior authorisation from the Commission. Upon judicial review, in two instances, by Judgment No. 9867/20.07.2009 and by Judgment No. 1509/05.02.2010, the Supreme Administrative Court disagreed with the Commission and annulled the decision, because it noted that a long-term rent agreement could constitute a concentration only where it led to the acquisition of all or part of an undertaking, and thereby achieved a structural change in the relevant market. As none of the landlords in the case in question operated in the fast-moving consumer goods markets, the leased properties did not constitute the acquisition of control (by way of the long-term lease of assets) over parts of the undertaking of the landlord. By its more recent case-law (Decision No. 955/14.09.2012. *Case KZK-727/2012, Eko Bulgaria*), the CPC seems not to have backed down completely from considering that a long term rent agreement of an essentially immovable asset (in this case a petrol station) could constitute a concentration, however it declined jurisdiction in this particular case on account of the holding that the rent agreement's duration of four years was insufficient to lead to a lasting change of control over part of the undertaking of the seller, and therefore the transaction did not constitute a concentration on this particular occasion.

In several earlier decisions, the CPC held that the granting of a concession to operate an existing facility could constitute a concentration within the meaning of the PCA and would therefore be subject to notification and clearance by the Commission. In its Decision No. 944/19.07.2011 on *Case KZK-551/2011*, the CPC reconfirmed this view and cleared the acquisition by LUKOIL Neftohim Burgas AD of sole control through a contract for the concession on the Operational Port Area Rosenets, which is part of port Burgas – a public transport port facility of national importance. The concession was granted by the Bulgarian government for a period of 35 years. The case provides an interesting insight into the interplay of the Commission's jurisdiction since, in addition to being the authority in charge of merger control, it has powers of administrative review over decisions issued by other authorities in public concession procedures.

Finally, the CPC seems to have expanded its interpretation of the concept of a "person or undertaking, controlling one or more undertakings" in its Decision No. 1488/13.12.2012 *Case KZK-663/2012, Ivan Angelov*, where the reasons seem to suggest that the authority will regard an individual who holds shares in undertakings, as an undertaking himself/herself, even if this shareholding is non-controlling. In other words, the CPC seemed to suggest that holding shares alone is an economic activity, which could constitute the business of an undertaking, and if such individual/undertaking acquires control of another undertaking or a part of it, then this would constitute a concentration for the purposes of Bulgarian competition law and, subject to meeting the relevant thresholds, it would need to be notified to the authority.

Key industry sectors reviewed, and approach adopted, to market definition, barriers to entry, nature of international competition etc.

The main economic sectors in the Bulgarian markets that were the focus of the Commission's attention in merger control cases were:
- trade with fast-moving consumer goods – three decisions in 2012;
- fuel retailing – three decisions in 2012; and
- electronics retailing – two decisions in 2012.

2012 saw a landmark case where a merger to monopoly was cleared unconditionally, following a phase 2 (extended) proceeding. By its Decision No. 64/19.01.2012 on *Case KZK-1471/2011, Gradski Transport EAD, Varna,* the CPC opened an extended investigation concerning the intention of the Varna city transport municipally owned public transportation operator to acquire its only rival Transtriumph, and thereby establish a 100% share in the market of mass public transit in the city of Varna. The CPC suggested a distinction between mass public transit, privately operated minibus transit lines and taxi services as three distinct public transportation product markets, confined geographically to the relevant city area. By its subsequent Decision No. 316/20.03.2012, the CPC unconditionally cleared the transaction. In its final decision it substantially confirmed its finding that mass public transit constituted a distinct relevant market, and that the concentration would result in a monopoly upon it. However, the CPC still authorised the transaction on a balance of positive and negative effects. In particular, the authority held that the transaction would allow the combined company to apply for and receive EU funding for a substantial new project to modernise mass public transit in Varna, ultimately to the benefit of consumers. Further, the CPC found that because the Varna Municipality was already setting the prices for individual tickets in Varna, both as regards the lines of its own company and as regards the lines operated by the acquired undertaking, an increase in prices could not be expected following the concentration. In essence, the CPC held that while the transaction would eliminate all competition from the market, it would be beneficial to consumers, without the risk of them suffering any substantial negative effects. Therefore the decision is not only important in authorising a merger to monopoly (for which there has been a previous precedent), but also in using consumer benefit as a justification of the clearance of a concentration that eliminates all competition in the relevant market.

Key economic appraisal techniques applied

The CPC's assessment of mergers, including its officially published Methodology, remains largely focused on market definition and market share analysis. Nonetheless, the CPC has always underlined that market shares are only the starting point of the analysis and a number of other factors, in particular the structure of the market and the nature and key driving forces of competition in it, may be decisive in respect of its final conclusions as regards the effects of the merger. In this respect the increasingly sophisticated analysis that the CPC employs, particularly in complex cases, drives it more and more towards more modern merger assessment techniques that increasingly move away from the focus on delineating markets and estimating shares, towards a more global view of the sources and effects of competition.

Approach to remedies (i) to avoid second stage investigation and (ii) following second stage investigation

In accordance with the PCA, the CPC may impose remedies, directly related to the implementation of the concentration, which are necessary to maintain effective competition and mitigate the negative impact of a concentration on the affected market.

In a phase 1 (accelerated) proceeding, remedies can be offered only by the notifying party, where they are called "changes" to the concentration. Presumably, such remedies may also be offered with the notification itself. If accepted by the Commission, they can be attached as conditions and obligations to the clearance decision following phase 1 review.

If the review of the merger extends into a phase 2 proceeding, the CPC may, on its own discretion, impose conditions and obligations attached to its clearance decision. While no strict procedure exists, the practice of the Commission shows that that even though it is not required by law to discuss proposed remedies, it does so in the interest of finding a workable solution to competition concerns. Such remedies may also be proposed by the notifying party and accepted by the Commission.

It should be underlined that the imposition of remedies is not linked directly to the merger test – creation or strengthening of dominant position – which would significantly impede effective competition. This has made it possible for the Commission to impose remedies even in cases which do not lead to the creation or strengthening of dominance, but which for various other reasons, could reduce effective competition (see Decision No. 63/25.03.2004 on *Case KZK-11/2004*). Thus the Commission, by using remedies, on occasions has moved closer to a 'significant impediment of effective competition' test, even though its national competition law still maintains the dominance test in the review of concentrations.

So far, the CPC's preference has been more towards behavioural, rather than structural remedies. This is due to the fact that local markets are usually less mature and more dynamic, and competition concerns related to mergers are less severe, so that behavioural remedies, in most cases, are sufficient to address them.

Peter Petrov
Tel: +359 2 8055 055 / Email: p.petrov@boyanov.com
Peter Petrov is a partner with Boyanov & Co., and leads the firm's competition practice. He has represented clients in a number of landmark merger cases in Bulgaria, in the finance, telecommunications, energy, pharmaceuticals, manufacturing, media, consumer goods, healthcare, tobacco, services and other industries. He is also actively involved in investigations of cartels and other prohibited agreements as well as dominance abuse, defending clients before the Bulgarian competition authority and the courts, as well as in competition advocacy work.

Meglena Konstantinova
Tel: +359 2 8055 055 / Email: m.konstantinova@boyanov.com
Meglena Konstaninova is an associate with Boyanov & Co., working in the field of competition law. She has worked on cases in the retail and consumer goods industries.

Boyanov & Co.

82, Patriarch Evtimii Blvd., Sofia 1463, Bulgaria
Tel: +359 2 8055 055 / Fax: +359 2 8055 000 / URL: http://www.boyanov.com

in this regard, named the shareholders of Complete as defendants. In its decision the Tribunal affirmed that dissolution is an available remedy, but indicated it would not be an acceptable remedy where it is intrusive, overbroad and unlikely to reverse the substantial prevention or lessening of competition. The Tribunal concluded that divestiture was an available and effective remedy, would assure certainty of the timing of a sale, and that an approved purchaser would ultimately be more likely to effectively compete in the market.

The decision in *CCS/Complete* underscores a number of key considerations that parties to a contemplated transaction should consider. First, regardless of whether a merger is subject to pre-merger notification, the Bureau may challenge the transaction for up to one year after its completion. Accordingly, regardless of transaction size, substantive due diligence is critical in mergers between competitors or between suppliers and customers. Second, the Tribunal's confirmation that dissolution is an available remedy for completed mergers should encourage parties to consider post-closing allocation of antitrust risk, particularly where the transaction is not subject to pre-merger notification under the Act. Finally, documents play an important role in the Bureau's review of mergers, and frequently play a role in both the length and outcome of the Bureau's assessment of the transaction and the Tribunal's decision.

CCS appealed the Tribunal's decision on various grounds and, despite finding that "the Tribunal erred in law in its section 96 analysis, notably by accepting a defective 'deadweight' loss calculation, by using an overly subjective offset methodology, by treating as qualitative effects certain quantitative effects which the Commissioner had failed to quantify, and by referring to qualitative environmental effects that are not cognisable under the Competition Act",[9] the Federal Court of Appeal dismissed the appeal.

After finding that the Tribunal "erred in law", the Court reassessed the matter based on the record before it and noted, in particular, that "the party bearing the burden of the offset analysis (in this case the appellants) must still demonstrate on a balance of probabilities that the gains in efficiency offset the anti-competitive effects."[10] In its ruling the Court stated that, "[t]hough the anti-competitive effects of the merger in this case have not been quantified, they nevertheless exist. Under an objective and reasonable offset determination, marginal and insignificant gains in efficiency cannot offset known anti-competitive effects even where the weight to be afforded to such effects is undetermined",[11] and that "it cannot be concluded that an anti-competitive merger may be approved under section 96 of the Competition Act if only marginal or insignificant gains in efficiency result from that merger. This approach is supported by the jurisprudence and by the very terms of subsection 96(1) of the Competition Act, which require that the gains in efficiency be both "greater than" and "offset" the anti-competitive effects".[12]

New developments in jurisdictional assessment or procedure

Revised thresholds for review

Pre-merger notification thresholds are indexed for inflation. As a result, the "size of transaction" threshold for pre-merger notification increased from C$77m to C$80m. Other than this minor change, there were no material changes to the jurisdictional threshold for merger review in the past year.

Mergers registry

In October 2011, the Bureau announced its intention to establish a public mergers registry.[13] While the proposed registry is not without controversy, primarily with respect to whether it is consistent with the statutory confidentiality protections under the Act, the Bureau began publishing results on the registry in February 2012.[14] The registry includes information respecting the parties to the transaction, the relevant industry, and the outcome of the review (i.e., whether the Bureau has issued either an advance ruling certificate or a no-action letter in respect of the transaction). The registry lists all transactions – both notifiable and non-notifiable – where the parties have requested either an ARC or a no-action letter, or have filed notifications.

Key industry sectors reviewed and approach adopted to market definition, barriers to entry, nature of international competition, etc.

Following the release of the revised *Horizontal Merger Guidelines* in the United States in 2010, the Bureau released a revised version of its *Merger Enforcement Guidelines* ("MEGs") on October 6, 2011.[15] The MEGs had been most recently updated in 2004. The revised MEGs reflect the results of round-table consultations conducted across Canada in 2010 and early 2011, consultations with foreign agencies and input from various bar associations (e.g., the Canadian Bar Association, the American Bar Association, etc.), the results of an internal review and responses to a draft version of the MEGs the Bureau had published on June 27, 2011.[16]

The revised MEGs build on the previous MEGs, with the stated objective of more accurately reflecting current Bureau practice and current legal and economic thinking. The revised MEGs clarify the Bureau's position in a number of areas, such as interlocking directorates, partial acquisitions, entry, efficiencies, monopsony power, coordinated effects and vertical issues.

In particular, the Bureau's methodology for determining whether certain transactions, such as joint ventures or strategic alliances, will be reviewed under the merger provisions, is likely to be of interest to parties following the recent introduction of civil competitor collaboration provisions to the Act. As indicated, the Bureau's challenge in *United Continental/Air Canada* under the merger provision of the Act involved a joint venture agreement where no purchase or lease of shares or assets was involved.

The revised MEGs are discussed more fully below under "Key policy developments and reform proposals".

With respect to its practice in reviewing mergers, the Bureau has, on several occasions, addressed the importance of entry and expansion, noting in *Transcontinental Inc./Quad/Graphics Canada, Inc.*, for example, that while the parties would face little competition in the national retail flyer printing market from existing regional printers in Canada, they would face increasing competitive pressure from US printers with facilities close to Canada.[17] Similarly, in *Canadian Tire/Forzani*, after considering the degree to which effective competition from national mass merchandisers and regional sporting equipment retailers would remain post-transaction, the Bureau concluded that certain retailers appeared to be well-positioned to expand their operations in the event of a potential exercise of market power by the merged entity.[18] The Bureau also found that barriers to expansion were "surmountable" in *Cardinal Health Canada Inc./Futuremed Healthcare Products Corporation*[19] and that competitors could quickly and easily reposition their offerings in *Chartwell Seniors Housing REIT and Health Care REIT Inc./Maestro Retirement Residences.*[20]

The Bureau has also recently reviewed several mergers with vertical implications. In *Olymel/Big Sky Farms* and *Maple Leaf/Puratone* the Bureau reviewed two proposed vertical mergers in the pork industry whereby Olymel and Maple Leaf sought to acquire the two largest independent hog producers in Western Canada (Big Sky and Puratone, respectively).[21] In its review the Bureau considered the ability and incentive of Olymel or Maple Leaf partially or totally to foreclose rivals' access to live hogs (input foreclosure) or to limit or cease purchases of live hogs from upstream competitors (customer foreclosure). The Bureau ultimately determined that the mergers were unlikely to lead to a substantial lessening or prevention of competition, as excess demand for hogs limited the ability to exercise market power upstream and effective remaining competition, including between Olymel and Maple Leaf, in the sale of pork primal cuts, limited the ability to increase market power downstream.

The Bureau similarly considered vertical issues in its review of BCE Inc. (Bell) and Rogers Communications Inc.'s proposed acquisition of Maple Leaf Sports and Entertainment, the owner of the Toronto Maple Leafs and the Toronto Raptors, among other sports teams and related businesses. Bell and Rogers are vertically integrated media and telecommunications companies providing a broad range of services including telecommunications services, internet access, television distribution services, and television, radio and digital media. Both companies are also broadcast distribution undertakings, Rogers via cable television and Bell via satellite and internet protocol television, as well as conventional and specialty television and radio broadcasters, including specialty sports broadcasting.

Approach to remedies (i) to avoid second stage investigation and (ii) following second stage investigation

Supplementary information requests

Where a transaction raises serious competition issues in Canada, it is much more difficult for the parties to avoid the issuance of a SIR. That being said, the issuance of a SIR does not signal that a remedy is inevitable. Indeed, among the 19 transactions where we are aware of the Bureau having completed its review after issuing a SIR, we understand that roughly one-half proceeded without any remedy.

In our experience, the likelihood and scope of a SIR depends on a number of factors, including: the public and media profile of the deal; the complexity of the industry; whether the transaction is subject to review in other jurisdictions; the degree and nature of competitive overlap; the extent to which historical business documents support or refute the "theory of the case"; the likelihood and timing of complaints from market participants; and the extent to which specific issues have been addressed to the Bureau's satisfaction during the initial 30-day statutory waiting period. The most important of these issues are the degree of competitive overlap and complaints from market participants.

Even if a SIR cannot be avoided entirely, parties may be able to reduce the burden of complying with a SIR by educating the Bureau about the parties' businesses, the transaction and the industry, by making business people available to address questions from the Bureau early in the review process, and by being responsive to potential Bureau concerns in parallel with the SIR compliance process.

Remedies

Remedies are required where a merger is likely to prevent or lessen competition substantially in one or more relevant markets. The guiding principle in determining an appropriate remedy was set out by the Supreme Court of Canada in *Canada (Director of Investigation and Research) v. Southam Inc.*, where the Court stated that the "appropriate remedy for a substantial lessening of competition is to restore competition to the point at which it can no longer be said to be substantially less than it was before the merger".[22] The Court also noted that "If the choice is between a remedy that goes farther than is strictly necessary to restore competition to an acceptable level and a remedy that does not go far enough even to reach the acceptable level, then surely the former option must be preferred. At the very least, a remedy must be effective. If the least intrusive of the possible effective remedies overshoots the mark, that is perhaps unfortunate, but from a legal point of view, such a remedy is not defective."[23]

As a matter of practice, the Bureau will first seek to negotiate a remedy with the parties prior to resorting to litigation. In seeking a remedy the Bureau prefers structural remedies, such as divestitures, over behavioural remedies, "because the terms of such remedies are more clear and certain, less costly to administer, and readily enforceable."[24] Structural remedies are also preferred by the courts, as noted by the Tribunal in *Canada (Commissioner of Competition) v. Canadian Waste Services Holdings Inc.*,[25] where the Tribunal stated: "once there has been a finding that a merger is likely to substantially prevent or lessen competition, a remedy that permanently constrains that market power should be preferred over behavioural remedies that last over a limited period of time and require continuous monitoring of performance. This is not to say that, in cases where both the respondents and the Commissioner consent, behavioural remedies cannot be effective".[26]

With respect to behavioural remedies, the Bureau views them as inadequate due to difficulty in monitoring the remedy, determining the appropriate duration for the remedy, and the direct and indirect costs associated with monitoring the remedy and its effect on market participants.[27] However, while standalone behavioural remedies are "seldom accepted by the Bureau", the Bureau has acknowledged that they "may be acceptable when they are sufficient to eliminate the substantial lessening or prevention of competition arising from a merger, and there is no appropriate structural remedy". Indeed, the Bureau has accepted non-structural remedies in recent matters, including in *United Continental Holdings/Air Canada*.[28]

In *United Continental Holdings/Air Canada,* the parties entered into a consent agreement with the Commissioner whereby they agreed not to implement their joint venture or to coordinate via existing "coordination agreements" on 14 Canada-US routes, and further to refrain from coordinating prices or the number of seats available at each price, pooling revenue or costs or sharing commercially sensitive information. Of particular note, the consent agreement will remain in force for so long as any of the coordination agreements between Air Canada and United Continental, or the joint venture, remain in force. While the remedy in *United Continental Holdings/Air Canada* is a non-structural remedy it is important to note that, as there was no structural component to the "merger", a structural remedy was not available in that case.

With respect to international transactions, the Bureau is likely to seek Canada-specific remedies where the transaction raises Canada-specific issues. However, where a transaction raises similar issues in Canada as in other jurisdictions, it is not uncommon for the Bureau to accept foreign remedies in Canada. For example, in *United Technology Corporation/Goodrich Corporation* the Bureau found that remedies agreed to in other jurisdictions would be sufficient to address any anticompetitive effects of the merger in Canada.[29] However, in that case, the Bureau's views on the sufficiency of the foreign remedy may have been coloured by the fact that the parties had no assets in Canada.

With respect to regulated industries, despite having expressed "serious concerns" regarding Maple Group's proposed purchase of the TMX Group, Alpha Group and Canadian Depository Services, the Bureau ultimately issued a no-action letter.[30] While the Bureau conducted a lengthy and extensive review of the proposed transaction, its concerns were adequately addressed by the recognition orders issued by the Ontario Securities Commission, the primary regulator for the Toronto Stock Exchange and Alpha. In that regard, the Bureau has noted that, while it had serious concerns, "the measures contained in the OSC's final recognition orders materially change the regulatory environment sufficient to substantially mitigate the Bureau's competition concerns".

Key policy developments and reform proposals

In the past year the Bureau has issued several key guidance documents respecting its approach to merger review, the issuance of SIRs, the impact of hostile transactions and the completeness of notifications. Each of these is summarised below:

Merger Enforcement Guidelines

On October 6, 2011 the Bureau issued revised MEGs which clarify the Bureau's position in a number of areas, such as interlocking directorates, partial acquisitions, entry, efficiencies, monopsony power, coordinated effects and vertical issues.

The MEGs are an important reference when considering the application of the merger review provisions of the Act to a proposed merger, and when determining what information should be provided to the Bureau to assist in its review of a proposed merger. While the MEGs do not represent a fundamental departure from the Bureau's traditional approach to merger review, they do provide useful guidance on the Bureau's current enforcement approach, which has evolved since the previous MEGs were issued in 2004.[31] Accordingly, the Bureau's substantive review of mergers going forward is unlikely to vary materially from its approach in recent years. However, given the breadth of topics addressed by the revisions, as well as the complex nature of the economic tools they formally introduce, the revised MEGs may result in at least some experimentation by the Bureau in their substantive review of mergers moving forward. A few of the key changes to the MEGs are discussed below.

Definition of merger

The MEGs include an expanded discussion of how the Bureau interprets the definition of a "merger" under the Act. The Act defines a merger to include the acquisition of a significant interest in the whole or a part of a business. The MEGs take an expansive view of what may constitute a significant interest as including transactions and appointments that result in the ability to materially influence the economic behaviour of a business – even where no voting or economic interest is being acquired.

Interlocking directorates and minority interests

In line with the expanded discussion of what constitutes a "merger" under the Act, the MEGs now contain an expanded discussion of the factors the Bureau considers when assessing the competitive effects of a merger involving interlocking directorates and minority shareholdings. Factors considered in this analysis include the extent to which the acquirer or interlocked directorate may induce the firms to compete less aggressively with one another, and whether access to confidential information may facilitate co-ordination between the two firms.

Market definition

The revised MEGs also take into account a number of the principles reflected in the recently revised US Guidelines, including clarification of the role of market definition within the Bureau's overall analytical framework for merger review. In particular, the revised MEGs note that market definition and the analysis of competitive effects are part of an iterative process, whereby evidence in respect of market definition and market shares is considered in assessing anticompetitive effects, while the results of effects-based analyses are used to hone the Bureau's definition of the relevant market. Moreover, the MEGs explain that the Bureau may not reach a firm conclusion on market definition where it is not necessary for the Bureau to conclude its analysis. That being said, the MEGs also note that market definition is still "generally undertaken" and "generally sets the context for the Bureau's assessment of the likely competitive effects of a merger".

Anticompetitive effects analysis

The revised treatment of market definition is accompanied by changes to the treatment of the anticompetitive effects analysis in the MEGs. In this regard, the MEGs have become more complex and sophisticated, explicitly contemplating different assessments depending on the nature of the products in the relevant market by, for example, adopting an approach to assessing differentiated product markets that is very similar to the approach adopted in the US (though they do not specifically reference the upward pricing pressure test adopted in the revised US Guidelines). In addition, the revised MEGs provide additional guidance on the evaluation of mergers in bidding and bargaining markets, recognising that if many firms are similarly situated to the merging parties in terms of meeting a buyer's requirements, a merger is unlikely to prevent or lessen competition substantially.

Entry/expansion

An area in which the revised MEGs introduce uncertainty is with respect to the relevant time frame for assessing competitive effects and entry. While the 2004 MEGs established two years as the relevant time frame, the revised MEGs no longer reference a particular period, instead referring to a vague concept of entry occurring "quickly enough to deter or counteract any material price increase owing to the merger." While the revised MEGs do note that a history of entry in a particular business is one mechanism for assessing the likelihood of entry occurring in a timely manner, they do not provide meaningful guidance on which factors could affect the relevant time frame for assessing these parameters. As a result of these changes, the ability to make effective arguments respecting likely timely entry following a merger may be diminished in the future.

Non-horizontal mergers

Unlike the US guidelines, the MEGs include a discussion of both horizontal and non-horizontal mergers (including both "vertical" mergers into upstream or downstream markets as well as "conglomerate" mergers into different but potentially related markets). In respect of non-horizontal mergers, the MEGs explain that the Bureau's focus will be on assessing whether the merger is likely to lead to foreclosure of inputs or customers, or could allow the merging firms to foreclose competitors by tying the sale of two products that are not both produced by the merged entity's competitors.

Efficiencies

The Act contains an explicit "efficiencies defence", which prohibits the Tribunal from issuing an order under the merger provisions of the Act, where the gains in efficiency likely to be brought about by the merger are greater than, and would offset, the likely anticompetitive effects, and those efficiencies likely would not be achieved if the order were made. This efficiencies defence has been the subject of considerable debate in Canada and was litigated extensively in the *Superior Propane* case, and was expanded upon in the recent Federal Court of Appeal decision in *CCS/Complete*.

The revised MEGs represent a departure by the Bureau from its previous interpretations of the statutory efficiencies defence. The old MEGs, and the Bureau's 2009 *Efficiencies Bulletin,* acknowledged that a wealth transfer resulting from an anticompetitive price increase may be considered an anticompetitive effect in some circumstances. In particular, the old MEGs explained "there are different ways in which the wealth transfer could be taken into account when evaluating a merger. One approach to the wealth transfer is the 'socially adverse effects approach', which attempts to quantify the portion of the transfer that is considered socially adverse". In contrast, the revised MEGs simply state "providing buyers with competitive prices and product choices is an objective of the Act". This indicates that the Bureau may intend to move away from its previous interpretation (notwithstanding that the previous interpretation was based on several Court of Appeal decisions in *Superior Propane*), instead seeking to leave its options open in taking a restrictive approach to the efficiencies defence in future cases.

Separately, the MEGs indicate that the Bureau will only consider efficiencies where the merging parties provide evidence of those efficiencies in a timely manner – in other words, where the Bureau believes a substantial prevention or lessening of competition is likely, unless the parties provide efficiencies evidence on a timeline the Bureau deems acceptable, the Bureau will apply for an order from the Tribunal without assessing the impact of efficiencies on the Tribunal's authority to issue that particular order.

Other bureau guidance

Merger Review Process Guidelines

In addition to the revised MEGs, the Bureau issued revised *Merger Review Process Guidelines,* which largely formalise the Bureau's practices in respect of the information-gathering processes used during merger review, particularly the SIR process, and appear to signal that the Bureau is prepared to issue SIRs with greater frequency.

Among other changes the revised guidelines: (i) de-emphasise the consideration that may be given to the burden imposed on merging parties when determining whether to issue an SIR and the scope of the SIR; (ii) no longer commit the Bureau to communicating preliminary views regarding a transaction as soon as reasonably possible, focusing instead on whether the need for an SIR can be obviated in a particular case; (iii) modify the parameters for consultation both before and after an SIR is issued (pre- and post-issuance dialogue) by focusing largely on identifying the sources of information at the pre-issuance stage, while leaving discussion of the terms of production (i.e., prioritising questions, custodians and information) to the post-issuance stage; (iv) standardise the practice of imposing a continuing production or "refresh" requirement (typically, at 30 and 90 days from the date the SIR is issued); (v) clarify where timing agreements may be used as an alternative to an SIR (e.g., more appropriate where the transaction does not meet the pre-merger notification thresholds under Part IX); (vi) confirm that the Bureau will no longer commit to a date for completing its review of a transaction under a timing agreement; and (vii) elaborate on the Bureau's approach to information-gathering in hostile transactions.

Hostile Transactions Interpretation Guidelines

The Bureau issued two interpretation guidelines relating its administrative practice in hostile bid situations. *Hostile Transactions Interpretation Guideline Number 1* sets out the Bureau's views on its responsibility to share information with the target of a hostile bid. Recognising the "sensitivities" involved in a hostile situation, the Bureau will "strive" to "equitably" share information with one party that it has shared with the other party. In the guideline, the Bureau recognises that the policy may be difficult to apply in a straightforward manner due to complexities that can arise in hostile acquisitions, and notes that it will be mindful of these complexities on a case-by-case basis.

Hostile Transactions Interpretation Guideline Number 2 sets out the Bureau's policies regarding the running of the waiting periods in circumstances where a hostile bid turns friendly following submission of the acquirer's pre-merger notification. Specifically, the Bureau's policy is that: where a transaction turns friendly after the acquirer has submitted its notification, the initial 30-day waiting period is unaffected; where the transaction turns friendly after an SIR has been issued, but before the acquirer certifies completeness of their response, the second 30-day period will not commence until both parties have certified the completeness of their responses; and where a transaction turns friendly after the acquirer has certified completeness of their response to an SIR, the second 30-day waiting period is not affected.

Pre-merger notification interpretation guidelines

Finally, the Bureau issued guidance regarding its policy on the completeness of notifications.[32] Although largely technical, two aspects of the guideline are of note. First, the guidelines provide clarity as to who is a "director" or "officer" of an unincorporated entity for the purposes of providing transaction-related documents as part of the notification, indicating that documents must be provided from a "person whose position is designated in a similar manner" to an officer or director. Second, the guideline explains what information can be withheld from the notification because it is confidential "by law", with the Bureau viewing information rendered confidential by private agreement as not confidential by law. Where parties are not willing to submit such information, they must submit an acceptable explanation as to why the Bureau's normal confidentiality protections would not be sufficient. Absent such explanation, the notification will be considered incomplete and the initial waiting period will not commence.

* * *

Endnotes

1. See section 65(2) of the Act.
2. See section 123.1 of the Act.
3. These thresholds are subject to adjustment for inflation, and annual adjustments are published in the Canada Gazette.
4. See section 110(3)(b), Competition Act.
5. The most recent data available from the Bureau, the *Merger Review Performance Report*, April 2012, only includes figures for the first nine months of the Bureau's 2011-2012 fiscal year rather than for the full year. A copy of the report is available at: www.competitionbureau.gc.ca/eic/site/cb-bc.nsf/vwapj/cb-merger-performance-report-apr-2012-e.pdf/$file/cb-merger-performance-report-apr-2012-e.pdf.
6. A "no-action letter" is a letter from the Commissioner indicating that the Commissioner is of the view that he does not, at that time, intend to make an application to the Tribunal under section 92 of the Act challenging the transaction. See section 123(2) of the Act.
7. Regardless of whether a merger triggers a pre-merger notification requirement under the Act, it can be challenged by the Commissioner for up to one year following completion.
8. *Remarks by Melanie L. Aitken, Commissioner of Competition*, Canadian Bar Association 2011 Fall Conference (October 6, 2011), available online at www.competitionbureau.gc.ca/eic/site/cb-bc.nsf/eng/03424.html.
9. Tervita Corporation v. Commissioner of Competition, 2013 FCA 28 at para. 163.
10. *Ibid*, at para. 167
11. *Ibid*, at para. 174.
12. *Ibid*, at para. 170.
13. Competition Bureau, *Remarks by Melanie L. Aitken, Commissioner of Competition*, (October 6, 2011), Keynote Speech at the Canadian Bar Association 2011 Fall Conference, Hilton Lac-Leamy, Quebec, available at: www.competitionbureau.gc.ca/eic/site/cb-bc.nsf/eng/03424.html.
14. Competition Bureau, *Monthly Report of Concluded Merger Reviews*, available at: www.competitionbureau.gc.ca/eic/site/cb-bc.nsf/eng/02435.html.
15. Competition Bureau, *Merger Enforcement Guidelines*, (October 6, 2011), www.competitionbureau.gc.ca/eic/site/cb-bc.nsf/vwapj/cb-meg-2011-e.pdf/$FILE/cb-meg-2011-e.pdf.
16. Competition Bureau, *Merger Enforcement Guidelines – Draft for Public Consultation*, (June 27, 2011), www.competitionbureau.gc.ca/eic/site/cb-bc.nsf/eng/03384.html.
17. Competition Bureau, *Competition Bureau Statement Regarding Transcontinental's Acquisition of Quad/Graphics Canada* (April 10, 2012) available at: www.competitionbureau.gc.ca/eic/site/cb-bc.nsf/eng/03451.html.
18. *Competition Bureau, Canadian Tire/Forzani Position Statement,* (October 5, 2011) available at: www.competitionbureau.gc.ca/eic/site/cb-bc.nsf/eng/03421.html.
19. Competition Bureau, *Competition Bureau Statement Regarding Cardinal Health's Acquisition of Futuremed,* (April 16, 2012) available at: www.competitionbureau.gc.ca/eic/site/cb-bc.nsf/eng/03458.html.
20. Competition Bureau, *Competition Bureau Statement Regarding Chartwell and Health Care*

REIT's Acquisition of Maestro Retirement Residences, (April 11, 2012) available at: www. competitionbureau.gc.ca/eic/site/cb-bc.nsf/eng/03456.html.

21. Competition Bureau, *Competition Bureau Statement Regarding Proposed Mergers of Pork Processors and Hog Producers* (December 17, 2012), available at: www.competitionbureau.gc.ca/ eic/site/cb-bc.nsf/eng/03519.html.

22. [1997] 1 SCR, at para. 85.

23. *Ibid*, at para. 89.

24. Competition Bureau, *Information Bulletin on Merger Remedies in Canada* (September 22, 2006), available at: www.competitionbureau.gc.ca/eic/site/cb-bc.nsf/eng/02170.html.

25. CT-2000/002, available at: www.ct-tc.gc.ca/CMFiles/CT-2000-002_0087_49PBY-982004-9241. pdf.

26. *Ibid*, at para. 110.

27. Competition Bureau, *Information Bulletin on Merger Remedies in Canada* (September 22, 2006), available at: www.competitionbureau.gc.ca/eic/site/cb-bc.nsf/eng/02170.html.

28. See, for example, *Commissioner of Competition v. The Coca-Cola Company,* (September 27, 2010) available at: www.ct-tc.gc.ca/CMFiles/CT-2010-009_Registered%20Consent%20 Agreement_2_45_9-27-2010_5925.pdf, and *Commissioner of Competition and Ticketmaster Inc. and Live Nation Inc.* (January 25, 2010), available at: www.ct-tc.gc.ca/CMFiles/CT-2010-001_ Consent%20Agreement_1_38_1-25-2010_9824.pdf.

29. Competition Bureau, *Competition Bureau Statement Regarding United Technology Corporation's Acquisition of Goodrich Corporation,* (July 26, 2012) available at: www.competitionbureau. gc.ca/eic/site/cb-bc.nsf/eng/03483.html.

30. Competition Bureau, *Competition Bureau Completes Review of Proposed Maple-TMX Transaction,* (July 4, 2012) available at: www.competitionbureau.gc.ca/eic/site/cb-bc.nsf/ eng/03480.html.

31. Competition Bureau, *Competition Bureau Issues Final Merger Enforcement Guidelines* (October 6, 2011), www.competitionbureau.gc.ca/eic/site/cb-bc.nsf/eng/03422.html.

32. See Competition Bureau, *Pre-Merger Notification Interpretation Guideline Number 13: Satisfying the Information Requirements set out in Section 16 of the Notifiable Transactions Regulations and Completeness of Notification*, available at: http://www.competitionbureau.gc.ca/eic/site/cb-bc.nsf/eng/03370.html.

Randall J. Hofley
Tel: +1 416 863 2387 / Email: randall.hofley@blakes.com
Randall Hofley is a partner with Blakes, Cassels & Graydon LLP, based in the Toronto and Ottawa offices. Randall's practice focuses on competition law, as well as federal laws regulating the communications, energy, financial services and transportation sectors. In addition to advising on transactions and conduct subject to the Competition Act, he has appeared as lead litigation counsel before the Competition Tribunal, the Canadian Radio-television and Telecommunications Commission, and Canada's Provincial, Federal and Supreme Courts in class action and other competition law-related matters. In addition to representing major domestic and international corporations in all aspects of the Competition Act, Randall has prosecuted major competition law cases as special counsel to the Commissioner of Competition, including major criminal cartel and pricing cases, and the only abuse of dominance matter to reach the Federal Court of Appeal and Supreme Court of Canada, the Canada Pipe case. He also represented the Commissioner on legislative/policy reform initiatives such as abuse of dominance, cartels, price maintenance, regulated conduct, and the intellectual property/competition law interface. Randall is the Chair of the Canadian Bar Association Competition Law Section's Criminal Matters Committee.

Micah Wood
Tel: +1 416 863 4164 / Email: micah.wood@blakes.com
Micah Wood is a partner with Blake, Cassels & Graydon, LLP based in the Toronto office. Micah advises international and Canadian clients on a wide variety of competition law matters, and has been involved in a number of large, high-profile mergers involving significant antitrust issues in industries as varied as telecommunications, media and advertising, consumer products, oil & gas, and medical devices. He has been involved in the negotiation of complex remedies and orders with the Competition Bureau and has appeared before the Competition Tribunal in contested proceedings. Micah's writing has included papers on merger law, abuse of dominance, the legal and economic analyses of network industries, the interrelation between economics and competition law in network industries, and the "efficiencies defence" in Canadian competition law. He is the former chair of the Law & Economics Committee of the National Competition Law Section of the Canadian Bar Association (CBA) and has made numerous contributions to the policy work of that and other CBA section committees.

Kevin H. MacDonald
Tel: +1 416 863 4023 / Email: kevin.macdonald@blakes.com
Kevin MacDonald is an associate with Blake, Cassels & Graydon, LLP based in the Toronto office. Kevin advises on all aspects of competition law, including mergers and acquisitions, marketing and distribution practices, abuse of dominance, criminal and civil investigations, and compliance matters. He also advises on foreign investment merger review under the Investment Canada Act. Kevin has advised international and Canadian clients on a wide variety of competition law matters, and has been involved in a number of large, high profile mergers in a variety of industries including insurance, oil and gas, financial services, consumer products, and healthcare.

Blake, Cassels & Graydon LLP

199 Bay Street, Suite 4000, Commerce Court West, Toronto, Ontario, Canada, M5L 1A9
Tel: +1 416 863 2400 / Fax: +1 416 863 2653 / URL: http://www.blakes.com

China

Feng Yao & Li Bo
Broad & Bright Law Firm

Overview of merger control activity during the last 12 months

Since the Anti-Monopoly Law of China (the "**AML**") came into force in 2008, the number of notifications regarding concentrations (or "mergers") of undertakings has increased year on year.[1] In 2012 (as of December 26, 2012), China's Ministry of Commerce ("**MOFCOM**") received approximately 201 merger control notifications filed in accordance with the AML, of which 186 were accepted and 154 were closed. The number of cases filed and accepted remains flat compared with 2011 level, during which MOFCOM received 205 notifications, with 185 accepted. But the number of closed cases (154 in total) shrank in 2012 from the 171 cases in 2011.

Share acquisition and joint venture are the two main types of transactions notified with MOFCOM. According to the statistics publicised by MOFCOM, most concentrations filed are share acquisitions. By the end of November 2012, there were 71 notifications involving share acquisition, accounting for 55% of all the cases; and joint venture only accounting for 36%, being 46 cases. This gap was even larger in 2011, during which there were 101 share acquisitions, accounting for 62% of all the cases, and 49 joint venture cases, accounting for 30%.

Notification by Types of Transactions (by the end of November 2012)

Type / Year	Share Acquisition		Joint Venture	
	Number of Notifications	Percentage	Number of Notifications	Percentage
2011	101	62%	49	30%
2012	71	55%	46	36%

From the perspective of nature (see table below), most concentrations filed were horizontal ones where the parties to these transactions were competitors in the first place. By the end of November 2012, there were 80 horizontal concentrations, accounting for 65% of all the cases closed; while in 2011 the number was 97, accounting for 60%.

Notification by Nature of Transactions (by the end of November 2012)

Nature / Year	Horizontal Concentrations		Non-Horizontal Concentrations	
	Number of Notifications	Percentage	Number of Notifications	Percentage
2011	80	65%	43	35%
2012	97	60%	65	40%

Among the 154 notifications closed in 2012, there were 142 cleared with no conditions, which accounted for 92% of all the notifications closed, and 6 cleared with conditions, accounting for 4%, and the rest (6 cases or 4%) were withdrawn. The 6 conditional clearances are summarised as follows:

1. Establishment of a JV by Henkel Hong Kong ("Henkel") and Tiande
- Both JV partners are significant players, active in upstream and downstream industries

respectively, i.e. Tiande is one of the two main suppliers in the worldwide upstream Ethyl cyanoacetate (ECYA) market. The two suppliers have a market share of 45-50% globally and in China, respectively, while Henkel has advantages in the downstream markets of CA monomers and adhesives in terms of brands, technologies, capitals and talents.

- Competition concerns in the vertical relationships between the transaction parties were identified and purely behavioural remedies adopted, which required that "Tiande [to] supply ECYA to all downstream customers based on fair, reasonable and non-discriminatory terms, particularly, Tiande shall not sell the products at an unreasonably high price, shall not supply ECYA to Weifang Dekel on preferential terms, and shall not exchange any competitive information with Henkel and Weifang Dekel".

2. Acquisition of Hitachi Global Storage Technologies ("HGST") by Western Digital Corporation ("WD")

- The notification took place in parallel with the Seagate/Samsung HDD case cleared in 2011.
- A hybrid of structural remedy and behavioural remedies adopted, where WD committed that it should "within 6 months from the promulgation of the Review Decision, divest the main 3.5-inch hard disk assets of Viviti (a wholly owned subsidiary of Hitachi active in HHD business) to a third party".

3. Acquisition of Motorola Mobility ("MMI") by Google Inc. ("Google")

- MOFCOM finds that Google's Android system has a dominant market position in the smart mobile terminal operating system market in China (73.99%).
- MOFCOM requires Google to license the Android platform on a free and open basis, and shall treat those OEMs that already consent not to conduct branching or deriving work for the Android platform on a non-discriminatory basis with respect to the Android platform. Google shall also continue to comply with MMI's current obligations of offering fair, reasonable and non-discriminatory ("FRAND") terms with respect to the patents of MMI. This is another case in which MOFCOM had concerns against the vertical relationship between the transaction's parties and as a result, purely behavioural remedies were imposed.

4. Acquisition of 33.6% Niuhai Holding Ltd. ("Niuhai") by Wal-Mart Stores, Inc ("Wal-Mart")

- The first published case involving an instance of control "*by way of contract or via other means*" due to application of the VIE structure, a contractual arrangement popular with foreign investors seeking to invest in many restricted sectors in China.
- Leverage effects were cited once again by MOFCOM in its review decision, under which Niuhai shall not utilise its self-owned network platform to provide network service to other transaction parties after the completion of this acquisition without obtaining the licence to operate value-added telecommunication business, and Wal-Mart shall not carry out the value-added telecommunication business through VIE structure currently operated by Yishiduo. It is understood that by imposing such conditions, MOFCOM is trying to eliminate the possibility of Wal-Mart's leverage of its competitive advantages in the physical store retail market to the on-line retail business.

5. Acquisition of Goodrich Corporation ("Goodrich") by United Technologies Corporation ("UTC")

- A high-profile transaction filed in eight jurisdictions, establishing a new standard for global regulatory cooperation and coordination. MOFCOM made its decision relatively early compared to the US and EU, which shows the confidence of MOFCOM in making its own decisions.
- Given the fact that the horizontal overlap between UTC and Goodrich in the market of aircraft AC generation systems would result in a combined share of 84% post transaction, MOFCOM required UTC/Goodrich to divest Goodrich's electric power systems business to a qualified buyer. The purely structural remedy is considered by MOFCOM as the first choice to address the horizontal competition concerns; as such the remedy would be more effective and easier to monitor compared with the behavioural remedies.

6. Establishment of a JV by ARM Holdings plc ("ARM"), Gemalto NV ("Gemalto") and Giesecke & Devrient GmbH ("G&D")

- A typical transaction with vertically-related markets involved, like Henkel/Tiande case, where there is vertical relation between the businesses of the parent of the JV and the business to be operated by the JV.

- In line with the EU decision, MOFCOM required ARM to abide by the non-discrimination rule, and release in the future the security monitoring code, as well as other information of its TrustZone technology that is necessary to develop TEE solutions, including relevant licences, licensing standards and conditions; and not to design its IP in such a way as to degrade the performance of third-party TEEs.

With the accumulation of experience in the past four to five years, MOFCOM appears to be more confident in issuing its own decisions, especially in the acquisition of Goodrich by UTC, in which MOFCOM's conditional clearance decision became the first approval among the major jurisdictions including EU and the US.

Similarly with the situation in 2011, however, a number of cases were delayed into Phase II review simply because of MOFCOM's lack of staff, and the lengthy opinion-solicitation process as well as other procedural issues, rather than having substantial competition concerns. In the past 12 months in 2012, efforts have been made by MOFCOM to improve and standardise its merger control review procedure, trying to make it more efficient. Although MOFCOM has yet to finish the legislative procedures for issuing the rules on the simplified review procedure, an internal fast-track review process has actually been implemented by MOFCOM in its practice. While not disclosed to the public, to our best knowledge and based on a rough estimate, around 10% of the accepted cases in 2012 have been reviewed and cleared under the internal fast track process. But the criteria adopted by MOFCOM in determination of the cases on which the fast-track process is applicable, are not clear.

Meanwhile, MOFCOM has improved its statistics transparency. In addition to the public announcement after every conditional clearance decision has been made, and the seemingly routine press conference being held every August and December, the Anti-monopoly Bureau of MOFCOM (the "**AMB**") also published, on November 16, 2012, a list covering all the transactions it cleared without conditions since August 1, 2008. It is stated that the AMB will disclose regularly all the transactions that are unconditionally cleared on a quarterly basis.

New developments in jurisdictional assessment or procedure

The general regime and practices under the AML for assessing the notifiability of a merger remain stable over the past years since the AML came into force. Similar to the EU Merger Regulation analysis, the two key questions of the notifiability analysis under the AML and the relevant regulations are:
(i)   whether the transaction constitutes "concentration"; and
(ii)   whether the turnover thresholds of the Parties to the transaction are triggered.

The notifiability analysis appears to be a clear-cut two-step test, while there are still certain practical issues that remain unclear under the current AML regime, such as the definition of "control", penalties on a pre-clearance implementation etc. Nonetheless, the new rules and the merger review decisions (especially those conditional ones) issued by MOFCOM during the last 12 months have shed some light on certain grey-area jurisdictional issues.

Implications of MOFCOM's mention of VIE structure

On August 13, 2012, following an eight-month review process, MOFCOM made a public announcement of its clearance decision, where MOFCOM conditionally cleared Wal-Mart's acquisition of control of Shanghai Yishiduo E-Commerce Co., Ltd. ("**Yishiduo**"), the owner of Yihaodian, the largest online supermarket in China. In fact, the control over Yishiduo is obtained by Wal-Mart through its acquisition of a 33.6% share in Niuhai Holding Ltd. ("**Niuhai**"), which in turn, has an indirect contractual control over Yishiduo through the Variable Interest Entity ("**VIE**") structure.

VIE structure is in essence a type of contractual arrangement, under which a foreign investor could, through its wholly owned foreign entity ("**WOFE**") in China, obtain actual control over a Chinese domestic company via a contractual relationship. The motive for foreign investors to adopt a VIE structure is to circumvent the restrictions (or even prohibitions) on foreign investment in certain industries/areas in China under the applicable foreign investment laws and regulations. The VIE structure is popular with foreign investors looking for investment opportunities in the Chinese internet and telecommunications market, especially the value-added telecommunications businesses for which an operational licence is necessary but not allowed to be granted to a foreign-invested enterprise.

One of the three conditions imposed by MOFCOM is: "*after the completion of this transaction, Wal-Mart shall not, through VIE structure, carry out the value-added telecommunication business that Yishiduo currently engages in*". The implications of MOFCOM's mention of the VIE structure are controversial among practitioners and counsel. For example, some believe that MOFCOM is insistent on the principle of foreign investment policies and that the restrictions on foreign investment in certain industries must be complied and cannot be circumvented by any means, including any contractual arrangements. But others are more optimistic,saying that MOFCOM's findings and rulings seem to suggest the PRC authorities, at least MOFCOM, will tolerate VIEs in the existing investments.

From the perspective of merger control review, MOFCOM's conditional clearance on the Wal-Mart/ Yishiduo acquisition is the first announced case that involves an instance of control "*by way of contract or via other means*", as provided in Article 20(iii) of the AML. Due to the VIE structure between Yishiduo and Niuhai Holding, Wal-Mart obtains control over Yishiduo by increasing its shares in Niuhai Holding from 17.7% to 51.3% post acquisition. We understand that through the decision, MOFCOM's attitude towards the VIE structure is quite clear that the VIE structure is NOT exempted from the merger control review.

MOFCOM merger control enforcement on SOE and JV

On November 10, 2011, MOFCOM conditionally approved the creation of a joint venture ("**JV**") between General Electric (China) Co., Ltd. ("**GE China**") and China Shenhua Coal to Liquid and Chemical Co., Ltd. ("**Shenhua**"). This was not only the first published merger control decision where a state-owned enterprise ("**SOE**") is involved, but also the first one regarding JVs since China's AML took effect.

Firstly, this conditional clearance decision, if interpreted together with the recent investigation on China Telecom and China Unicom by the National Development and Reform Commission, the sister agency of MOFCOM, has displayed the attitude of the Chinese enforcement agencies that transactions involving SOEs are not immune from the antitrust scrutiny under the AML regime. MOFCOM's willingness to increase its enforcement over SOEs shown in this case, is also a positive reaction against the alleged SOEs' opting-out of the merger control review process by the overseas/ private business sector. These enforcement activities show that efforts are being made by Chinese competition enforcement agencies to ensure that the AML regime is a non-discriminatory one that holds the SOEs accountable to the same criteria as private enterprises.

Secondly, while not expressly stipulated in the AML and the pertinent regulations and MOFCOM rules as to whether the JV would be considered as a qualified "concentration" under the AML and subject to the merger control review, based on practitioners' experiences, MOFCOM considers JVs to be a type of notifiable transaction under the AML. MOFCOM's position then has been officially affirmed by the GE/Shenhua review decision.

Increasingly lengthy pre-initiation process

According to MOFCOM's practice, after the formal submission of the notification materials by the notifying party(ies), typically there is a commentary process before the clock of the formal procedure starts ticking, during which MOFCOM will review the submission and raise one (or more) rounds of questions. The notifying party(ies) must respond satisfactorily in writing to those questions before MOFCOM would accept the filing as complete, thus initiating the formal "Phase 1" procedure and all associated timelines.

This pre-initiation process had been becoming increasingly long in MOFCOM's practice in 2012. Under most circumstances (no matter how "simple" the case is), it would take around one month for MOFCOM to finish its preliminary review on the notification materials and issue its first round of comments/ questions to the notifying party(ies). Such pre-initiation process, as well as the similarly prolonged review process after the initiation, are attributed to the shortage of staff in the review departments of the AMB, and MOFCOM's greater care in reviewing some complicated mergers, which have in turn materially slowed down the timeframe of MOFCOM's review. This is evidenced by the 10% decline in the number of the closed cases in 2012 (154 in total) compared with that in 2011 (171 in total).

Key industry sectors reviewed and approach adopted to market definition, barriers to entry, nature of international competition etc.

In general, from the perspective of the industry sector involved, most concentrations filed in 2012 involve the manufacture industries, including petro-chemicals, chemicals, machinery manufacture, auto, vehicles, aircraft, mines, etc. The number of cases involving the manufacturing sector decreased by 30% in 2012 (74 cases) compared with the 107 cases in 2011.

According to the recent practice of the AMB, some key industry sectors have been paid close attention by MOFCOM, including the mining, agricultural commodities, and other industries in relation to the important raw materials. These sectors are deemed to be strategically meaningful to the national economic development and public interests in China, which are some other important objectives of the AML in addition to the competition-oriented objectives. As a result, the companies seeking M&A opportunities in these sectors should be alerted if the deal will likely trigger the filing thresholds in China.

Key economic appraisal techniques applied e.g. as regards unilateral effects and co-ordinated effects, and the assessment of vertical and conglomerate mergers

Since the review process in a merger review under the AML, in particular the assessment approach and process of the AMB, is not transparent to the notifying party(ies), very few developments in respect of the economic analysis have been revealed in the AMB's practice.

However, it is worth noting that in the Wal-mart/Yishiduo case, which was conditionally cleared in August 2012, MOFCOM explicitly cited the "leverage effect" once again since its decision blocking Coca-Cola/Huiyuan deal in 2009. Although this kind of theory has rarely been applied by agencies in other major jurisdictions like the US and EU, MOFCOM decisions' repeated reference to leveraging suggests that MOFCOM might intend to establish a conglomerate effects theory of its own. However, the real trend of MOFCOM's practice, in terms of this potential theory of harm, needs to be further observed in the future.

Approach to remedies

To date, MOFCOM has cleared 16 transactions subject to the relevant remedy measures. It is worth noting that among the 16 conditionally cleared cases, there are only 6 from 2008 to 2010, and the remaining 10 have occurred in 2011 and 2012. This upward trend indicates that MOFCOM has become more confident and skillful in imposing remedy measures to address competition concerns in the last two years, notwithstanding that some of the remedy measures are controversial.

Key issues when devising remedies in China

As far as MOFCOM is concerned, effectively eliminating or reducing the anti-competition effect or, in other words, effectively preserving competition, is the key point for appropriate remedies. By proposing remedies, MOFOCM should be convinced that such remedies are feasible and practicable in terms of time, cost, and supervision. Therefore, when devising remedies, the following issues shall be taken into account[2], or MOFCOM may challenge or even reject remedies proposed:

- Whether the proposed remedies are able to directly address the competition concerns raised by MOFCOM;
- whether the proposed remedies are able to effectively eliminate or reduce the effect of eliminating or restricting competition in China as a result of the concentration;
- whether the proposed remedies are able to be implemented and monitored in practice within MOFCOM's effective jurisdiction; and
- whether the proposed remedies can successfully and expeditiously preserve competition within an anticipated timeline.

However, while understanding the competition concerns of MOFCOM is the premise of devising remedies, there is a lack of statutory rules in China as to when and how MOFCOM shall come up with its competition concerns. To some extent, it is difficult for merger parties to identify the issues MOFCOM is concerned about in a timely manner. In practice, the merger parties normally will not receive a written statement of issues; instead, they will need to orally communicate with MOFCOM through frequent and close contact as well as meetings to understand the problem or any potential issues. Only after that can either an appropriate defence or an effective proposal of remedies be devised.

In addition to competition concerns, in practice, MOFCOM may request proposed remedies to address other non-competition issues, or to achieve objectives other than competition-oriented objectives, such as issues under industry policies, balance between the various interested parties, etc.

MOFCOM's preference for structural remedy in horizontal mergers and behavioural remedy in vertical mergers

In practice, based on the former conditional clearance cases, where the merger involves competition concerns arising from horizontal overlaps, for example, with a significant increase in market share, and the creation or increase of a dominant market position, MOFCOM may prefer a structural remedy, because such remedy typically can effectively and efficiently resolve the problem concerning the change of the market's structure as a result of the horizontal merger. Consistent with the common definition of structural remedies applied in other major jurisdictions, structural remedies basically involve divestiture of a certain business or selected assets. In past cases in China, generally a divestiture may contain: (1) an existing business that can be separately operated; (2) subsidiaries, branch entities or business sections; or (3) selected assets.

On the other hand, where competition concerns come from a vertical relationship or a JV, for example, the foreclosure of raw materials suppliers or customers, a behavioural remedy is normally acceptable to MOFCOM. Especially in JV transactions where JV partners are active in upstream and downstream industries respectively, such as cases of GE/Shenhua (2011) and Henkel/Tiande (2012), MOFCOM adopted behavioural remedies.

It is worth noting that the approach of accepting purely behavioural remedies by MOFCOM is somehow different from the practices in the EU or the US. As indicated in the EC's guideline, behavioural remedies are applied only where either a structural remedy is not available, or the structural remedies may work better with a supplement of behavioural remedies. But in China, MOFCOM is relatively more likely to accept behavioural remedies, particularly in vertical mergers[3]. In the total 16 precedents of conditional clearances in China, purely behavioural remedies were used in as many as 10 cases.

Procedures of remedy negotiations

At present, the *Rules on the Review of the Concentration of Undertakings* only stipulate several principles; no specific guideline or implementation rule with regard to the negotiation of remedies has been promulgated yet. Therefore, it is difficult for the merger party to properly set expectations on the whole procedure, the specific time schedule or the rights and obligations during the remedy negotiation. However, on the other hand, there exists significant flexibility for the negotiation between the merger party and MOFCOM; therefore, taking the initiative, devising an active strategy, maintaining good communication as early as possible and full cooperation shall usually win the merger party more time and space for negotiation.

Based on our experiences in the past two years, in practice, remedies are usually proposed by the merger party, while rarely by MOFCOM taking the initiative. Generally, MOFCOM shall raise competition concerns regarding a notified concentration and require explanation and clarification from the merger party. In the event that the defence of merger party cannot eliminate MOFCOM's competition concerns, MOFCOM will request the party to propose remedies. After the proposed remedies are submitted for consideration, MOFCOM will conduct assessments and tests to determine whether the proposed remedies can effectively eliminate or reduce the anti-competition effects, generally by consulting the third parties by means of written questionnaires or meetings, including related government authorities and industry associations, competitors, upstream and downstream industries, consumers etc.

Considering that MOFCOM will not disclose the methods and process of its assessment, in order to receive feedback in an expedient manner, the merger party could submit a written application to MOFCOM to hold a meeting to learn the assessing opinions, or keep timely and close contact with the case team of the AMB and seek opportunities for opinions. According to MOFCOM's recent practice, MOFCOM would usually inform the merger party of its opinions on the proposed remedies or modification suggestions via meeting or telephone, instead of a written notice. In general cases, the remedy proposal will go through several rounds of negotiations and modifications before it is finalised.

Key policy developments

In 2012, MOFCOM continued to seek to standardise the review procedure and promote statistical transparency in the merger control regime. There are two important developments, among others, of MOFCOM's efforts in 2012 that we would like to highlight here:

The new notification form

On 6 June, 2012, MOFCOM officially promulgated a new notification form ("**New Form**") with detailed introduction on how to fill it out. Before the promulgation of this New Form, the notifying parties only had a rough list of information required by MOFCOM, and a very simple notification form. The lack of guidance to fill out the old form, and the absence of uniform interpretation to the requirements of MOFCOM, brought about various problems, e.g. improper notifying parties, lack of necessary information for the case team for evaluation, or how to organise the notification materials. The New Form has reflected MOFCOM's enforcement experiences in the past four to five years; it is more than a formal change, as it also clarifies some substantive legal issues of merger filling under the current AML regime.

- *Clarifications on important legal concepts*

Before the New Form has been issued, the AML and the pertinent regulations keep silent on definitions on several important concepts in the merger filing. The most important clarification in the New Form is the definition of "undertakings to the concentration", which also relates to the concept of the "notifying party".

In the New Form, MOFCOM makes it clear that "undertakings to the concentration" shall be those undertakings that will have control or be able to exercise decisive influence after the transaction. The undertakings may decide which party(ies) will act as the notifying party(ies), while the other undertakings to the concentration are those undertakings that participate in the transaction but do not have control or decisive influence of the entity post-transaction.

MOFCOM deems the control, power and decisive influence as the key factors to differentiate the "undertakings to concentration", and the other undertakings participating in the concentration, and the two groups of parties will bear different information disclosure obligations, according to the specific requirements in the New Form.

- *More specific information requirements*

Generally, the New Form is quite complex and detailed when comparing with the old one, adding a great deal of specific information requests (with 50 endnotes explaining the information requests), which expressly require the parties to provide more detailed factual information, as well as more comprehensive competition analysis.

Another highlight is that the New Form has added the items of "studies, analyses and reports that are internally prepared by transaction parties or prepared by third parties" ("**Study**"). Before issuance of the New Form, it used to be controversial whether an internal study could be served as an acceptable data in the review. The New Form serves as a positive answer by MOFCOM. Meanwhile, the New Form seems to regard a wide range of the Studies as acceptable.

For the definition of product market, the New Form introduces the code of product and service issued by the National Bureau of Statistics of China (NBSC) for a preliminary definition, which is believed to be a convenient tool for MOFCOM. Also, MOFCOM requires the parties' clarification on the neighbouring market definition for the first time, in addition to the well-known horizontal overlap and vertical relationship.

- *More focus on competition analysis*

The New Form goes down in a clear logic – the parties that will take control in the transaction and the parties that will not; the detailed description of the transaction; and then the market analysis, including definition of market; analysis of these defined markets; the supply and demand structure; market entry and at last the possible efficiency, which is the most important part of the New Form (it takes 6 sections (sections 7-12) out of the 19 sections of the New Form). This is consistent with the logic adopted by the other major jurisdictions in the world, and demonstrates the improvement of MOFCOM's ability in the merger control review.

In addition, the New Form explicitly requires that the HHI/CRn index be applied to the analysis on the impact of the concentration on market competition. Also, the New Form requires that reasons be provided if the notifying party(ies) are not able to provide the HHI index (endnote 39 of the New Form).

In recent practice, MOFCOM frequently emphasises the importance for the parties to follow the requirements of the New Form. Although it was initially anticipated that the New Form would make the preparation of a PRC filing more burdensome, the transparency it brings to the parties in preparation of the filing is also of important value to large companies seeking clearance for notifiable transactions in China.

Statistics transparency

Since the AML came into effect, the AMB holds a press conference every August (the anniversary of the AML) and December to update on the performance of AML on the year. In the past 12 months, MOFCOM has made further efforts to promote statistical transparency.

In 2012, in addition to this routine conference, MOFCOM published all 458 cases that it cleared without conditions from August, 2008 to the end of September 2012, including the parties and the nature of concentrations (JV, share acquisition etc.).[4] Mr. Shang Ming, the Director General of the AMB, declared at last December's press conference that they will publish the list of unconditional clearance cases on a quarterly basis in the future. Actually, the list for the fourth quarter of 2012 is available now.[5]

Although efforts have been made by MOFCOM to promote the transparency of the case statistics, a more transparent review process is still eagerly awaited by both the practitioners and the business sectors.

Reform proposals

MOFCOM has been considering, at least, two sets of proposed rules which are expected to be internally finalised in the near future. One is in relation to the restrictive conditions formulation (from the negotiation, assessment to determination and implementation of remedies), and the other is in relation to the fast-track review process.

Remedy negotiations

Due to the absence of systematic legislation regulating the negotiation, assessment, determination and implementation of the remedy measures, MOFCOM in practice refers to the experiences and practices of EU. It is understood that MOFCOM is considering promulgating a template of proposed text for the conditions to be attached, which may assist merger parties in devising remedies to meet the requirements by MOFCOM, in terms of both the format and the content.

In addition, according to Mr. Shang Ming, the Director General of the AMB, in the year-end routine press conference at the end of 2012, MOFCOM is planning to formulate the *Rules on the Restrictive Conditions to the Concentration of Undertakings* in 2013, and it is envisaged that such rules will cover the entire procedure for devising remedies in both substantive and procedural aspects including the proposal, assessment, implementation as well as the re-examination. This will help the merger parties better understand their rights and obligations during the remedy negotiation, and also ease concerns regarding the unpredictability and uncertainty of the entire process and MOFCOM's practice.

Simplified procedures

Given the increasingly lengthy review and approval process as the result of shortage of case handlers and heavy workload of MOFCOM, as well as the complicated procedure for opinion-solicitation (from both relevant government authorities and the other stakeholders), most cases were not cleared until into Phase II, and MOFCOM has faced complaints from the merger parties as well as the practitioners for a while. Some simplified procedures, with greatly reduced information requirements and simplified opinion-solicitation process, have been long called for.

MOFCOM has been working on formulating simplified procedures, according to Mr. Shang at the AMB routine press conference at the end of 2012. It is expected that MOFCOM will primarily base its classification of the cases on the market share and HHI/CRn index for identifying cases to be reviewed under the simplified procedure.

* * *

Endnotes

1. According to MOFCOM, there are 16 notification closed in 2008, this number in 2009 is 78, 109 for 2010 and 171 for 2011.
2. Article 12 of the *Rules on the Review of the Concentration of Undertakings* ("***Review Rules***") promulgated by MOFCOM in November 2009, provides some key principles the Chinese authority shall consider when evaluating proposed remedies. According to Article 12, "*The restrictive conditions proposed by the undertakings involved in the concentration shall be appropriate to eliminate or reduce the effect of excluding and restricting competition so that the concentration of undertakings has or may have, and shall be realistically operational. The written version of the restrictive conditions shall be clear and definite so that the effectiveness and feasibility of these conditions can be thoroughly reviewed.*"
3. Purely behavioural remedies are applied even in some horizontal mergers as well, such as Uralkali/Silvinit (2011) and Seagate/Samsung (2011).
4. See http://images.mofcom.gov.cn/fldj/accessory/201211/1353031118730.pdf.
5. See http://fldj.mofcom.gov.cn/aarticle/zcfb/201301/20130108512781.html.

Feng Yao
Tel: +86 10 8513 1810 / Email: yao_feng@broadbright.com
As one of the four founding partners of Broad & Bright, Ms. Yao Feng's focus of practice includes anti-trust, international trade, customs and FDI.
Her clients range from private companies to governmental departments from Korea, Japan, the United States and European Union countries. Yao has represented the Chinese government in WTO dispute-settlement proceedings, advising clients on legal issues arising from import and export control, FDI and anti-trust matters.
In her position in MOFTEC Yao handled antidumping disputes, FDI issues and participated in trade treaty negotiations and trade law drafting. As well as her private practice she serves as a governmental expert advising on WTO rules implementation, OECD steel negotiation, trade barrier issues and antitrust law legislation.
In recent years, Yao have represented over 100 antitrust filings in China, representative clients include GE, Sumitomo, Carlyle, Kraft Food, Acer, Oracle, CVC, Bassell, BCI, Avery, Dynamic, Volkswagen, HGV, Goldman Sachs, SPX, Kent, Coca-Cola/Huiyuan, Hanwha, UTC, InBev/ANHEUSER-BUSCH, KKR, etc.

Li Bo
Tel: +86 10 8513 1840 / Email: bo_li@broadbright.com
After receiving a Juris Master degree from Renmin University School of Law, Mr. Li Bo joined Broad & Bright Law Firm in October, 2005. He has nearly eight years' practising experience as a lawyer admitted in China.
As a senior associate in the firm's competition and international trade group, Mr. Li Bo's practice cover competition law, international trade matters, foreign investment and M&A. His recent focus includes advising international clients in antitrust filings in China and antitrust compliance matters under the AML. Mr. Li's particular experience in merger control review and competition law compliance bring him a special advantage in advising clients in China as a part of the global filings in large cross-border transactions.
So far, Mr. Li has, with the firm's competition team, represented over 80 antitrust filings in China; representative clients include Siemens, MediaTech, Shell, UTC, GE, Kraft Food, Acer, Oracle, UTC, Shell, Seagate, KKR, International Paper, etc.

Broad & Bright Law Firm

Suite 701, CBD International Plaza, No.16 Yong'andongli, Jianguomenwai Avenue, Chaoyang District, Beijing, 100022, China
Tel: +86 10 8513 1818 / Fax: +86 10 8513 1919 / URL: http://www.broadbright.com

Colombia

Alfonso Miranda Londoño
Esguerra Barrera Arriaga S.A.

Brief introduction to Colombian competition law

Like most countries in Latin America, Colombia issued a first tier of antitrust legislation at the end of the 50s, under the political and academic influence of the US and the European Union. However, competition laws were not applied in this first era, mainly due to the economic protectionist model, which did not favour a competition environment.

The evolution of antitrust laws in Colombia can be divided into two main phases, which can be, in turn, subdivided into many others depending on the depth and detail in which the analysis is conducted.

The first phase began with Law 155, 1959, which contained the first comprehensive regulation of Antitrust Law in Colombia, and ended with Special Decree 2153, 1992, which reorganised the Competition Authority and structured the anticompetitive conducts into several categories including: (i) the general prohibition; (ii) the anticompetitive agreements; (iii) the anticompetitive acts; (iv) the conducts of abuse of the dominant position; and (v) violation of merger control regulations. The 1991 Political Constitution was issued during this phase. This event had an enormous significance for competition law in Colombia, because the new Constitution established Free Economic Competition as an economic right for everyone, which imposes responsibilities.

The second phase began when Decree 2153, 1992 was issued, and it can be said that we are still living in this new phase, which has now lasted for twenty (20) years. During this time period, Law 1340, 2009 was issued. The most important aspects of this law are the following:

- The Superintendence of Industry and Commerce (hereinafter referred to as SIC) was appointed as the National Competition Authority, with an almost exclusive jurisdiction for the application of the Competition Laws in Colombia.
- The law clarifies the rules for the application of Special Competition Regimes in coordination with the General Competition Regime.
- The law calls for a stronger application of Competition Advocacy and coordination between public authorities, for the purposes of application of the Competition Laws.
- The law modifies the thresholds and the procedure for merger review.
- The law requires that, in case that an investigated party decides to offer a settlement to SIC, it will only have the opportunity to propose it during the first stages of the procedure, so that SIC does not have to go through the whole investigation only to have to analyse a settlement proposition at the end.
- The law includes a leniency programme aimed at fostering collaboration from the companies and the administrators involved in anti-competitive conducts. Effective and timely cooperation from companies and the natural persons involved in the investigated conducts, can grant them partial or total immunity from the sanctions that SIC can impose.
- The law allows a more active participation of third parties in the investigations for anti-competitive practices and in the merger review procedures.
- The fines that can be charged by SIC were increased considerably. Now, they can go up to US $31,527,647[1], or to the equivalent of 150% of the profits generated by the anti-competitive

conduct for the companies. Natural persons can also be charged with fines that can go up to US $630,552[2].

- The new law expanded the statute of limitations for imposing fines in antitrust investigations from three (3) to five (5) years.
- Lastly, the Law created special mechanisms for State intervention in the agricultural sector. Eventually, these mechanisms may be used in order to exclude conducts and situations from the application of competition laws.

Several laws have been issued after the application of Law 1340, 2009 started. Though they don't have the importance of the mentioned law, they introduced interesting changes that are worth describing.

The first one is Law 1474, 2011, better known as the "Anticorruption Statute". Article 27 of this law applies criminal law to bid-rigging agreements in bids related to the public sector. Before the law, bid-rigging agreements were considered only as anti-competitive practices under number 9 of article 47 of Decree 2153, 1992, and now they are categorised as a crime when the affected bid affects State funds. As a direct consequence of the issuing of this law, Colombian Antitrust Law ventures in the field of the criminal repression of anti-competitive conducts, with the consequences that this decision carries.

According to the second paragraph of the mentioned article, the persons accused of this criminal infraction that are accepted in a leniency programme by SIC, are also eligible for obtaining benefits within the criminal procedure, consisting in the reduction of a third of the imposed penalty, a reduction of 40% of the imposed fine and a five- (5) year restriction prohibition to contract with State entities.

The second statute that has introduced changes to the Competition Laws is Law-Decree 019, 2012, better known as the "Anti-Bureaucracy Statute". Its general objective is to introduce efficiency in administrative proceedings in order to eliminate unnecessary steps, delays and permits. In order to accomplish this objective, the statute eliminates or modifies unnecessary procedures and requirements in State proceedings. It is based in articles 83 and 84 of the Politic Constitution, which include the principle of "good faith" and prohibit public authorities from requiring permissions, requisites or licences in addition to those imposed by law, for the activities of private persons and companies.

The named decree modifies some of the procedures that must be followed in the investigations and procedures carried out by SIC.

Merger control in Colombia

The Merger Control legislation in Colombia is set forth mainly in Law 155, 1959, Decree 2153, 1992, Law 1340, 2009, Circular No. 10 of the Superintendence of Industry and Commerce, Resolution 75837, 2011 which refers to the economic thresholds for review, and Resolution 35006, 2010, modified by Resolution 52778, 2011, which contains the guidelines for presentation of antitrust filings pursuant to the New Competition Law, 1340, 2009. Merger regulations for specific sectors are contained in other statutes.

The Organic Statute for the Financial System (Decree 663, 1993) governs mergers in the financial and insurance sectors. Legislation for mergers between airlines is basically contained in article 1866 of the Commerce Code and article 3.6.3.7.3 of the Colombian Aeronautic Regulation – RAC.

The Superintendence of Industry and Commerce – SIC is the National Competition Authority in Colombia and is also the main authority for merger control. SIC is an administrative entity controlled by the Government. The Superintendent can be freely appointed and removed from office by the President of Colombia.

Pursuant to article 2 of Law 1340, 2009, SIC has been now granted the power to review mergers in all sectors of the economy with two exceptions: (i) reorganisation operations in the financial sector which are reviewed by the Financial Superintendence, which must hear the opinion of SIC and must apply the conditions that SIC recommends, if any; and (ii) operational agreements between airlines, which are reviewed by the Aeronautic Authority.

According to article 9 of Law 1340, 2009, merger transactions that have to be informed and require previous authorisation (waiting period) from SIC in Colombia, are those that:

(i)   Are entered into by companies that are dedicated to the same activities, or participate in the same vertical value chain.

(ii) Together or separately had operational income or own assets anywhere in the world, in the year previous to the transaction, in an amount that meets the thresholds that SIC has established. Right now the notification thresholds are defined in Resolution 75837, 2011, in an amount in monthly minimum wages, equivalent to approximately US$31m.

(iii) Have an individual or joint participation in the relevant market(s) affected by the transaction of 20% or more.

If the economic thresholds pointed out in (ii) are met but the market participation threshold is not, then the transaction is deemed authorised, and needs only to be previously **notified** (no waiting period) to SIC. Mergers that do not meet the above-mentioned economic thresholds are not subject to merger control.

Clearance is not required when the transaction is carried out between companies that belong to the same corporate group.

According to article 9 of Law 1340, 2009, all transactions that consist of acquisitions, mergers, consolidations or integrations (whatever the legal form of the transaction) between companies dedicated to the same activities or participating in the same vertical value chain, which assets and sales individually or jointly meet the economic thresholds, and have a 20% or more market participation as explained above, require to be **informed** to SIC and previously authorised (waiting period). If the economic thresholds are met but the joint or individual participation of the companies in all the markets in which they participate is below 20%, the transaction is deemed as authorised and needs only to be **notified** to SIC (no waiting period). The new 2009 law has made it totally clear that SIC will review both horizontal and vertical transactions. Currently there is a discussion going on as to whether merger control applies to conglomerate mergers in which there is no market overlap, but it seems that this is not the case, since the new 2009 law did not refer to those cases.

The interpretation of SIC is that a merger transaction amounts to an entrepreneurial concentration that needs authorisation from the competition authority, when the companies involved (two or more) cease to participate independently in the market and are therefore **permanently** controlled by the same management or decision centre, whatever the legal structure designated for that purpose.

The SIC has not issued any particular doctrine on when joint ventures are caught; however, as pointed out above, the interpretation of SIC is that there is an entrepreneurial concentration when control over two companies or undertakings that were participating independently in the market is acquired **permanently** by the same management or decision centre, whatever the legal structure designated for that purpose. In this sense, only joint ventures that create a sort of **permanent** undertaking should be subject to merger control.

Colombian law offers two definitions of control: one is found in the Commerce Code and applies to corporations; the other is in the Competition Law and refers in a broader way to undertakings. According to the broader definition, control is the possibility of influencing, directly or indirectly, the business policy of a company or undertaking, the initiation or termination of the activities of the company, the variation of the activities to which the company is dedicated, or the use or disposal of the essential assets needed for the activities of the company.

The definition of corporate control includes both internal and external control. Pursuant to article 261 of the Commerce Code, internal control shall be considered to exist when a company, directly or through other subsidiaries, owns more than 50% of the capital stock of another company or owns or commands enough voting stock to appoint the majority of its directors. External control, on the other hand, exists when, by way of a contract or other relationship different from the ownership of stock, one person or company can exercise a dominant influence over a corporation.

The Merger Antitrust Legislation does not apply to transactions that do not imply the acquisition of control.

In reference to foreign mergers, it must be said that Colombia adheres to the effects theory, meaning that foreign transactions that produce effects in the Colombian market are subject to SIC review. The same legislation governs both domestic and foreign mergers. SIC doctrine requires authorisation of foreign mergers where both parties to the merger market their products, directly or indirectly, in Colombia. Under the former doctrine of SIC, clearance was not necessary for foreign mergers, when the products of one or both of the merging parties were sold in Colombia by independent companies that assumed the risk and made the decisions associated with the import and sale of the products. Nevertheless, it must be considered that this doctrine has been overruled after the SABMiller – Bavaria merger. In this case, SIC requested an antitrust filing, even though independent importers sold the products and brands of SABMiller.

Overview of merger control activity during the last 12 months

Principal cases

In the past few years, SIC cleared some big acquisitions: the sale of the national telecommunications company – *Telecom*, to the Spanish operator – *Telefonica*; the transaction *Procter & Gamble – Gillette*, the sale of the supermarket chain – *Carulla*, to the French controlled chain – *Éxito*[3]; the sale of the main national newspaper *El Tiempo*, to the Spanish *Planeta* Group; the sale of the national steel producer – *Acerías Paz del Río*, to the Brazilian conglomerate *Grupo Votorantim*; the sale of the only PVC resin producer – *Petco* to the Mexican manufacturer – *Mexichem*, and the subsequent sale of the main PVC tube manufacturer – *Amanco*, also to *Mexichem*; the acquisition of *Petro Rubiales* by *Pacific Stratus Energy,* the sale of *Aluminio Reynolds Santodomingo* to the Arfel Group, the sale of *Bavaria* to *SabMiller*, the sale of the drugstore business of *Éxito/Cafam* to *Olímpica*, and the transaction between *Colgate* and *Unilever* for the sale of the detergent brands, *inter alia*. In the case of the main cigarette manufacturer *Coltabaco*, SIC initially approved the transaction presented with *Phillip Morris* as a buyer, but the companies could not comply with the structural conditions imposed and the merger failed. The transaction was later approved with *BAT* as a buyer.

However, not all the important transactions were cleared. SIC objected to the *Procter & Gamble – Colgate* transaction related mainly to the *Fab* brand, and the *Postobón – Quaker* transaction, related to the *Gatorade* brand. In both cases the main debate between SIC and the petitioners was related to the definition of the relevant market. In the *P&G – Colgate* transaction SIC decided, at the last moment, to narrow the relevant market of powder detergents, departing from the market for washing products (including powder and bar soap) presented by the companies.[4]

In the *Postobón – Quaker* transaction, SIC narrowed the relevant market to include only isotonic beverages. In this case, SIC not only forbade the transaction, but also launched an investigation in order to establish whether the parties had closed the transaction before SIC approved the deal.[5]

General statistics

The general record of SIC for merger review is as follows:

Year	Informed	Notification	Authorised	Remedies	Objected
1998	132	0	132	0	0
1999	118	0	118	0	0
2000	126	0	123	2	0
2001	121	0	93	3	0
2002	104	0	70	9	1
2003	62	0	47	3	0
2004	97	0	90	2	3
2005	103	0	98	3	0
2006	112	0	98	4	3

Year	Informed	Notification	Authorised	Remedies	Objected
2007	83	0	62	3	1
2008	81	0	74	2	0
2009	76	13	53	0	0
2010	10	59	32	0	1
2011	36	19	0	0	0
2012	76	53		1	0
Total	**1337**	**144**	**1090**	**32**	**9**

From this table we can see that in 14 years the authority has reviewed 1,337 transactions (transactions that have been **informed**). From the total number of transactions presented, the authority made a decision in 84.59% of the cases, which means that 15.41% of the transactions were desisted.

It is also important to note that, since the economic threshold was raised in 2006, the number of transactions was reduced by 25%; when it was raised again in 2009 it was reduced by an additional 22%, and the numbers did not improve when the threshold went back down in 2011. Also, since law 1340, 2009 created the new notification (no waiting period) procedure, the number of transactions that are informed (waiting period) has been reduced significantly: in 2009, already 14% of the total transactions were notified and in 2012 the number of notifications is 70% of the total transactions reviewed. This means that in the year 2012, approximately 70% of the transactions that met the economic threshold created a market concentration below 20%, or so the interested parties claim, because we have no statistics as to the number of those notifications that are actually under investigation for failing to inform the transaction.

New developments in jurisdictional assessment or procedure

The highlights in the evolution of SIC's doctrine regarding mergers during the past few years are the following:

- In 2009, SIC issued Resolution 69901 raising again the economic thresholds for antitrust filing. It was then mandatory to inform those operations in which the value of the assets or sales of the merging companies in Colombia (individually or jointly considered) were equal or superior to US $40m. The application of these thresholds reduced the number of informed transactions significantly as said before.
- In 2011, SIC issued Resolution 75837, 2011, lowering again the economic threshold to US $31m.
- Since the *Pavco – Ralco* transaction, SIC started to impose structural as well as behavioural conditions in order to subdue restrictions on competition and authorise complex transactions. Structural conditions require divestiture of brands, installed capacity, etc. Behavioural conditions, on the other hand, require the elimination of exclusivity, obligation to supply, etc. Nowadays, SIC applies all kinds of conditions but prefers the structural ones. This practice will continue, for the new 2009 law allows for the application of conditions.[6]
- The *Cementos Andino – Cementos Argos* transaction was authorised by SIC based in the *Failing Industry Doctrine*. Even though this kind of defence had been considered before, it was not until the cement merger that SIC laid down the characteristics and requisites for application of the *Failing Industry Doctrine*.[7]
- SIC developed a doctrine for review of vertical concentrations. It also concluded that operations such as the sale of a brand or the creation of a new company by two previous competitors amount to an economic concentration that needs authorisation from SIC. As mentioned before, under the new 2009 law, it is clear, that vertical integrations will be reviewed if they meet the thresholds. It is important to point out that the 20% market participation threshold will trigger the need to **inform** (waiting period) the transaction to the authority, if the threshold is met in any of the vertical markets affected by the merger.

- During the years previous to Law 1340, 2009, SIC claimed jurisdiction over mergers between public utilities companies. It also disputed the review of mergers between Cable TV companies. As mentioned before, the new law leaves no doubt in the sense that SIC is the merger authority in the mentioned sectors of the economy.
- In recent cases, SIC has challenged the decision of the interested parties to file a short **notification** (no waiting period) and has initiated investigations in order to establish if the parties should have filed an **information** which requires a previous authorisation (waiting period) of the merger, before it can produce effects in the Colombian market.
- In 2010, SIC decided the merger between the *Regional Port of Buenaventura, TECSA and the Port Operators*, in which was accepted for the first time the efficiency exception provided by the law, for those merger transactions that create an important concentration of the market but result in efficiencies and reduction of costs that cannot be achieved otherwise. The transaction was approved without conditions, based on the efficiency exception.

Assessment of vertical and conglomerate mergers

There is no explanation in the law of the reasoning and analysis that SIC should use in merger cases, and the guidelines that the authority issued in 2009 do not shed light to that effect. SIC has been working on new guidelines, but they are not official yet. However, through the analysis of cases, it is possible to identify some general points in the analysis:

- SIC defines the general market based in the product market and the geographic market. The product market will be defined narrowly using the hypothetic monopolist test *(SSNIP Test)*, in order to isolate the group of products (goods or services) that behave as perfect or imperfect substitutes of the product affected from the merger.
- In the supermarket cases: *Éxito – Carulla; Éxito – Cafam and Éxito/Cafam – Olímpica*, SIC used the Isochronal Test in order to define the relevant geographic market of the different supermarket chains within the large cities. The isochronal was rated at ten (10) minutes time of transportation.
- SIC will consider and evaluate the competitive pressure that arises from perfect and imperfect substitutes, as well as from potential competition coming from national or international players. In 2011, SIC authorised the *Caterpillar – Bucyrus* transaction, in which the authority considered competitive pressures from a relevant market larger than Colombia, which comprised a substantial part of Latin America.
- SIC will calculate the participation of the merging companies in the relevant market and apply concentration indexes like HHI and CR4 in order to evaluate the effect of the merger. In markets that present a *leader – follower* structure, SIC has also used the *Stackelberg Model* in order to assess market power before and after the merger takes place.
- SIC will then evaluate the different kinds of barriers for entering the market including import tariffs and duties, transportation costs, excess capacity, cost of building a plant in the country, etc., in an effort to evaluate the contestability of the market or the likelihood of entry of new competitors.
- If the parties have proposed conditions to the transaction, SIC will evaluate them and discuss them with the merging parties. In some cases SIC will modify substantially the conditions offered by the parties and in general will prefer structural to behavioural remedies. Most likely, SIC will require divestment of part of the business.
- It is not very clear what particular set of circumstances will trigger an objection or a conditional approval; but most likely it will be a negative mixture of the above elements.
- This means that a merger that increases concentration in the relevant market to a high degree, with no perfect or even imperfect substitutes of the product, no potential competition in sight, high barriers to entry, scarce contestability and no possible structural remedies, will probably be prohibited.
- Having said that, it is important to remember that in its whole history SIC has prohibited less than 1% of the informed mergers.

As said before, for some years now, SIC has been applying reasoning and analysis similar to those developed both in the European Union and the United States. There is much debate as to the use of economic tools, such as the concentration indexes, which were prepared for developed economies, without adjustment to the size and specific characteristics of the Colombian economy. It has to be considered that most markets in a developing economy are small and already concentrated, but this circumstance does not mean that there is no competition or that it will become impossible for new competitors to enter the market.

From the lines of merger cases that have been objected or conditioned it is possible to deduct that SIC has moved from the *"Market Dominance Test"* it used initially, into a more comprehensive *"Substantially Lessening of Competition Test"*. It is now clear under the new 2009 law that SIC has the capacity to review vertical mergers. There is much debate in regard to the possibility of the authority to review conglomerate mergers.

Non-competition issues, such convenience, political considerations, labour loss, etc., are not relevant in the merger review process and will not be considered or discussed by SIC.

As said before, the substantive test for clearance is not described in the law. It has been developed by SIC based on the US and EU experiences and guidelines. SIC defines the relevant market based in the product market and the geographic market. The product market will be defined narrowly using the hypothetic monopolist test (*SSNIP Test*). The geographic market has been defined using the *Isochronal Test.* SIC will consider the competitive pressure that arises from perfect and imperfect substitutes, as well as from potential competition coming from national or international players. SIC will calculate the participation of the merging companies in the relevant market and apply concentration indexes like HHI and CR4 in order to evaluate the effect of the merger. In some cases, SIC has also used the *Stackelberg Model.*

SIC will study the barriers to entry and the contestability of the market. In its analysis SIC will take into consideration actual and potential competition including imports and the possibility of new entrants to the market. In case the data shows that the transaction produces an important increase in concentration and that it can substantially lessen competition, SIC will consider possible remedies. Remedies have to be presented and substantiated by the merging parties.

There is no doubt that during the past few years SIC has gone a long way in the study and control of mergers, as recent cases indicate. However, there is a great deal of uncertainty as to what kind of analysis SIC or any of the other authorities is going to apply in the review of mergers.

In compliance with the new 2009 law, SIC should issue guidelines for mergers, which help to explain and illustrate its decision-making process, for the benefit of the parties to the merger. The guidelines that were issued in 2009 only explain the procedure and the information-gathering process, they do not shed light over the substantial test that SIC will apply.

Approach to remedies to avoid second stage investigation

It is important for the merging companies to identify early in the review process if the transaction should be subject to remedies in order to offer them, at least in a general way, so that the authority is aware of the intention or willingness of the parties to discuss them. In those cases, when SIC finds that the proposed transaction may pose undue restrictions to competition, but believes there are options to correct such distortion, it will authorise the merger provided certain remedies are undertaken.

Such conditions or remedies have ranged from elimination of exclusivity for distributors to the obligation of producing for a competitor at variable cost, allowing a competitor to use a percentage of installed capacity, and even the obligation to divest part of the business. SIC has proven to prefer structural remedies, such as divestments to conduct, or behavioural remedies.

SIC customarily requires that the parties comply with structural remedies within a certain time limit (generally, less than one year). Compliance of behavioural remedies is also required for a limited period of time (generally, no more than three years). Pursuant to article 11 of Law 1340, 2009, SIC must review periodically if the parties have complied with the conditions and obligations imposed.

Traditionally, SIC has required that an external auditor verifies the full compliance of the remedies and presents reports to the authority from time to time. Finally, SIC requests that the merging parties put in place a bank or insurance bond to guarantee the full compliance of the remedies.

SIC has not made distinctions in regard to the imposition of remedies in foreign-to-foreign mergers.

Key policy developments

Law 1340, 2009, substantially changed merger control.

Change in the Authority

As explained above, Law 1340, 2009 appointed SIC as the National Competition Authority, with capacity to decide over mergers in all sectors of the economy, but for the transactions in the financial sector and the aeronautic sector, which are decided by the Financial Superintendence and the Aeronautic Authority respectively, with the particularities previously described.

Change in the thresholds

Law 1340, 2009 added the market participation threshold to the previously existing economic thresholds (US $31m in assets or operational income, considered worldwide). As has been explained above, the market participation threshold divides the transactions in which the interested parties have a joint or individual market participation equal or superior to 20% of the market, in which case they need to be **informed** (waiting period); from those other transactions in which the interested parties have a joint or individual market participation below 20% of the market, in which case they need to be **notified** (no waiting period).

Procedure is divided in two stages

Pursuant to Law 1340, 2009, the merger review procedure is now divided into two stages. It is considered that mergers that pose no threat to competition and need no conditions should be decided in Stage I, whereas complex transactions that restrict competition will pass to Stage II and probably will need conditions in order to avoid objection or prohibition. The duration of Stage I is thirty (30) working days and the duration of Stage II is three (3) months.

Stage I

SIC Resolution 35006, 2010, as amended by Resolution 52778, 2011, points out the specific information that the merging parties must provide to SIC. The list is very detailed. It includes information concerning the transaction itself, the companies involved, market participations and conditions, other competitors, consumers, barriers to entry, and other information that may aid SIC to properly evaluate the effects of the transaction. It is important to note that SIC can abstain from considering the merger until the information is complete. The main steps in this stage are as follows:

- The petitioners file a pre-evaluation petition, together with a succinct description of the transaction.
- Within the following three (3) days, SIC will evaluate if the transaction needs to be reviewed. In case it decides the transaction does not need review, it will end the proceedings.
- If the transaction needs review, within the three- (3) day period SIC will order a publication in a newspaper of ample circulation, so that any interested parties can file the information they deem relevant for the analysis of the transaction.
- The petitioners can request to SIC to abstain from the publication, for reasons of public order, and SIC may accept the petition and keep the transaction and the procedure confidential.
- SIC has thirty (30) working days (45 calendar days in most cases)[8] to study the transaction and decide whether the transaction poses no risk to competition, in which case it will approve it; or if the review proceedings must continue.

Stage II

- If the procedure continues, SIC will inform the regulation and the control agencies in the special sectors involved in the merger transaction. Those entities will have the opportunity to offer SIC their technical advice in regard to the transaction under study, within ten (10) working days of the notification, and can also participate in the proceedings at any point. Their opinion is not binding for SIC, but if SIC is going to depart from that opinion, it must justify its decision.

• Within fifteen (15) days of the continuation of the proceedings, the authorities and other interested parties must file with SIC any information they deem relevant for the decision. They can also propose conditions and other measures that can help to mitigate the anticompetitive effects of the transaction.

• SIC can request the authorities and interested parties to add, explain or clarify the information they have filed.

• Within this fifteen- (15) day period, the petitioners can review the information filed by the authorities and third parties, and prove against it.

• Within the three (3) months following the date in with the parties have filed all the information requested, SIC will have to make one of three possible decisions: simple authorisation; conditioned authorisation (clearance with remedies); or objection.

• According to Colombian Law, in case SIC surpasses this deadline, the transaction is considered automatically approved (positive administrative silence) and the Authority loses competence over the case. However, it must be pointed out that there have been only a couple of such cases in twenty (20) years, which means it is most unlikely to occur.

• In case that at any time within the proceedings, the parties to the merger remain inactive for two (2) months, SIC will consider that the petition for authorisation of the transaction has been desisted.

Consequences of *gun-jumping*

Mergers carried out without previous clearance from SIC are considered an infraction of antitrust laws and the companies and their administrators are subject to fines. Fines are expressed in minimum monthly wages. The maximum fine that SIC may enforce amounts up to US $31m for the companies and US$ $500,000 for the administrators[9]. In addition to that, if SIC considers that the transaction produces an undue restriction on competition and must be prohibited, it could order to reverse the operation. Finally, it must be considered that an operation carried out in violation of competition laws can be declared by a judge absolutely null and void, which can have important economic repercussions. It must be pointed out that, for merger purposes, SIC is not a judicial authority. Such a declaration has to be obtained through an ordinary process before the general jurisdiction.

It is therefore important to convey that a foreign merger that meets the above mentioned thresholds, should not produce effects in the Colombian territory until it has been approved by SIC. There is not yet a clear doctrine in regard to the closing of foreign transactions before obtaining clearance with SIC, with a *"carve out provision"* or a *"hold separate agreement"* for Colombia. However, it is advisable to have such clauses and any other elements that help to assure SIC that the transaction will not have effects in Colombia before it has been cleared by SIC.

Involvement of other parties or authorities

Third parties have not been allowed to participate in the merger review process, that is, they are not allowed to review information revealed by the merging parties, they are not notified of the decisions and are unable to file a reconsideration plea. Nevertheless, third parties can and do present documents and express their opinions, that SIC may or may not take into account. If considered necessary, SIC may ask third parties to render testimony or to disclose information that might prove useful in order to review the transaction.

All the information included in the antitrust filing by the parties is considered strictly confidential.

The Colombian economy is open to foreign investment. However, there are exchange, tax, labour, securities and special sector requirements that need to be checked with local councils before entering into a transaction.

Reform proposals

Because of the wideness of the Merger Control Rules, it is important that SIC issues additional guidelines that deal with the substantial test that the authority will apply, including the definitions and requisites for the application of the *Efficiency Exception* and the *Failing Industry Defence.*

Endnotes

1. Before this law was issued, the maximum fine that could be imposed to the companies was of US$630,552.
2. Before this law was issued, the maximum fine that could be imposed to the administrators was of US$94,583.
3. *Carulla – Exito.* Resolution 34904 of December 18 of 2006.
4. *Procter & Gamble – Colgate.* Resolution No. 28037, issued on November 12th, 2004.
5. *Postobón – Quaker.* Resolution No. 16433, issued on July 23rd, 2004.
6. *Pavco – Ralco.* Resolution 4861 of February 27 of 2004, Resolution 22338 of August 8 of 2003, Resolution 5013 of March 10 of 2004.
7. *Cementos Andino – Cementos Argos.* Resolution 13544 of May 26 of 2006.
8. According to article 62 of Law 4, 1913, unless explicitly stated otherwise, when laws and official acts refer to terms of days, they are understood as working days.
9. Law 1340, 2009, Article 25.

Alfonso Miranda Londoño
Tel: +57 1 312 2900 / Email: amiranda@esguerrabarrera.com

Alfonso Miranda Londoño is a lawyer from the Javeriana University Law School in Bogotá, Colombia. He specialised in Socioeconomic Sciences at the same University, in Banking Law at Los Andes University (also in Bogotá) and obtained his Masters Degree in Law (LL.M) from Cornell University (1987). He is the Director of the Law and Economics Department at the Javeriana University Law School, the co-founder and Director of the Centre for Studies in Competition Law – CEDEC, and a Professor of Competition Law at the Javeriana University.

He is the partner who leads the Competition Law practice at Esguerra Barrera Arriaga, which is the result of the integration of two prestigious and renowned law firms founded in 1977 and 1990. Its partners possess vast consulting, litigation and academic experience, and several of them have occupied high positions in the Colombian government.

Esguerra Barrera Arriaga S.A.

Calle 72 No. 6-30 Piso 12, Bogotá D.C., Colombia
Tel: +57 1 312 2900 / Fax: +57 1 310 4715 / URL: http://www.esguerrabarrera.com

Cyprus

Polyvios Panayides & Alexandros Economou
Chrysses Demetriades & Co. LLC

Overview of merger control activity during the last 12 months

In the course of 2012, the Commission for the Protection of Competition of the Republic of Cyprus (the "CPC") has mainly focused its high-profile activity on antitrust enforcement under the Protection of Competition Law which deals with cartels and abuses, with particular emphasis on the food, telecoms and consumer goods sectors. In fact, with respect to using the available antitrust tools, the CPC has actually been quite active.

On the other hand, the activity of the CPC in 2012 on the merger control front was mainly of a procedural nature. This may be because:

- most of the concentrations were of an international nature that had little or no impact on the relevant Cyprus markets; and
- the concentrations involving Cypriot-based parties mostly involved consolidation of relatively competitive sectors such as banking (including cooperative banks), car distributors and food and consumer product distributors.

Nonetheless the number of concentrations that were notified to the CPC in 2012 was 47, as compared to 33 in 2011.

The trend of notifications is on the increase compared to the previous year, bringing an additional workload for the CPC; however this increase should mostly be attributed to foreign-to-foreign transactions of international groups which do not necessarily have a physical presence in Cyprus. This is mainly because the relevant criteria do not require that any of the parties has a physical presence in Cyprus or that all parties to a concentration have activities in Cyprus.

It is also notable that there were no prohibition decisions by the CPC during 2012, nor were there any decisions that imposed commitments on the parties concerned. In fact, no concentration that was reviewed by the CPC in the relevant period led to a phase II investigation. However, it appears that a number of notifications which *prima facie* raised competition concerns may have been withdrawn by the parties.

In terms of European cooperation, on 5/11/2012 the CPC decided to request the referral to the European Commission of the proposed concentration between the two main Greek airline companies, Aegean and Olympic, pursuant to article 22(1) of the EU Merger Regulation. The said concentration, which had been notified to the CPC on 30/10/2012, did not have a European dimension. A parallel notification for the said concentration was also filed in Greece.

New developments in jurisdictional assessment and procedure

The Control of Concentrations Law, Law 22(I)/1999 (the "Cyprus Merger Control Law") imposes a legal obligation to notify a concentration which fulfils the following criteria:

(i) The aggregate worldwide turnover achieved by each of at least two of the participating undertakings exceeds €3,417,202.88; **and**

(ii) at least one of the participating undertakings is engaged in commercial activities within Cyprus; **and**

- at least €3,417,202.88 out of the aggregate worldwide turnover of all the participating undertakings relates to the disposal of goods or the supply of services within Cyprus.

The above thresholds, which can be triggered relatively easily, have remained the same for the last years.

In addition, there is a residual (political) power vested in the Minister of Trade and Industry to decide to request a notification even if the above thresholds are not fulfilled, if he considers that a concentration is of "major importance". The relevant provision of the Cyprus Merger Control Law provides that "the Minister may, even if in relation to a specific concentration the conditions set above are not satisfied, declare by an Order that the said concentration is of major importance, and in such a case the provisions of the law shall apply". This power was not exercised in the course of 2012.

Given the nature of the Cyprus economy, being a small economy with low levels of manufacturing, dependent on a high level of imports of goods, an obligation to notify in Cyprus can be triggered with regard to a large number of multinational mergers, where at least one of the parties has commercial activities in Cyprus. Moreover, in recent years there has been an increase in the number of concentrations affecting the services sectors on which the Cyprus economy primarily depends.

In 2012 there were no significant, if any, developments in the jurisdictional assessment or procedure. However, in line with the European practice, the CPC followed the approach of other European jurisdictions to require a notification in situations of a change from joint to sole control (see the *Carrefour Marinoulos* concentration, Decision 22/2012). Almost always, when it comes to dealing with legal issues of a jurisdictional nature, the CPC follows the precedents of the European Commission and the relevant Jurisdictional Notice (e.g full functionality, change of control and attribution of turnovers to parents of a joint venture).

If there are no affected markets in Cyprus (i.e if horizontal overlaps are below 15% and verticals below 25%), the parties need only file a short Form CO. From a practical point of view, the CPC has in fact been very swift at clearing simplified cases, often doing so before the phase I deadline.

It needs to be emphasised that the fact that only one of the undertakings concerned has a real presence in Cyprus (or that the other has minimal or no presence) is not a ground to be exempted from the obligation to notify. During 2012, the CPC applied the Cyprus Merger Control Law strictly, and did not exempt parties from the obligation to notify concentrations that led to zero or minimal effects on competition. As mentioned above, it is not a prerequisite for triggering the obligation to notify to have a branch or subsidiary in Cyprus. In fact, the test is whether the parties engage in the "disposal of goods or the supply of services within the Republic".

Formally speaking, there are no pre-notification discussions in Cyprus, however it is advisable to consult with the service of the CPC at an early stage if jurisdictional uncertainties are encountered. Unlike most European jurisdictions, pursuant to the Cyprus Merger Control Law, the obligation to notify is only triggered after the signing of the (binding) agreement bringing about the concentration or the relevant public offer (if it is the case). Before these events take place, the CPC will be unable to accept a notification. Should the jurisdictional thresholds be met, the parties will have to file a notification within seven days from the relevant triggering event. Therefore, from a practical point of view, the parties and their legal advisors need to undertake a jurisdictional assessment at an early stage of the corporate negotiations.

In the event of a failure to notify a concentration that meets the applicable criteria, the CPC can impose a lump sum fine of up to €85,000 (plus up to €8,500 for every day the infringement continues). If also the concentration is partially or completely implemented ahead of regulatory clearance, the CPC may additionally impose a fine of up to 10% of the total turnover of the participating undertakings (of preceding financial year) plus up to €8,500 per day for each day the infringement continues.

In the event that the CPC detects a failure to notify a concentration (or if the parties themselves inform the CPC on their own initiative of a historic breach of the Cyprus Merger Control Law), the CPC will take enforcement action against the parties that failed to comply with their legal obligation. The CPC will not exempt from enforcement action negligent breaches. Although the CPC will pursue all cases involving such infringements, and will normally ask the parties to file a notification irrespective of the fact that the transaction has been put into effect, the CPC is generally lenient in terms of the level of fines. This practice was also maintained in 2012.

The CPC imposed fines for failure to notify and for putting into effect concentrations without a clearance decision being first issued, on numerous occasions in the course of 2012, but the fines can generally be characterised as relatively lenient compared to other EU jurisdictions and the practice of the EU Commission. The CPC decisions in the course of 2012 that we reviewed imposed fines of €5,000-10,000. It cannot however be excluded that the trend of imposing high fines in other national/EU jurisdictions for breaches of the duty to notify is also followed by the CPC in the future.

Key industry sectors reviewed, and approach adopted, to market definition, barriers to entry, nature of international competition etc.

The Merger Law sets out the criteria to be considered when assessing a concentration. These include:
(a) the structure of the affected markets;
(b) market position;
(c) economic power;
(d) alternative sources of supply of the products or services and any substitutes;
(e) supply and demand trends;
(f) barriers to entry; and
(g) interests of consumers.

The CPC only assesses relevant markets within Cyprus. In its 2012 decisions the CPC maintained its practice of referring very often to European Commission precedents, especially with respect to identifying the relevant product market definition.

The CPC, being mostly faced with mergers that do not *prima facie* raise competition concerns, chose to leave the relevant geographic and product markets open in most cases, though in some instances it has indicated a preference for a specific definition.

More specifically, one can detect a preference of the CPC to assess concentrations by reference to a national (i.e. Cyprus-wide) geographic market definition for almost all sectors. This is possibly due to the small size of Cyprus and the generally harmonious conditions of competition and regulation throughout Cyprus.

For example, in sectors such as retail banking, the CPC opted for a national market definition, in view of the common regulatory framework and the generally consistent entry barriers in all regions. This approach was also observed in a number of concentrations between locally based cooperative banks which had a presence only in specific (local) regions of Cyprus (see Decisions 56/2012 and 4/2013) but also with respect to the recent concentrations between Greek banks Eurobank/National Bank of Greece (Decision 61/2012) and Emporiki Bank of Greece/Alpha Bank (Decision 53/2012) which had a national presence throughout Cyprus.

The approach of the CPC to prefer a national market definition was also noted in the P.M. Tseriotis Ltd /Tryfon Distributors (Decision 31/2012) and the Laiko-Cosmos Trading Ltd JV (Decision 30/2012), which involved concentrations between consumer goods distributors/wholesalers.

Given the current banking crisis facing Cyprus, it is likely that local consolidation between undertakings will continue to increase in 2013, especially in sectors such as banking and other financial services sectors. Further consolidation between players active in the consumer and food sectors will likely take place as well. Further increased merger activity in these sectors, between players that have an important local presence, could trigger more significant competition challenges for the CPC.

Key economic appraisal techniques applied

The key substantive test, as stated in the Cyprus Merger Control Law, is whether the proposed merger "creates or strengthens a dominant position in the affected markets within the Republic".

Because most mergers are cleared at phase I, there is little analysis in the context of assessing each of the above criteria in the published decisions. The approach that can be observed from recent decisions of the CPC, is that it mainly focuses on market shares rather than on other economic criteria and tests, such as risks of collusion or spillover effects on neighbouring markets. Especially when assessing full-functional joint ventures relevant to the food and consumer goods sectors, the CPC could apply additional economic tests; nevertheless the existing approach will likely be followed by the CPC, as the said sectors are expected to continue contracting in 2013 and 2014.

Approach to remedies (i) to avoid second stage investigation and (ii) following second stage investigation

There were no significant developments in 2012 with respect to the approach to remedies, since all cases the CPC reviewed were cleared at phase I.

The practice of the CPC for mergers that go into a phase II investigation, or where there appear to be concerns at an early stage of phase I, follows a negotiated approach involving discussions with the parties to remove the incompatible elements of a concentration, either through amending the structure of the transaction or by offering commitments and remedies (such as divestments).

Key policy developments

No policy developments have been reported in 2012.

Reform proposals

There are currently no published proposals to reform the merger approval regime in Cyprus.

It is not excluded, however, that amendments of the merger regime will be tabled in the near future, more particularly by reason of the increased number of foreign-to-foreign transactions that are being notified, which in almost all cases pose no competition concerns. As regards the relevant financial thresholds, which *prima facie* may appear to be low, one could argue that these are satisfactory given the size of the Cypriot economy. Another area that may lead to reform could relate to the obligation to notify within seven days of signing the agreement bringing about the concentration, and the related inability to notify at an earlier stage of the corporate process.

Polyvios Panayides
Tel: +357 25 800 000 / Email: polyvios.panayides@demetriades.com
Polyvios' practice mainly covers Competition and EU law, as well as commercial/corporate litigation and dispute resolution.

Prior to joining Chrysses Demetriades & Co. LLC, Polyvios worked for over five years as an official of the European Commission in Brussels. From this position he was actively involved in a number of high-profile competition cases, mainly in the energy sector (Electricity, Natural Gas and Oil).

During the 2012 Cyprus Presidency of the Council of the European Union, he represented the Republic of Cyprus before European legislative bodies discussing a proposed EU Directive on the gathering and transfer of evidence. As part of this task, he chaired a Council Working Group and represented the Council at the trilogues with the European Parliament.

Alexandros Economou
Tel: +357 25 800 000 / Email: alexandros.economou@demetriades.com
Alexandros is a partner at the firm and heads the EU Law Section of the Company/Commercial Department. Alexandros specialises in all aspects of EU and CY competition law and in selected aspects of EU law; in particular Internal Market issues, data protection, consumer protection laws, and the protection and exploitation of trademarks.

In 2002 Alexandros provided direct consultation services to the Chairman of the Commission for the Protection of Competition under a fixed term contract. He was responsible, amongst others, for the closing of the Competition Chapter (*acquis communautaire*), and for all interaction with DG Competition, the ICN, the OECD and other authorities and organisations.

For several years Alexandros lectured, amongst others, European Internal Market (University of London external LL.M. course) and EC Competition Law at Intercollege (now European University of Nicosia). He is also a frequent speaker at events organised by the Cyprus Academy of Public Administration (of the Ministry of Finance) as part of a team of experts in EU matters.

Chrysses Demetriades & Co. LLC

13 Karaiskakis Street, Limassol 3032, Cyprus
Tel: +357 25 800 000 / Fax: +357 25 342 887 / URL: http://www.demetriades.com

European Union

Alec Burnside & Anne MacGregor
Cadwalader, Wickersham & Taft LLP

Overview of merger control activity during the last 12 months

Numbers of notifications

During calendar year 2012, there were 283 cases notified to the European Commission's Directorate General for Competition ("DG Comp" or "the Commission") under Council Regulation (EC) No 139/2004 on the control of concentrations between undertakings ("the Merger Regulation"). This is fewer than 2011 (309), more than 2010 (274) and 2009 (259), but substantially fewer than 2008 (347).

Of the cases notified in 2012, five were withdrawn, four in Phase I and one in Phase II (M.6362 *Cin/ Tirrenia Business Branch*). This is a substantial decrease on 2011 where 10 were withdrawn, nine in Phase I and one in Phase II.

Phase I clearances

In 2012, there were 254 Phase I clearance decisions. DG Comp issued: 170 simplified procedure clearances (all without commitments); 75 Phase I clearances without commitments under the normal procedure; and nine clearances under the normal procedure with commitments. This is a decrease on 2011, when there were 299 Phase I clearance decisions issued.

The percentage of notified cases dealt with under the simplified procedure remains in the majority: 60% in 2012; 62% in 2011; 52% in 2010; 55% in 2009; and 55% in 2008.

Phase II investigations

In 2012, nine cases were put into Phase II, i.e. an "in-depth investigation", an increase of one case on 2011.

In 2012, there were seven Phase II clearances, six with commitments (M.6266 *J&J Synthes*, M.6286 *Südzucker/ED&FMan*, M.6458 *Universal/EMI*, M.6410 *United Technology/Goodrich*, M.6471 *Outokumpu/Inoxum* and M.6497 *Hutchison/Orange Austria*) and one without (M.6314 *Telefonica/ Vodafone JV*). At the end of 2012, there were four ongoing Phase II investigations: M.6570 *UPS/ TNT Express*, M.6663 *Ryanair/Aer Lingus*, M.6690 *Syniverse/Mach* and M.6576 *Munksjö/Ahlstrom*. *UPS/TNT Express* was subsequently prohibited on 30 January 2012. During 2011, there were five Phase II clearances: four without remedies (M.5907 *Votorantim/Fischer JV*, M.6101 *UPM/Myllykoski and Rhein Papier,* M.6106 *Caterpillar/MVM* and M.6214 *Seagate Technology/The HDD Business of Samsung Electronics*), and one with remedies (M.6203 *Western Digital Ireland/Viviti Technologies*).

Between 2010 and 2012, the following interesting statistics emerge. Of the 20 Phase II cases, there were 13 statements of objection issued and approximately nine oral hearings. All those cleared with remedies required extensive divestments. There were voluntary extensions under Article 10(3) in 14 cases[1]. In seven cases, the maximum possible under Article 10(3) of 20 days was used. In nine cases, remedies were submitted after working day 55 in Phase II, triggering a 15-day extension.

New developments in jurisdictional assessment or procedure

Planned review of the simplified rules

In early 2013, the Commission unveiled a roadmap[2] which should eventually lead to more cases being notified under the simplified procedure. Although the document is the first step by the Commission to achieve changes on this issue, it is a welcome move. The proposed improvements aim to reduce the administrative burden on businesses by allowing more deals to be notified using a Short Form filing. First, the Commission intends to increase market share thresholds for both horizontal and vertical transactions from the current 15% and 25%, to 20% and 30% respectively. Second, it is considering allowing simplified treatment of horizontal transactions with very small market share increments, in line with the "safe harbour" provisions of the Commission's Horizontal Merger Guidelines. Finally, the Commission will streamline its notification and referral forms (Form CO, Short Form and Form RS) which will reduce the amount of required information. The Commission expects that these changes will raise the number of total notifications treated under the simplified rules by around 10%, to 70% of the total. A public consultation for this initiative is expected in spring 2013.

Upward referral requests by Member State authorities

The use of Article 22 (three or four cases per annum) is now increasingly coordinated between Member State competition authorities, with more of them "joining" other Member States' requests than in earlier years. This means that in cases where the Merger Regulation thresholds are not met, and even if the parties themselves do not have the option to seek upwards referral in advance of notification because they have a notification obligation in only one or two Member States, the case may still end up in Brussels if it affects trade between Member States, or threatens to significantly affect competition in the territory of the Member State making the request. This is beyond the control of the companies concerned, and can make for a significant extension of the timeline for clearance, increasing legal uncertainty.

For pre-notification upwards referral requests under Article 4(5), which parties have the option to make if the transaction qualifies for national review in three or more Member States, there were 22 such requests made in 2012 and only one case in which a Member State authority blocked the request.

Commissioner Almunia has raised the question of whether the European Competition Network (ECN) model can be applied in the sphere of merger control to bring about more cooperation among competition authorities. In November 2011 DG Comp published a set of *Best Practices on cooperation between EU National Competition Authorities in Merger Review*, aimed at fostering cooperation and facilitating information-sharing between national competition authorities ("NCAs") within the European Union, for mergers that are not reviewed at an EU level but require clearance in several Member States. The consent of the parties to the transaction is required before confidential information can be exchanged between authorities.

Downwards referral requests

In 2012 there were 13 pre-notification Article 4(4) downward referrals to Member State competition authorities at the request of notifying parties, none of which were refused.

For post-notification downward referrals under Article 9, in 2012 there were two requests made by Member State authorities, resulting in one full referral and one partial referral. In M.6497 *Hutchison/ Orange Austria*, the Commission, considering itself to be the best placed authority, refused a referral request from Austria even though it fulfilled the legal requirements for referral.

Lack of review of acquisitions of minority shareholdings not conferring control

In a speech in March 2011 Commissioner Almunia acknowledged that there "is probably an enforcement gap" at the EU level concerning transactions involving the acquisitions of minority shareholdings that do not give rise to a "change of control" within the meaning of the Merger Regulation, and announced that he had instructed DG Competition to study the matter. Following up in a November 2012 speech, the Commissioner outlined that there are two options for merger control law reform for cases involving non-controlling minority shareholdings. The first would be a selective system, whereby the Commission identifies the cases that may raise specific competition problems; the other would be a mandatory notification system. The Commissioner indicated his preference for the first option, but it is unclear when the Commission might put forward a proposal for the Council to amend the Merger Regulation on this point.

Key industry sectors reviewed, and approach adopted, to market definition

Exchange derivatives sector

M.6166 *Deutsche Börse/NYSE Euronext:* Prohibition Decision

The Commission's 1 February 2012 prohibition of the proposed tie-up between the operators of the world's two largest derivatives exchanges (Eurex, operated by Deutsche Börse and Liffe, operated by NYSE Euronext) brought to 22 the number of transactions blocked under the Merger Regulation since it came into force in 1991. The merger would have created a near-monopoly in European financial derivatives traded globally, with the companies controlling 90% of global trade. A critical factor was that the parties were each other's closest competitor. The Commission found that due to high barriers to entry, new competitors were unlikely to sufficiently enter the markets so as to constrain the behaviour of the merged entity.

Market definition in this case was crucial and much debated between the notifying parties and the regulator. The Commission found that there were two separate markets for derivatives; "over-the-counter" derivatives (OTC) and "exchange-traded" derivatives (ETD), the relevant market in this case being the market for ETDs. The investigation indicated that OTCs and ETDs are not substitutable. ETDs are highly liquid, relatively small in size and fully standardised contracts in their terms, whereas OTCs are larger and the contracts may be customised. Moreover, some ETD users are not authorised to operate in the OTC market.

The Commission also found that Eurex and Liffe operate closed "vertical silos", linking their exchanges to their own clearing house. Thus, the merger would have created a single silo, trading and clearing more than 90% of the global market of European financial ETDs. Due to the advantages flowing from the ability to clear ETDs in a single clearing house, customers would be reluctant to trade at other exchanges, creating a barrier to entry.

The parties argued that benefits to consumers would arise from increased liquidity. However, the Commission reasoned this was unlikely to occur directly as a result of the merger. The parties further claimed customers would benefit from having to post less collateral for security, but the Commission deemed these benefits to be overrated and not specific to the merger. Although efficiencies were vigorously argued, the Commission decided that any efficiencies that might arise would not outweigh the harm to consumers from the merger.

The parties offered to sell Liffe's single stock equity derivatives products where these competed with Eurex. However, the Commission judged this divestment to be too small to be viable on a stand-alone basis. In the problem area of European interest rate derivatives, the companies did not offer to sell overlapping derivatives products, but only access to the merged company's clearing house for some categories of new contracts. There were also concerns as to the feasibility of such an access remedy.

The adoption of the prohibition decision in this case was notable for the fact that the Commissioner for the Internal Market, Michel Barnier, took the very unusual procedural step of entering a "waiting reserve" on the case a few days before the full College of Commissioners met to adopt the decision formally. At the meeting itself on 1 February 2012, it was reported that there was considerable discussion on the case, although ultimately the prohibition decision was adopted as expected by the full College. Technically only a majority vote of Commissioners is required for the adoption of Phase II decisions, and it is extremely rare for there to be an actual vote at such meetings.

Deutsche Boerse brought an action appealing the prohibition decision in the General Court in Luxembourg on 12 April 2012. Perhaps looking ahead at potential future transactions, NYSE Euronext, on the other hand, decided not to appeal: on 20 December 2012 the US stock market operator Intercontinental Exchange (ICE) and NYSE Euronext announced an agreed merger.

Steel sector

M.6471 *Outokumpu/Inoxum–ThyssenKrupp*

This deal was notified on 10 April 2012 and went into Phase II on 21 May 2012, with the European Commission at that point finding "potential serious competition concerns in markets for the production and distribution of stainless-steel flat products, where the merged entity would have very high market shares", noting that "only three integrated producers of stainless-steel flat products would remain". On 7 November 2012, the Commission approved the deal with commitments.

Finnish stainless steel company Outokumpu initially offered to sell its Swedish melting and coil operations in Avesta, Nyby and Kloster as well, as part of its European sales network. This was rejected by the Commission and was not included in the commitments which were ultimately accepted. The package was changed and improved on 9 October 2012 to include divestments of Inoxum's stainless steel mill in Terni, Italy, and some stainless steel service centres. The regulator found that these would provide the purchaser with a fully-integrated, stand-alone production and distribution business with access to all major EEA countries. The final version of the commitments included, at the option of the purchaser, the divestment of Terni's forge and a large bright annealing line. The Commission ultimately found the transaction did not raise concerns in the distribution of stainless steel products, only in its supply.

Barroso suggestion of early notice of competition cases of broader importance

Both the *Deutsche Börse/NYSE Euronext* and *Outokumpu* cases prompted European Commission President Barroso to suggest in November 2012, at the College of Commissioners meeting at which the *Outokumpu* Phase II decision was adopted, that all Commissioners should receive early notice of competition cases that might have an impact on broader EU policies.

In *Outokumpu*, there was great political interest in the transaction, given its potential impact on the numerous industries in Europe that rely on stainless steel. *Deutsche Börse/NYSE Euronext* was examined against a backdrop of significant legislative reforms in the financial services sector being driven by DG Internal Market.

Mining sector

M.6541 *Glencore/Xstrata*

The £39bn deal between commodities trader Glencore and mining giant Xstrata, announced in February 2012, and notified to the European Commission on 2 October 2012, raised concerns on the market for the supply of zinc in Europe. Glencore was the largest supplier of zinc in the EEA on the basis of an off-take agreement with Nyrstar, a relationship covering some of Xstrata's EEA output and production from Glencore's own smelter and imports. Glencore also controlled Pacorini, the owner of a London Metal Exchange (LME) approved storage warehouse in New Orleans, and a large amount of exports. Xstrata was the second-largest producer of zinc metal in the EEA.

In the 2006 *Xstrata/Falconbridge* case, the Commission had found that Glencore controlled Xstrata at that time because it was "in a position to exert a decisive influence on Xstrata's strategy and operations". At the time of announcing its acquisition of Xstrata in early 2012, Glencore owned 34% of Xstrata. There was initially a jurisdictional discussion as to whether the deal would require notification to the European Commission, because it was unclear whether in 2012 Glencore still had "control" over Xstrata with its stake within the meaning of the Merger Regulation. Ultimately, the deal was notified in Brussels, after an eight-month long pre-notification period.

Glencore achieved a Phase I clearance with remedies by offering to terminate its "off-take" deal with zinc producer Nyrstar. Glencore also committed not to buy any zinc metal from Nyrstar or to engage in any other practices which would have the effect of materially restricting Nyrstar's ability or incentive to compete with Glencore for a period of ten years. Finally, Glencore committed to sell its 7.79% stake in Nyrstar.

Telecommunications sector

M.6497 *Hutchison Whampoa – Hutchison 3G Austria/Orange Austria*

On 7 May 2012, Hutchison notified the acquisition of Orange Austria. A Phase II investigation was opened on 29 June 2012, with the Commission citing "significant competition problems by removing Orange as a competitor in the retail market for end consumers, and on the wholesale market for network access and call origination". The transaction meant that the number of players in the wholesale and retail mobile services in Austria would be reduced from four to three, with the merged entity enjoying a 22% market share.

On 21 August 2012, Hutchison submitted remedies, including the opening up of its network to virtual mobile operators wishing to enter the Austrian market, by offering to grant lower wholesale rates, and an upfront deal with a virtual mobile network operator. However, this was deemed insufficient to achieve an early Phase II clearance, and the Commission issued a Statement of Objections on 21 September 2012, outlining doubts over Hutchison's potential to raise the prices at which it offered mobile services to consumers. On 19 October 2012, Hutchison bolstered its remedies offer.

The final remedies package included a commitment to divest 2.6GHz radio spectrum rights to an interested new market entrant. This new mobile network operator will also acquire additional spectrum 800MHz frequency reserved for the new entrant by the Austrian telecom regulator in a 2013 auction. This combination would enable the operator to provide a competitive mobile broadband network. Secondly, Hutchison committed to provide wholesale access to its network for up to 30% of its capacity to up to 16 mobile virtual network operators in the next 10 years. This was an up-front commitment, meaning that the acquisition cannot be completed before a wholesale access agreement has been entered into. On this basis, the Commission conditionally cleared the transaction on 12 December 2012.

Hutchison illustrates the Commission's preference for structural remedies over access remedies. The access remedy first offered was deemed insufficient and ultimately a divestment was required.

M.6281 *Microsoft/Skype*

Microsoft's acquisition of Skype, announced on 10 May 2011, was notified to the Commission on 2 September 2011 and unconditionally cleared on 7 October 2011. The Commission's investigation revealed that overlaps in the area of consumer communications were present in video communications due to Microsoft's Windows Live Messenger. However, there were no competition concerns, as there were many players active on the market. In enterprise communications, Skype was found to have a limited market presence and did not compete with Microsoft's Lync, which is used mostly by large enterprises.

The Commission also checked for possible conglomerate effects, since the parties were active in neighbouring markets. It researched the possibility of Microsoft hindering Skype's interoperability with competing services, and tying its own products (e.g. Windows operating system) with Skype, thereby limiting the ability of other players to compete. However, it was found that Microsoft would have no incentive to hinder interoperability, as Skype seeks to be accessible on as many systems as possible. On the issue of bundling, the majority of customers who buy a PC with Skype pre-installed are registered Skype users, and most of them subsequently download a different version.

Interested third parties Cisco and Messagenet have appealed the clearance decision to the General Court in Luxembourg, arguing the Commission misjudged the network effects which eliminate incentives to offer operability with competing products.

M.6690 *Syniverse/Mach*

The €550m acquisition by Syniverse of fellow telecommunications technology company MACH, announced on 30 June 2012, was notified to the European Commission on 16 November 2012 and went into Phase II on 20 December 2012. The parties are the leading players in the market for data clearing and both are present on the market for financial clearing, MACH being the market leader.

In its investigation to date, the Commission has looked at various issues, including whether there are any costs when switching providers, whether any new entrants to the market have failed in the past five years, and whether operators would switch to in-house data clearing if the merger resulted in price increases. The Commission has also looked into whether companies would object to using a competing operator's in-house data-clearing services. At the time of going to press, the deadline for the Commission's decision was set at 15 May 2013.

Airline sector

M.6663 *Ryanair/Aer Lingus*

In the latest in the convoluted saga involving Ireland's two airlines, which has been running since 2006 and yielded a prohibition decision under the Merger Regulation in June 2007, Ryanair announced a third hostile takeover attempt of Aer Lingus on 19 June 2012. This occurred just days after the

UK's Competition Commission opened an in-depth investigation into Ryanair's 29.8% minority shareholding in Aer Lingus, following a referral to it by the UK's Office of Fair Trading. Ryanair notified the proposed takeover to the Commission in Brussels on 24 July 2012.

The case went into Phase II on 29 August 2012 after the Commission found that on a large number of routes, mainly out of Ireland, the two airlines are each other's closest competitor and barriers to entry are high, with a higher number of overlaps than at the time of the 2007 prohibition. The deadline for decision by the Commission is 6 March 2013; at the time of writing, a succession of remedy proposals had been submitted.

In parallel, Ryanair has been arguing in the UK that the UK Competition Commission's investigation into its minority stake should be suspended until EU merger control proceedings have finished. It bases its arguments on the Member States' Treaty "duty of sincere cooperation" with the European Commission, meaning they should not run parallel investigations into the same subject matter, so as to avoid conflicting decisions. The UK Competition Commission and Aer Lingus are arguing in response that the minority stake does not form part of the EU's review, which involves a separate transaction – the full takeover of Aer Lingus. The UK's Competition Appeal Tribunal agreed that the Competition Commission could continue its investigation, as did the UK's Court of Appeal on 13 December 2012. Ryanair has now sought permission from the UK Supreme Court to appeal the matter further.

M.5830 *Olympic Air/Aegean Airlines*

In what might be called the second repeat airline saga, in October 2012, Marfin Investment Group Holdings announced the signing of an agreement for the sale of its portfolio company Olympic Air to Aegean Airlines for €72m. The European Commission will shortly have to review the merger of the two Greek airlines for the second time: it prohibited the first attempt in January 2011. Although the Commission did not have original jurisdiction to look at the latest transaction (the new deal is structured as an outright sale, so Marfin's turnover falls out of the turnover calculation this time), in late 2012 the Greek and Cypriot competition authorities both made upwards referral requests to Brussels under Article 22(5) of the Merger Regulation.

Although Aegean is no longer active on two of the 2011 problem routes, the parties still compete head-to-head on many Greek domestic routes. The parties' joint appeal to the General Court against the 2011 prohibition decision remains pending.

M.6447 *IAG/bmi*

On 30 March 2012 the European Commission granted conditional Phase I clearance of the acquisition of bmi by IAG. Approval was contingent on the release of 14 daily slot pairs at London Heathrow (LHR) in order to facilitate new entry, and the promise to carry connecting passengers to feed the long-haul flights of competing airlines out of LHW. The Commission found that without the commitments, the transaction would have led to high market shares and even monopolies on a number routes out of LHR. It took the view that slots and other incentives, such as the acquisition of grandfathering rights after a certain period, should facilitate entry. Finally, a feeder arrangement ensured passengers would continue to have a choice to use airlines other than IAG when connecting at LHR. Interested third party Virgin has filed a challenge to the clearance decision in the General Court. Clearance came against the background of indications that bmi would not be able to survive for the duration of a Phase II inquiry.

Package delivery sector

M.6570 *UPS/TNT Express:* Prohibition Decision

On 19 March 2012 UPS announced that it would acquire competitor TNT Express. The transaction was notified to the European Commission on 15 June 2012, going into Phase II on 20 July 2012.

The Commission issued a Statement of Objections on 1 November 2012. It limited its concerns to the market for intra-EEA international express package delivery, in other words, next-day parcel delivery from one EEA country to another EEA country. Although there were overlaps in some domestic express parcel markets, and on some intercontinental routes, the Commission chose not to pursue those aspects.

The Commission contended that the transaction would raise competition concerns because it would result in the removal of a close competitor. Essentially there are only four global "integrated" express parcel companies in the world (DHL and FedEx being the other two), and this would have been a four-to-three transaction. A key distinguishing feature of integrated express parcel companies is that they control all the infrastructure on which the parcel travels, from the moment of pick-up until the moment of delivery. Ownership, or at least control, over night air uplift is essential.

Whilst the Commission found that non-integrators do offer some intra-EEA express parcel services (e.g. DPD and GLS), its investigation revealed that they failed to provide any true competition. Further, amongst the four integrators, FedEx was found to have a far lesser presence in the EEA than UPS, TNT Express and DHL, so that it was judged to exercise only a weak competitive constraint on the merging parties.

Following UPS's reply to the SO, and an oral hearing on 12 November 2012, the list of problematic countries was much shorter by the time UPS came to make a remedies offer. On 29 November, UPS offered remedies comprising the divestment of TNT subsidiaries including assets, consumer contracts and personnel in 12 countries, and access to UPS' air network (TNT Express had lined up the ASL Aviation Group to buy its airline, conditional upon the deal with UPS closing). UPS improved its commitments offer on 16 December 2012, and again in early January 2012. At the same time, UPS was understood to be talking to DPD as a potential buyer of the divestment package, FedEx having expressed no interest.

Following a state of play meeting with the Commission on 11 January 2013, UPS and TNT Express announced on 14 January that they anticipated that the regulator would prohibit the deal. That decision was formally adopted on 30 January 2013.

Other sectors

M.6266 *Johnson & Johnson/Synthes*

This medical devices transaction was notified to the European Commission on 27 September 2012 and went into Phase II on 3 November 2012. On opening its in-depth investigation, the Commission felt that "the proposed transaction would combine two of the leading suppliers of spine devices and would strengthen the position of Synthes as the current market leader in trauma and cranio-maxillofacial (CMF) devices, and of Johnson & Johnson in-shoulder devices, in a substantial number of EEA member states".

A Statement of Objections was issued on 25 January 2012. At that stage, the Commission only had remaining concerns on the market for trauma products. On 21 February 2012, J&J submitted commitments, offering to sell its DePuy trauma products business. The transaction was then conditionally cleared on 19 April 2012, and DePuy was sold shortly thereafter to Biomet, Inc.

M.5549 *EDF/Segebel-SPE-Centrica*

This case involved EDF's acquisition of Centrica's subsidiary Segebel, which in turn owns a 51 per cent shareholding in the Belgian electricity company SPE-Luminus. The deal was notified on 23 September 2009 and was given Phase I conditional clearance on 12 November 2009. EDF committed to immediately divest the assets of one of its companies in charge of the development of these power stations. In addition, if EDF had not invested in a second planned power station by June 2012, or no decision to invest had been taken, EDF committed to divest the assets of the company in charge of the project.

On 17 May 2010, the Belgian consumer group "Test Achats" brought a General Court annulment action against the Commission's clearance decision. On 12 October 2011, the General Court ruled that Test Achats, as a consumer association, had the right to be heard during a merger control procedure conducted by the Commission, as long as the merger related to goods or services used by final consumers, and on condition that it made an application to be heard by the Commission in writing following notification of the deal. Here, Test Achat had asked to be heard two months prior to notification, but the court said it should have engaged with the EU regulator after formal notification of the transaction on 23 September 2009. The court also ruled that third parties cannot challenge a Commission decision not to refer a case to a national regulator.

In an interesting codicil to the original conditional clearance decision, on 5 September 2012, EDF took the European Commission to court to annul its decision refusing to give the firm more time to comply with its commitment obligations. EDF also applied for interim measures, which were refused on 16 October 2012. EDF has now filed an appeal on the interim relief point with the ECJ.

M.6410 *United Technologies/Goodrich*

The transaction was notified to the Commission on 20 February 2012 and went into Phase II on 26 March 2012 due to concerns over the merged entity's extremely high market shares in engine controls and power generators used in aircraft.

On 26 July 2012, the Commission cleared the acquisition subject to the divestment of Goodrich's electrical power generation and engine controls for small engines businesses. In addition, Rolls Royce was granted the option to acquire Goodrich's lean-burn fuel nozzle R&D project. During the investigation, Rolls Royce announced a buy-out of Goodrich's share in Aero Engine Controls, which held all Goodrich's activities for engine controls for large engines. This, in combination with the engine controls for small engines business divestment, removed the entire overlap between UTC and Goodrich in the engine controls market.

M.6381 *Google/Motorola Mobility*

This $12.5bn acquisition of smart phone and tablet developer Motorola Mobility by Google, the search engine and developer of the Android mobile operating system, was notified to the Commission on 25 November 2011 and cleared unconditionally on 13 February 2012.

The issue was whether Google would be likely to prevent Motorola's competitors from using its Android operating system. The Commission found that Android helps spread Google's other services and therefore Google would not restrict the use of Android solely to Motorola, a relatively minor player. Secondly, all smartphones adhere to telecommunication standards, for example 3G, and Motorola holds patents that are essential to comply with these standards – access to such standard-essential patents is crucial for players on the smartphone market. However, the Commission found the transaction would not materially change this situation. Finally, the Commission investigated whether Google would be able to use those patents to obtain preferential treatment for its services.

At the time of the unconditional clearance decision in this case, Commissioner Almunia cautioned technology companies generally against abusing the power that standard-essential patents (SEPs) confer, and threatened to act against Google and others if they disregard fair-licensing commitments. The Commission has recently increased its scrutiny of SEPs, notably issuing Samsung with a Statement of Objections in an Article 102 dominance investigation on 21 December 2012.

Key economic appraisal techniques applied

M.6203 *Western Digital/Hitachi* is a good example of the Commission's use of economic analysis. This merger would have reduced the players in the hard disk drive industry from four to three, and in some markets from three to two. First, qualitative methods were employed, revealing that HDD customers need multiple sources of supply. This need was then confirmed by the economic analysis undertaken by the Chief Economist's Team. This revealed that the presence of a third supplier was crucial for competition, so as to keep prices stable. Bidding data also showed that Hitachi participated in most bids and was an important competitor, whose removal would lead to higher prices. Ultimately, divestments allowing a competitor to replace Hitachi as the third supplier in the market were sufficient for the merger to be cleared.

In October 2011 DG Comp published provisionally applicable *Best Practices on the Submission of Economic Evidence.* These aim to ensure that the economic data submitted by parties, during both anti-trust and merger control procedures, meets certain standards. Guidance is given on how economic models should be built, and parties are encouraged to inform the Commission of the kind of empirical analysis they consider appropriate in each case. The document also recommends that parties should consult early on the type of data available. Since the Best Practices were published, the Commission has sent more draft information requests than previously, seeking to tailor its requests to data which is actually available.

Approach to remedies

Viability of remedies remains paramount

As the discussion of a number of commitments cases above indicates, the viability of remedies packages remains paramount in the Commission's determination of whether to accept or reject them, such that in some cases the parties may have to include more in their packages than would be strictly required to address the concerns identified.

In M.6458 *Universal/EMI,* the Commission considered that the £1.2bn acquisition by market leader Universal of EMI's recording business would lead to competition concerns in the wholesale of physical and digital recorded music at the European level. To obtain Phase II clearance, Universal undertook to divest a significant number of music catalogues and assets. Significantly, the rights divested were worldwide, so that prospective buyers would be able to exploit the assets in a viable and competitive way, despite the fact that concerns were only raised at the European level. Furthermore, two-thirds of the divested music catalogues had to go to a single buyer experienced in the music industry to ensure credible competition. The requirement to divest global rights follows the approach in the earlier case of M.6459 *Sony/Mubadala Development/EMI Music Publishing.*

Key policy developments

There were no notable key policy developments in 2012 in the sphere of European merger control.

Reform proposals

Since taking office in early 2010, Commissioner Almunia has not brought forward any concrete legislative proposals to amend the Merger Regulation or its Implementing Regulation. The initiatives in relation to minority shareholdings, and extension of short-form filings, mentioned above, remain at an early stage.

* * *

Endnotes

1.   Cases in which a decision is still pending have not been taken into account.
2.   http://ec.europa.eu/governance/impact/planned_ia/roadmaps_2013_en.htm#COMP

Alec Burnside
Tel: +32 2 891 8181 / Email: alec.burnside@cwt.com

Alec Burnside is the Managing Partner of Cadwalader in Brussels. He has practised EU competition law in Brussels for over two decades, focusing on merger control. He has handled leading and sensitive cases across many sectors, spanning financial services, IT, consumer products, energy, natural resources, manufacturing, military, pharmaceuticals, transport and logistics, and telecoms.

Among recent and prominent transactions, he advised Deutsche Börse on its proposed merger with NYSE Euronext; Aer Lingus on its successful defences of Ryanair's hostile takeover bids, and court appeals; Billiton on its merger with BHP; and British American Tobacco and DHL on successive acquisitions. Alec is frequently sought out for comment in the media, and as an author and speaker.

Alec studied at Downing College, Cambridge; College of Law, London; and Institut d'Etudes Européennes, Brussels. He is a Solicitor of the Senior Courts of England and Wales and a foreign member of the Brussels Bar.

Anne MacGregor
Tel: +32 2 891 8166 / Email: anne.macgregor@cwt.com

Anne MacGregor is Special Counsel in Cadwalader's Brussels office. She has been practising EU trade and competition law in Brussels since 1994 and specialises in European and multijurisdictional merger control on international transactions across a variety of industry sectors, including parcel delivery, airlines, packaging, chemical distribution, mining, energy, pharmaceuticals and software.

Among recent and significant transactions, Anne has advised Deutsche Börse, Deutsche Post DHL, Aer Lingus, Abbott Laboratories, Ashland, iSoft, CVC private equity and Vattenfall.

Anne tutors in EU competition law at the Vrije Universiteit Brussel (VUB) and studied at the Australian National University, Canberra and the University of Hamburg. She is admitted to practise in England and Wales, New York, and Australia, and is a registered foreign lawyer with the Brussels Bar.

Cadwalader, Wickersham & Taft LLP

22-28 Avenue d'Auderghem, 1040 Brussels, Belgium
Tel: +32 2 891 8100 / Fax: +32 2 891 8106 / URL: http://www.cadwalader.com

Finland

Leena Lindberg & Petteri Metsä-Tokila
Krogerus Attorneys Ltd

Overview of merger control activity during the last 12 months

Pursuant to the Competition Act (948/2011, *fi: kilpailulaki*) a concentration must be notified to the Finnish Competition and Consumer Authority ("FCCA") if:
- the combined worldwide turnover of the parties exceeds €350m; and
- the turnover of each of at least two of the parties accrued from Finland exceeds €20m.

The applicable substantive test is the significant impediment to effective competition ("SIEC") test, which is intended to be equivalent to the SIEC test provided in the EU Merger Regulation. Other substantive merger control rules, including the definition of a concentration, are mostly in line with European Union rules.

The Finnish Competition Authority merged with the Consumer Agency on 1 January 2013, forming the new FCCA, but this has no notable practical effects on merger control. The abbreviation FCCA is used throughout this article whether reference is made to the new Authority or the old Finnish Competition Authority.

During calendar year 2012, 24 concentrations were notified to the FCCA. This number is roughly in line with the typical yearly number of notifications, which has been around 15-35 notifications since the current jurisdictional thresholds came into force in 2004. In 2011, 27 concentrations were notified to the FCCA.

In 2012, the FCCA reviewed 22 concentrations:
- Nineteen of these cases were cleared unconditionally during the so-called Phase I investigation. In Phase I investigations, the FCCA must decide whether further investigations are required within one month from the receipt of the notification. If the acquisition clearly does not have restrictive effects on competition, the FCCA must approve the concentration. The average amount of days spent on Phase I investigations in 2012 was 15.
- Three of these cases were subject to Phase II investigations. These entailed a merger in the field of production and selling of ready-made concrete, and concrete and other building materials products *(Rudus Oy / Lemminkäinen Rakennustuotteet Oy)*; a merger in the field of agricultural trade *(DLA International Holding A/S / Hankkija-Maatalous Oy)*; and a merger in the field of plastic pipes, fittings, wells and other similar products designed for the construction and infrastructure technology *(Uponor Oyj / KWH-Yhtymä Oy / Joint venture)*. In Phase II, the FCCA has three months from taking the decision to further investigate the proposed concentration, after which it may attach conditions on the implementation of a concentration, approve it without conditions, or propose that the Market Court prohibits the concentration. Two of the above-mentioned cases were cleared unconditionally in Phase II.
- One of the Phase II cases, *Uponor Oyj/KWH-Yhtymä Oy/Joint venture*, is still pending. The parties have significant market shares in the market of plastic pipes, fittings, wells and other similar products. They also produce a wide range of these products, while smaller competitors only produce a more limited range. The FCCA has concerns over the significant market shares of the proposed concentration, the already strong position of the parties, especially in products made from plastic, as well as possible barriers to entry. In Phase II, the FCCA will further investigate

the role of substitute materials for plastic, as well as the impact of imported products, to assess the competitive situation fully. Further, with the approval of the parties, the FCCA requested the Market Court to extend the Phase II investigation for one extra month. The FCCA found out during its investigation that the parties were also active in sales to industrial customers; information that was not provided in the original notification.

- During 2012, the FCCA has not made any decisions of inapplicability nor carried out any proceedings for failure to notify a concentration. No concentrations were referred to the European Commission by the FCCA or *vice versa*, and no new applications to amend or repeal commitments given in earlier cases were made. One such application is still pending.

New developments in jurisdictional assessment or procedure

The new Competition Act entered into force on 1 November 2011. With the new Act, substantive merger control rules were fully harmonised with the EU Merger Regulation (139/2004). The applicable substantive test is now whether the concentration significantly impedes effective competition in the Finnish markets or a substantial part thereof, in particular, as a result of the creation or strengthening of a dominant position (the SIEC test). The FCCA has also published its own Guidelines on Merger Control, which are to a great extent in line with the European Commission's Guidelines.

The FCCA's Guidelines provide a general framework for the substantive assessment of concentrations under the Finnish merger control rules. The assessment is, as a starting point, in line with the SIEC assessment used in other jurisdictions. Pursuant to the Government Bill for a Competition Act (88/2010), the applicable substantive test is intended to be equivalent to the SIEC test provided in the EU Merger Regulation and practice of the European Courts, and the Guidelines of the European Commission may be used for interpretative purposes when assessing concentrations in Finland.

However, it is noteworthy that the Competition Act does not contain a provision exactly similar to Article 2(4) of the EU Merger Regulation, which deals with joint ventures leading to co-ordination of the parent companies' behaviour. Despite the fact that no such provision exists, in connection with introducing the SIEC test in 2011, it was assumed that such co-ordinated effects will now be examined under the SIEC test. According to the FCCA's Guidelines, the SIEC test offers a better chance to address the possible negative competitive effects that might arise due to a joint venture between competing parent companies. Further, the Guidelines state that the SIEC test also addresses so-called "gap situations" in oligopolistic markets more efficiently than the previous test based on creation or strengthening of dominance.

On the procedural side, Phase I of the notification process takes one month, at the most, and Phase II takes three months, at the most. The Market Court may extend Phase II by no more than two months. The FCCA deems an extension of Phase II proceedings appropriate only in exceptional situations. The FCCA does not require the consent of the parties to ask for an extension of Phase II from the Market Court, but in line with its previous practice asked for such consent in *Uponor Oyj/KWH-Yhtymä Oy/ Joint venture*. Should the parties resist an application, the Market Court may grant the extension only if weighty reasons exist.

Further, the FCCA has the power to freeze its own procedural deadlines ("stopping the clock") if the parties fail to provide information required by the FCCA or the information provided is inadequate or erroneous. The preparatory works of the Competition Act state that the provision is intended to be applied in situations where the parties are withholding information deliberately. In practice, the FCCA did not apply these provisions during 2012.

However, in the Finnish process, the FCCA does not at any stage have to find the notification complete. According to the Competition Act, the deadline does not start to run if the notification is essentially incomplete, or if essential changes in the notified facts take place, and these changes have an essential impact on the assessment of the concentration. A change in facts is deemed essential if the parties knew or should have known about these facts when submitting the notification. Further, since there is no statement when a notification can be considered incomplete, it is possible that the authority will refer to incompleteness of the notification if essential new facts appear. However, in *Uponor Oyj/KWH-Yhtymä Oy/Joint venture*, where the notification lacked information relating to sales to industrial customers, the FCCA asked the Market Court to extend Phase II instead of declaring the notification incomplete.

Key industry sectors reviewed and approach adopted to market definition, barriers to entry, nature of international competition etc.

The FCCA does not have any predefined key sectors or key policy areas in merger control. The Competition Act itself includes sector-specific rules for concentrations in the employee pension insurance, pension funds and insurance funds sectors, pursuant to which a concentration on those sectors must first be approved by the Financial Supervisory Authority. A separate notification to the FCCA is not required if the Financial Supervisory Authority has asked for the FCCA's statement during its investigations and the FCCA has found in its statement that no impediment for the approval of the concentration exists. Further, the Competition Act also stipulates that a merger in electricity markets may be prohibited if the combined share of the transmission operations of the parties to the concentration, and the entities or facilities controlled by them or in control of them, exceeds 25% of the amount of electricity transmitted at 400V in the transmission grid on a national level. Thus the FCCA may intervene with a concentration in the electricity sector if the 25% market share is exceeded and demonstrating significant impediment on effective competition is not required.

Based on the FCCA's strategic and operational focuses agreed annually with the Ministry of Employment and the Economy, the FCCA continues to focus on reducing the harm caused by concentrated retail trade. During the past few years, the FCCA has investigated several concentrations in the food industry. In these cases, the FCCA has been especially interested in both the industry and retail level of the food supply chain, both of which are rather concentrated in Finland. No other significant trends, or a particularly high number of concentrations within a certain sector, have emerged except for the apparently growing concentration in the insurance sector, where three concentrations have been cleared during the last 12 months *(OP-Pohjola cooperative / Business operations of Skandia Life, Local Insurance Mutual Company / Tapiola General Mutual Insurance Company and If Insurance Company Oy / Business operations of Tryg Forsikring A/S Finnish branch).*

In its decisions, the FCCA has lately also investigated the negative competitive structure of the markets and has taken into account issues such as whether the structural and economic links between the major market players affect the incentives of the companies in question. These assessments have led to joint dominance and facilitating practices becoming one of the FCCA's interest areas in merger control. Due to the concentrated markets in Finland, joint dominance has been a focus area in a number of major cases.

It is also noteworthy that due to Finland's slightly isolated location from the rest of Europe and the effects this might have on cross-border trade, especially geographic markets are defined somewhat differently than in EU practice. The FCCA tends to take national markets as a starting point, and extensive economic and statistical evidence on wider markets is required to convince the FCCA that the markets are wider than national. Mere reliance on EU cases finding EU- or EEA-wide or broader markets will not suffice in this respect.

The Competition Act does not include a provision similar to Article 3(5) of the EU Merger Regulation, according to which notification is not required in certain temporary arrangements where credit institutions or other financial institutions or insurance companies hold, on a temporary basis, securities they have acquired in an undertaking with a view to reselling them ("warehousing structures"). The FCCA states in its Guidelines that because the Competition Act does not include provisions exempting temporary ownership arrangements, these transactions have to be notified in Finland, provided that the other criteria applicable to the obligation to notify are met.

Pursuant to the Decree by the State Council on the obligation to notify a concentration, less information about the relevant markets is required if the parties are not competitors in any markets where their combined market share is at least 15%, or they do not have a vertical relationship at all, or the market share of neither party to the concentration and the entity or foundation part of the same group in such vertical markets does not exceed 20%.

Further, in individual cases, the FCCA may grant waivers to the obligation to notify if the effects of a concentration for competition are likely to be minor, or if the information prescribed to be given is unnecessary, in certain parts, for the assessment of a concentration. In such cases, a short-form notification is available. The notifying party may ask the FCCA to approve the use of the short notification form before notifying the concentration in informal negotiations, or may alternatively notify the concentration straight with the short-form notification. In the latter case, the FCCA may ask for normal detailed notification, which must then be provided. The short-form notification is accepted, for example, in cases where companies who accrue turnover from Finland set up a joint venture with no connection to the Finnish markets.

In practice, concentrations that clearly raise no concerns are cleared rather quickly. The FCCA has sometimes issued clearances within a week.

Similarly to the EU rules, the concentration may be notified prior to the actual signing if the parties can sufficiently reliably show their intention to merge. Sufficiently reliable intent may be expressed by signing a letter of intent, memorandum of understanding or by announcing publicly the bid regarding the relevant shares. The planned concentration must, however, be concrete enough for the FCCA to investigate it on the basis of provided information. The FCCA has the obligation to immediately begin investigating the concentration after the notification has been made, as the time limits start to run.

The FCCA has the power to propose that the Market Court imposes fines up to 10% of the turnover of the preceding year for implementing a concentration without notifying it ("gun-jumping"), but in practice such proposals have not been made. This seems to suggest that the FCCA is not especially keen on proposing fines because of pre-implementation if the failure to notify has not been intentional and if the concentration in question does not have any actual competitive effects.

Key economic appraisal techniques applied, and vertical and conglomerate mergers

The competitive effects of concentrations are assessed on the relevant product markets and geographic markets. In its investigations, the FCCA assesses the market definition presented by the notifying party and third parties in their answers to the FCCA's requests for comments and information on certain claims deriving from the market definition.

After the market definition has been finalised, the competitive effects of the merger are assessed. This includes an assessment of the current market situation, market entry and possible barriers to entry, as well as other factors that balance the market power of the merging entity (e.g. customers' bargaining power). Where appropriate, efficiency gains resulting from the concentration will also be taken into account, but it remains for the notifying parties to demonstrate that the concentration leads to efficiency gains that benefit consumers.

In general, the assessment of the effects of a concentration on the markets can be characterised as a general assessment of many factors, with the purpose of estimating the effects of the merger on a future market situation. As the SIEC test, which has been applied for a year now, focuses more strongly on competitive effects and less on market shares and structural considerations, market definition and market shares will still remain important but not necessarily decisive factors in the assessment. The FCCA has stated that its investigations will focus more on the economic basis of concentrations and on the likely conduct of the market actors following the merger.

A recent example of assessing the relevance of market entry and barriers to entry can be found in the FCCA's decision in *Rudus Oy / Lemminkäinen Rakennustuotteet Oy*. The parties were active in, *inter alia*, ready-made concrete and other concrete products. The geographic markets regarding ready-made concrete were defined local in scope, and while the national combined market share of the parties did not raise serious concerns, in some local markets the merging parties' combined market shares were as high as 85%. The FCCA opened a Phase II investigation to further investigate the proposed concentration's effects on competition.

The parties claimed there was excess capacity in the markets and entry was fairly easy, so no significant impediment to effective competition could arise. Drawing from the Commission's Horizontal Merger Guidelines, the FCCA noted that when entering a market is sufficiently easy, a merger is unlikely to pose any significant anti-competitive risk. After assessing entry conditions in-depth, the FCCA noted that especially in those areas where the combined market shares of the parties were highest or where other market participants had noted that the concentration would cause competition problems, there had either been recent entries by third parties or there were plans to enter the market. Based on this finding, the FCCA concluded that the concentration would not significantly impede effective competition in ready-made concrete markets despite the combined high market shares, and after assessing the concentration's effects on competition in other markets, cleared the concentration without remedies.

A recent example of a merger leading to efficiencies can be found in the FCCA's decision in *DLA International Holding A/S / Hankkija-Maatalous Oy,* a concentration in the field of agricultural trade. DLA acquired control in Hankkija-Maatalous Oy from Suomen Osuuskauppojen Keskuskunta (SOK), leaving the latter with a minority ownership of 40%. Hankkija-Maatalous was, prior to the acquisition, wholly owned by SOK and was responsible for developing SOK's agriculture business and SOK's Agrimarket chain, which, in turn, is a chain specialising in agriculture production materials, farming machines and gardening business. Retail co-operatives that are part of the Agrimarket chain were not included in the concentration and remained separate undertakings in the field of agricultural trade. However, these co-operatives planned to continue co-operating with Hankkija-Maatalous in certain operations after the acquisition. Prior to the acquisition, DLA owned Yrittäjien Maatalous Oy and Melica Oy, companies also active in the field of agricultural trade. DLA, in turn, is partially owned by Danish Agro A.m.b.A. The FCCA had initial concerns that the concentration might significantly impede effective competition in various Finnish agricultural product markets and opened a Phase II investigation.

During the Phase II investigation, the FCCA noted that the retailing of Hankkija-Maatalous may become more effective after the acquisition, because in the future the company is able to benefit from the bigger procurement volumes of the Danish Agro Group. According to the FCCA, this and the strengthening bargaining power of the concentration may ultimately show as more affordable sales prices to the end-customer. After assessing other competitive effects, the FCCA came to the conclusion that despite the high combined market shares of the concentration on some markets, and the fact that other retail co-operatives belonging to the same association of undertakings as SOK could not be regarded as creating significant competitive pressure, as long as SOK owns a minority of Hankkija-Maatalous, the concentration did not cause a significant impediment to effective competition and thus cleared it without remedies.

Otherwise, during the first year of applying the SIEC test, no significant cases have emerged where effects on competition have been assessed with econometric models, or at least the FCCA has not made public in its decisions whether it has applied such models or not. However, the FCCA has not only trained its existing staff extensively on the SIEC test, but has also recruited new staff specialising in competition economics during 2012. Further, the authority has publicly stated that it is also establishing an external group of economists to consult when assessing the effects of notified mergers. Together these developments mean that the FCCA is better prepared to carry out complex econometric analysis if required, and it can be expected that such analyses will be carried in the future in appropriate cases.

Assessment of vertical and conglomerate mergers

The FCCA deals briefly with vertical and conglomerate mergers in its Guidelines. The FCCA notes that non-horizontal concentrations are generally less likely to significantly impede effective competition than horizontal mergers. Further, the FCCA states that non-horizontal mergers often provide substantial scope for efficiencies. However, negative effects on competition, especially in the form of foreclosure, co-ordinated or non-co-ordinated effects, may also arise from vertical or conglomerate mergers. The FCCA describes these briefly in its Guidelines. In general, due to the introduction of the SIEC test, vertical and conglomerate mergers are assessed similarly to the EU Merger Regulation and no noteworthy differences exist.

In *Lohja Rudus Oy Ab / Abetoni Oy,* the FCCA examined a number of possible negative vertical effects of a concentration in the markets for cement and concrete. The FCCA was particularly concerned about the effect of the strong market position of Finnsementti, a dominant undertaking in the cement market, in relation to Abetoni's firm position in the ready-mixed concrete market. The FCCA also examined whether the acquisition favours Abetoni in the raw material purchases with regard to competitors, and whether Finnsementti's position will be further reinforced when Abetoni is transferred to the same group. In addition, the FCCA examined the strengthening of Lohja Rudus' market position in the closely related ready-mixed concrete market. The possibility of Lohja Rudus to tie the sales of ready-mixed concrete and aggregates to the sales of Abetoni's products in land construction projects was also under review. However, after an in-depth Phase II investigation, the FCCA found no evidence of such effects and approved the concentration unconditionally.

Similar vertical effects were also investigated in the recent *Rudus Oy / Lemminkäinen Rakennustuotteet Oy* case. Finnsementti Oy, which belongs to the same group as the buyer, Rudus Oy, still had a significant market share of 70-80% in producing and selling of cement, which is one of the main crude materials for concrete. Several market participants had noted that the already strong position of Finnsementti would be further strengthened and competition would be reduced in the cement markets after the merger. Additionally, the target was also active in manufacturing step-ladder units, which also use cement as their crude material. After assessing the production costs of these units, the FCCA came to the conclusion that the competitive situation would not change materially and there still remained parties that were not dependent on the supplies of Finnsementti.

In *Suomen Posti (Finnish Post) / Atkos Printmail Oy,* the FCCA examined the vertical effects of the merger on the postal and printing markets. In the FCCA's view, the proposed concentration could have caused negative competitive effects on these markets, because the acquirer could have favoured Atkos Printmail over its competitors in the future, which, in turn, would have strengthened the already dominant acquirer's market position. Suomen Posti committed to keep Atkos Printmail as a separate subsidiary and not to transfer its current business operations to Suomen Posti. The remedies were straightforward and offered already in Phase I, which made it possible to clear the concentration without opening a Phase II investigation.

Approach to remedies (i) to avoid second stage investigation and (ii) following second stage investigation

Where a merger raises competition concerns, in that it could significantly impede effective competition, the notifying parties can propose commitments to the FCCA in order to resolve the competition concerns. The FCCA has a duty to consider these remedies, and if the remedies proposed by the notifying parties are deemed sufficient for eliminating the competition concerns associated with the merger, the parties are asked to commit to the remedies in writing. The FCCA is responsible for ensuring that the remedies are implemented as agreed. Since the FCCA's primary responsibility is to find an agreeable solution, it cannot ask the Finnish Market Court to prohibit a merger if the remedies proposed by the notifying parties are sufficient for eliminating the competition concerns identified.

In practice, the FCCA is always willing to meet the parties and discuss informally the proposed concentration and possible commitments.

The Competition Act presupposes that mainly structural remedies should be used in merger control cases. The FCCA has also stated that it favours structural remedies over behavioural ones and tends to refrain from accepting the latter. *NCC Roads Oy / Destia* is a good example of this policy. The parties had proposed behavioural remedies or limited structural remedies only, while the FCCA required clear structural ones. Further, the fulfilment of the proposed remedies was uncertain and their implementation would have required constant surveillance by the FCCA. When sufficient remedies were not offered, the FCCA made a proposal for the Market Court to prohibit the merger.

In its prohibition proposal to the Market Court, the FCCA referred to the European Commission's practice as well as to the case-law of the Court of Justice of the European Union to support structural remedies. The FCCA stated its view that behavioural remedies are generally difficult to supervise and that this is the case especially where the FCCA in practice would have ended up supervising whether the merged entity sold asphalt mass to third parties with reasonable prices or not. Further, the FCCA has never approved a divestment commitment that need not be adhered to, on the grounds that suitable buyer or tenant cannot be found. In earlier cases, the parties have committed to abandon the concentration if the divestment requirement could not be fulfilled *(Metsäliitto/Vapo)*. Alternatively, secondary commitments have also been given in case primary commitments could not be fulfilled *(Carlsberg / Orkla)*.

However, recent examples of clearing concentrations based on behavioural remedies only exist where they are found appropriate and sufficient to counter the problems identified (*Terveystalo Healthcare Oy / ODL Terveys Oy* in 2011). To address the FCCA's concerns concerning the hospital services of Oulu and the medical services in Kajaani and Kemi-Tornio, the parties offered such behavioural commitments that allowed the customers to have the opportunity to purchase operations conducted in private hospitals also from doctors outside the concentration. Additionally, Terveystalo undertook to follow the same national prices as elsewhere in the more competitive parts of Finland with regard to the medical services offered to private customers in the region of Kajaani and Kemi-Tornio. The FCCA was of the opinion that without these commitments, price increases pertaining to the services would have been imminent.

The FCCA may issue a conditional clearance decision during Phase I or Phase II. However, clearing a concentration conditionally does not affect the FCCA's procedural deadlines. Because of this, most conditional decisions are postponed until Phase II. However, some examples of conditional clearance decisions already in Phase I exist. These have taken place especially when the notifying party has submitted its commitments and the information necessary to investigate the concentration to the FCCA already before submitting its official notification. These kinds of open pre-notification discussions make it possible for the FCCA to evaluate the concentration already before the procedural deadlines start to run.

Commitments and appeals

It is also noteworthy that pursuant to the Competition Act, the FCCA has the duty to negotiate the commitments or remedies with the parties, but it cannot make commitments binding that the parties have not proposed. If the FCCA does not accept the commitments proposed, it must make a proposal to the Market Court to prohibit the concentration. Further, a notifying party cannot appeal a decision by which the commitments it has given have been ordered to be followed, nor can it appeal the conditional approval decision in itself.

In practice this means that if the company is unwilling to submit commitments, or is unwilling to approve commitments, the FCCA has stated it will have to approve the concentration, the only course of action available is for these cases to proceed to the Market Court as a prohibition proposal. A good example of this is the *NCC / Destia* case, where the commitments proposed by the parties were not sufficient to address the competitive concerns, a view upheld by the Market Court.

If the Market Court does not agree with the FCCA's proposal to prohibit the concentration, it has the power to impose conditions it sees as suitable to address the competitive concerns. The decision of the Market Court may be appealed to the Supreme Administrative Court. It is also noteworthy that third parties retain a right to appeal a conditional merger control decision if they are considered to be affected by the decision in the sense specified in the Finnish Administrative Judicial Procedure Act. However, in practice, third parties in a merger control case have never been considered to be in such a position.

Pursuant to the Competition Act and earlier practice of the Supreme Administrative Court *(Sonera / Loimaan Seudun Puhelin)*, the Market Court can prohibit a concentration only based on a proposal by the FCCA. An appealing party can thereby not have a concentration prohibited. Hence, the only effect an appeal might have is the removal of a single commitment or the whole remedies package.

Key policy developments

No significant developments relating to merger control have taken place during 2012, since the new Competition Act entered into force in November 2011.

Reform proposals

The FCCA continues to focus on reducing the harm caused by concentrated retail trade. The daily consumer goods trade is particularly noteworthy, as it is the most concentrated in Europe, with 80% of the market controlled by two retail chains. To address the issue of potential abuse of market power by these chains, the Government issued on 20 December 2012 a much-debated Bill to amend the Competition Act. The proposal would add a new provision stipulating that an undertaking in the daily consumer goods trade would have a dominant market position if its market share exceeds 30%. However, the Bill explicitly states this new provision has no effect on control of concentrations, as the applicable substantive test in the Competition Act is equivalent to the SIEC test provided in the EU Merger Regulation.

No other reforms have been proposed.

Leena Lindberg
Tel: +358 29 000 6371 / Email: leena.lindberg@krogerus.com
Leena Lindberg, a partner and co-head of Krogerus' competition practice, advises clients on competition law assignments. Prior to joining Krogerus, Leena worked with the Finnish Competition Authority (FCA) for 14 years, where she served also as a member of the board of directors. Among her responsibilities was managing the asphalt cartel investigation that led, in September 2009, to the largest infringement fines ever imposed in Finland. Additionally, Leena was in charge of the FCA's merger control team and handled many merger and antitrust cases in the Market Court and the Supreme Administrative Court. Her other international experience includes working for the European Commission's Directorate General for Competition. She is ranked by Chambers Europe where 'clients assert that she has the view from both sides, and can explain the thinking behind certain authority actions more clearly'.

Petteri Metsä-Tokila
Tel: +358 29 000 6249 / Email: petteri.metsa-tokila@krogerus.com
Petteri Metsä-Tokila, a partner at Krogerus' competition practice, specialises in competition law, regulatory issues and commercial agreements. He regularly advises clients in assignments heard before competition authorities and the Finnish Market Court. Petteri has especially strong expertise in distribution matters and horizontal co-operation, as well as in merger control. Additionally, he counsels both private and public sector entities in public procurement matters. He is ranked by Chambers Europe where it is noted that he 'assist[s] in Krogerus' most important competition cases, and is known for his compliance work'.

Krogerus Attorneys Ltd

Unioninkatu 22, 00130 Helsinki, Finland
Tel: +358 29 000 6200 / Fax: +358 29 000 6201 / URL: http://www.krogerus.com

France

Pierre Zelenko
Linklaters LLP

Overview of merger control activity during the last 12 months

Following the Law of Modernisation of the Economy dated 4 August 2008 (the **"LME"**), the French Competition Authority (the **"Autorité"**) has been in charge of French merger control since 2 March 2009. It issued useful Guidelines in December 2009 (the **"Guidelines"**), whose main provisions are in line with the EU Commission's practice, but also contain some differences. The Autorité has announced that it will amend the Guidelines in the coming months after an open process of public consultation.

Statistics

The summary table below shows relevant indicators of the Autorité's activity in 2011 and 2012.

The immediate comments raised by this table are that:

- there has been a decreasing trend in notifications in 2012 compared to 2011 and 2010, probably due to the slowdown in economic activity;

- the number of conditional clearances has increased in 2012 compared to 2010 and 2011 in absolute value as well as in percentage. While conditional clearances represented a rate of around 3.5% of all merger decisions in 2010/2011, they reached 5.5% in 2012;

- the EU Commission made three Article 9 (ECMR) referral decisions (Eurovia/Tarmac[2], Veolia/Transdev[3] and Univar/Eurochem[4]) and four Article 4§4 (ECMR) referral decisions (HTM/Saturn[5], Point P/Brossette[6], SNCF/Keolis[7] and Carrefour/Guyenne-Gascogne[8]) to France in three years, which is a significantly higher rate than in other Member States during that period. That statistic could give rise to several interpretations, the one favoured by the Autorité being that it proves the EU Commission's trust in this national merger control authority. It can be noted that no downward referral to France had occurred between 2004 and 2009 on the basis of Article 9 (ECMR). This is therefore a rather new trend, confirmed again by the two referrals in 2012 on the basis of Article 4§4 (ECMR).

Merger Control – Autorité de la concurrence / Statistics 2011-2012

	2011	**2012**
Number of notifications	231	169[1]
(including number of referrals from the European Commission)	2 • Decisions 11-DCC-87 of 10 June 2011, HTM Group/Media Concorde SNC and • 12-DCC-41 of 23 March 2012, Point P SA/Brossette S.A.S	2 • Decisions 12-DCC-129 of 5 September 2012, SNCF/Keolis and • 12-DCC-63 of 9 May 2012, Carrefour/Guyenne Gascogne
Number of decisions	215	185

Table continues overleaf

	2011	2012
Number of Phase II openings	2 • Geodis/Tatex (the transaction lapsed) • COFEPP/Quartier Français Spiritueux (see decision 11-DCC-187 of 13 December 2011)	3 • Castel Frères SAS/groupe Patriarche (see decision 12-DCC-92 of 2 July 2012) • Vivendi-GCP/Direct 8-Direct Star (see decision 12-DCC-101 of 23 July 2012) • Vivendi-Groupe Canal Plus/TPS-CanalSatellite (see decision 12-DCC-100 of 23 July 2012)
Conditional clearances after Phase I	6 • Decision 11-DCC-150 of 10 October 2011, Agrial/Elle & Vire • Decision 11-DCC-134 of 2 September 2011, Groupe Bernard Hayot/Cora Martinique SAS • Decision 11-DCC-114 of 12 July 2011, Banque Fédérative Du Crédit Mutuel/Est Républicain • Decision 11-DCC-102 of 30 June 2011, Rubis/Société Antillaise des Pétroles Chevron • Decision 11-DCC-87 of 10 June 2011, HTM Group/Media Concorde SNC • Decision 11-DCC-34 of 25 February 2011, GDF Suez/Ne Varietur, CI2E	9 • Decision 12-DCC-154 of 7 November 2012, Eurotunnel/Actifs de Sea France • Decision 12-DCC-129 of 5 September 2012, SNCF/Keolis • Decision 12-DCC-59 of 4 May 2012, Groupe Parfait/Leclerc Lamentin • Decision 12-DCC-58 of 4 May 2012, ITM A N/Financière RSV • Decision 12-DCC-57 of 4 May 2012, ITM Alimentaire Nord/Tilguit, Ludivan and Vanlube • Decision 12-DCC-48 of 6 April 2012, ITM/Sofides • Decision 12-DCC-42 of 26 March 2012, Coopérative Champagne Céréales/Coopérative Nouricia • Decision 12-DCC-41 of 23 March 2012, Point P SA/Brossette S.A.S • Decision 12-DCC-20 of 7 February 2012, Électricité De Strasbourg/Enerest
Conditional clearance after Phase II	1 • Decision 11-DCC-187 of 13 December 2011, COFEPP/Quartier Français Spiritueux	2 • Decision 12-DCC-101 of 23 July 2012, Vivendi-Canal+/Direct 8-Direct Star • Decision 12-DCC-100 of 23 July 2012, Vivendi-Canal+/TPS-CanalSatellite

New developments in jurisdictional assessment or procedure

Regarding assessment and procedure, several issues have been clarified during recent months.

<u>Strict monitoring of the implementation of remedies</u>

The Autorité's landmark decision 11-D-12 of 20 September 2011, sanctioning Canal+ for failure to implement the remedies it had given to obtain clearance of its acquisition of TPS in the market for pay TV, will probably be regarded as 2012's most important decision. Not only did the Autorité oblige Canal Plus to re-notify this acquisition, but it also imposed a fine of €30m (reduced to €27m by a decision of the Conseil d'Etat of 21 December 2012) whereas the preceding fine for such an infringement was only €250,000 (imposed on another TV channel, TF1). In doing so, the Autorité sent a clear message to all companies committing to remedies that they should carefully implement them within the deadlines imparted. This strict verification of the implementation of remedies could be seen as the counterbalance of the Autorité's open approach to creative behavioural remedies while other competition authorities, such as the European Commission, seem more reluctant to accept undertakings other than clear-cut structural ones.

The Autorité's decision 12-D-15 of 9 July 2012 imposed a fine of €1m on a smaller company, Bigard, for failure to implement the remedies on which the clearance of its acquisition of Socopa was conditioned. This decision provides yet another example of the Autorité's strict monitoring of the implementation of remedies.

First use of injunction powers

The Autorité used its injunction powers for the first time. As mentioned in the previous paragraph, the Autorité withdrew its clearance of the Canal+/TPS/Canalsatellite merger due to the parties' failure to implement the remedies they had given. When clearing this merger again, the Autorité estimated that reverting to the situation of 2006 (date of the merger) was not an option but considered at the same time that the proposed remedies were insufficient, and consequently imposed injunctions on the parties, pursuant to Article L. 430-7 III of the French commercial code. Canal+ appealed this decision before the Conseil d'Etat, which rejected its plea for annulment (decision of 21 December 2012) as well as its petition for interim measures (decision of 22 October 2012). In the framework of this Canal+ saga, it is also interesting to note that, before the Conseil d'Etat rendered its decision, the Conseil Constitutionnel had to verify whether the internal organisation of the Autorité complied with the French Constitution, as the parties had raised concerns about this. In its 2012-680 decision of 12 October 2012, the Conseil Constitutionnel confirmed the constitutionality of the rules organising the functioning of the Autorité.

Review of simple cases

First, the Autorité has proven its pragmatic approach as regards simplified filing forms/accelerated procedures. It must be recalled that there is no legal obligation for the Autorité to handle certain cases in less than the standard 25 working days. However, in its Guidelines and in different public speeches, the Autorité had stated that it would endeavour to reach a decision in a shortened timeframe of 15 working days for cases without any specific competition issues. This reduced timescale was further opened specifically to investment funds (whose transactions rarely have an impact on competition).

Nevertheless, it is our experience that the Autorité has proved flexible when handling simple cases in significantly reduced timeframes. A survey of the last ten decisions on private equity transactions shows that such transactions have been cleared in less than 20 working days, on average. However, the timing of the review of such transactions also depends on the workload of the Autorité at the time.

In its annual report for 2011, the Autorité stated that the simplified notification forms have proved sufficient to clear such simple cases, and that it took the decision to issue simplified clearance decisions in such cases so that the legal waiting period could be further reduced.

Other notable developments

Four additional points are worth noting:

- The issue of warehousing, addressed by the EU General Court in a recent *Odile Jacob* ruling[9], is also mentioned in the Guidelines[10], with a direct reference by the Autorité to article 3, paragraph 5 of Regulation n°139/2004 and to the approach adopted by the EU Commission. There is also a specific provision about warehousing in the retail sector[11] according to which, when the identity of the ultimate purchaser is unknown and when there are no clear and binding agreements for the resale, the Autorité takes a more cautious view with respect to intermediate transactions. This was illustrated by an operation that was presented by the parties as provisional but was assessed by the Autorité as a concentration in its own right[12].
- While the recent period could have provided a good opportunity to apply the failing firm criteria to

certain acquisitions concerning targets undergoing financial difficulties, the strict and cumulative criteria have proved difficult to meet and, while presumably taking the situation of the target into account, the Autorité has applied a classic merger control analysis to acquisition of companies under liquidation or *redressement judiciaire*[13].

- The Autorité fined Colruyt, a Belgian company, €392,000 for failure to notify a transaction[14]. This is one of the rare cases of a fine for such a violation. It has given the Autorité the opportunity to decide that such infringements are subject to a five-year limitation period (which was not mentioned in the law).

Key industry sectors reviewed, and approach adopted, to market definition, barriers to entry, nature of international competition etc.

Two sectors have particularly fuelled the Autorité's merger control decisional practice this year.

The TV sector

The most interesting sector this year has probably been the television broadcasting sector. Beyond the extensive litigation proceedings (described in more detail above) to which the Canal+/TPS/Canalsatellite decisions gave rise, the Canal+/Direct 8-Direct Star Phase II clearance was granted subject to interesting remedies.

Firstly, Canal+ committed to limit the acquisitions of rights for American movies, American TV series and French films, in order to prevent itself from using its buying power to drain the most attractive rights from the market. However Canal+ can supply the merged channels with attractive programmes, to the benefit of television viewers. The Parties have therefore undertaken to limit "output deals", combining acquisitions of both free-to-air and pay TV rights to a single American studio among the six majors (Universal, Paramount, Warner, Sony, Fox and Disney).

Secondly, the merging parties committed to organise separate negotiations for pay TV and free-to-air TV rights for films (French and international) and TV series, with specific staff in a separate company dealing with the acquisition of broadcasting rights for free-to-air TV. Furthermore, Groupe Canal Plus committed not to practise/grant any form of bundling, subordination, benefit or financial consideration between acquisitions of free-to-air broadcasting rights and acquisitions of pay TV broadcasting rights regarding American movies and TV series.

Thirdly, the parties committed to limit the acquisitions by Direct 8 and Direct Star of StudioCanal's library movies to levels reported prior to the merger, to limit the term of assignment of rights to six months, and not to grant these channels any preferential terms compared to competing free-to-air channels.

Finally, they committed to sell free-to-air broadcasting rights they may have acquired for major sports events, within the framework of transparent and non-discriminatory tender procedures involving all relevant broadcasters, organised by an independent pre-approved trustee.

All of these commitments were undertaken by the Parties for a five-year term. This case testifies again to the Autorité's open-minded approach to creative behavioural remedies.

The retail sector

In terms of volume, mergers in the retail distribution sector have triggered several notifications. Indeed, as in the past few years, the retail sector generated quite a lot of notifications, and accounts for 102 of the 184 clearance decisions of 2012. This is partly due to the lower thresholds set by the LME for retail stores (in short, turnover achieved in France exceeding €15m instead of €50m). ITM alone accounted for 44 decisions in 2012.

Most of those merger cases in retail distribution were cleared within short timeframes, which meant that the Autorité's resources were not engulfed by this administrative burden.

This being said, in certain of these decisions, the Autorité addressed challenging issues, as testified by the number of conditional clearances in 2012.

Five of the remedy decisions rendered by the Autorité in 2010 and 2011 concerned retail distribution:
- In decision 12-DCC-41 of 23 March 2012, the Autorité cleared the acquisition of Brossette by

Point P subject to the divestiture of 22 points of sales (on 360 points of sale).
- In decision 12-DCC-48 of 6 April 2012, the Autorité cleared the acquisition of Sofides by ITM subject to the divestiture of 5 points of sale (on 20 points of sale).
- In decision 12-DCC-59 of 4 May 2012, the Autorité cleared the acquisition of Leclerc Lamentin by Groupe Parfait subject to reduction of the size of the Long Pré hypermarket to 2,450 square metres.
- In decisions 12-DCC-58, ITM Alimentaire Nord/Financière RSV and 12-DCC-57 ITL Alimentaire Nord/Tilguit, Ludivian et Vanlube of 4 May 2012, the Autorité allowed ITM to carry out those acquisitions, subject to ITM's divestiture of a big hypermarket in Beauvais.
- All these decisions were based on detailed analyses of the local markets. Where the transactions were to result in high market shares in certain areas, the Autorité conditioned its clearance upon the divestiture of a sufficient number of points of sale to make sure that competition would not be harmed.

Regulated sectors

Beyond the media and retail distribution sectors, regulated sectors such as energy continue to be closely monitored by the Autorité, as well as by several other competition authorities across Europe. This year again, there was an important case cleared in Phase I with remedies, in which the Autorité cleared the acquisition of Enerest (the incumbent gas supplier in the Strasbourg area) by Électricité de Strasbourg, its counterpart in the electricity sector. This case was particularly interesting as, for the first time, the Autorité carried out a detailed analysis of the barriers to entry relating to bundled gas and electricity offers.

Key economic appraisal techniques applied

With regard to economic appraisal, it must first be stressed that the Guidelines not only refer frequently to economic theory, but also include a specific annex offering practical recommendations for the submission of economic studies. This signals the firm resolution of the Autorité to use detailed economic analysis when reviewing complex merger cases.

This coincided with the setting up of a team of economists, now including seven economists and headed by a chief economist, that is involved whenever a merger raises complex competition issues.

The first Phase II case handled by the Autorité (*TF1/TMC-NT1*[15]) was one of the transactions that required the most thorough economic assessment, because of the mutual influences of the markets for broadcasting rights and advertising on TV, and on the supposed ability to build on the market share of a strong channel (namely TF1) to develop two smaller general interest channels (TMC and NT1). The assessment involved the analysis of several scenarios for different segments of TV advertising (unilateral effects) as well as of possible conglomerate effects. The transaction was cleared through a detailed set of behavioural remedies further detailed below.

As regards economic appraisal of concentrations, it is also noteworthy that, in two recent conditional decisions to date (Rubis/Chevron[16] and Crédit Mutuel/Est Républicain[17]), the theory of harm relied almost exclusively on non-price effects:
- In the *Rubis/Chevron* case (petrol stations in the overseas *départements* of Guadeloupe and French Guiana), the Autorité had concerns that the merger would result in a lower quality of services (Rubis gave divestiture commitments).
- In the second case (regional press in eastern France), the Autorité feared horizontal effects which would have led to a reduction in the quality and diversity of the regional press. The parties gave behavioural commitments not to harmonise the content of the press titles.

However, the new "GUPPI" test for carrying out the economic analysis in the retail sector does not seem to have been adopted by the Autorité, which seems to rely on more practical analysis of the percentage of the local turnover of a retail point of sale that is subject to competition from other retail points of sale in the same area. It is worth mentioning that the Autorité has made a reference to the GUPPI test in the *Castel Frères/Patriarche* case[18], without however following the parties' assessment of the result of such test.

Approach to remedies (i) to avoid second stage investigation and (ii) following second stage investigation

The number of Phase II proceedings handled by the Autorité in 2012 (three) has remained significantly lower than the number of Phase I conditional clearances (nine). This would tend to show that both notifying parties prefer to seek an acceptable solution with the Autorité in Phase I than drift towards a Phase II. This may be partly explained by the Autorité's open-minded approach to creative and behavioural remedies, that address the issues identified and focus on them without jeopardising too significantly the synergies of the mergers in question.

Behavioural remedies

However, following either Phase I or Phase II proceedings, one of the most distinctive features of the Autorité when it comes to merger remedies is its willingness to assess and accept behavioural commitments (whereas the European Commission gives a clear and almost systematic preference to divestiture commitments).

As mentioned above, the Autorité had to assess a large merger in the TV broadcasting sector, namely the acquisition of Direct 8-Direct Star by Canal+, described in more detail above.

The Autorité also had to review in 2010 the acquisition by TF1 of TMC and NT1, which would have strengthened the TF1 group's position in the markets for broadcasting rights and advertising (around 40-50%).

According to its press release, *"the Autorité nevertheless found that with nearly 50% market shares, the TF1 group maintained a dominant position in this market that could only be strengthened by this acquisition, given the seemingly considerable growth potential of TMC and NT1, and despite their currently very low market shares (less than 2% in all)"*.[19]

The remedies offered by TF1 were essentially behavioural and spanned a period of five years (with apparently flexible review clauses). In short, TF1 undertook to facilitate the circulation of broadcasting rights for the benefit of competing channels, to renounce any kind of cross-promotion on TF1 of the programmes shown on the acquired channels (TMC and NT1), and to handle separately the advertising business of TF1 on the one hand, and of TMC and NT1 on the other.

The *Électricité de Strasbourg/Enerest* decision in 2012 provided yet another example of a complicated transaction cleared through behavioural remedies only. In this case, the Strasbourg area's incumbent electricity provider was acquiring its gas counterpart, thus creating a very strong local entity with extremely high local market shares in gas and electricity, which would be the only supplier holding the right to offer regulated gas and electricity tariffs. This transaction was cleared with unprecedented behavioural remedies consisting in: (i) prohibiting the new entity resulting from the merger from offering gas and electricity jointly where one of the two sources of energy was subscribed at a regulated tariff; and (ii) for the open market, obliging the new entity to open its client books to competitors to enable them to compete with offers as well targeted to their prospect's needs as those of the new entity.

Innovative remedies

In addition to behavioural remedies, the Autorité has proved that it can be open to innovative commitments.

In this regard, the single commitment that was most widely commented on in the past few months is certainly the creation of a "competition stimulation fund", proposed by Veolia Transport and Transdev, in order to remedy the Autorité's concerns that their merger could reduce the incentive for smaller competitors to participate in public tenders.

This *Veolia/Transdev*[20] case involved the merger of two of the three national leaders in urban and intercity passenger transport. The Autorité identified competition concerns in five local markets for intercity transport and in the national market for urban transport. The concerns on local markets were addressed mostly by "standard" divestitures, but it proved more difficult for the Autorité to deal with the national market for urban transport, because this market is organised through public tenders launched by local public entities which own the assets concerned (vehicles, garages etc.). Therefore, the Autorité could not directly strengthen competitors through divestitures, but it had to ensure that future public tenders would see credible competitors facing the merged entity.

The Autorité accepted the parties' innovative and unprecedented remedy to finance a competition stimulation fund (amounting to €6.54m) designed to allow the relevant public authorities to finance two types of measures:

- compensating all or part of the response expenses for rejected candidates following calls for tenders, thereby encouraging more competitors to take part in them; and
- the use by local and regional authorities, especially small ones, of project management assistance services, in order to help them improve their knowledge of the networks and obtain the best prices in the framework of the tenders that they organise.

Another example of innovative and unprecedented remedies accepted by the Autorité is provided by the *GDF SUEZ/Ne Varietur* case[21] (following Phase I proceedings). The Autorité considered that the acquisition of sole control by GDF SUEZ of one of its few competitors in the market for delegated management of district heating networks would have a significant impact on competition. The Autorité's concerns focused on three local areas, which were already highly concentrated and where the additions of market shares were significant. The decision was conditional upon behavioural remedies offered by GDF SUEZ (i) to allow certain local authorities in these areas to unilaterally terminate their delegation contracts with Ne Varietur, and (ii) to allow one competitor in the market to unilaterally terminate one of its subcontracts. Therefore the Authority preferred a free choice by the customers (in that case local authorities) to imposing divestiture remedies.

It remains to be seen how such innovative remedies could work in other cases, and what further innovative remedies the Autorité's merger practice will endorse in the coming years. What remains certain, however, is that in France, as with many other competition authorities, a well prepared and explained set of remedies proposed in Phase I is the best way to avoid Phase II proceedings for cases that raise competition issues. The significant number of conditional clearances granted after Phase I in 2012 testifies to this again.

Key policy developments

Role held by the Minister for the Economy

As mentioned above, pursuant to the LME, the Autorité has now replaced the DGCCRF (a directorate reporting to the Minister for the Economy) in terms of jurisdiction over merger control cases.

It would, however, be incorrect to state that, following the LME, the Minister for the Economy has lost all prerogatives in merger control. While entrusting the Autorité with the main role with respect to merger control, the French legislation provides two important possibilities of intervention. Firstly, following a Phase I clearance, the Minister for the Economy can ask the Autorité to reconsider the need to carry out an in-depth examination (Phase II). Secondly, at the end of a Phase II, The Minister for the Economy can decide to overrule the Autorité's decision on the grounds of public interest considerations. As far as we know, there has been no such official intervention of the Minister for the Economy in a merger control case.

The possibility of interference from the Minister for the Economy in merger control is one of the significant areas of uncertainty for French practitioners when they are faced with a complex case, all the more since there are no precedents and little guidance in this respect.

Another area of policy development that is worth mentioning is the focus on competition in French overseas territories, mainly the five *Départements d'Outre-Mer* (the **"DOM"**). We have already mentioned the lowered thresholds concerning these geographic areas. This has led mechanically to a number of notifications which enabled the Autorité to assess the level of competition in the DOM. And indeed, out of the seven commitments decisions taken by the Autorité in 2010, two concerned DOM exclusively: (i) the above-mentioned *Hoio/Delhaize* case in Martinique; and (ii) the acquisition by Tereos of Groupe Quartier Français[22] in May 2010, which raised concerns in the market for wholesale distribution of sugar in the overseas *département* of La Réunion. Tereos committed to divest local assets and to sign a 20-year supply contract to enable a third party to develop a competing business.

The June 2011 Rubis/Chevron case (already mentioned above) provides a third example of a conditional clearance exclusively addressing competition issues in French DOMs (Guadeloupe and French Guiana).

But, even more interestingly, in one of the first significantly developed decisions issued by the Autorité, the *Banques Populaires/Caisses d'Epargne* case in 2009[23], clearance was granted on the basis of only one remedy concerning the overseas *département* of La Réunion (the new group committed to maintain the legal independence and management autonomy of three local branches for a period of five years). This speaks volumes about the particular interest of the Autorité regarding competition in the DOM, since this case related to a merger between two nationwide banks which, contrary to the three previous cases, led to overlaps in several other geographic areas across France besides La Réunion.

The Autorité announces that its merger control Guidelines are to be amended

To clarify its new approach to merger control, the Autorité issued updated Guidelines in 2009, building upon the former guidelines issued by the DGCCRF, while adding several further provisions.

It would be too long to describe all those provisions. One good example of clarification which it is interesting to stress is the assessment of ancillary restrictions.

The Autorité is now encouraging merging parties to signal *"those restrictions whose compatibility with competition law seems doubtful, either because of their form, their scope, their combination with other restrictions, or the general competitive landscape"*[24]. While the European Commission no longer reviews or clears such ancillary restrictions, the Autorité provides more legal certainty in this respect. This is particularly interesting for the merging parties because (i) the status of these ancillary restraints was less clear at the time when the DGCCRF had jurisdiction for merger control cases, and (ii) legal certainty following the review of such clauses is high, since the same Autorité is also in charge of anticompetitive practices. One example of such a review is provided by the Berto/ Lovefrance case[25], in which the Autorité considered that a non-compete clause of 10 years could only be regarded as directly related and necessary to the transaction for a duration of three years.

Other interesting new developments in the Guidelines include the introduction of a simplified form and the review process of simple cases; useful explanations on the application of the new and specific lower thresholds; and procedural methodology relating to the submission by the parties of economic analyses.

The Autorité has announced its intention to amend these Guidelines soon, organising, as for the previous ones, a broad and open consultation of all stakeholders, including representatives of professional associations, companies and law firms. It remains to be seen what the changes will be.

Reform proposals

Some procedural aspects may be clarified in the coming new Guidelines. It will be interesting to see if there are such developments.

Beyond this, several interesting questions could be mentioned:
- Will the role played by the Minister for the Economy (as developed above) remain limited and devoted to exceptional cases?
- Will the Autorité grant the *"accusé de complétude"* (confirming that the notification was complete on the day it was filed and that the Phase I legal waiting period effectively started on that date) more quickly than it usually does now?
- Will the Autorité extend its use of injunction powers to a significant number of cases in the future?
- Despite the Canal+ case, will the Autorité remain open to behavioural and creative remedies, although they are more difficult to monitor than clear-cut structural undertakings?

* * *

Endnotes

1. This does not include the 11 clearance decisions which were not yet published when this table was prepared.
2. Decision 10-DCC-98 of the French Competition Authority of 20 August 2010.
3. Decision 10-DCC-198 of the French Competition Authority of 30 December 2010.
4. Decision M.814 of the European Commission of 16 July 2010.
5. Decision 11-DCC-87 of the French Competition Authority of 10 June 2011.
6. Decision 12-DCC-41 of the French Competition Authority of 23 March 2012.
7. Decision 12-DCC-129 of the French Competition Authority of 5 September 2012.
8. Decision 12-DCC-63 of the French Competition Authority of 9 May 2012.
9. European Commission, press release No 84/10 of 13 September 2010.
10. See paragraph 64 of the Guidelines.
11. See paragraph 591 of the Guidelines.
12. Decision 11-DCC-02 of the French Competition Authority of 17 January 2011, ITM Alimentaire/ Leman.
13. See decisions 10-DCC-90, Caravelle/Girard and 10-DCCC-42, 3 Suisses International/Quelle-La Source of the French Competition Authority.
14. Decision 12-D-12 of the French Competition Authority of 11 May 2012, Colruyt.
15. Decision 10-DCC-11 of the French Competition Authority of 26 January 2010.
16. Decision 11-DCC-102 of the French Competition Authority of 30 June 2011.
17. Decision 11-DCC-114 of the French Competition Authority of 12 July 2011.
18. Decision 12-DCC-92 of the French Competition Authority of 2 July 2012.
19. http://www.autoritedelaconcurrence.fr/user/standard.php?id_rub=368&id_article=1338.
20. Decision 10-DCC-198 of the French Competition Authority of 30 December 2010.
21. Decision 11-DCC-34 of the French Competition Authority of 25 February 2011.
22. Decision 10-DCC-51 of the French Competition Authority of 28 May 2010.
23. Decision 09-DCC-16 of the French Competition Authority of 22 June 2009.
24. See paragraph 486 of the Guidelines.
25. Decision 09-DCC-74 of the French Competition Authority of 14 December 2009.

Pierre Zelenko
Tel: +33 1 56 43 56 43 / Email: pierre.zelenko@linklaters.com
Pierre Zelenko is a partner in the Competition/Antitrust practice of Linklaters in Paris, specialising in EU and French competition law (merger control, cartels, abuses of dominant position, litigation before the European and French Competition Authorities, horizontal cooperations, vertical restraints). Pierre graduated from the École Nationale d'Administration (ENA), the École Supérieure de Commerce de Paris (ESCP), the Institut d'Études Politiques de Paris (Sciences Po), and earned a PhD in Philosophy of Law at the Paris Sorbonne University and a PhD in Economics at the École des Hautes Études en Sciences Sociales (EHESS).

Transactions in which Pierre has been involved include the acquisition of International Power by GDF SUEZ, the acquisition of joint control by la Caisse des dépôts et consignations over La Poste, the acquisition of Ne Varietur by GDF SUEZ, the acquisition by Lyonnaise des Eaux of several water distribution companies, the creation of the Atmea joint venture between Areva and Mitsubishi in the nuclear reactor sector, and the merger between Suez and Gaz de France.

Linklaters LLP

25 rue de Marignan – 75008 Paris, France
Tel: +33 1 56 43 56 43 / Fax: +33 1 43 59 41 96 / URL: http://www.linklaters.com

Germany

Jan Heithecker
Wilmer Cutler Pickering Hale and Dorr LLP

Overview of merger control activity during the last 12 months

According to a press release by the German Federal Cartel Office (FCO) of 18 December 2012 (at the time of writing at the end of February 2013, the detailed FCO activity report for 2011/2012 had not been published yet), there were "around 1,200" merger control notifications to the FCO in 2012, of which 21 led to phase II investigations.

"Around 1,200" notifications in 2012 marks a certain increase over 2011, where there were, according to an FCO press release of 21 December 2011, "more than 1,100" merger cases notified, of which 15 went to a phase II in-depth examination, two were ultimately prohibited, and two were cleared only against far-reaching commitments.

In previous years, according to the FCO activity reports, the number of merger control notifications received by the FCO had developed as follows: 987 notifications in 2010; 998 notifications in 2009; 1,675 notifications in 2008; 2,242 notifications in 2007; 1,829 notifications in 2006; 1,687 notifications in 2005; 1,412 notifications in 2004; and 1,366 notifications in 2003.

The increase from 2004 to 2007 was mainly due to increased merger activity in the economy. However, the decrease from 2008 to 2009 was not only due to decreased merger activity but also to the introduction of the second domestic turnover threshold in the amount of €5m, which took place in March 2009.

New developments in jurisdictional assessment or procedure

One development that is important, in particular to international companies that need to deal with German merger control, is actually a non-development, namely the still outstanding update of the FCO's 1999 guidelines on the assessment of domestic effects of foreign transactions, which has been pending since the introduction of the second domestic turnover threshold in March 2009. This is unfortunate because the second domestic turnover threshold so far applies only to straightforward transactions, and notably not to joint venture constellations and many other constellations comprising several parallel and/or indirect acquisition acts. When such more complicated transaction structures are contemplated by large foreign companies with some activities in Germany, whether or not a notification to the German FCO is required often hinges on whether the transaction has a sufficient domestic effect in Germany under section 130(2) of the German Act against Restraints of Competition (ARC) or not.

Another continuing critical jurisdictional issue is the concentration type of acquisition of a "competitively significant influence" under section 37(1) no. 4 ARC, for which no FCO guidance is available. Many other elements of the jurisdictional assessment under German merger control are similar to EU merger control, for which guidance is available, but the concept of "competitively significant influence" cannot be found anywhere but in Germany. It is not an exaggeration to say that with this concept, Germany has the lowest threshold worldwide with regard to transaction types caught by merger control. Today many international companies in particular (including their internal and external counsel) simply do not know (and frankly cannot even imagine) that, depending on the circumstances, even the acquisition of a very small shareholding (e.g. 13.75% in the A-Tec case of 2008) can require a merger control notification in Germany. To eliminate the presumably very large number of resulting violations of the suspension obligation under German merger control, the FCO should issue detailed and reliable guidance regarding the interpretation of a "competitively significant influence" as soon as possible.

A further key development from the point of view of international companies is about to enter into force as part of the imminent eight ARC amendment law (for more details, see the "Reform Proposals" section at the end of this chapter). The so-called market-related *de minimis* exception is supposed to be removed from the jurisdictional thresholds and to be limited to the substantive assessment.

To recall the context, under the ARC as it currently stands, German merger control is applicable only if all four of the following conditions are met:
- the proposed transaction comprises at least one concentration in the meaning of section 37 ARC;
- the aggregate annual turnovers of the undertakings concerned by the concentration exceed the revenue thresholds in section 35(1) ARC, i.e. €500m worldwide for all undertakings concerned combined, €25m in Germany for at least one undertaking, and €5m in Germany for at least one other undertaking concerned;
- inapplicability of the company-related *de minimis* exception in section 35(2) no. 1 ARC, i.e. no undertaking concerned is an independent undertaking with less than €10m worldwide annual revenue; and
- inapplicability of the market-related *de minimis* exception in section 35(2) no. 2 ARC, i.e. annual total sales in Germany on the relevant market exceed €15m (or the relevant market has not yet existed for at least five years).

Because currently, the *de minimis* market exception is part of the jurisdictional rules in section 35 ARC, if a proposed transaction concerns only one market that is (or several markets that each are – even taking into account the FCO's "bundling theory" under which the FCO may combine several neighbouring relevant markets specifically for the purposes of the assessment under section 35(2) no. 2 ARC) *de minimis* under section 35(2) no. 2 ARC, then German merger control does not apply to the proposed transaction altogether, so that no merger control notification is required. In contrast, in the future version of the ARC, the market-related *de minimis* exception will be transferred from section 35 ARC to section 36(1) ARC, which contains the substantive assessment criteria. As a consequence, unlike today, in the future even those mergers that only concern one or several *de minimis* markets will have to be notified to the FCO.

From a policy point of view, it is questionable whether this extension of the scope of application of German merger control is warranted, in particular if one takes into account that the threshold of €15m of total annual sales by all market participants in Germany already captures rather small economic sectors. Thus, to properly focus German merger control on sectors that are significant from an economic point of view, this threshold should be increased.

In any event, from the point of view of legal certainty, this amendment is to be welcomed, because in practice, the applicability of the *de minimis* market exception is very often uncertain due to lack of clarity with regard to the delineation of the relevant product market. Very often, there is at least one rather narrow conceivable product market definition under which the €15m threshold is not exceeded, and at the same time at least one somewhat wider conceivable product market definition under which that threshold is exceeded.

What is more, by its order of 14 October 2008 in case no. KVR 30/08 "Faber/Basalt" (and subsequent decisions), the Federal Court of Justice (FCJ) had held that when the *de minimis* market clause is decisive for the jurisdictional question of whether or not a transaction has to be notified to the FCO, then it has to be interpreted very narrowly by way of "a high-level review that excludes only such markets for which there is from the outset no doubt that the substantive merger control conditions are not met". In addition, in its judgment of 1 February 2012 in case VI-Kart 6/11 "Lenzing/Kelheim", the Higher Regional Court (HRC) Düsseldorf, which is the competent first instance court for all FCO decisions, explicitly held that the legal uncertainty created by the potential application of the *de minimis* market clause to the jurisdictional analysis was to be borne by the merging parties, rather than by the FCO.

This case law had introduced two different legal standards for the application of the market-related *de minimis* clause, which is very questionable from a legal point of view. Moreover, this case law created extreme legal uncertainty with regard to the market-related *de minimis* exception for the merging parties, to the point where it was virtually impossible for the merging parties to rely on this exception to justify a non-notification of a transaction to the German authority. It is thus to be welcomed that the imminent legislative changes will remove this legal uncertainty and the need for two different legal standards with regard to one and the same provision.

Key industry sectors reviewed and approach adopted to market definition, barriers to entry, nature of international competition etc.

The in-depth phase II merger control investigations that the FCO conducted in 2012 concerned the following industries and had the following outcomes:

- Clearances without remedies concerned the gas sector (Gazprom/VNG and ESW AG/ESW Gasvertrieb GmbH), aquavit and other caraway liquors (Ratos/Pernod Ricard), safety syringes (Becton Dickinson/Safety Syringes), blood transfusion technology (Fresenius Kabi AG/Fenwal Holdings Inc.), metal container coatings (Akzo Nobel Coatings International B.V./Metlac Holding S.r.l.), automotive industry procurement (GM/PSA), inland ports (Häfen Köln/Neuss - Düsseldorfer Hafen), and rail vehicle systems (H. H. Thiele/Vossloh).
- A phase II clearance with remedies was granted with regard to reusable plastic packaging containers (OEP/Linpac RTP).
- The FCO's prohibition decisions concerned porous concrete (Xella/H+H International), hospitals (Klinikum Worms/Hochstift Worms), viscose fibres (Lenzing/Kelheim), and savings banks (Haspa Finanzholding/Kreissparkasse Lauenburg).
- There were (at least) three further phase II investigations in which the FCO raised competitive concerns. In one of them, which concerned agricultural magazines (Landwirtschaftsverlag GmbH; Münster/Landwirtschaftsverlag Hessen GmbH/Fachverlag Dr. Fraund), the parties withdrew the notification. Another one of them, which concerned cable TV (Kabel Deutschland/Tele Columbus), led to a prohibition on 22 February 2013). The third one concerns hospitals (Asklepios/Rhön-Klinikum) and was still pending at the end of February 2013.

In many cases in which the FCO raised concerns, it delineated relevant geographic markets narrowly, e.g. to be regional or even local rather than national, or even EU-wide or worldwide. This was, for example, the case for the abovementioned cases relating to porous cement, agricultural magazines, savings banks and hospitals. Generally, it can be said that also in 2012, the FCO continued to tend to delineate relevant markets in terms of both products and geographies rather narrowly, if compared to other competition authorities such as e.g. the European Commission.

The most significant general development in 2012 with regard to the substantive competitive assessment under German merger control law is the introduction of the concept of "future potential competition" by the FCJ in a case concerning regional newspapers. In its "Haller Tagblatt" judgment, the FCJ refined the concept of potential competition under German merger control by distinguishing between current potential competition and future potential competition. In addition, the FCJ provided clarifications with regard to the standards of likelihood that need to be met by future factual elements in order to be taken into account in merger control decisions. In order to understand the quite subtle differentiations introduced by the FCJ, it is necessary to consider the details of the decided case.

The facts of the case were as follows: The owner of Zeitungsverlag Schwäbisch Hall GmbH (ZSH), who was approaching retirement age, intended to sell all shares in ZSH to Neue Pressegesellschaft mbH & Co. KG (NPG). ZSH was the only newspaper publisher active in the county of Schwäbisch Hall, and published there the subscription newspaper "Haller Tagblatt" (with on average 17,300 copies sold per day) and the advertisement paper "KreisKurier". NPG already owned controlling shareholdings in several other regional press publishers, one of which was the only newspaper publisher active in the county of Crailsheim, and published there the subscription newspaper "Hohenloher Tagblatt" (with on average 14,400 copies sold per day) and the advertisement paper "Hohenloher Wochenpost"; and another of which was the only newspaper publisher active in and around the town of Gaildorf, and published there the subscription newspaper "Rundschau für den Schwäbischen Wald" (with on average 4,700 copies sold per day). The county of Crailsheim and the town of Gaildorf, where NPG was active, are geographically neighbouring the county of Schwäbisch Hall, where ZSH was active.

Already for decades, both NPG and ZSH had been members of the "Südwest Presseverbund" cooperation scheme, by way of which 17 local press publishers procure one centrally produced supra-regional newspaper section, and 14 of these publishers also jointly market the advertisements in that part of the newspaper (in the case of the "Haller Tagblatt", the externally procured supra-regional newspaper section and the self-produced local newspaper section were about the same size). Within the "Südwest Presseverbund", NPG had the task of producing the supra-regional newspaper section for all cooperation members. Thus, ZSH had been procuring the supra-regional newspaper section from NPG already since 1978. In addition, NPG printed, at its usual prices, the "Haller Tagblatt" for ZSH, and ZSH also cooperated with NPG with regard to accounting and data processing.

By decision of 21 April 2009 (case no. B6 - 150/08), the FCO had prohibited the merger, arguing that the merger would have permanently removed potential competition between ZSH and NPG, so that the merger would have strengthened the already existing dominant positions that ZSH and NPG held in the local newspaper, and newspaper advertisement markets in Schwäbisch Hall, Crailsheim and Gaildorf, respectively.

By judgment of 22 October 2010 (case no. VI Kart 4/09), the HRC Düsseldorf had annulled the FCO decision. The HRC Düsseldorf had held that while it was correct that each of ZSH and NPG already held dominant positions in local newspaper and newspaper advertisement markets in Schwäbisch Hall, Crailsheim and Gaildorf, respectively, it was incorrect to assume that the merger would have strengthened these dominant positions. The HRC Düsseldorf argued that due to the absence of actual or current potential competition between NPG and ZSH, the FCO's prohibition decision would have been lawful only if there had been "based on concrete factual elements, a high likelihood" that within the "prognostic period" under German merger control, i.e. approx. 3-5 years following the merger, the following developments will take place: (i) Rather than NPG, an independent third party acquires ZSH; (ii) the said third party is in a position to participate in a cooperation scheme, with regard to the supra-regional newspaper section and to advertisements, that is different from the "Südwest Presseverbund"; (iii) as a consequence, the said third party has an economic incentive to take ZSH out of the "Südwest Presseverbund" cooperation scheme and have it participate in a different cooperation scheme; and (iv) based on the participation in such different cooperation scheme, the said third party has an economic incentive to let ZSH compete against NPG in the county of Crailsheim, and in and around the town of Gaildorf. In the view of the HRC Düsseldorf, the FCO's factual findings did not meet this "high likelihood" standard, and the FCO was wrong to base its prohibition decision on the mere "theoretical possibility" that the developments (i) through (iv) could take place within the prognostic period.

By its second instance judgment of 19 June 2012 (case no. KVR 15/11), the FCJ upheld the judgment of the HRC Düsseldorf even though it disagreed with the HRC's findings about the applicable probability standard. The FCJ held:

- There is case law that supports a "high likelihood" standard in merger control, but this standard applies only to changes in the applicable laws or to other changes of the framework conditions under which competition takes place. None of the abovementioned developments (i) through (iv) constitute changes to the framework conditions. Rather, these changes are all brought about by market participants and do not require any changes to the framework conditions. Thus, the HRC Düsseldorf was wrong to apply the "high likelihood" standard to developments (i) through (iv).
- Due to the absence of actual or current potential competition between NPG and ZSH, the decisive question is whether there will be any "future potential competition" between them. This question asks for two prognostic assessments that build upon each other: First, the assessment of the likelihood that certain factual developments will occur that could enable competition. Second, assuming that these factual developments take place, an assessment of the likelihood of significant actual or potential competition. The probability standard on which each of the two prognostic assessments have to be based is the regular probability standard under German merger control, namely whether there is "based on concrete factual elements, some likelihood".
- Even though the FCJ held that the HRC applied an incorrect probability standard, it did not annul the HRC judgment. This is because in the assessment of the FCJ, the FCO's factual findings with regard to the likelihood of the abovementioned developments (i) through (iv) not only did not meet

the (wrong) "high likelihood" standard, but they also did not meet the (correct) "some likelihood" standard. Thus, the FCJ agreed with the HRC judgment in so far as the FCO was wrong to prohibit the merger merely on the basis of the "theoretical possibility" that the developments (i) through (iv) could take place within 3-5 years following the merger, so that the annulment of the FCO decision was correct.

While the distinctions between current and future potential competition, and between different applicable probability standards that are discussed above, may at first sight seem very subtle, these distinctions are likely to be of considerable practical importance in the future. This is in particular because under established case law, the applicable legal standard for a strengthening of an already existing dominant position is very low.

Key economic appraisal techniques applied e.g. as regards unilateral effects and co-ordinated effects, and the assessment of vertical and conglomerate mergers

In 2012, there were no key developments with regard to economic appraisal techniques under German merger control law.

In general, it must be noted that in recent years, the FCO has undertaken considerable efforts in response to criticism that had been voiced in the international antitrust community about the FCO's alleged disregard of economic analysis. In today's FCO, just like in the Directorate General Competition of the European Commission, all important investigations are co-conducted by the FCO's Chief Economist (currently Mr Christian Ewald) and his team.

One prime example of the FCO's awareness of and participation in the worldwide dialogue in competition economics is the 230-page FCO's report of May 2011 regarding the results of its car fuel sector inquiry. In this report, the FCO examines its empirical observation of regular ups and downs of gas prices at German gas stations on the basis of detailed econometrics, and specifically of the various economic theories discussing so-called Edgeworth cycles. While certain results of the FCO's investigation may be debatable – the HRC Düsseldorf did not agree with the FCO's conclusion that the five leading gas station chains in Germany form a jointly market-dominant oligopoly, but its judgment to that effect was annulled by the FCJ – there cannot be any doubt that the FCO is applying competition economics at a high level of sophistication.

The FCO's increased economic sophistication is also illustrated by the fact that there have recently been more unconditional clearances in cases involving high market shares, e.g. in the abovementioned cases regarding inland ports and metal container coatings.

The FCO's approach to unilateral effects and co-ordinated effects, and its assessment of vertical and conglomerate mergers, is set out in detail in the FCO's "Guidelines on market dominance in merger control", which were finalised in March 2012 but circulated in draft form and widely discussed already in 2011. By far most of the concepts and criteria explained in these guidelines are very similar to the European Commission's guidelines on the assessment of horizontal mergers and on the assessment of non-horizontal mergers, and deviations under German merger control are quite limited. These FCO guidelines also display a high level of sophistication of economic analysis, in particular with regard to the assessment of joint market dominance.

Approach to remedies (i) to avoid second stage investigation and (ii) following second stage investigation

In 2012, there were no key developments with regard to remedies under German merger control law. In general, the following characteristics of the remedy negotiation process under German merger control law are notable:

The FCO expects remedies to be proposed by the parties, but in many cases, the competitive concerns raised by the FCO will go a long way to determining the content of any successful remedies. The FCO cannot accept remedies in phase I but only in phase II, but this is in practice not a considerable obstacle because contrary to e.g. the European Commission, the FCO has considerable flexibility with regard to when and for how long it enters into phase II. Thus, there is no strict timetable for remedy offers in Germany, contrary e.g. to the strict deadlines that are prescribed in the European Commission's Remedies Notice.

In fact, there is also no written guidance on the required content of remedies, but the basic principles (in particular the need for full solution of the competitive problem, as seen by the authority in the respective stage of the investigation, as well as preference for a divestiture of a viable business to a viable buyer in a viable process) are the same in German merger control as in EU merger control. One key difference between the merger regimes is that under section 40(3) ARC, remedies can be accepted by the FCO only if they do not require permanent monitoring of the behaviour of the merging parties, which normally means that contrary to the established Gencor case law at the EU level, remedies in German merger control must be structural rather than behavioural.

As regards the implementation of remedies, there are several model texts on the FCO's website (namely for suspensive conditions, dissolving conditions and obligations to be attached to the clearance decision as well as for the mandate of the divestiture trustee) which the FCO generally requires the parties to follow. While the FCO's standard practice initially was to implement remedies only by dissolving conditions, it now increasingly often insists on suspensive conditions, which are effectively similar to a fix-it-first solution requirement.

Key policy developments

In recent years, the FCO's focus has somewhat shifted away from merger control and towards other areas of competition law enforcement. This is due not only to the fact that there are fewer notifications, but also to changed policy priorities. In particular hard-core cartel prosecution has recently gained in importance, as is illustrated by the fact that in 2012, the FCO conducted 14 dawn raids at 72 premises and imposed total fines of €248m on 57 companies and 31 individuals. Dominance abuse cases (in particular with regard to municipal water supplies) and sector inquires (still pending with regard to food retail; concluded in 2012 with regard to milk, recycling systems, road asphalt and district heating) played an important role. In addition, based on a new law that entered into force on 12 December 2012, market transparency units will be put in place for car fuel, electricity and heating gas. Overall, it can be said that while merger control certainly continues to be an important part of the FCO's overall activity, the relative importance of merger control within the FCO's overall activity has somewhat decreased in recent years, and this is not likely to change in the near future.

One key policy development that deserves special attention from the point of view of (although it does not directly pertain to) merger control is the FCO's increasing enforcement of prohibitions of companies that are jointly owned by competitors. In this context, two FCO inquiries are noteworthy:

In September 2012, the FCO's first decision division published a 110-page report on the results of its road asphalt sector inquiry. In the report, the FCO found that out of 268 road asphalt production plants active in the various local markets in Germany, only 56 are sufficiently independently owned, whereas all others are indirectly co-owned by more than one of the four main competing supplier groups Werhahn, Strabag, Eurovia and Kemna and are thus *prima facie* problematic under section 1 ARC, the German equivalent to section 101 TFEU. To identify the problematic ownership structures, the FCO proceeded as follows:

- As a starting point, the FCO used the constellation (which it calls "A cases"), where at least two shareholders of the jointly owned company are active on the same product and geographic market as the jointly owned company. For this constellation, there is, under established FCJ case law, a rebuttable presumption of a restriction of competition violating section 1 ARC.
- As "B1 cases" the FCO then defined the constellation where at least two shareholders of the jointly owned company are active on the same product and geographic market, but only one of these shareholders is active there through a controlled subsidiary, whereas the other shareholder(s) only has/have a non-controlling minority interest in that market.
- "B2 cases" were defined by the FCO as the constellation where only one shareholder of the jointly owned company is active in the same product and geographic market but at least one other shareholder is active on a geographically neighbouring market.
- "B3 cases" were defined by the FCO as the constellation where none of the shareholders of the

jointly owned company is active in the same geographic market as the jointly owned company, but where there are other geographic markets in which at least two of the shareholders of the jointly owned company compete head-on against each other.

* Finally, "C cases" were defined by the FCO as those constellations where, even though none of the constellations A or B1 through B3 is present, there is or may be an excessive flow of information from the jointly owned company to one or several of its shareholders who compete with the jointly owned company.

The sector inquiry report concludes by saying that the shareholders of the identified problematic jointly owned companies will be granted roughly one year's time to dissolve the problematic ownership structures voluntarily. To the extent that the relevant shareholders will refuse to dissolve the structures voluntarily, the FCO announces the commencement of formal proceedings to achieve the required disentanglement measures by way of formal orders. It remains to be seen whether all future formal orders based on the abovementioned new cases B1 through C will withstand court scrutiny.

On 21 November 2012, the FCO's third decision division concluded an inquiry by adopting a formal decision prohibiting a jointly controlled 51%:49% joint venture, Brenntag Germany Holding GmbH and CG Chemikalien GmbH & Co. Holding KG. It argued that both parent companies were active on the same relevant product and geographic markets (various chemicals trading markets in various regions of Germany) as the joint venture, and jointly had market shares of 30-40%, so that the coordination between the parent companies through the joint venture violated section 1 ARC and Article 101 TFEU. In its line of argument, the FCO's third decision division also explicitly refers to the abovementioned road asphalt sector inquiry report.

Reform proposals

During 2012, a draft law to amend the ARC was debated in public and in the parliament and (almost completely) finalised. The considerable significance of this amendment law is apparent already from the fact that since the entering into force of the ARC in 1958, this is only the eighth major ARC amendment law. The original plan to have this law enter into force was not accomplished due to still on-going negotiations in the conciliation committee of the two houses of the German parliament, but the remaining items under debate are minor. The most important changes with regard to merger control that will be brought about by the eighth ARC amendment law are the following:

* Just as Article 2 of the EU Merger Regulation was changed in 2004, section 36(1) ARC will be changed so as to feature in the future as the general substantive test the "significant impediment to effective competition" (SIEC) but to also retain the "creation or strengthening of a market dominant position" as one example, separated from the general test by "in particular". However, unlike the European Commission, the FCO has already stated that it will actively continue to use the market dominance test wherever appropriate, rather than to rely solely on the new SIEC test. In addition, in the opinion of the FCO, under German competition law, "market dominance" is and will continue to be a different concept from "market dominance" under EU law and jurisprudence. Thus, the effect of the introduction of the SIEC test in German merger control will likely be limited to closing the enforcement "gap" that, according to most scholars, the "market dominance" test left with regard to unilateral effects below the threshold of market dominance.

* To align German even further with EU merger control, provisions will be inserted into the ARC that are equivalent to Article 5(2)(2) – cumulation of several concentrations within a two-year period, Article 7(2) – exemption from the suspension obligation in case of public bids, Article 10(3) – extension of the three-month deadline for phase II by one month when the parties first offer remedies, and Article 10(4) – stop-the-clock provision for formal information requests necessitated by the parties' behaviour.

* The market share threshold for the rebuttable presumption of single dominance (which is relevant not only for merger control but also, and in particular, for the prohibition of the abuse of market dominance) will be increased from one third (33.3%) to two fifths (40%) of the market. This is in line with the abovementioned greater economic sophistication of the FCO's decision-making practice.

- The market-related *de minimis* exception will be transferred from the jurisdictional assessment in section 35 ARC to the substantive assessment in section 36 ARC (for details, see the section "New developments in jurisdictional assessment or procedure" above).
- Against the declared opposition of the FCO, the legislator enacts several provisions with the declared objective to enable small and medium companies in the press sector to merge with larger partners more easily: the factor by which press turnovers are multiplied is reduced from 20 to 8; the company-related *de minimis* exception will in the future also be applicable to press mergers; and a special version of the failing company defence with lower evidentiary burdens will be introduced specifically for press mergers.

Jan Heithecker
Tel: +49 30 2022 6307 / Email: jan.heithecker@wilmerhale.com
Jan Heithecker is a partner at Wilmer Cutler Pickering Hale and Dorr LLP ("WilmerHale"). Having spent several years in WilmerHale's Brussels office, today he works in the Berlin office and has a general EU and German competition law practice with a special emphasis on EU and national merger control and EU State aid law. In the field of merger control, he regularly advises and represents clients in proceedings before the EU Commission and the German Federal Cartel Office and has acted in numerous complex proceedings before both authorities. He also has extensive experience in handling multi-jurisdictional filings within and outside the EU. His clients belong to a variety of industries, including aviation, defence, energy, environmental services, industrial process technology, machine building, manufacturing, media, medical technology, measurement technology, and raw materials. He graduated from the University of Munich in 1994, was admitted to the bar in 2000, and received a Ph.D. degree from the University of Jena in 2002.

Wilmer Cutler Pickering Hale and Dorr LLP

Friedrichstr. 95, 10117 Berlin, Germany / Ulmenstr. 37-39, 60325 Frankfurt/Main, Germany
Tel: +49 30 2022 6400 / Fax: +49 30 2022 6500 / URL: http://www.wilmerhale.com

Greece

Emmanuel J. Dryllerakis & Cleomenis G. Yannikas
Dryllerakis & Associates

Introduction[1]

A new competition law

As of April 2011 Greece has a new law, "*re. protection of competition*", under the serial number 3959/2011[2]. It replaced the long-lived Law 703 of the year 1977, which was introduced long before Greece became a Member of the then EEC. Both the new and the old law are modelled upon European legislation. Articles 1 and 2 of both laws literally translate the then Articles 85 & 86 of the Rome Treaty, later 81, 82, and now Articles 101, 102 of the TFEU, to prohibit any agreement, concerted practices or decisions of associations as well as the abuse of dominant position. The new law does not introduce radical changes. Basically it integrates the changes of the past, as developed during all these long years, especially the ones introduced in 2009. The later changes are the ones which changed, in many ways, the operation of the Hellenic Competition Commission.

The old law originally totally exempted mergers from the jurisdiction of the Hellenic Competition Commission. This is something which is not surprising for a country suffering from a lack of units of a certain size and which, even today, gives tax and other incentives for mergers. Gradually, but systematically, the concept of merger control prevailed to reach a point where the law expresses, in general, the concept of European Law not only in substance but also in the procedure followed.

Only major concentrations fall under the jurisdiction of the Hellenic Competition Commission, which examines whether they significantly impede competition, as analysed below.

The Hellenic Competition Commission (HCC)

The HCC is the Independent Authority which not only enforces Articles 1 and 2 of the law but also Articles 5-10, which deal with the merger control of mergers with a national dimension. In this capacity, the HCC has the decisive power to verify whether there is a significant impact on competition from the concentration and can decide whether to allow or prohibit it, or to accept remedies or impose conditions.

The HCC is exclusively competent to apply merger control provisions in all market sectors[3], but for specific liberalised industries, such as telecoms and energy, there are separate National Regulatory Authorities ("*EETT*", "*RAE*") for these fields, which are also assigned with the application of competition rules, including merger control provisions, in co-operation with the HCC. L.3959/11 (Article 24 par. 2) specifies the terms of co-operation between the authorities, given that in most cases co-ordination is required.

There also used to be a separate authority for cases of sea transportation ("*RATHE*"), although this was abolished in 2004. Competence now lies with the HCC for such cases as well, but L.3260/2004 provides that an expert from the Ministry of Development, Competitiveness and Shipping must participate in the hearings and the deliberations of the HCC, as a non-voting member.

The HCC is also competent to handle mergers with a Community dimension, which are referred to it by the European Commission, as per the provisions of EU Regulation 139/2003. Reference will be made below (under "Recent HCC Decisions on Concentrations") to two recent cases where such referral has taken place.

The HCC comprises eight members: the President; the Vice President; and six more members, four of whom are full-time, exclusive employment executives ("*Rapporteurs*").

Before 2009 the composition and the role of the HCC was quite different. Apart from the President, who was a full-time, exclusive employment executive, the other members had no relations with the organisation of the HCC. Some of them were designated by Business Associations, while the remaining were appointed by the supervising Minister of Development, among qualified individuals. Therefore, the HCC consisted of two parts, the Service (General Directorate of Competition) and the (independent) Committee, which had no other relation with the Service but for being assigned the task to review and approve or reject the Recommendation Reports of the Service. The umbilical cord of the two parts was the President, who not only presided over the Committee, and actually had a double vote, but at the same time was the Head of the Service. Under this scheme, the HCC has been assigned quasi-judicial tasks, although, being a part of the Administration and not of the judiciary, the only exception is the double role of the President.

On the contrary, under the current structure, the HCC is a single organ and the *Rapporteures* (the members of the HCC) are assigned the cases. They then prepare, in co-operation with the Service, a Statement of Objections, which constitutes the basis of the examination of the case by the HCC. A *rapporteur* participates in the hearing and the deliberations, but he/she does not vote, according to the last amendment.

Pre-merger notification

Thresholds. Concentrations which fall under the definition of the law (Article 6) are subject to a pre-merger notification. If they are implemented prior to the clearance by the HCC or contrary to the prohibition decided by the HCC, the undertakings concerned are subject to serious sanctions, i.e. penalty and possible invalidity of the concentration. A penalty is also given for late notification, even if the parties did not yet implement the concentration or if the concentration was finally approved.

Merger control is exercised when a concentration exceeds the following turnover thresholds:

(a) the combined aggregate worldwide turnover of all the undertakings concerned is at least €150m; and, cumulatively,

(b) the aggregate turnover of each of at least two of the undertakings concerned in the Greek market exceeds €15m.

The above thresholds apply for all market sectors except for mass media, where special legislation (L.3592/07) defines the respective thresholds as follows:

(a) the combined aggregate worldwide turnover of all the undertakings concerned is at least €50m; and, cumulatively,

(b) the aggregate turnover of each of at least two of the undertakings concerned in the Greek market exceeds €5m.

Deadline – Notifying party. While EU Regulation No.139/2004 does not set any notification deadline, and while it is in the parties' interest to move quickly in order to get clearance and implement the merger, in Greece, notification must be made within 30 days from the entry into an agreement or the publication of an offer or an exchange, or the obligation from the undertaking to acquire participation, which secures the control of another undertaking. Up until the new law, the deadline was only 10 working days, which was really tight for proper notification.

Parties to a concentration, which consists of a merger or in the acquisition of joint control, shall notify the concentration jointly. In all other cases, the notification shall be effected by the person or undertaking acquiring control of the whole or part of one or more undertakings.

Definition of concentration. A concentration shall be deemed to arise where a change of control on a lasting basis results from the merger of two or more previously independent undertakings or parts thereof, or the acquisition of direct or indirect control of the whole or part of undertaking(s) regardless of the way this acquisition is affected. Article 5 of L.3959/11 follows the definitions of Regulation (EC) No.139/2004.

Both stock and asset deals can be considered as a concentration, once they lead to the acquisition of control. Cases of a change of control (e.g. turning from joint to full control) do also constitute a concentration to be notified once the above thresholds are met.

Creation of a joint venture constitutes a concentration, only if the new entity performs all the functions of an autonomous economic entity on a lasting basis. Otherwise, it would be a co-operative joint venture, falling under the scope of Article 1 (Article 101 TFEU) and possibly qualifying for exemption.

Substantive test. Greek law, following the EU substantive test (SIEC), provides that a concentration is prohibited if it may lead to a significant impediment of competition in the whole or a substantial part of the Greek market, especially by creating or strengthening a dominant position.

Therefore, market share is to be examined, but it is not the only decisive criterion. In the framework of the test adopted, the law itself specifies the basic criteria to be considered thereof, i.e. structure of the relevant markets, actual or potential competition, barriers to entry, market position of the participating undertakings, available sources of supply and demand, consumers' interest and efficiencies, etc.

The above test applies in all market sectors, except for mass media where special law (L.3592/2007) provides for dominance test. For the purposes of this law, "dominance" is translated into a market share from 25-35%, depending on the case.

Turnover calculation. The turnover for the calculation of the thresholds comprise the amounts derived by the undertakings concerned (as the case may be in the national or international market) in the preceding financial year from the sale of products and the provision of services falling within the undertakings' ordinary activities after deduction of sales rebates and of value-added tax and other taxes directly related to turnover. The aggregate turnover of an undertaking concerned shall not include the sale of products or the provision of services between any of the undertakings within the group of companies (intra group)[4].

Where the concentration consists of the acquisition of parts, whether or not constituted as legal entities from one or more undertakings, only the turnover relating to the parts which are the subject of the concentration shall be taken into account with regard to the seller or sellers.

The aggregate turnover of an undertaking concerned shall be calculated by adding together the turnover of the "group"[5].

Special rules apply for the calculation of the turnover, in the case that the participating undertakings are banks or insurance companies (Article 10 par. 3). Again, these rules follow the respective European framework.

Approval by the Minister. Under the previous law, in case the HCC prohibited a merger, the interested parties had the right to request approval of the concentration from the competent Minister of Development. Such request would not lead to a new competitive assessment by the Minister to challenge the decision of the HCC. On the contrary, the law itself provided that such approval would be granted on the basis of different criteria, i.e. the overall economic interest of this merger (that it could be for "political" reasons). This possibility, which had been used only once throughout the 35-year life of the law, has now been abolished under the new law. Once a merger is prohibited, the parties may only appeal against the decision of the HCC before Court (see below under "Judicial protection").

Post merger notification. The current law also abolishes the obligation for post-notification to the HCC of concentrations of undertakings, the share of which in the Greek market was at least 10%, or their aggregate turnover in Greece was at least €15M. Such concentration did not require any approval by the HCC but it should be notified within one month after its closing. It was intended to be a tool for market mapping, i.e. to follow up the trends of the market, but it did not work so. It ended up adding an unnecessary workload to the HCC and for this reason it was abolished in the past and reinstituted. Hopefully the repeal will now be final. When the notification obligation was in force, failure to comply was subject to a fine.

The procedure

<u>Notification form</u>. The content of the notification is defined by a decision of the HCC. The latter has issued a new draft notification form (Decision No. 523/VI/2011), together with a separate form for submitting remedies (Decision No. 524/VI/2011). The format of these templates generally follows the guidelines of the European Commission and the purpose is to make the minimum information they have to substantiate as part of the notification clear to the notifying parties. The notification form must be submitted in Greek, together with all supporting documents and the receipt of the filing fee, which currently amounts to €1,100. A summary of the notification must also be published in a daily financial newspaper, as well as in the website of the HCC, so that any third party (competitor, supplier, customer, customer's association) may take knowledge of the transaction and express its comments to the HCC.

Without filling in and submitting the notification form properly, the notification is not complete, the deadlines for the submission are not met and the deadlines for the HCC to issue its decision(s) will not commence. Depending on the extent of omission, it may be considered as a failure to notify.

<u>Two-phase examination</u>. Within a month from receipt of proper notification, the President of the HCC has to issue an Act to certify that the concentration concerned does not fall within the scope of the law.

If the concentration falls within the scope of the law, the concentration may be examined in **one** or **two phases**, in line with the practice defined by EU Regulation No.139/2004.

Where the HCC finds that the notified concentration does not raise serious doubts as to its compatibility with the competition requirements of the relevant national markets, the HCC issues a decision approving the concentration within a month from the date of notification, i.e. within the same period granted for the verification that the concentration is within or outside of the scope of the law.

Where the HCC finds that the concentration raises serious doubts, its President issues a decision initiating the Phase-II proceedings, which is notified to the interested parties. This decision has to be issued within a month from notification. Following this decision, the *rapporteur* prepares his recommendation within 45 days from the initiation of Phase-II proceedings and the HCC has to decide within ninety (90) days to approve or prohibit the concentration. If the HCC fails to issue a decision within this period of 90 days, the concentration is deemed as approved. Both the 45- and 90-day deadlines start as of the initiation of the Phase-II examination, instead of the notification date under the previous law.

In summary, the first month from the notification is the most critical. Within this period, the following developments will or may occur: the concentration will be declared as not falling within the scope of the law; the concentration will be approved if it does not raise serious doubts that it will significantly impede competition; or a Phase-II proceeding will be initiated, i.e. it will be decided whether a full investigation has to follow. The total maximum period, provided that the notification is complete (see 'Extension, suspension or interruption of deadlines', below) and no remedies have been submitted (see 'Modifications and remedies', below), is a month[6] plus 90 days, i.e. 118-121 days depending on the length of the month.

<u>Extension, suspension or interruption of deadlines</u>. The legal deadlines may be extended if the notifying undertakings are in agreement. Also the deadline is extended by 15 days in case the HCC accepts a delayed proposal of remedies. If the notification is incorrect or misleading, or if the format of notification has not been completed properly, so that the HCC cannot evaluate the notified concentration, then the deadlines start when the notifying parties have been advised of their failure from the HCC. This notice from the HCC must be given within seven (7) days from the notification. The deadlines are also suspended when the undertakings do not meet their obligation to supply information, provided that the participating undertakings are advised by a notice communicated to them within 2 days from the expiration of the deadline to supply the information. The deadline period restarts from the submission of the information requested[7].

<u>Modifications and remedies</u>[8]. Within 20 days after the submission of the Recommendation of the

rapporteur, the parties have the right to propose remedies to remove the serious doubts as to its compatibility with the competition in the relevant market. Although the possibility of making modifications was introduced in 1995[9], the term "remedies" was added by the new law. The HCC may, in exceptional cases, accept the proposal of remedies after the expiration of the above deadline. In this case, the deadline of 90 days may be extended by 15 days, reaching 105 days in total.

Conditions. The HCC may approve the notified concentration, attaching to its decision conditions and provisions to ensure compliance of the participating undertakings with the commitments undertaken by them, with a view of rendering the concentration compatible with the provisions of the law requiring that the concentration must not raise serious doubts on its significant impact to competition in the national market or, in the case of a joint venture, the latter operates as an autonomous unit[10].

The HCC may threaten the participating undertakings with fines if they fail to comply with the conditions and provisions in the framework of the remedies.

Derogations. The prohibition of its implementation prior to its clearance does not prevent a concentration in certain cases:

a)   In case of the acquisition of control following a public offer[11] or other stock exchange transactions under the proviso that the relevant actions are notified in time (i.e. within 30 days from the date of the transactions) and the buyer does not exercise its voting rights related to the acquired titles except (after special permit by the HCC) in order to maintain the value of its investment.

b)   By special permission of the HCC, to avoid serious damages to one or more of the undertakings participating in the concentration or to a third party.

Revocation. In addition to the general rules of the administrative law regulating the revocation of legal or illegal administrative acts, the new law maintains special rules concerning the decision approving the implementation of a concentration. It maintains the provision allowing revocation of the HCC decision based on inaccurate or misleading data[12]. The revocation in case the participating undertakings in the concentration violate any condition or accepted remedy is specifically regulated,[13] allowing as well the HCC to take any measures to dissolve the concentration or to restore prior conditions or to split the merged enterprises or to order the sale of the acquired shares or assets. The above arrangement applies as well in case of concentrations implemented without approval.

Sanctions

Apart from its authority to revoke any decision approving a concentration and to restore conditions in the relevant national market, the HCC may impose fines, the size of which depends on the kind of violation. In this respect the fine amounts to:

(a)   at least €30,000 and up to 10% of the aggregate turnover (a.t.o.) in case of violation of the obligation of the undertaking to notify in time a concentration subject to prior notification, regardless of whether failure was not intentional but due to light negligence;

(b)   the same as (a) for the implementation of the concentration before the approval is granted;

(c)   up to 10% of the a.t.o. of all participating undertakings, which do not comply with the undertaken remedies; and/or

(d)   up to 10% of the a.t.o. of all participating undertakings for failure to comply with the conditions of the HCC decision in the framework of the approved concentration.   ·

In addition, the law provides for criminal sanctions, which are cumulative to the fines imposed by the HCC. Article 44 §1 provides for a fine ranging from €15,000 to €150,000 to be imposed by the criminal court to anyone who violated the provisions on merger control or does not comply with the relevant decisions of the HCC. The criminal character of the offence is eliminated for the culprits or the accomplices who notify the HCC, the prosecutor or any other competent authority of the violation, submitting any evidence of the offence as well.

Statute of limitation

Article 42 of the new law provides that any violations of the law are subject to a five-year statute of limitation[14], which starts on the date the violation was committed. In case of a continuous violation or a repeated violation, it starts on the date the offence ceased.

Contrary to EU Regulation No.1/2003 which clearly only refers to the violation of Articles 101 & 102 TFEU, the above provision, speaking for *"any violations of the law"*, appears to also cover infringements of Greek merger control provisions. Such a provision on the limitation period is absent from the respective EU Regulation 139/2004, but is indirectly found in Regulation 2988/74 (Article 1), which remains applicable for any competition infringements other than those falling under Regulation 1/2003[15].

The main question is whether late notification and/or prior implementation of a merger would be considered to be a continuous violation or not. It must be noted that issues of a statute of limitation have not been tackled by the HCC in merger cases.

Still though, the general rule of the administrative law should apply, which does not allow for the revocation of an illegal act after the lapse of a reasonable time; a period of 5 years is always considered as such.

The statute of limitation is interrupted by any act of the HCC (or EC) in the framework of the investigation of the violation or of the procedures related with the specific violation, including but not limited to written requests of the HCC or another authority for providing information or orders for audit (or dawn raids), assignment of the case to a *Rapporteur*, servicing of an SO or of a Recommendation Report, etc. The interruption starts from the communication of the relevant act to at least one of the undertakings participating in the violation and applies to all accomplices. The deadline for completion of the statute of limitation is suspended during the time that the act or decision of the HCC, in relation with the case, is pending before courts. In any case, the statute of limitation is completed upon the lapse of 10 years (i.e. double the basic period of prescription).

Strictly legally speaking, the statute of limitation is an institution of the civil law and it refers to claims against a person. The term is not compatible with the public law terminology, where the authorities do not exercise any right but they perform their duties in accordance with the law. Therefore, in terms of administrative law, we should refer to a peremptory deadline, following the lapse of which the HCC is deprived of its authority to act and enforce the specific provisions of the law.

Judicial protection

The enforceable decisions of the HCC are subject to appeal (application for annulment) directly to the Athens Appellate Administrative Court. In merger cases, an appeal would normally challenge a decision of the HCC that either prohibited a merger or fined the undertaking for the alleged violation of merger control provisions (e.g. late notification). Still, we had a case in the past where a third party successfully challenged the approval of a merger in court.

The court examines both the legality and the substance of the decision, which may be annulled in full or in part. This includes the reduction of a fine (if any), something which is not unusual at all. In contrast, the annulment of the decision is not as common and in many cases this is due to technicalities, due to the inability of the HCC to adhere strictly to administrative procedural rules.

The appeal does not suspend the payment of the fine or the enforcement of other conditions or remedies imposed by the opposed decision. The court may, though, suspend enforcement, in full or in part, conditionally or unconditionally, in extreme cases, for example in an unfounded decision or due to a complete inability of the undertaking(s) to pay the fine. A provision strongly contested as unconstitutionally limiting is the authority of the court to suspend the fine up to 80%.

The decision of the Appellate Court is subject to appeal (cassation) before the Supreme Administrative Court (*Conseil d'Etat*) for legal reasons only (i.e. the wrong application of the law, assuming as correct the factual basis accepted or the dictum not supported by reasoned arguments). Exceptionally as well, the law allows the suspension of the contested decision of the Appellate Court by the *Conseil d'Etat*.

In case that the decision of the HCC is totally annulled, the case may be re-examined anew by the HCC, which will re-judge the case based on the conditions prevailing in the market at the time of re-examination. A new or supplementary notification will be required if the conditions of the market have changed or the data submitted needs to be updated (Article 8 § 13). This is a new provision introduced by the current law and as a result increases the discretionary authority of the HCC, as the decision of the court is based on different facts than the ones which will be the basis for the re-examination of the notification for a second time.

Recent HCC decisions on concentrations

Overview of M&A activity. Last year has been characterised by the further deepening of the financial crisis in Greece.

In this sense, the surrounding financial environment has heavily affected M&A activity and there have been only a few recent deals that have occurred, mainly referring to the banking sector. Therefore, one could note that last year's activity of the HCC has mainly focused on behavioural cases of Articles 101, 102 TFEU, as well as on its advisory powers (issuance of opinions mainly on liberal professions and removal of regulatory obstacles to competition).

Banking sector. In the banking sector, consolidation through M&A activity has been long-awaited and one may note that this year there have been significant movements, due to the deteriorating circumstances with the Greek economy and the Greek banks. Recently (in August 2011), Alpha Bank and EFG Eurobank announced a friendly merger and the deal was notified to the HCC, which cleared the deal upon remedies. However, the deal was later abandoned by the parties, due to changing circumstances in their financial conditions.

Following that, there have been new rounds of negotiations and combinations in the Greek banking system, which ended in the formation of three main groups: a) NBG has agreed its merger with Eurobank Ergasias SA, which appears still to be in the pre-notification stage; b) Alpha Bank has been declared the preferred bidder for the purchase of Emporiki Bank from Credit Agricole. This deal has been recently notified to the HCC and is also expected to be cleared in the next few months; and c) Piraeus Bank has acquired state-owned Agricultural Bank of Greece (its "healthy" part) and Geniki Bank (member of Societe General Group). The last two acquisitions by Piraeus Bank have been already cleared by the HCC without any remedies or concerns.

Aegean/Olympic-II. One of the recent highlights for M&A deals in Greece would certainly be the second attempt for the concentration between Aegean Airlines and Olympic Air. Following the 2011 prohibition by the European Commission, Aegean Airlines announced on October 2012 a new agreement with Marfin Investment Group SA for the purchase of 100% of the share capital of Olympic Air S.A. The significance of this deal is again based on the intended formation of one consolidated Greek air carrier, following the international tendency for consolidation in the aviation industry. The deal aims to create a stronger national carrier with potential international standing. The deal has a different structure, i.e. it leads to acquisition of sole control by Aegean Airlines over Olympic Air, while previously there would be joint control of three groups of shareholders over the merged entity. Therefore, there is no European dimension this time and, as far as the EU is concerned, the transaction was only to be notified in Greece and Cyprus. However, the European Commission requested for the upwards referral of the case and it is currently pending before the DG Comp. It is expected that the European Commission shall examine the changing circumstances at all levels.

Supermarket retail sector. Another deal referred to the exit of Carrefour from the Greek market. The HCC, by its Decision No. 544/VII/2012, cleared the concentration, consisting in the acquisition of sole control over the company "Carrefour-Marinopoulos General Trading Co. SA" by Marinopoulos Group. The HCC held that the concentration does not raise serious doubts as to its compatibility with competition rules governing the functioning of the Greek market, given that it only concerns a change in the structure and the quality of control over the company Carrefour-Marinopoulos (a change from joint to sole control), with no material change in the market structure and conditions of competition currently prevailing in Greece.

* * *

Endnotes

1. Reference to an Article in the text without any other identification is deemed to refer to the new law 3959/2011.
2. Under the Greek system, laws voted in the Parliament have a continuous numbering. The first number is the number of the law and the second is the year of publication in the Government Gazette.
3. Including mass media, for which special rules apply only as to the thresholds and the substantive test (L.3592/07).
4. The notion of the group is not used in the law. Instead there is a clear definition of when an undertaking has control over another undertaking: a) if an undertaking has directly or indirectly: i) a participation of more than 50% on the share capital; ii) the majority of the voting right; iii) the right to appoint or revoke the majority of the members of the board of directors (administration); or iv) the right to manage the cases of those undertakings; b) if an undertaking has the rights or powers mentioned hereinabove in cases i to iv (both ways, i.e. controlling and under control; and c) if there is more than one undertakings that jointly have the above rights.
5. Again the term "group of companies" is not used in the law. See herein above endnote number 4.
6. I.e. 28,29,30 or 31 days depending on the month.
7. Article 8 § 12, Article 3, 4 & 5, Article 38.
8. Article 8 § 8.
9. L.2256/1995 Article 2 § 5.
10. Article 8 § 8 , 7 § 1, 5 § 5 and 1 § 3.
11. See L.3461/2006.
12. Article 8 § 14.
13. Article 9 § 4.
14. The new provision resolved a controversial issue, in cases of violation of Articles 1 & 2 of the law (equivalent to 101, 102 TFEU). Up until this provision, the HCC denied to accept the concept of prescription, as well as to apply at least the direct-effect provision of Article 23 § 2a of Regulation 1/2003. On the contrary, theory as well as some court decisions argued that many generally accepted principles applicable in administrative law require the Administration to act timely i.e. within reasonable time and not at any time. In addition for violations of Articles 1 & 2 of the law, corresponding to Articles 101 & 102 of the TFEU, the rule of uniform application and interpretation of European and national law would advocate to this direction.
15. See e.g. COMP/M.4994-ELECTRABEL/COMPAGNIE NATIONALE DU RHONE, 10.06.2009, referring to the previous regime of Regulation 4064/89.

Emmanuel Dryllerakis
Tel: +30 21 1000 3456 / Email: ed@dryllerakis.gr
Partner and one of the Administrators of Dryllerakis & Associates. He is specialised in competition law, being involved in most of the major competition cases in Greece. Mr. Dryllerakis is also active in the fields of corporate law, contracts, telecoms, corporate financing and privatisation. He graduated from the Law School of Lille II University in 1995 and from the Athens University Law School. He is a member of the Athens Bar, the International Bar Association, the Hellenic Society of Tax Law & Fiscal Studies and the Competition Law Association. He is qualified to practice before courts of all degrees, including the Supreme Courts. Mr. Dryllerakis is an author and/ or contributor to several local and international publications on competition law and a speaker in competition conferences. He speaks Greek, English and French fluently.

Cleomenis Yannikas
Tel: +30 21 1000 3456 / Email: cy@dryllerakis.gr
Partner of Dryllerakis & Associates. Member of the firm's competition team, having handled numerous antitrust cases before the Hellenic Competition Commission. He is also active in corporate law, M&A and investment incentives, having considerable experience in major M&A and project finance deals with international profile. He graduated from the Athens University Law School in 2002. He is a member of the Athens Bar and qualified to practice before Courts of Appeal of all jurisdictions. Mr. Yannikas is an author and/or contributor in several local and international publications on competition law, corporate law and investment incentives. He speaks Greek, English and German fluently.

Dryllerakis & Associates

25 Voukourestiou str., 106 71 Athens, Greece
Tel: +30 21 1000 3456 / Fax: +30 21 1000 5200 / URL: http://www.dryllerakis.gr

Hungary

Anikó Keller & Bence Molnár
Szecskay Attorneys at Law

Overview of merger control activity during the last 12 months

Between September 2011 and November 2012, the Hungarian Competition Office (the "**HCO**") issued 30 decisions in merger cases. This means almost a 20% decrease in the number of concentrations above the thresholds, compared to the preceding period. The number of notifications is not publicly available.

Three concentrations were cleared in the second stage, 25 cases were cleared in the first stage. There have been two cases where the participants failed to notify the HCO about the transaction and the HCO investigated the concentration *ex officio*. In one of these cases *(Vj-27/2011 ELMIB/ DunaCent)*, the HCO established that it did not have to be notified of the concentration under the Competition Act; in the other case *(Vj-04/2011 Ispotály Management/HungaroCare)*, the HCO established that it should have been notified of the concentration and imposed a fine for the failure to do so.

Obligations have only been prescribed in one case *(Vj-066/2011 Magyar RTL/ IKO Televízió)*.

We are not aware of any concentrations notified to the HCO that were not cleared by the HCO. Nor are we aware of any referrals between the European Commission and the HCO.

New developments in jurisdictional assessment or procedure

We are not aware of any development in jurisdictional assessment.

In late 2011 and 2012, the HCO issued three instruments that are relevant for the procedure of the HCO in merger control cases. These are: (i) the new notification form; (ii) the information memorandum on pre-notification meetings; and (iii) the information memorandum on simplified decisions without any reasoning.

The new notification form is applicable to concentrations notified to the HCO not earlier than February 1, 2012. First of all, the new form requires different amounts of information in respect of the direct participants, in respect of the indirect participants with (supply, production, sale, *etc.*) links to Hungary and in respect of (groups of) indirect participants not related to Hungary at all. This is a more sophisticated (and reasonable) approach compared to the old form. Another great change is that the form requires the applicant to identify all the reasonably possible market definitions where (horizontal) overlaps or (vertical) relations may arise. If activities with significant overlaps or relations are identified (significance being measured on the market shares) then detailed information shall be provided on the relevant markets, and on the effects of the concentration on them. However, if the overlaps or relations are not significant at all, it is not necessary to provide extensive information on the markets (except on the market sizes and shares).

Pre-notification meetings with the HCO were normal and very practical before the issuance of the memorandum on this issue. However, the memorandum now clearly sets out the framework of these meetings and what should be expected. *e.g.:* no minutes are taken of the meetings; the applicant may send the draft notification form to the HCO before the meeting; market definitions may be discussed and clarified, *etc.* In comparison to the practice of the EU Commission, the aim of such pre-notification discussions is not to "complete" the notification and delay the filing, because the 30-day deadline applies regardless of the outcome of the pre-notification discussion, and failure to meet the deadline is subject to fines.

The HCO has been entitled to issue *simplified decisions* since February 1, 2012, based on the reference of the Competition Act to a specific section of Act CXL of 2004 on the General Rules of Administrative Proceedings and Services. According to this section, a decision without reasoning and information on legal remedies can (but does not have to) be issued if: (i) the authority satisfies the request of the applicant in its entirety; and (ii) there is no opposing party, or the rights and legal interests of opposing parties are not affected. (Under Hungarian law, competitors are not considered opposing parties in the proceeding on the approval of concentrations.) The mentioned information memorandum sets out the cases where it will not issue such a simplified decision, even if the above two conditions are met. Such cases are, for example: (i) if the cooperation of another authority is mandatory; (ii) if a full (rather than a simplified) proceeding is conducted, or the decision about whether the procedure is simplified is not made in accordance with the respective notice of the HCO; (iii) if an obligation or condition is prescribed; (iv) if there are ancillary restraints that are not necessary for the concentration and the HCO deems it necessary to highlight this; (v) if the notification was filed late; (vi) if fundamental questions of the case have to be clarified (*e.g.* whether it is a concentration, the identification of the participating groups of undertakings, jurisdiction of the HCO, calculation of turnover); and (vii) if the HCO wishes to publish the reasons of the decision due to increased public attention, acquisition of control by a state entity or a local government, or the fact that the decision contains conclusions important for the interpretation of the law. It is clear from the above that a simplified proceeding does not necessarily mean a simplified decision. The fact that the HCO may issue a simplified decision has two consequences: first, the fact that no reasoning is given may shorten the time within which a concentration is approved by a few working days. Second, the absence of published reasoning will cause the situation that market-definitions accepted by the HCO in such cases will not be available publicly, thus less guidance for future concentrations will be available from the previous practice of the HCO.

In addition, we would like to highlight a case where, due to the parties' failure to notify the HCO, the latter investigated the concentration *ex officio*: this is case *Vj-04/2011 Ispotály Management/ HungaroCare*. The reason for the failure to notify was the incorrect interpretation of the Competition Act by the parties in connection with the necessity of clearance regarding the acquisition of indirect and joint control over the target company in addition to the acquisition of direct and sole control. This very same interpretation error happened several times in the practice of HCO (see Vj-24/2006, Vj-100/2009). Therefore, we think it is worth mentioning it briefly.

In this particular case, Ispotály Management Kft. (Ispotály) acquired direct and sole control over HungaroCare Intézeti Gyógyszertár Kft. (HungaroCare). Ispotály was jointly controlled by Hungaropharma Gyógyszerkereskedelmi Zrt. (Hungaropharma) and Kókai Tanácsadó Kft. (Kókai).

The parties identified Ispotály's as the buyer's and HungaroCare's as the target's groups of undertakings, where, due to a lack of sole control, the parent companies were not to be included in the buyer's group of undertakings in accordance with Section 15 of the Competition Act. Based on this, the parties found that the relevant turnover thresholds, above which notification to the HCO is mandatory, were not met. This was, however, only true in respect of the acquisition of direct and sole control by Ispotály. Notably, simultaneously with the acquisition of direct and sole control over HungaroCare by Ispotály, Hungaropharma and Kókai acquired indirect and joint control over HungaroCare. Since, according to item b) of Section 23(1) of the Competition Act, a concentration of undertakings is effected where a sole undertaking or <u>more than one undertaking jointly acquires</u> direct or <u>indirect control</u> of the whole or parts of one or more than one other undertaking which have been independent of them, the turnover thresholds relating to the group of undertakings of Hungaropharma and Kókai should have also been assessed. The HCO did this in its procedure initiated *ex officio* and found that, in relation to the acquisition of indirect and joint control by Hungaropharma and Kókai, the relevant turnover thresholds were met and, therefore, although the parties failed to notify the HCO, the transaction was subject to the latter's clearance.

Key industry sectors reviewed and approach adopted to market definition, barriers to entry

Among the concentrations approved in full proceedings, *Magyar RTL Televízió Zrt. / IKO Televisions Kft. (Vj-066/2011)* is worth introducing. The acquiring party is Magyar RTL Televízió Zrt., a member of the RTL-group, and Hungary's largest commercial TV broadcasting company (a "media service provider" as defined under EU law), having a concession over one of the two national commercial (terrestrial) TV broadcasting rights. The acquired participant, IKO Televisions Kft., is the broadcaster of several smaller TV-channels, available via cable-reception.

Before January 1, 2011, the concessionaire of one of the national commercial broadcasting rights was not allowed to acquire a controlling interest in any other broadcasting entity. The concentration could come about due to the fact that this restriction was lifted, therefore it can be regarded as unique. Accordingly, the HCO examined the market's and the participants' status in detail.

The HCO identified two main markets related to the transaction: the sale and purchase of advertising time between advertisers and broadcasters (or their sales houses); and the sale of TV programmes by the broadcasters to the TV programme-distributors (*e.g.* cable companies making the broadcast available to the audience) for fees. The audience is the final element in both chains. The HCO also established that the markets of media services are so-called two-sided markets, due to the fact that the media product is sold both to the audience and the advertisers, and these two kinds of demands are highly dependent on each other.

In its decision, the HCO examined two markets: the distribution of TV broadcasts; and the TV advertisements market.

Regarding the relevant product markets within the distribution of TV broadcasts, the HCO established that most channels are substitutable with other channels within their genre, however certain channels are "must have" channels. Such "must have" channels are the two national commercial broadcasting channels, *i.e.* RTL Klub and TV2, and certain other channels may potentially also belong here. "Must have" channels are so important for the audience that they cannot be substituted, even if there is another within the same genre. Therefore, the HCO established that RTL Klub forms a separate product market for the purposes of TV-programme distribution services. The relevant geographic market is national in all cases.

Regarding the relevant product markets within the TV advertisements markets, the HCO established that the purpose and structure of advertising is different on the two national commercial channels (RTL Klub, TV2) from that on the smaller cable channels. Therefore, the two national commercial channels form a separate relevant product market. The relevant geographic markets are also national for the broadcasting services.

Due to the above, namely that the acquiring participant's channel forms a market that is separate from the acquired participant's channels, the HCO could not identify horizontal and vertical effects, only significant portfolio effects.

Regarding programme distribution, the HCO found that no harmful effects on competition are likely, due to the structure of the market, as there are relatively few barriers to entry to the cable-channel (broadcasting) market, and media regulation.

Regarding the advertising markets, the HCO established that the bundled sale of both the advertising time of RTL and the cable channels could cause the lessening of competition. Therefore, the HCO found it necessary to counterbalance such effects by obligations. The HCO did not find it necessary to prohibit bundled sales of advertising time, but it is prescribed in the decision that: (i) separate sale of the advertising time of RTL Klub and of the acquired channels shall be maintained; and (ii) the fees, discounts and conditions in respect of separate sales shall be reasonable and free of unjustified discrimination. The applicant also undertook to create, operate and make available to the HCO a documentation system that enables the HCO to monitor compliance. The obligations expire as of December 31, 2013.

Key economic appraisal techniques applied, assessment of vertical and conglomerate mergers

We are not aware of any sudden shift or change in the economic appraisal techniques applied. In our view, the HCO mainly follows the practice of the European Commission in merger control matters.

In September 2010, the HCO issued a non-binding memorandum on the relevant aspects in evaluating non-coordinative horizontal effects of a concentration. This memorandum does not have the authority of an HCO notice (the issuance of which is authorised by the Competition Act). The memorandum provides three levels of assessment, as described below.

First phase of the evaluation: Market shares

In most cases, the **market shares** provide information on whether a more detailed analysis is needed. However, the analysis of market shares may not be sufficient if the market changes swiftly or a transaction (*e.g.* a tender) is capable of significantly altering the market.

Second phase of the evaluation: Horizontal effects

If, based on the analysis of market shares, it cannot be stated clearly that there will be no significant (detrimental) effects to competition, the HCO examines the **horizontal effects** of the concentration. For this analysis, the HCO differentiates between three main types of the market: (i) markets of relatively homogenous products; (ii) markets of differentiated products with prices set without respect to customers; and (iii) markets with individualised prices. (Of course, the HCO does not seek to force any market into one of the categories.)

(i)   In case of *homogenous products,* the HCO mentions the following methods for the analysis of the effects: *(a)* examination of structural indexes, *i.e.* market share, based on either income, or volumes sold, or production capacities; *(b)* price-concentration analysis; and *(c)* examination of the effects of the presence of a competitor to another competitor's pricing.

(ii) In case of markets where *products are differentiated* but prices of a single participant are standardised (*e.g.* chocolate bars, newspapers, internet access packages), the HCO takes into account that the same relevant market is segmented by the fact that certain products are better substitutes to each other than other products. Therefore, there is a greater price (cross-) elasticity (and more intense competition) between products that are closer substitutes to each other, and nude market shares do not give a fair view of competition. Due to this, a concentration between participants with more substitutable products may have a more detrimental horizontal effect on competition than a concentration of more distant participants. The HCO notes that due to potential entries to the market and the hypothetical situations that shall be taken into account, customer queries and surveys are often the means of discovering market behaviour. The HCO takes into account the difficulty of comparing prices of relatively different products. This difficulty may often be solved by identifying the elements of the prices, or creating an artificial average price. Price-concentration analysis and the examination of the effects of the presence of a competitor on another competitor's pricing are also used on differentiated markets. The HCO also pays attention to the fact that the participants may compete in factors other than prices, such as marketing or innovation.

(iii) *Markets with individual prices* have two main (proto) types, according to the HCO: *(a)* markets where products are similar, but single customers may receive individual discounts; and *(b)* markets where rare auctions or biddings with great value generate demand for the product/service. The HCO points out that, in the first case, analysing methods used for homogenous markets and differentiated markets may be well adopted. In the second case however, different methods are necessary for markets with big unique transactions. Prices applied towards individual customers or (if necessary) in individual transactions shall be collected from customers. According to the HCO, market shares on this market are less representative and longer trends shall be analysed, due to the fact that the winner of bidding may "take it all" for a certain period. Therefore, it may be important to precisely explore the rules of the individual biddings and the relations between the participants. For example, the number of tenders where certain market participants *actually compete* may describe whether they are actual competitors or not. According to the HCO, close competitors often have *close positions* at the outcome of the biddings, thus outcome analysis may also give a description of the market. The HCO also takes into account whether prices offered by an undertaking change whether a competitor undertaking is also participating in the bidding/auction.

Third phase of the evaluation: Pro-competitive effects and defences

Finally, if anticompetitive effects of the concentration have been identified, the HCO deliberates the

potential pro-competitive effects. These are categorised in the memorandum as follows:

(i)   *New entrants.* New entrants can counterbalance anticompetitive effects if the entrance is: *(a)* likely to happen; *(b)* happens soon enough after the concentration; and *(c)* has an impact sufficient enough to counterbalance anticompetitive effects. When investigating the possibility of new entrances, events in the past (entrances and exits) and the possibilities to enter (minimal costs, return rate, minimum market share necessary to compete effectively, chance to reach such market share) must be taken into consideration. If such information is available, the HCO investigates whether there is any undertaking that is likely to enter the market.

(ii) *Buyer power.* The HCO takes the position that it is not enough if there is a certain buyer power on the market. Customers having buyer power must cover a sufficiently large part of the market. The HCO notes that on markets without a possibility to discriminate prices, there is a greater probability that buyer power will be effective. It is important that buyers have a strong bargaining position, and the loss of a buyer is a significant loss for the sellers. There is less chance that buyer power is effective if the costs of changing business partners (suppliers) are high.

(iii) *Increase in efficiency.* The HCO takes into account that a concentration may have effects decreasing costs or otherwise increasing efficiency. However, following the horizontal guidelines of the European Commission (2004/C 31/03 – OJ C 31, 2004.2.5.), four conditions must be met to accept such argumentation: *(a)* only such improvements may be taken into account that would not occur without the concentration; *(b)* improvements shall be represented in decreasing prices; *(c)* improvements must be verified by calculations, not just arguments; and *(d)* improvements that are more likely to happen in the close future are more convincing. Furthermore, increases in efficiency shall match the anticompetitive effects and effectively counterbalance them.

(iv) *Failing firm defence.* It may be argued that the intensity of competition would also decrease without the concentration, due to the fact that the acquired undertaking would also disappear from the market due to its poor financial situation. The HCO notes that this argumentation may only be accepted with certain restrictions, namely: (a) it cannot be expected that the failing firm would be replaced by a new entrant; and (b) it is likely that the assets and production of the failing firm would actually disappear from the market. It is the obligation of the concentrating parties to prove such conditions.

In the memorandum summarised above, the HCO describes its methods for analysing non-coordinative horizontal effects. However, the analysis of coordinative effects also forms part of the HCO's practice, as shown above in the summary of the *Holcim/Východoslovenské stavebné hmoty* case.

Approach to remedies (i) to avoid second stage investigation and (ii) following second stage investigation

Pursuant to Notice 3/2009 of the Head of the Hungarian Competition Office and the President of the Competition Council on simplified and full proceedings, if commitments or obligations are attached to the clearance, the concentration will be investigated in a full proceeding and will therefore consist of two stages. However, the HCO may exceptionally accept commitments in the simplified proceeding as well, provided that:

(i)   the competition problem can be easily identified;

(ii) the remedy for the competition problems can be simply assessed;

(iii) the notification filed by the applicant already contains the commitment for the competition problem foreseen and not disputed by the applicant; and

(iv) with the commitments, the concentration meets the requirements set out in the same Notice for simplified proceedings.

The Head of the HCO and the President of the Competition Council issued a Notice on prescribing conditions and obligations in merger clearances (Notice 1/2008). As explained in the Notice, a condition may be a *condition precedent* (the clearance is not effective until the condition is fulfilled) or a *condition subsequent* (the clearance is annulled if the condition is not fulfilled). *Obligations* do not affect the effectiveness of the clearance, but the HCO may revoke the clearance on non-compliance. The HCO points out that these are only the forms, so the same behaviour may be prescribed in any of the above three constructions, depending on the circumstances of the case.

The HCO has set the following principles for prescribing remedies:

- The condition or obligation shall be applied to solve only the competition problems that are caused by the concentration.
- The condition or obligation may only be prescribed if the applicant has offered the remedy as a commitment or accepted it before adopting the final resolution. If neither is the case, the HCO does not prescribe the condition/obligation not agreed to by the participant, but rather denies the concentration.
- The condition/obligation shall be clear, unambiguous, precise and enforceable, and compliance shall be verifiable.
- The HCO continuously negotiates with the applicant and (if necessary) foreign competition authorities.

Pursuant to Notice 1/2008, the HCO prefers *structural remedies over behavioural remedies.* As a third category of remedies, the HCO often prescribes *obligations to provide information,* most likely about the fulfilment of other conditions and compliance with other obligations. The Notice also explains the practice of the HCO in connection with divestitures.

We are not aware of any circumstances where the HCO's actual practice deviates from the above policy statements.

Reform proposals

We are not aware of any reform proposals.

Anikó Keller
Tel: +36 1 472 3000 / Email: aniko.keller@szecskay.com
Anikó Keller is a Hungarian attorney admitted to the Budapest Bar Association. She joined Szecskay Attorneys at Law in 2003.

She currently specialises in competition law, state aid, advertising law, consumer protection, data protection, employment law and commercial law.

She received her JD, *summa cum laude,* from Eötvös Loránd Faculty of State and Legal Sciences in 2000 and a postgraduate diploma in a King's College London postgraduate course on European Union Competition Law in 2012.

Anikó Keller is member of the German-Hungarian Jurist-Union and the Hungarian Self-Regulatory Advertising Board and author of a number of articles on competition law. Chambers Europe 2011 recognised her as an "Associate to watch". She is fluent in English and German.

Bence Molnár
Tel: +36 1 472 3000 / Email: bence.molnar@szecskay.com
Bence Molnár is a Hungarian attorney candidate admitted to the Budapest Bar Association. He joined Szecskay Attorneys at Law in 2008.

He currently specialises in competition law, banking regulatory law and corporate law.

He received his JD, *cum laude*, from Eötvös Loránd Faculty of State and Legal Sciences in 2009. During his university years he was a member of Mathias Corvinus Collegium (2004-2009), where he researched the law of fiduciary transactions and trusts. In 2007-2008 he studied at the University of Groningen in the Netherlands on an Erasmus scholarship, where he studied the law of international organisations, international contracts law and private international law.

He is fluent in English and German.

Szecskay Attorneys at Law

Kossuth tér 16-17, H-1055 Budapest, Hungary
Tel: + 36 1 472 3000 / Fax: +36 1 472 3001 / URL: http://www.szecskay.com

India

Farhad Sorabjee & Amitabh Kumar
J. Sagar Associates

Overview of merger control activity during the last 12 months

Upon notification of Sections 5 and 6 of the Competition Act, 2002 (**"Act"**) on 1 June, 2011, the approval of the Competition Commission of India (**"CCI"**) for all combinations (acquisitions, merger, amalgamation, de-merger) which meet the asset or turnover thresholds prescribed under the Act has become mandatory.

The implementing regulations, namely The Competition Commission of India (Procedures in regard to the transaction of business relating to Combinations) Regulations 2011 (**"Combination Regulations"**) and The Competition Commission of India (General) Regulations, 2009 (**"General Regulations"**) were notified on 1 June, 2011 and 21 May, 2009 respectively.

As the Act envisages a suspensory regime, concern was expressed by various stakeholders that approaching the CCI may delay the transaction. However, this apprehension has been successfully dispelled by the CCI, as is evident from the following:

(a) In the last 12 months, the CCI has received 81 Form I (short form) notices and has approved a total of 79 combinations, with the other two pending. A total of 96 combination applications have been approved between the date of notification of the merger provisions and 1 January, 2013.

(b) The CCI has approved all the subject combinations within a period of 30 days, excluding the time taken by the parties to the combination to respond to queries posed by CCI, or for offering modification.

It is evident that the CCI has made serious and successful efforts to ensure that its process of reviewing merger filings and approving combinations is rapid and non-obstructive.

(c) It is of note that the CCI also recently approved a combination subject to amendment of the Business Transfer Agreement by incorporation of the modifications proposed by the parties to the combination before the CCI.

(d) The CCI has been vested with the power to impose a penalty for failure to make a filing required under the Act, which can be as high as 1% of the total turnover or the assets of such a combination, whichever is higher. To date, the CCI has entertained nine belated notices but has refrained from levying any penalty as a concession to the relative newness of the merger control law. It is likely that this lenient approach will not continue and penalties will commence being imposed.

As per information available in the public domain, only two Form II (long form) filings have been made and are currently pending approval.

As of 31 December, 2012, four Form III filings, which are essentially *post facto* intimations to be furnished by public financial institutions, foreign institutional investors, banks or venture capital funds within seven days from the date of acquisition, have been filed with the CCI.

New developments in jurisdictional assessment or procedure

To clarify issues and overcome uncertainties regarding merger filing requirement, the CCI notified the Competition Commission of India (Procedures in regard to the transaction of business relating to

Combinations) Amendment Regulations 2012 (**"Combination Regulations 2012"**), which came into effect from 23 February, 2012. A few of the relevant amendments are:

(a) The earlier exemption granted to the holding of not more than 15% of the total shares or voting rights of a company through acquisition in the ordinary course of business or for investment purposes, not leading to control, has been enhanced to up to 25% of the total shares or voting rights. Acquisitions with future conversion provisions would also include the effects of such future conversions in computing the 25% holding.

It may be relevant to point out here that the CCI has observed in one instance that since the conversion option (to be exercised any time within ten years) contained in the Zero Coupon Optionally Convertible Debentures (ZOCDs) entitles the holder to receive equity shares of the target companies, the ZOCDs are shares within the meaning of Section 2(v)(i) of the Act, and the subscription to ZOCDs amounts to acquisition of shares of the target companies.

(b) A filing exemption for certain intra-group acquisitions already existed. The Combination Regulations, 2012 now provide that mergers or amalgamations relating to subsidiaries wholly owned by a group also qualify for exemption.

(c) It is important to note that the Combination Regulations, 2012 express a preference for a filing of Form II where the parties have combined market shares exceeding 15% in a horizontal combination, and individual or combined market shares of 25% in a vertical combination.

(d) If, on a review of a filed Form I, the CCI finds this inappropriate and directs the parties to file Form II instead, such filing of Form II shall be treated as a fresh filing and the timelines applicable to the review of this Form II shall commence from the date of filing the form.

In terms of the Combination Regulations, there are certain categories of combinations listed in Schedule I to Regulation 4 of the Combination Regulations, 2012, which are stated to ordinarily not be likely to cause an appreciable adverse effect on competition in India and, therefore, notice need not normally be filed in terms of the provisions of the Act. It is incumbent upon the parties to a combination which they expect to fall in those categories to undertake a careful base analysis and determine whether the proposed combination will cause an appreciable adverse effect on competition in India. There are no objective tests or guidelines provided by the CCI to undertake the said analysis, and no adequate body of precedent which crystallises the position.

Entry 10 to Schedule I concerns foreign transactions. This Entry provides that in respect of "a combination referred to in Section 5 of the Act", notice need not normally be filed because they are ordinarily not likely to cause an appreciable adverse effect on competition in India provided the following conditions are met:

(a) the combination is taking place entirely outside India;
(b) the combination has insignificant local nexus; and
(c) the combination has insignificant effect on markets in India.

Therefore, the basic condition precedent for availing the benefit of Entry 10 to Schedule I is that the said transaction should amount to a "combination in terms of Section 5 of the Act". In order to meet the asset or thresholds prescribed under the Act, the parties to the combination would have to have a local nexus. Once this is established, the questions that remain to be ascertained are:

(a) whether the local nexus is insignificant; and
(b) whether the combination has insignificant effect on markets in India.

There is neither any guidance nor any precedent on what the term "insignificant local nexus and effect" means. Hence, the parties to the combination would have to make their assessment of whether it is sustainable to contend that the proposed combination is likely to have an "insignificant local nexus and effect". Parameters such as the percentage of the combined asset base or total turnover of the parties to the combination *vis-à-vis* the other competitors may be taken into consideration. It is of interest that in the case of the acquisition of the global nutrition business of Pfizer Inc. by Nestlé S.A., the CCI observed that notwithstanding the absence of any horizontal overlap between the products/ services of the enterprises involved in the combination, the possibility existed that an acquisition could cause an adverse effect on competition by removing a potential competitor from the market. In the said case, the CCI required Nestlé to furnish information so it could assess any adverse effect on competition due to the loss of potential competition.

The Central Government has by a notification dated 4 March, 2011 exempted the acquisition of small targets [with assets of less than INR 250 crore in India (US$50 million approx.) or turnover of less than INR 750 crore in India (US$150 million approx.)] from the provisions of section 5 of the Act and accordingly no filing needs to be made with the CCI for such acquisitions.

However, the benefit of the abovementioned *de-minimis* threshold has been diluted by the Combination Regulations, 2012, which provide that in instances of an indirect sale of a business unit/assets of an entity by way of its/their transfer into another entity and subsequent onward sale of such transferee to the acquirer, the assets and turnover of the original owner of the business unit/assets shall also be included for assessing whether the transaction is entitled to the benefit of the exemption notification. This has so far led to a few filings where the target itself is small, but the original owners had large assets or turnover.

The Act does not define the term de-merger. In the absence of a definition, there is uncertainty regarding:

(a) whether there is a requirement for filing in relation to a de-merger; and

(b) if a filing is so required, whether a de-merger would fall under section 5(a) *(acquisitions)* or 5(c) *(mergers and amalgamations)* of the Act.

In some decided cases, the CCI has approved mergers and de-mergers which form part of the same integrated transaction, though there was no filing involving only the de-merger portion of the transaction. In a recent case, the CCI recorded that the transaction involved two de-mergers, acknowledged the filing was made only in respect of the merger/ amalgamation and not for the de-mergers involved in the series of steps involved in the integrated transaction. In another case, the CCI has noted de-mergers as well as the amalgamation in the series of steps involved in the integrated transaction notified. While approving the transactions, the CCI held that the combination falls under Section 5(c) of the Act *(mergers and amalgamations)*. In a further ruling, the merger as well the de-mergers were noted by CCI, and the CCI again held that the proposed combination fell under Section 5 (c) of the Act. Recently, in the order dated 18 September 2012, CCI has approved the restructuring of a group involving two demergers and a slump sale, stating that the proposed combination falls within the ambit of Section 5 (c) of the Competition Act, 2002. This treatment of demergers is indicative that demergers are likely to be treated in the same manner as mergers.

The position regarding the treatment of joint ventures, and any distinction between greenfield and brownfield joint ventures, remains unclear. Section 5 of the Act also does not provide any indication as to how the thresholds prescribed in the Act are to be applied to joint ventures. The CCI has entertained a filing for acquisition where the notice related to a jointly controlled company. This clearly suggests that joint ventures are included in the merger control provisions of the Act, but does not provide any guidance on how the jurisdictional thresholds are to be applied.

There is also a lack of clarity as to which enterprise of a joint venture will be treated as the target in order to conclude whether the benefit of the target exemption notification can be availed of. It may be noted that in a recent order of the CCI, as the assets were transferred by one of the parties to the proposed joint venture prior to the acquisition of equity share capital of the joint venture by the acquirers, the value of assets and turnover of the transferor was attributed to the value of assets and turnover of the joint venture.

Further, the filing requirement for both greenfield and brownfield joint ventures would have to be determined on a case-by-case basis in view of the Regulation 5(9) of the Combination Regulations, 2012, mentioned above.

Key industry sectors reviewed and approach adopted to market definition

As of 31 December, 2012, the CCI has not exercised its *suo motu* power to inquire into a combination and has approved all the combinations in respect of which notices have been filed by the parties to the combination. Therefore, it is premature to say that the CCI is focusing on any particular industry sectors. It may be mentioned that there is an amendment to the Act pending before Parliament which, if passed, would allow differing thresholds to be set for different sectors. A few of the industry sectors reviewed by the CCI under the notification regime are as follows:

(a) insurance;
(b) broadcasting, media and entertainment;
(c) nutrition;
(d) automotives and automobiles;
(e) power;
(f) asset management and portfolio management services;
(g) infrastructure;
(h) banking and financial services;
(i) information technology and information technology enabled services;
(j) hospitality;
(k) telecommunications and wireless services;
(l) pharmaceuticals;
(m) construction and project development;
(n) mutual funds;
(o) shipping;
(p) travel and aviation; and
(q) print media.

Section 20(4) of the Act, enlists various economic factors to be considered by the CCI to determine whether the combination would have appreciable adverse effect on a combination in the relevant market, such as:

(a) actual and potential competition from imports;
(b) extent of barriers to entry;
(c) level of combination in the market;
(d) extent to which substitutes are available or are likely to be available in the market;
(e) market share in the relevant market of the persons or enterprise in a combination, individually and as a combination;
(f) likelihood that the combination would result in the removal of a vigorous and effective competitor or competitors in the market; or
(g) nature and extent of vertical integration in the market.

There are also certain non-economic factors provided for in Section 20(4) of the Act such as:

(a) nature and extent of innovation;
(b) relative advantage, by way of the contribution to economic development, by any combination having or likely to have appreciable adverse effect on competition; and
(c) whether the benefits of the combination outweigh the adverse impact of the combination.

From a review of the orders of the CCI, it has taken into consideration factors such as the business of the parties to the combination, market shares of the parties, entry barriers, level of combination and the removal of potential competitors.

Key economic appraisal techniques applied

The orders of the CCI on combinations do not detail the economic appraisal techniques applied by it in its analysis. The assessment of the combinations is undertaken by the CCI considering the factors enlisted in Section 20(4) of the Act, such as those enumerated above. It is likely that economic analysis will be discussed in orders passed as and when a filing goes to Phase 2.

Approach to remedies (i) to avoid second-stage investigation and (ii) following second stage investigation

To date, the CCI has not initiated any second-stage investigation. The CCI has also so far shown little inclination to aggressively probe information provided.

However, to minimise the chances of a second-stage investigation and a consequent delay in approval, it is advisable that the parties to the combination carefully examine and analyse the extent of information which should be furnished to the CCI in the initial filing itself. Detailed information, including reports of independent third parties analysing the feasibility of the proposed combination, documents evidencing the rationale for entering the proposed combination, the structure of the market, etc. should be considered for filing and furnishing to the CCI at the outset.

In case of doubt, a pre-merger consultation may also be sought with the CCI. However, the opinion rendered by the CCI at such consultation is non-binding on the CCI.

Key policy developments

The review and approval of combinations by the CCI is so far almost entirely filing-driven. Although the CCI has been vested with the power to *suo motu* inquire into a combination within a year from the date on which the combination took effect, the CCI has so far refrained from exercising this *suo motu* power.

Reform proposals

The Competition (Amendment) Bill, 2012 was introduced in the Lok Sabha on 7 December, 2012, but has not yet been passed. It proposes several important amendments, including:
(a) turnover shall include value of goods and services excluding the taxes, if any, levied on the sale of such goods or provision of services;
(b) the Central Government in consultation with the CCI has the power to specify different value of assets and turnover for any class of enterprise; and
(c) the outer limit of the mandatory suspensory regime for combinations has been reduced from 210 to 180 days, thus curtailing the time for a Phase 2 investigation.

Additionally, the Competition Policy of India which, as per the information available in the public domain, awaits approval from the Government, has the following basic elements:
(a) set of policy initiatives designed to increase competition in the domestic market;
(b) designed to prevent unwanted Government intervention and anti-competitive business practices;
(c) ensure competitive neutrality;
(d) belief in the market, unless natural monopolies necessitate *ex ante* regulation, in which case the sector regulation should have a sunset clause; and
(e) facilitates communication between the competition agency and sector regulators.

Farhad Sorabjee
Tel: +91 22 4341 8502 / Email: farhad@jsalaw.com
Farhad Sorabjee, Partner, is an experienced trade lawyer and litigator and heads the firm's competition law team in Mumbai. Farhad acted in the very first cartel activity investigation filed before the Competition Commission of India, the first substantive abuse of dominant position complaint, and acts in several investigations before the Commission. He has appeared and argued before diverse authorities including the Competition Commission, Tribunals, High Courts and the Supreme Court of India. He advises and acts variously on merger control issues and filing. Farhad has written variously in both Indian and international publications on several aspects of competition law, and is part of the India task force of the American Bar Association Anti-trust Section involved in the representations made by the ABA to the Competition Commission from time-to-time.
Farhad's full c.v. can be found at http://www.jsalaw.com/our-people/People-Details. aspx?PeopleId=MzQx-rD8aJRQH4DI%3d

Amitabh Kumar
Tel: +91 11 4937 0648 / Email: amitabh.kumar@jsalaw.com
Amitabh Kumar, Partner and a retired Indian Revenue Service Officer, has handled diverse assignments in the sphere of Regulation, Public Finance and Policy in an illustrious carrier of 31 years. He also has consulting experience with multi-lateral organisations. As the first Director-General of the Competition Commission of India (2004-2009), he was involved in the Policy and Regulatory Framework. He assisted the Government in drafting the Competition (Amendment) Bill, 2007 and nine implementing regulations, besides contributing to the authority's Competition Advocacy initiative. Recently, he was member of a committee appointed by the government to recommend a National Competition Policy document and amendments to the Competition Act, 2002. At JSA, he has handled complex cases of abuse & cartels besides merger filings and organising competition compliance programmes. Over the past two-and-a-half years, he has handled the matters of a large private container train operator in litigation before the competition authority.
Amitabh's full c.v. can be found at http://www.jsalaw.com/our-people/People-Details. aspx?PeopleId=NDgw-5XbTi644Wb0%3d

J. Sagar Associates

Vakils House, 18 Sprott Road, Ballard Estate, Mumbai – 400 001, India
Tel: +91 22 4341 8600 / Fax: +91 22 4341 8617 / URL: http://www.jsalaw.com

Ireland

Helen Kelly & Kate Leahy
Matheson

Overview of merger control activity during the last 12 months

If merger activity is an indicator of economic performance, any economic recovery being experienced in Ireland is slow and fragile. In 2012, the number of merger filings to the Competition Authority ("Authority") fell for a second year in a row to a total of 33 filings. By comparison, there were 40 filings in 2011, 46 in 2010, 27 in 2009, 38 in 2008, 72 in 2007 and 98 in the 'Celtic tiger' peak of 2006. However, the overall downward trend masks a significant increase in activity towards the end of 2012. While only one filing was submitted to the Authority during January and February 2012, when the Eurozone debt crisis intensified with the downgrade of nine Eurozone sovereign ratings, there was a step-change in the last quarter of 2012 when 14 out of 33 mergers (42%) were notified.

No Phase II investigations were initiated by the Authority during 2012 (or 2011). Even in this context, it is unusual that the merger of greatest note during 2012 was not mandatorily notifiable to the Authority. *Eason/Argosy* is the first case where Authority intervention led to the withdrawal of a non-notifiable merger that was advanced so far as a signed purchase agreement. A press release by the Authority states that the merger would have reduced the number of wholesalers of new books in Ireland from two to one. It further states that the parties alerted the Authority of their proposed merger post-signing and the parties subsequently withdrew the merger for competition reasons. At the time of the parties' decision to withdraw in October 2012, the Authority had not published any record of an investigation under its general jurisdiction to review all agreements for competition law compliance, which applies in relation to non-notifiable mergers. However, the Authority's report indicates that a decision to commence proceedings against the parties had been made prior to the parties' decision to withdraw. This case demonstrates the need for parties to conduct an early and detailed analysis of non-notifiable transactions that present potential competition issues, and to evaluate the appropriate strategy for interaction with the Authority.

During 2012, no merger approvals were issued by the Minister for Finance under section 7 of the Credit Institutions (Financial Support) Act 2008 ("Credit Institutions Act"). The Act was introduced at the height of the 2008 financial crisis and provides the Minister for Finance with powers to review mergers involving credit institutions where he/she is of the opinion that the proposed merger is necessary to maintain the stability of the financial system in the State, and there would be a serious threat to the stability of that system if that merger or acquisition did not proceed. 2011 saw the first merger control approval by the Minister pursuant to this Act.

Only one determination published by the Authority during 2012 (*Millington/Siteserv M/12/002*) makes reference to a target company being in financial difficulty, and "failing firm" arguments were not addressed in this case or in any other. In previous years, cases involving firms in difficulty have not led to any new failing firm analysis, but rather have involved the Authority expediting its normal review process from one month to shorter periods including, on one occasion, to ten working days to deal with the timing realities where firms are in liquidation or receivership.

The Authority has the power to extend the one-month statutory timescale for a Phase I investigation by issuing a Requirement for Further Information that 'stops the clock'. During 2012, this tool was employed by the Authority on two occasions. The longest period between notification and clearance during 2012, resulting from issue of a Requirement for Further Information, was 79 days (*United Care/Pharmexx M/12/017*). To put this timescale in context, the average duration of a Phase II investigation by the Authority in the period 2003-2011 was 113 days.

New developments in jurisdictional assessment or procedure

Ireland's merger control regime, as set out in Part 3 of the Act, is mandatory and imposes a prohibition on the merging parties putting a merger into effect prior to Authority clearance.

The Consumer and Competition Bill is expected to be published in the first quarter of 2013. It is expected to introduce significant changes to the procedure and tests applicable to media mergers (see 'Reform proposals' below). The Authority has sought changes to some procedural issues also (see 'Reform proposals' below).

One area of on-going interest is the issue of implementation of a transaction prior to clearance. The Authority has always been implacably opposed to implementation prior to clearance. However, the way in which the merger regime operates so as not to permit notification prior to conclusion of a binding agreement/announcement of a public bid, and the absence of a discretion to exempt implementation prior to clearance, causes real difficulties for merging parties. The Authority has suggested that the Act be amended to allow early notification of transactions, reducing the number of occasions where this issue arises.

Issues around implementation prior to clearance came under renewed focus in December 2010 when the Authority criticised the implementation of a notified merger, *Stena/DFDS* (M/10/043). In this case, the merger, which was notified to both the UK's Office of Fair Trading and the Authority, signed and completed on the same day so that the authorities were considering an implemented merger. While this did not raise concerns under the UK's voluntary merger control system, where "hold separate" undertakings are relatively commonplace, it did raise Authority concerns.

The Authority issued a stern press release as follows:

> *"Stena Acquisition of Certain Assets of DFDS A/S Void*
>
> *By implementing the acquisition of certain assets of DFDS A/S before receiving clearance from the Competition Authority, Stena AB (Stena) and DFDS A/S, have infringed section 19(1) of the Competition Act 2002. Consequently, as provided for by section 19(2) of the Act, this acquisition is void.*
>
> *[...]*
>
> *Dr Stanley Wong, Member of the Competition Authority and Director of the Mergers Division, said: "It is not acceptable for parties to implement a notifiable merger or acquisition prior to obtaining approval from the Competition Authority. Any such merger or acquisition is void."*
>
> *The Competition Authority will proceed to assess the notified transaction in accordance with the provisions of the Competition Act 2002."*

The merger was subsequently treated by the Authority as a proposal to put an acquisition into effect and cleared by the Authority following a Phase II Investigation.

However, it is clear that this case is not unique. The main practical difficulty that arises in multijurisdictional transactions involving Ireland is that the merging parties may wish to sign and complete a transaction simultaneously, or may have received all other clearances and may not wish to delay completion solely in order to gain Authority clearance. Merging parties who are considering implementation prior to clearance must consider their strategy carefully.

Unfortunately, there are no clear cut mechanisms to avoid a breach of the implementation prohibition where merging parties wish to implement a transaction prior to clearance. One mechanism often considered is to try and "carve out" the Irish aspects of the proposed transaction so that, although it would be put into effect elsewhere, it would not be put into effect in Ireland until clearance was obtained. However, the Authority does not tend to recognise a "carve-out" of the Irish aspects of the transaction as remedying a breach of the Act. In *Aviva/CGU International Insurance plc/Gresham Insurance* (M/05/013), while the Authority did not find that a "carve-out" employed by the parties was such as to prevent the entire transaction being void, it did note that the effect of the "carve-out" was to prevent the transaction having any effect in Ireland until Authority clearance was issued. However, the Authority accepted that a "warehousing" structure prevented a breach of the Act in *Heineken/ Scottish and Newcastle* (M/08/11). The structure involved the transfer to an investment bank, pending the Authority's clearance, of voting rights in a NewCo that would purchase a business as a first step in the transaction, whose aim was to divide a business between the two shareholders in NewCo.

Another mechanism sometimes considered is to provide the Authority with "hold separate" undertakings. There have been a number of cases where the merging parties have informed the Authority that they will "hold separate" until clearance is issued by the Authority, including *Stena/ DFDS*. However, in all of the reviewed cases the Authority has still taken the view that a breach of the Act has occurred. The Authority has not, to date, taken any action against the parties in such circumstances.

In *Noonan Services/Federal Security* (M/09/014) the purchaser acquired the competing security services business of the target in both Ireland and Northern Ireland. The transaction was completed prior to clearance, subject to a hold separate agreement.

In both the public version of the determination and the press release which was issued on completion of the Authority's review, the Authority made reference to the fact that the parties had completed prior to clearance and had therefore breached the Act so as to result in the transaction being void. It was apparent from both documents that the Authority was dissatisfied with the parties' actions, as evidenced by the reference in both documents to its recommendation that the merger control regime be amended to provide for a substantial fine for breach of section 19 of the Act.

The current situation gives the Authority a number of options where there is implementation prior to clearance. In particular, if the Authority were to become aware that merging parties were considering completion, it could seek a court injunction in the Irish High Court.

An Irish court may be minded to grant such an injunction where the Authority is able to demonstrate that its preliminary examination of the merger gives rise to grave SLC concerns, or where the Authority suggests that it may find it necessary to prohibit the merger on SLC grounds or approve it subject to conditions. It is also possible that the Authority could initiate the action solely on the grounds that the parties would breach their statutory obligations.

If the Authority were to be successful in obtaining an injunction in the Irish courts preventing completion taking place, a court order would then be served on the merging parties, or such of their subsidiaries that carry on business in Ireland, requiring them to refrain from completing the proposed transaction prior to receipt of Authority clearance. Non-compliance with the terms of the court order could result in a finding of contempt of court against the parties.

A finding of contempt of court could result in personal liability for the directors of the Irish entities (the court in such instance could require the directors of the companies in question to remedy any breach or bring the relevant companies into compliance with the court order).

Another issue that has to be taken into account is the risk to the merging parties where the merger is ultimately blocked. Section 26(4) of the Act provides that where the parties to a merger contravene a determination of the Authority prohibiting a merger, the parties will be guilty of an offence, punishable by fines of up to €10,000, or to imprisonment for a term not exceeding two years. Section 26(4) also provides for additional daily default fines for each day of continued contravention.

While there is a lack of clarity on the correct statutory interpretation of section 26(4), because it relates to the commission of a criminal offence, it must be read restrictively, so that the Authority's determination must first be in place before any contravention can occur. There has been no judicial interpretation of section 26(4) or precedent as regards this matter. The Act provides only that the determination shall state that the merger may not be put into effect.

As part of a general consultation on reform of the Act initiated in late 2007 (see further below), the Department of Enterprise, Trade and Employment, now the Department of Jobs, Enterprise and Innovation ("Department"), which is responsible for competition legislation, has been asked to consider proposals to alleviate the problems surrounding this issue. Proposals include: (i) allowing notification of transactions prior to the conclusion of a binding agreement, as is the case under the EU Merger Regulation, where there is a good faith intention to merge; and (ii) granting an exemption from the obligation not to complete a merger where there are good reasons for allowing implementation.

In its submissions to the Department on amendments to the Act, the Authority sought an ability to allow early notification of transactions, and the insertion of a civil penalty in the form of a "substantial fine", for implementation of a merger prior to clearance. It is to be hoped that a more flexible approach to this problem might be considered by the relevant Minister, so as to include, for example, a discretion to allow implementation in certain circumstances, and/or to avoid the imposition of penalties in appropriate cases.

In terms of new developments in jurisdictional assessment during 2012, the only case of note is (*Manwin/RK Netmedia M/12/014*) where the published determination notes that the Authority rejected the parties' submission that the merger was non-notifiable on the basis that one of the undertakings involved did not carry on a 'media business' within the terms of the jurisdictional test for media mergers under the Act (see 'Reform proposals' below). Specifically, the Authority held that the target company which compiled adult entertainment content mainly for internet transmission was 'providing a broadcasting service' for the purposes of section 11(a) of the Act.

Key industry sectors reviewed and approach adopted to market definition, barriers to entry, nature of international competition etc.

Industry sectors most likely to be subject to merger control review by the Authority are mergers involving financial services. This reflects the facts that the Irish merger control system is mandatory, and the only relevant factor is the turnover of the undertakings involved and not substantive overlap, such that the high proportion of such mergers is more a factor of the number of financial institutions carrying on business in Ireland and their high turnover, rather than the approach of the Authority to market definition or to any other substantive concern. Within this industry sector, private equity buyers featured strongly in 2012 with nine out of the 33 mergers notified (30%) involving such entities.

It is expected that media mergers will continue to feature prominently, due to the disapplication of turnover thresholds for all media mergers, although only two media mergers were notified in 2012, and both were cleared following a Phase I review by the Authority (without conditions), i.e. with no competition issues or plurality concerns following review by the Minister for Jobs, Enterprise and Innovation. There remains some level of frustration that so many media mergers continue to be caught by the Act, imposing an unnecessary regulatory burden on such businesses. However, there is no indication of a desire to modify the scope of the current media merger system so as to enable such mergers to escape merger control review (see 'Reform proposals' below).

Other industry sectors which featured prominently in 2010, 2011 and 2012 include the pharmaceutical sector and the food and drink sector. The latter sector was the subject of six merger control determinations during 2012 and has also produced the only merger control determination which has been the subject of an appeal to date – in August 2008, the Authority prohibited the proposed acquisition by Kerry Group plc of the consumer foods division of the former Dairygold Co-operative (*Breeo Foods Limited and Breeo Brands Limited M/08/009*). The Authority's prohibition decision was overturned on appeal by Kerry Group to the High Court, based in part on the Court's critique of the Authority's approach to market definition which had focused on very narrow segments within certain food sectors such as natural and processed cheese. During 2010, the Authority made an application for a priority hearing of its appeal, in turn, to the Supreme Court. However, this application was not granted. There was a 'case management' hearing on 13 July 2012, where counsel for Kerry Group submitted that the appeal was 'moot' because the merger had already been implemented by the parties on foot of the High Court appeal decision, an argument which was refuted strongly by counsel for the Competition Authority on the basis that the decision was a matter of significant public interest. As of the time of writing, the Supreme Court case is still awaiting a hearing date.

Based on the information available at the time of writing, approximately 23 of the 33 filings submitted to the Authority involved a target business that had a substantial base in Ireland. Once again, this reflects the mandatory turnover thresholds that apply in Ireland.

In terms of the approach to market definition, during 2012 the Authority continued its established practice of exercising restraint and not reaching firm conclusions on market definition where possible. This practice was confirmed by the following extract from a Powerpoint presentation by Ibrahim Bah, then Head of the Mergers Division of the Authority at the IBA Conference in October 2012: "*Plausible to find 'no SLC' without defining markets... Finding 'SLC' probably requires identifying markets where harm is likely*". In any event, the Authority did go through the process of identifying potential market definitions in each and every 2012 decision. The Authority took a firm position on market definition in one of the eight cases notified during 2012 that involved horizontal overlaps.

During 2012, we have perceived certain changes in the Authority's approach to case analysis, which may reflect the new leadership from Professor Stephen Calkins, who has been Director of the Mergers Division of the Authority since December 2011. It appears that there has been closer analysis of cases involving no overlaps or minimal overlaps. This is reflected in greater use of informal information requests. For example, the determination in *Pallas/Crossgar M/12/010* states that "the Authority requested and received, on an on-going basis, further information and clarifications", and the horizontal overlap in this case was described in the notification as '*de minimis*' and occurred in a market that the Authority described as 'fragmented'. Similarly, consideration was given to arguments relating to 'loss of a potential competitor' in cases involving no overlap (see *Southbank Media/Travel Channel M/12/004*). Yet another indicator of this trend is the fact that a Requirement for Further Information was issued in a case involving no overlap and, in that case, the impact was an extension of the review period from one month to over two months.

Key economic appraisal techniques applied, and the assessment of vertical and conglomerate mergers

The Authority's *Guidelines for Merger Analysis* have been in place since December 2002. The Authority initiated a public consultation in December 2010 with a view to reviewing and updating these Guidelines. No revised Guidelines have yet been issued but these are expected later this year following publication of the Bill and coming into operation of that legislation.

The Authority is very influenced by the work of the International Competition Network (the "ICN") of which it is an active member, and also of the EU, UK and USA competition authorities. The Authority appears minded to follow the new US DOJ and FTC approach, as set out in their 2010 Horizontal Guidelines, to reduce the importance currently afforded to the SSNIP test and market definition, describing it as "not always necessary and a pre-requisite to the conduct of a competitive effect analysis". The Authority has consistently reviewed mergers by emphasising unilateral and coordinated effects as the main theories of harm, and this position is not likely to change in any new guidelines. However, we might expect a more complete discussion of efficiencies, including consideration of the extent and probability of cost efficiencies, and evidence of such efficiencies and the likely distribution of efficiency gains among consumers, staff and shareholders.

In terms of specific appraisal techniques used during 2012, the Authority typically used the Herfindahl-Hirschman index (HHI) as a step in cases involving overlaps. The issue of written questionnaires to the top five customers of the merging parties is another technique, which was used in *Airtricity/ Phoenix M/12/006* and *United Care/Pharmexx M/12/017*. In the former case, the questionnaire was issued only to customers in the area of overlap where the parties' combined share was greatest, at *c.*11%, and the feedback was used to support the Authority's conclusion that the merger raised no significant competition issues. In *United Care/Pharmexx*, the Authority placed even more significant weight on the detailed views expressed by customers in response to their questionnaire in deciding to clear a four-to-three merger in a "*highly concentrated*" market, on the basis that the remaining two competitors of the merged entity "*will be credible competitive constraints*".

Approach to remedies (i) to avoid second stage investigation and (ii) following second stage investigation

The Authority is willing to consider remedies in each of Phase I and Phase II. Where remedies are voluntarily suggested by the merging parties in Phase I, this increases the period for the Authority review from a one-month period to 45 days. While the Authority states that it prefers for remedies to be set out as early as possible in the process, there is some frustration among practitioners that the Authority's internal processes are not well suited to an early engagement on such matters. This can lead to mergers moving to Phase II even where there is an appropriate remedy offered early in Phase I (as the Authority does not allow itself sufficient time to consider the issues).

The Authority's preference when considering mergers is where possible to identify an available structural remedy and then to consider behavioural remedies. In practice, structural remedies are rare. Where behavioural remedies are adopted, the Authority prefers those which require the least possible oversight role by the Authority itself in demonstrating compliance. In the last Phase II merger involving remedies, *Metro/Herald* (M/09/013), the Authority imposed a requirement that an annual report be submitted by the independent Chairperson reporting on compliance. This mechanism has worked satisfactorily to date.

The Authority has not to date published any guidelines in relation to remedies. However, its approach to the small number of cases in which structural remedies have been imposed to date (for example, *Premier Foods/RHM* (M/06/098) and *Communicorp/Emap* (M/07/040)) has increasingly relied on both EU and UK guidance, and has required the appointment of an independent trustee with a mandate to oversee and, if necessary, enforce the divestiture process.

As part of its commentary on the proposed reform of the Act by the Department, the Authority has proposed that the time period for Phase II be extended from three months to four in all cases (see 'Reform proposals' below) and by a further period of 15 days in event that remedies are considered during Phase II.

Key policy developments

There are no new policy developments in Irish merger control as such. The Competition (Amendment) Act 2012 introduced certain changes to strengthen competition law enforcement powers and sanctions, but did not impact on merger control rules or policy.

The new disciplines imposed on the State as a result of the EU/IMF Memorandum of Understanding in November 2010 and change of Government in March 2011 seem to have introduced a possible new commitment to, and focus on, the role of competition and the need for a new, strong, merger control regime. One significant step taken during 2012 was the recruitment of one new case officer by the Authority, with up to seven new case officers potentially being recruited in 2013, which could lead to a re-energised Authority. However, there has recently been a significant management change at the Mergers Division with the departure of experienced division manager, Ibrahim Bah, towards the end of 2012.

The Government is due to amend the Act to facilitate the merging of the Authority and the National Consumer Agency. The Consumer and Competition Bill was due for publication in the last quarter of 2012, but was delayed and is now due to be released during the first quarter of 2013. However, this change is unlikely to cause any change to merger control policy as it is not envisaged that there be any change to the SLC test, which is a consumer welfare test.

Reform proposals

There are a number of proposals for reform which could impact on Irish merger control rules.

Media mergers

Changes to the Act during the first quarter of 2013 are expected to include changes to the media merger control regime to take account of recommendations contained in the 2008 Report of the Advisory Group on Media Mergers ("Report").

However, while the Report recommends that the Act be amended to provide for a separate system of notification of media mergers to the Minister for Jobs, Enterprise and Innovation for clearance, we understand that it is likely that the Minister for Communication will take the role of the Minister for Jobs, Enterprise and Innovation. While the Authority would continue to review the competition aspects of media mergers under the SLC test, media mergers would require an additional notification to the Minister for Communications (on a specific notification form and attracting a separate fee) who would apply a statutory test (discussed below) to ensure that the merger is not contrary to the public interest.

The Report proposes that media mergers which fall within the jurisdiction of the EU Merger Regulation should also be notified to the Minister of Communications for approval. This would appear to provide for a specific mechanism (not currently provided for under the Act) for the application in Ireland of Article 21(4) of the EU Merger Regulation, which allows Member States to take "appropriate measures" to protect legitimate interests, including media plurality.

The Report defines a proposed new statutory test to be applied by the relevant Minister in a review of media mergers, i.e.: "whether the result of the media merger is likely to be contrary to the public interest in protecting plurality in media business in the State". Plurality of the media is defined in the Report as including "both diversity of ownership and diversity of content".

The Advisory Group also recommends the adoption of a revised set of "relevant criteria" to be considered in applying the above test, including the likely effect of the media merger on plurality; the undesirability of allowing any one individual/undertaking to hold significant interests within a single sector or across different sectors of media business in the State; the consequences for the promotion of media plurality of the Minister intervening to prevent the merger; and the adequacy of other mechanisms to protect the public interest.

The Report recommends that these criteria should be supplemented by more detailed statutory guidelines to be issued by the relevant Minister. Such guidelines are intended to assist the undertakings involved in knowing how the Minister will apply the "relevant criteria". It is proposed that the guidelines would contain indicative guidance on levels of media ownership and in particular, cross-media ownership, that would generally be regarded as unacceptable. They would also provide for concrete indicators of diversity and plurality which might operate as a "sort of checklist" which the parties to a media merger would be invited to address in their notification. Examples given include demographic audience information and market share data, shareholder information, compliance by the parties with industry codes of good practice, and whether the parties have a "record of truthful, accurate and fair reporting".

Should the Government implement the proposals contained in the Report and reflect comments by the Minister for Communications, parties will require a separate approval from the Minister for Communications prior to implementation of a media merger. The Report suggests a two-phase system for review, in which Phase I would last until 30 days after the date of notification to the Minister or the decision of the Authority / European Commission / Broadcasting Authority of Ireland (to which TV and radio mergers must also be notified), whichever is the later (i.e. effectively a two-month period for mergers notified to the Authority).

At the end of this period, the Minister may decide to: (i) approve the media merger on the basis that it does not contravene the public interest test; (ii) approve the media merger with conditions; or (iii) proceed to a Phase II examination.

It is proposed that Phase II should last no more than four months from the date of the Phase I decision. In addition, at any stage in the process (Phase I or II), the Minister would be entitled to look for further information and extend time limits by the time required to respond.

In the event of a Phase II review, the Report calls for the establishment of a five-person Consultative Panel comprised of experts in law, journalism, media, business or economics, to advise the Minister on the application of "relevant criteria" (and to replace the existing role of the Authority in this regard).

At the end of Phase II, unless concluded in the intervening period by a Ministerial decision, the Minister shall decide whether to approve, approve with conditions or block a media merger.

The Report also recommends the on-going collection and periodic publication by the Government of information in relation to media plurality in the State.

The long-awaited legislative proposal based on the recommendations of the Report is scheduled to be published in the first quarter of 2013.

Other proposed reforms

In its response to the Department of Jobs, Enterprise and Innovation's public consultation on a general reform package for the Act, the Authority requested that a number of changes be made to the Act, including changes to the merger control provisions in Part 3.

The more important changes suggested by the Authority include:

- Proposal to allow notification in advance of conclusion of a binding agreement (as is currently the case), allowing notification based on a "letter of intent", for example. In making this proposal, the Authority made reference to the European Commission's requirement for there to be "a good faith intention to conclude an agreement".
- Proposals to introduce "more appropriate sanctions". At the moment the sanctions for breaching various elements of Part 3 of the Act, including knowing and wilful failure to notify a notifiable transaction within the statutory one-month period and breach of a provision of a binding commitment or a conditional clearance determination, are criminal offences under the Act. It is, in the Authority's view, more appropriate that the sanctions for these infringements are civil. The Authority is also seeking civil sanctions for implementation of a transaction prior to clearance for the first time.
- Proposal to include partial investments At the moment the Act refers to mergers that involve a change in decisive control. The Authority has noted a suggestion in the literature and case law that there is a case for analysis of partial investments – i.e. those that fall short of decisive control. The Authority makes some tentative proposals for discussion on this issue, although it makes no definitive recommendations.
- Proposals to extend time limits for review. The Authority has two major suggestions: (i) to extend a Phase II review from three to four months; and (ii) to enable it to "stop the clock" during Phase II following a requirement for further information.
- Proposal to review the media merger provisions. The main suggestion (consistent with recommendations of the 2008 Report) is to remove the Authority from having to opine on "public interest criteria" in media mergers, as it "is not within its area of competence". The Authority also notes that even with recent revisions to the Media Order, media mergers with little nexus to the State are still captured under the Act, and it is thus proposed to introduce revisions to resolve this issue.

Helen Kelly
Tel: +353 1 232 2000 / Email: helen.kelly@matheson.com
Helen Kelly is a partner and head of the EU, Competition and Regulatory Law Group
at Matheson. Helen's practice focuses on EU and Irish competition and regulatory law.
Helen specialises in EU and Irish merger control work.
Helen is a graduate of Trinity College Dublin and the London School of Economics
and is a solicitor in Ireland and England and Wales.
Helen regularly publishes articles and speaks at leading conferences. Helen has
contributed articles to a number of publications including Global Competition Review,
IFLR and the European Lawyer. Helen has frequently been recognised as one of
Ireland's leading EU competition and regulatory lawyers in international legal reviews.

Kate Leahy
Tel: +353 1 232 2000 / Email: kate.leahy@matheson.com
Kate Leahy is a solicitor in the EU, Competition and Regulatory Group at Matheson.
Kate completed her training in a leading city firm in London and joined the EU,
Competition and Regulatory Group in October 2011. Kate specialises in advising
on EU and Irish competition law, as well as regulatory law, public procurement law,
merger control and State aid. She has made notifications and submissions to, among
others, the European Commission, Irish Government Departments, the Competition
Authority, the UK Office of Fair Trading, and sectoral regulators in Ireland and the
UK.
Kate is a committee member of the Irish Society for European Law and a tutor of the
Law Society of Ireland's consumer law and competition law courses for apprentice
solicitors.

Matheson

70 Sir John Rogerson's Quay, Dublin 2, Ireland
Tel: +353 1 232 2000 / Fax: +353 1 232 3333 / URL: http://www.matheson.com

Israel

Dr David E. Tadmor & Shai Bakal
Tadmor & Co.

Overview of merger control activity during the last 12 months

The decline in the number of mergers notified to the Israeli Antitrust Authority ("the IAA") following the global economic crisis continued in 2012. While the average number of notifications in the years 2006-2007 was around 240, the number declined to 181 in 2008, 160 in 2009, and in 2010 only 153 new notifications were made. While in 2011 there was an increase in the number of merger filings to 195 merger notifications, in 2012 the number declined significantly to a record low of around 135 (the exact number could be closer to 140 notifications since the number of merger notifications which were withdrawn by the parties is yet to be available).

During this time, the relevant filing thresholds have not changed, which indicates that the M&A activity in Israel has not yet recovered from the negative impact of the global economic crisis. Another explanation could be that the market is starting to grasp the more conservative approach of the new General Director. Parties to transactions that are more complicated from an antitrust perspective abandon them before they reach the formal filing stage.

* * *

The Israeli Restrictive Trade Practices Law ("the Antitrust Law") sets a general procedural framework which applies to all mergers. There is no formal division of the investigatory process into different phases and all mergers must be reviewed by the General Director up to 30 days from the date the merger notifications were filed. The term may be extended by the Antitrust Tribunal or by consent of the merging parties. If the General Director does not render a decision within the prescribed time period, consent to the merger is deemed to have been given.

In 2011, 85% of the mergers were decided within the 30-day period and in 15% of the mergers, the period was extended. These figures have been stable in recent years.

While the Antitrust Law sets a general procedural framework which applies to all mergers, in practice the IAA screens merger notifications upon filing and classifies them to one of the three following categories: "green" (clearly benign mergers); "yellow" (mergers that merit more detailed analysis); and the "red" (mergers that are seemingly anticompetitive).

In 2011, 85.9% of the mergers were labelled "green" and were cleared within two weeks on average; 9.95% of the mergers were labelled "yellow", with decisions being issued within two months on average; and 4.2% of the mergers were labelled "red" and were decided within three months on average. The parallel data for 2012 is not public yet, but we expect the average time for merger review to be extended, in light of the General Director's tendency to apply stricter policy towards mergers, as well as an increase in the amount of data that the IAA seeks as part of its merger investigations.

* * *

According to the Antitrust Law, the General Director has the power to either approve the transaction, block the transaction (if there is a reasonable likelihood that the merger will significantly harm competition in a relevant market), or approve the transaction subject to conditions (if such conditions can eliminate the harm to competition). Of the 134 mergers regarding which the IAA issued a decision in 2012:

- 92.5% of the mergers were cleared without conditions.
- 4.5% of the mergers were approved with conditions.
- 3% of the mergers were blocked by the General Director. An estimated 4%-6% of the transactions were withdrawn by the parties before any decision was given, mainly because the IAA indicated that it is likely to block the deal.

An analysis of the IAA's track record during the last decade shows that the relative share of mergers that are blocked is stable, ranging from 0%-2% at most, with another 1%-3% of the notifications withdrawn. The higher percentage of mergers that were blocked or withdrawn in 2012 (more than twice the average number in the past decade) seems to mark the beginning of a new hawkish approach towards mergers by the General Director. It thus appears that the appointment of the new General Director, Prof. David Gilo, had a substantial influence on the IAA's merger control policy.

On the other hand, there is an evident decrease in the use of remedies by the IAA. While in the years 2000-2005 around 18% of the merger decisions included remedies, the number decreased to only 6%-8% in the last years, with 2011 posting the lowest share ever for such decisions (2.6%). Although the number increased to 4.5% in 2012, it is still lower than the number prevailing during the last decade. The decline in use of remedies, especially behavioural remedies, is in line with the new IAA's guidance on remedies – see "Key policy developments" below.

New developments in jurisdictional assessment or procedure

The main policy document in the area of merger procedure has remained the **"Antitrust Commissioner's Pre-merger Filing Guidelines"** published in 2008 ("the Pre-merger Guidelines"). The IAA recently had a chance to elaborate on one of the issues addressed by the Pre-merger Guidelines. In 2012 the IAA blocked the transaction between Isrotel Ltd., a major hotels operator in Israel's southern city Eilat, and Laxan Israel Ltd., which owns a hotel in Eilat. The parties agreed that Isrotel will manage Laxan's hotel for a period of 10.5 years with an option to extend the period twice, for 5 years each time. In addition, Isrotel was granted the option to purchase 25% of the hotel. The parties argued that such an agreement does not fall under the definition of "merger transaction", since the management period is not indefinite. The General Director blocked the merger, and rejected the parties' claims that the transaction was not subject to the merger control supervision. Citing the pre-merger guidelines, the General Director stated that any transaction that confers control over important competitive parameters of the services rendered by one firm (such as the quality of service and the infrastructure of a hotel) in the hands of another firm, might be deemed as a merger. The length of the management agreement is yet another factor to be considered, but it does not need to be indefinite. In the case of Laxan and Isrotel, the General Director held that the agreement between the parties was a long term agreement, which conferred the type of control that is normally attributed to mergers.

With a very limited number of cases that are brought each year before the Antitrust Court, merger procedure was pretty much shaped by the IAA and only rarely was the IAA's practice contested in court. In recent years, the IAA's practice was twice contested in an area which had long awaited judicial guidance – the nature and scope of the IAA's duty to reason its decisions in the field of mergers.

It has been the IAA's position for many years that when it approves a merger (with or without conditions), it is only required to provide the "bottom line". According to the IAA, it is required to provide a reasoned opinion only if it blocks a merger.

This position of the IAA is not clear of doubts. Under the Law for Administrative Procedure (Decisions and Reasons) 1958 (the "Reasoning Law"), a governmental authority which refuses to exercise its authority, must provide the applicant with the reasons for its decision.

The IAA's practice was first contested a few years ago in AT 515/04 **Cellcom Israel Ltd. V. The**

General Director (2005). In Cellcom, the IAA approved a transaction by which Bezeq, Israel's leading telecom firm, increased its share in Pelephone (one of three Israeli mobile carriers) from 50% to 100%. Cellcom, another mobile carrier, appealed the approval before the Antitrust Court requesting, among other things, that the IAA will reason its decision to ignore Cellcom's plea to block the merger or impose conditions upon it.

The Court ruled that it will be unnecessary and impractical to impose on the IAA a duty to reason every merger decision. The Court further explained that the Reasoning Law did not apply – at least not directly – on a refusal by the IAA to block a merger at the request of a third party. The Antitrust Court implied that the outcome may have been different had it been the merging parties that requested the IAA to reason its decision. The Court explained that in such a case the Reasoning Law would seem to apply, since a conditional approval generally means that the original request of the merging parties was effectively denied.

In 2010, the IAA's practice was once again contested - this time by a merging party. In AT 803/08 **Teraflex Compounds (1994) Ltd V. The General Director** (2010), the IAA approved a merger between Israel's sole manufacturers of PVC mixture: Teraflex and Kafrit. The decision was subject to conditions, one of which was the mandatory licensing of IP rights to interested third parties. Teraflex, the buyer in this transaction, preferred to waive the transaction in light of these conditions, but it was contractually compelled to complete the transaction and thus appealed the decision seeking – rather oddly – that the Antitrust Court will block the merger altogether.

Teraflex argued, among other things, that the IAA was legally required to issue a reasoned decision explaining why such conditions were imposed and why were they preferred over an outright objection to the merger (which would have allowed Teraflex to terminate the merger agreement).

The Court upheld the General Director's decision, stating it was based on solid economic and legal grounds. The Court further stated that the IAA's position was elaborately explained to Teraflex in an oral hearing which was held prior to the issuance of a formal decision. In these circumstances, the Court found the IAA's position reasonable and valid. The Court did not analyse the IAA's position in light of the Reasoning Law, which requires the relevant authority to explain its position in writing. It seems that the Court adopted a restrained approach, leaving the IAA broad discretion in shaping merger procedure, as long as its actions do not seem to cause grave injustice. The Antitrust Court's ruling was upheld by the Supreme Court in 2012, though the Supreme Court's decision addressed other issues.

A different and more critical approach was adopted by the Antitrust Court in an interim decision in AT 36014-12-10 **Kniel Packaging Industries Ltd. V. The General Director** (2011). This decision contested a different practice of the IAA, which was to first "stop the clock" with an unreasoned objection to the merger, which is followed by a reasoned opinion only after several weeks have passed. Naturally, this practice made it more difficult for the merging parties to launch a timely appeal on the IAA's decision to block a merger, which many times meant abandoning the merger altogether.

In *Kniel*, the IAA issued an unreasoned decision after four-and-a-half months of investigation, stating that it will need an additional 45 days to issue the reasoned decision. Kniel appealed to the Court and, although the request was denied for technical reasons, the Court criticised the IAA, stating that it is expected to render reasoned decisions in an expedite manner, especially when it investigates mergers for such a prolonged period. The decision sent a clear message that the Court has the power to exert judicial review on administrative and procedural decisions of the IAA and that it will not hesitate to intervene when it deems it appropriate. In its final ruling in *Kniel*, given in 2012, the Court addressed another important issue in which there is a pressing need for clarity – the burden of proof in an appeal on the General Director's objection to a merger. The Israeli Supreme Court expressed in the past contradicting opinions in this respect (these were made as *obiter dictum*). The Antitrust Court in *Kniel* assumed that the burden of proof lies with the General Director. Only once the General Director established a reasonable likelihood for significant lessening of competition does the burden shift to the merging parties to prove a defence (such as efficiency defence, failing firm, etc.).

* * *

The Antitrust Law sets a mandatory filing regime, which is enforced by the IAA. A breach of the mandatory filing requirement is a criminal offence and a source of potential civil liability. The likely impact of the transaction on competition may have some weight with the IAA, when it determines the type of enforcement actions that will be launched against the merging parties.

An important development in the area of merger enforcement was the publication, in July 2012, of the **"IAA's Guidelines Regarding the Use of Enforcement Procedures of Monetary Payments"**, which stated that the illegal execution of non-horizontal mergers would normally be sanctioned by a monetary payment (an administrative tool), rather than the criminal penalties, which legally could be applied. Illegal horizontal arrangements are still subject to criminal enforcement.

In 2011, the IAA entered a consent decree with Station Holdings Ltd. and The New Tel-Aviv Bus Terminal Co. Ltd., who allegedly breached the mandatory filing regime. While the IAA found no competitive issues with the merger, the parties were required to pay 400,000 NIS (around US$120,000)

In January 2013, the IAA announced that it will allow electronic filing of merger notifications, in order to make the filing process more efficient. Moreover, public companies will no longer be required to submit financial reports and prospectuses as part of their merger notifications.

Key industry sectors reviewed, and approach adopted, to market definition, barriers to entry, nature of international competition etc.

In 2012, the food sector took, once again, centre stage of the IAA's attention, following the social unrest that erupted in 2011. In 2012, the IAA promoted legislative initiatives aimed at restricting large suppliers and retail chains. The IAA approved several mergers in the food sector, but required the merging parties to divest branches in locations where it considered that competition might be harmed. For example, the IAA approved the sale of "Maman" discount chain to Israel's second-largest retail chain, "Mega", subject to divestiture in two cities where the IAA thought there was a threat of harm to competition. In December 2012, the IAA approved a major retail merger between "Bitan Wines" heavy discount chain and "Almost Free" heavy discount chain, creating Israel's third-largest retailer, subject to an obligation to sell a branch in one of the overlapping locations.

2010 and 2011 were very busy years for the IAA in the telecommunications sector. The IAA contributed to several governmental reforms initiated by the Ministry of Telecommunications, mainly in the cellular market, such as the bids to introduce two additional MNOs (currently Israel has three), facilitating entry of MVNOs, and changes in the interconnection fees between mobile carriers.

These regulatory changes were accompanied by significant structural changes in the market and the gradual formation of four telecommunications groups. These changes were brought about by the aspiration of local telecoms to become a 'one stop shop' for all their customers' needs. This desire was accomplished in two principal ways: natural growth of incumbent players to new or adjacent markets; and mergers between firms with activities in complementary telecom markets.

The IAA was somewhat hesitant about the effects of such structural changes. The theory of harm which the IAA explored was that, over time, it will become difficult for smaller firms, operating only in one market, to compete with the "full line service" of the telecom groups. If that were the case, the number of players in the telecom markets will decrease over time, with only the four groups remaining. The barriers to entry will then become significant, since any newcomer would need to enter, simultaneously, into several markets. According to this theory, once they are shielded from outside entry, the four telecom groups would have both the incentive and the ability to adopt parallel pricing behaviour.

A review of the IAA's track record on telecom mergers shows that merging parties were allowed to combine their operations in complementary markets and to form telecom groups that are capable of providing a full line telecom service to their customers. This may indicate that the IAA could not have sufficiently established the theory of harm presented above. Instead, the IAA focused on a traditional antitrust analysis, dealing with concrete horizontal (and, to a lesser extent, vertical) overlaps.

The IAA's approach is best illustrated by two major telecom mergers: the acquisition of "Bezeq" the Israeli Telecom Corporation Ltd by 012 Smile Telecom Ltd; and the acquisition of 012 Smile Communications Ltd by Partner Communications Ltd.

In 2010, the IAA approved the acquisition of Bezeq, a proclaimed monopoly in several telecom markets, by 012 Smile, which was mainly active in the ISP and the international calls services market. The merger was approved after 012 Smile's overlapping activities were divested. The IAA did not seek to prevent the combination of complementary services or non-significant horizontal and vertical overlaps between the parties.

In 2011, a merger between Partner and 012 Smile, which formed Israel's fourth telecom group, was unconditionally approved. Partner was a significant player in the mobile market and a fringe player in the ISP and domestic calls market. 012 Smile was a significant player in the ISP and international calls markets and a less significant player in the domestic calls market. The IAA cleared the merger after thorough investigation, concluding that the overlaps between the parties were not likely to injure competition. This conclusion stems from the relatively low barriers to entry in these markets, and the fact that merging firm was subject to competition from other telecom groups.

The merger directly confronted the IAA with the theory presented above, since the merger involved the combination of several complementary services that were offered by "semi telecom groups". It was clear that the merger was a significant headway towards a 'four telecom groups' structure of the Israeli telecommunications market. The IAA allowed this combination to go ahead, probably because it came to realise that the theory of harm associated with telecom groups was, at least at this point, speculative in nature.

Another core issue, which was analysed carefully by the IAA in the Partner-012 Smile merger, was the potential loss of competition in the mobile market. The IAA had long perceived the mobile market, in which competition was held between three players, as concentrated and not sufficiently competitive. At the time the merger was notified, there were regulatory reforms aimed at introducing new competition to the market either as MVNOs or MNOs. 012 Smile was seemingly a natural candidate to enter the market in either of these paths. The core issue which the IAA struggled with was, therefore, whether the Partner-012 Smile merger would eliminate a potential competitor from the mobile market and whether such elimination would result in significant injury to the competition in that market. The IAA cleared the merger, probably having concluded that 012 Smile was not the only potential competitor to the market.

In 2012 there were fewer mergers in the telecom market and no notable merger decision in this area.

* * *

In 2010/2011, there were also several mergers in the electric appliances and consumer electronics retail sector. Prominent examples are the merger between Electra Consumer Products Ltd. and Mini-line Ltd., the merger between Newpan Ltd. and Mini-line Ltd. and the merger between Newpan and "Wholesale Electricity" (Sofer & Ben Eliezer Group).

Newpan is one of Israel's largest importers of electric appliances and consumer electronics. In addition, Newpan has a minority interest in two retail chains of electric appliances: "Best Buy"; and "Big Box". In 2010, Newpan requested the IAA's approval to acquire 33.3% of the shares in "Wholesale Electricity", a chain of electric appliances and consumer electronics retail stores which competed with "Best Buy" and "Big Box". The IAA concluded that Newpan's cross-ownership of a minority stake in these chains was unlikely to significantly impede competition, given the limited aggregate market share of these firms and the existence of competition from other market participants.

The IAA was of a different view when, in the same year, Electra Consumer Products Ltd. and Mini-line Ltd. attempted to merge. Both parties imported and marketed electric appliances and consumer electronics for home use. The merger was investigated by the IAA for several months, during which time several market participants publicly expressed concern over the parties' alleged ability to foreclose competing importers from their powerful retail chains. The IAA concluded that importers needed access to nationwide retail chains, which are an essential advertising platform for new electrical appliances. The IAA argued that Electra and Mini-line were two out of very few such relevant platforms and, thus, that the merger posed real danger to competition. The IAA was willing to approve the merger subject to divestment of a nationwide chain ("Shekem Electric" or "A.L.M"), but the parties preferred to withdraw their application.

In 2011, Mini-line filed again, this time to merge with another competitor – Newpan. This transaction too was investigated for months by the IAA, which once again concluded that the aggregate share of the merging parties in the retail segment raised material concerns. The IAA approved the merger in August 2011, subject to divestiture of Newpan's minority stake in the "Best Buy" retail chain. The IAA revoked the divestiture in late 2012, under the failing firms doctrine, after concluding that "Best Buy" could not be competitively sustained other than as a subsidiary of Newpan.

The series of mergers in the electric appliances and consumer electronics retail sector continued in 2012 and many of them were approved by the IAA. Thus, the IAA approved, subject to conditions (which were not published), a merger between Ace Auto Depot Ltd., Ace Marketing Chains – Consumer Products Ltd. and Electra Consumer Products (1970) Ltd. Other mergers were approved with no conditions, *inter alia*: a merger between Pilab M.M Reparation and Service Ltd., C.S.B. Zafon Electric Appliances 2001 Ltd., C.S.B. Electrical Appliances Ltd. and Ratfon Services Ltd.; a merger between Newpan and Fishman Chains Ltd.; a merger between Electrodan Commerce Ltd. and Exit Electronics Ltd.; and a merger Newpan Pro Ltd., Kahana Audio Ltd. and N.K. Ltd.

Key economic appraisal techniques applied

The substantive test under section 21(a) of the Antitrust Law is "reasonable likelihood that, as a result of the proposed merger, competition in the relevant market may be significantly harmed or that the public would be injured".

In assessing the possible competitive outcome of a merger, the IAA usually applies the same methodology that the relevant US and EC authorities use. The IAA would normally define the relevant market and then, if necessary, assess the relevant market shares of the parties, the existence of barriers to entry and expansion in the market, as well as other economic factors which may indicate how likely it is that the merger would result in either unilateral or coordinated effects.

The definition of the relevant market is mostly based on qualitative evidence, usually obtained by conversations with the merging parties and other market participants, internal documents, surveys, public records, information from other governmental agencies and much more. In cases where the qualitative analysis is not sufficiently informative, the IAA may seek to strengthen the qualitative analysis by a quantitative analysis (critical loss analysis, price correlations, etc.).

The IAA increased the use of econometric analysis in recent years, but the analysis is still fundamentally qualitative. The IAA attributes special importance in merger investigations to direct evidence, such as natural experiments, internal documents and market surveys.

In 2011, the IAA published the **"Guidelines for Competitive Analysis of Horizontal Mergers"** (see "Key policy developments" below), which describe the theoretical economic and legal foundations upon which the IAA's merger review is based.

According to these guidelines, the core purpose of merger review is to prevent the creation or enhancement of market power. The guidelines further explain that such market power can be exercised either unilaterally ("merger to monopoly") or collectively. The guidelines further explain that, in order to assess the competitive effects of a contemplated merger, the following steps will be carried out:

First, the IAA will identify the relevant product and geographical markets in which the merging companies operate. The definition of the relevant market is based on the hypothetical monopolist test, which is implemented using practical indices such as differences in the functional use of the products, price differences, price correlation, the perspectives of market participants, differences in quality, etc.

Second, the IAA will identify the players in the market, their market shares and the level of concentration before and after the merger.

The guidelines stress that the merger investigation does not rest solely on static analysis. Therefore, when the initial assessment yields that the merger raises significant concerns, the IAA will enter a more detailed analysis of the "dynamic aspects", i.e. the possibility that the new entry or expansion of existing players in the market will mitigate the immediate and potentially harmful effects of the merger.

The analysis of entry and expansion will focus on a variety of entry and switching barriers, including regulatory barriers, scale economics, network effects, strategic behaviour by incumbent firms, branding, access to essential inputs and much more.

If the analysis results in a conclusion that the merger is anticompetitive, the IAA will examine whether there are available remedies that can eliminate the potential harm to competition.

If such remedies are unavailable, the IAA will block the merger, unless one of the following rare situations is proven by the parties:

- **Efficiency defence** – if the IAA is convinced that there are efficiencies directly resulting from the merger that outweigh the potential harm to competition, the merger will be approved. In order to enjoy the efficiency defence, one must meet certain conditions: (a) the efficiency must be merger-specific, in the sense that the parties cannot obtain similar efficiencies in any other way; and (b) the efficiency must be significant, timely and such that the benefits will mostly be passed on to the consumers and outweigh the harm inflicted on them by the loss of competition.

- **The failing firm doctrine** – this doctrine refers to situations by which the acquired entity is financially unsustainable and would likely exit the market, even absent the merger. In such cases there is no casual link between the merger and the injury to competition. In 2010, the IAA published guidelines detailing the legal basis and the practical requirements to meet the defence (see "Key policy developments").

Approach to remedies (i) to avoid second stage investigation and (ii) following second stage investigation

As we previously explained, the merger control procedure in Israel does not have a formal classification method. However, it is not uncommon for parties seeking swift approval for complicated mergers to offer upfront remedies, attempting to expedite the review process. An excellent example for such an approach is the Bezeq-012 Smile merger mentioned above.

In that case, the parties identified several overlapping areas which were seemingly meaningful and would possibly have required a lengthy review. In order to avoid such lengthy proceedings, the parties suggested divestment of the overlapping activities at the outset.

However, it is more common that remedies are discussed only if the IAA reaches a tentative conclusion that the proposed merger may significantly lessen competition in the market. In such cases, the parties may propose remedies that will eliminate the harm to competition or, alternatively, the IAA may stipulate the conditions that are required in order to have the merger approved, and these can then be discussed with the parties.

In 2011, the IAA issued guidelines for merger remedies detailing key principles of its remedies policy – see "Key policy developments" below. In a nutshell, the new guidelines express a preference for structural remedies over behavioural remedies. Interestingly, the clear majority of remedies imposed until 2011 were behavioural, while in 2011 and 2012 most cases involved structural remedies.

Key policy developments

In 2011, the IAA has published several key policy documents in the area of mergers.

The first policy document is **"Guidelines for Competitive Analysis of Horizontal Mergers"** which describes the method the IAA will use to analyse the competitive effects of horizontal mergers on competition (see detailed explanation in "Key economic appraisal techniques applied" above).

The second policy document is **"Guidelines on Remedies for Mergers that raise a Reasonable Concern for Significant Harm to Competition"**.

The document outlines the governing legal principles in the area of merger remedies, out of which two stand out: (a) the IAA is authorised to request remedies only if the merger, as it was originally proposed, raises a real danger that competition will be harmed significantly. In other words, the IAA may impose conditions only for mergers that it can otherwise block; and (b) remedies are preferable whenever they are capable of mitigating the harm to competition.

The guidelines explain that the decision of and what sort of remedies are suitable in a particular case is based on the specific circumstances. The following considerations serve an important role in such analysis:

- The theory of harm to competition, which the remedies aim to disrupt. Different theories of harm will likely require different solutions. For instance, a remedy which may be optimal to eliminate potential vertical issues may not help in solving a significant horizontal overlap.
- How effective is the remedy? From a set of different remedies, the IAA will prefer the more effective one. The IAA further explains that the more difficult it is to effectively address the potential harm to competition, the more likely it is to block a merger altogether. Such situations may arise when the injury to competition can be manifested in many, in part unpredictable, ways.
- The ability to enforce the remedy and to monitor deviations of the parties from such remedy. The IAA will generally prefer remedies that are easy to enforce and require less monitoring.
- The resources required for such enforcement and monitoring.
- The remedy duration. In general, the IAA will prefer remedies that can be achieved in a single-shot or within a definite time frame over remedies that are ongoing over time.
- The ability of the merging parties to comply with the remedy. The IAA will see if it is sufficiently probable that the merging parties will be capable of complying with the remedy imposed. The IAA will tend not to impose remedies whose execution depends on the actions of their parties (for example – if a third party's approval is needed to execute the remedy).

The guidelines show that, given such considerations, it will generally prefer structural remedies over behavioural remedies. The IAA alleges that structural remedies are normally more effective as they deal with the disease and not merely the symptoms, do not require complex and ongoing monitoring, require less pubic resources and are executed within a defined, normally short, period. The IAA acknowledges, though, the fact that in certain instances behavioural remedies, or a mix of behavioural and structural remedies, would be more appropriate.

In 2010, the IAA published another policy document – **"Guidelines Regarding the Failing Firm's Doctrine"**. The guidelines explain that when a firm is insolvent and will likely exit the market regardless of the merger, there is no causal link between the merger and the competitive harm that will follow its inception. For the failing firm's defence to exist, the following conditions must be met: (a) the firm's chances to survive as an independent player in the market (including through debt restructuring and similar proceedings) are very slim; (b) there is no alternative buyer to whom the sale of the company is less anticompetitive; and (c) the merger is better, from a competition point of view, than letting the firm exit the market. While the IAA rarely acknowledges the failing firm's doctrine, several mergers were approved under this doctrine during the years.

As stated above, 2012 seems to mark a change of direction in the IAA's approach, towards applying stricter criteria to proposed mergers. This impression is supported by the unprecedented numbers of blocked mergers and of withdrawals of merger notifications. Even more can be learned from explicit statements made by the new General Director, Prof. Gilo (for example, in the recent annual IAA conference). These statements show that the IAA does not only intend to block mergers that harm competition significantly, but also mergers in markets posing a trend towards higher concentration, as well as mergers which raise more remote concerns for diminished actual or potential competition.

Reform proposals

There have been no reform proposals in Israel in 2011/2012 in the field of mergers.

Dr David E. Tadmor
Tel: +972 3 684 6000 / Email: david@tadmor.com

Dr Tadmor, a former General Director of the Israel Antitrust Authority (IAA), is the founding and managing partner of Tadmor & Co., a growing first tier antitrust firm. Dr Tadmor was named by Chambers as being in the top class of antitrust lawyers in Israel and as being "in a league of his own" and "the first port of call".

David's practice includes the representation of many leading multinational and Israeli clients in a large variety of industries.

During his time as a General Director (1997-2001), the IAA trebled in size and much of the foundation for Israel's competition law and enforcement policies was laid. As General Director, David introduced the IAA to the competition committee of the OECD, which has since included the IAA as an observant.

In the past, David was a senior partner at Caspi & Co., a leading Israeli firm; a member of the Antitrust Court and a corporate attorney with the New York law firm of Wachtell, Lipton, Rosen & Katz (1988-1993).

Shai Bakal
Tel: +972 3 684 6000 / Email: shai@tadmor.com

Shai Bakal's practice covers all areas of Antitrust Law and Regulation. Shai regularly advises and represents leading corporations in Israel and abroad with respect to complicated antitrust matters such as mergers, joint ventures, restrictive trade practices and dominant position cases. Shai's practice includes representing clients in major antitrust cases before the IAA and in litigation before the Antitrust Tribunal, as well as representation before other governmental agencies.

Prior to joining Tadmor & Co., Shai practised law at the legal department of the IAA (2002-2007), where he was in charge of different sectors, including the food sector, retailing and IP. He was later appointed as the head of the IAA's mergers team. During his term at the IAA, Shai drafted several key policy documents, including the "Antitrust Commissioner's Pre-merger Filing Guidelines" and the "Antitrust Commissioner's Position on Commercial Arrangements Between Suppliers and Large Retail Chains". Shai has unique expertise and vast experience in merger control issues and, in particular, in cross-border transactions.

Tadmor & Co.

5 Azrieli Center, The Square Tower 34th floor, 132 Begin Road, Tel Aviv 67021, Israel
Tel: +972 3 684 6000 / Fax: +972 3 684 6001 / URL: http://www.tadmor.com

Italy

Mario Siragusa & Matteo Beretta
Cleary Gottlieb Steen & Hamilton LLP

Overview of merger control activity during the last 12 months

The number of concentrations notified to the Italian Competition Authority (*Autorità Garante della Concorrenza e del Mercato*, the "ICA") in 2012 (434) was lower than in 2011 (532), and in 2010 (495) but, in absolute terms, remained quite high. For the period considered in this publication (June 2011 – December 2012, the "Reference Period"), the mergers reviewed by the ICA were 787.

These figures can be explained by the alternative nature of the two turnover thresholds set forth in Article 16(1) of Law No. 2 87/1990 (the "Antitrust Law")[1] and by the fact that a mandatory notification is also triggered upon acquisition of targets with a trivial/negligible presence in Italy if the acquiring undertaking alone meets the first turnover threshold (which makes reference to the *aggregate* Italian turnover of all the undertakings involved).[2] As a result, undertakings are frequently subject to (barely justifiable) procedural burdens and related costs, including possible fines for violation of the reporting obligation, for transactions with little or no impact in Italy.

However, as of January 1, 2013, the turnover thresholds set forth in Article 16 of the Antitrust Law must be cumulatively met. In other words, an obligation to file a mandatory notification is triggered only when *both* thresholds are met. As a consequence, a considerable number of mergers will no longer be reportable to the ICA.[3] (For a more comprehensive description of the new legislation, see below under 'Key policy developments').

In more detail, in the Reference Period:[4]

* 742 cases were cleared during the so-called "Phase I" (*i.e.*, the ICA issued a decision declaring that no further investigation was required because the notified transaction did not create or strengthen a dominant position as a result of which effective competition would have been significantly impeded);
* 21 notifications resulted in a decision of inapplicability[5] (*i.e.*, a decision finding that the notified transaction: (i) did not fall within the scope of the Antitrust Law because it did not amount to a concentration within the meaning of Article 5 of the Antitrust Law; or (ii) had Community dimension and, thus, fell within the European Commission's exclusive jurisdiction; or (iii) did not meet the turnover thresholds set forth in Article 16 of the Antitrust Law);
* in seven cases the ICA opened an in-depth investigation (so-called "Phase II"), because the notified transaction could have been prohibited under Article 6 of the Antitrust Law (6 of which were cleared subject to remedies);[6]
* in one case the ICA opened proceedings for failure to comply with the conditions imposed, pursuant to Article 19(1) of the Antitrust Law;[7]
* in 14 cases the ICA opened proceedings for failure to notify a concentration pursuant to Article 19(2) of the Antitrust Law;[8] and
* in one case (*Compagnia Aerea Italiana/Alitalia Linee Aeree-Airone*)[9] the ICA adopted a decision imposing post-transaction conditions under Law Decree No. 134/2008.[10]

Finally, in one case (*CVA-Compagnia Valdostana delle Acque/Deval-Vallenergie*), the ICA revoked a prohibition previously imposed. Particularly, on August 4, 2011, the ICA had prohibited the acquisition of sole control of Vallenergie S.p.A. ("Vallenergie") and Deval S.p.A. ("Deval") by CVA-Compagnia

Valdostana delle Acque S.p.A. ("CVA")[11].

The proposed transaction concerned the markets for electricity in Valle d'Aosta, a region in the North of Italy. In particular, the ICA had found that the transaction raised a number of concerns with respect to the local markets for (1) the retail supply of electricity to domestic final users, and (2) the retail supply of electricity to non-domestic final users, *i.e.*, small businesses. The post-merger entity would have reached a share in excess of 90% in both markets, the remaining 10% being fragmented among several minor competitors.

The ICA also had found that potential competition was hindered by significant legal barriers to entry. To reduce the price of electricity, the local regulation granted distributors a 30% refund to be directly applied in the customers' invoices, provided that they complied with local technical specifications. In the ICA's view, to comply with these specifications, new entrant distributors would have had to implement substantial changes to their payment systems, which would have ultimately rendered the refund inefficient. Therefore, according to the ICA, new entrants would not have benefited from this policy and, as a result, entry into the markets by new operators and/or the migration of CVA's customers towards other operators would have been highly unlikely.

Based on the foregoing, the ICA had concluded that the proposed transaction would have created a dominant position capable of substantially lessening or eliminating competition in the regional market for the retail supply of electricity to domestic and non-domestic customers.

Notably, the ICA prohibited the transaction notwithstanding the fact that CVA had undertaken not to modify the prices applied to customers for a period of two years, with a possibility for the ICA to require an extension of the commitments up to four years, maintaining that such proposed behavioural commitments concerning CVA's future pricing policy did not address the competition concerns stemming from the transaction. In this regard, the ICA had expressly referred to paragraph 17 of the European Commission notice on remedies[12], pursuant to which: *"commitments in the form of undertakings not to raise prices [...] will generally not eliminate competition concerns resulting from horizontal overlaps"*.

However, following the amendment of the regional law regulating the market for electricity, the parties re-notified the transaction. On November 16, 2011, in light of the amended legal framework, the ICA cleared the transaction.[13]

In fact, on October 19, 2011, the local regulation was amended and the intermediation of distributors eliminated. According to the new provisions, the discount would directly be granted by the local authority to the customers requesting it. The ICA, thus, found that the new regulatory framework had eliminated the competitive disadvantage for new entrants. By allowing the distributors active in different geographic markets to benefit from the discount, the new provisions made their entry into the local market of Valle d'Aosta economically viable. The ICA, thus, considered that potential competition from other distributors was sufficient to significantly reduce any market power of the merged entity, regardless of its monopolistic market share.

New developments in jurisdictional assessment or procedure

In the Reference Period, no significant developments occurred. However, three ICA reform proposals concerning the jurisdictional assessment of certain concentrations and the substantive merger control test were recently brought to the attention of the Italian Government. Such reform proposals are aimed at putting an end to a number of inconsistencies between the Italian merger control regime and the system laid down at the EU level by Regulation 139/04[14] (the "EU Merger Regulation"). (These reform proposals are described more in detail under 'Reform proposals', below).

Key industry sectors reviewed, and approach adopted, to market definition, barriers to entry, nature of international competition etc.

During the Reference Period, the Italian transportation sector has been under the spotlight. Particularly, the ICA reviewed two mergers concerning operators active in air transportation for passengers;[15] and two mergers between operators active in maritime transportation for passengers, vehicles, and cargo.[16] All these cases involved markets characterised by high administrative barriers to entry, limited resources and high startup costs. The main remedy imposed on notifying undertakings has been the divestiture of strategic slots, in order to facilitate access to the market by competitors and new entrants.

Key economic appraisal techniques applied

The substantive test under Article 6(1) of the Antitrust Law measures *"whether a concentration creates or reinforces a dominant position on the Italian market capable of eliminating or restricting competition appreciably and on a lasting basis"*.

The ICA's substantive appraisal takes into account a number of factors including: (i) the position in the market of the undertakings concerned; (ii) the structure of the relevant markets; (iii) the existence of barriers to entry; (iv) the competitive position of the domestic industry; (v) the conditions of access to supplies or outlets; (vi) the alternatives available to suppliers and users; and (vii) the supply and demand trends for relevant goods and services. In assessing the competitive effects of a merger, the ICA employs a market-based approach that attempts to determine the existing parameters and dynamics of competition on the affected market, and predicts the effect of a given transaction on that market. The ICA compares the competitive conditions in the post-merger scenario with those that would prevail absent the merger, and endeavours to determine whether the merging firms will face sufficient residual competition to make it unprofitable to increase prices or decrease output.

The starting point in the ICA's assessment is represented by the merged entity's market shares. However, the ICA also takes into account other important factors including market concentration, number and strength of competitors, barriers to entry, characteristics of demand and the degree of vertical integration.

In *Bolton Alimentari/Simmenthal*,[17] the ICA, for the first time, took into account the Gross Upward Pricing Pressure Index (GUPPI), a tool aimed at measuring the unilateral merger price effects in markets for differentiated products.[18] In particular, the GUPPI measures the *"Upward Pricing Pressure"*, which reflects the unilateral incentive for the merged firm to increase prices, by calculating the value of sales diverted to one merging firm's product (*"diversion ratio"*) due to a post-merger increase in price of the other merging firm's product. The "GUPPI analysis" departs from the traditional structural approach focused on the assessment of the merged entity's market shares.[19] It may, thus, be used as a counter-argument in the hand of notifying parties charged with the finding of high market shares or, on the contrary, as a threat for merging parties whose products are regarded as very close substitutes (regardless of the merged entity market share).[20]

Approach to remedies

During the Reference Period, in one instance[21] remedies were offered in Phase I, with a view to secure clearance, while, as seen above, six conditional clearance decisions were adopted following a Phase II investigation. More in general, the ICA has traditionally shown a particular favour for a "negotiated" approach with the notifying parties. This is true also with respect to procedures concerning abuses of dominance and (though, to a lesser extent) cartels, where the ICA makes large use of "commitments" under Article 14-*ter* of the Antitrust Law. The favour for a "negotiated" approach may be justified also in light of the importance that the ICA gives to the exposure of its activity to the media. In recent years, the ICA has made significant efforts to promote its achievements, especially among consumers, and the publicity normally given to remedies (and to their envisaged pro-competitive effects) serves this purpose. It will be interesting to see whether the favour for the "negotiated" approach will be confirmed under the presidency of the new ICA Chairman Mr Giovanni Pitruzzella, who has recently replaced Mr Antonio Catricalà.[22]

As regards the analysis of the most important "remedy" cases dealt with by the ICA in the Reference Period, the following should be noted.

On November 30, 2011, the ICA opened an investigation into the merger between Italy's flagship carrier Alitalia and its main competitor Air One[23] after expiry of the three-year suspension of the operation of national merger control rules, provided for by Law Decree No. 134/2008.[24] Particularly, by means of Law Decree No. 134/2008, the Italian government had adopted *ad hoc* urgency measures exempting from merger control scrutiny those "*concentration operations* [that] *fulfill major public interests*". The exemption was due to last for a period no longer than three years, after which, according to the law, "*any possibly ensuing monopoly positions must end*".

The merger had taken place in December 2008 and involved a vehicle company owned by a group of Italian investors, Compagnia Aerea Italiana ("CAI"), which was established for that purpose. The transaction consisted in CAI's acquisition of: (i) certain assets of the Alitalia Group (which at that time was under special administration); and (ii) sole control over the companies of the Air One Group. The ultimate aim of the merger was to prevent Alitalia's default by creating a new Italian airline combining Alitalia's main operating assets and Air One. Nonetheless, the transaction led to an overlap between the parties' activities on a number of domestic and international routes, with very significant aggregated market shares on several routes, but only behavioural remedies could be imposed in order to "*prevent the risk of prices or other contractual conditions being imposed that would be unduly burdensome for consumers*". The ICA, given the provisions laid down by Law Decree No. 134/2008, was in fact barred both from prohibiting the transaction and from imposing structural remedies such as the divestiture of airport slots. Accordingly, on December 3, 2008, the ICA adopted a decision ordering a number of price control and consumer protection remedies for a period of three years.[25] As the three-year suspension period was elapsed, the ICA opened an investigation to ascertain whether the 2008 transaction created or strengthened a dominant position on certain routes and whether any such dominant position persists to date.

The ICA first stated that the relevant markets should have been defined according to the Commission's consolidated approach to market definition in air transport of passengers, the point-of-origin/point-of-destination pair approach ("O&D"), adding that, despite their proximity, the three Milan airports (Linate, Malpensa, and Orio al Serio) could not (either in 2008 or today) be considered substitutable and should have been therefore identified as distinct markets at least in relation to domestic flights. The ICA then identified seven international routes and 22 domestic routes where the transaction had determined an overlap between the parties' activities.

Turning to the competitive effects of the merger, the ICA held that, as regards international routes, in light first and foremost of CAI's limited market share and of the competitive pressure from other carriers, the transaction did not distort competition. As regards the domestic routes, the ICA relied on EU and national precedents, which consider the control of at least 60% of the daily flights operated on a given route to be a threshold of concern that may trigger the application of structural remedies.[26] The ICA identified 18 domestic routes where CAI came to operate at least 60% of daily flights post-merger (on most routes, CAI controlled 100% of the daily flights).[27] The ICA added that, of these 18 routes, those having Milan Linate as their origin or destination raised particular concerns due to the high entry barriers resulting from regulatory constraints on the allocation of slots at that airport, and in light of CAI's 70% overall share of total available slots.

On April 11, 2012, the ICA closed its investigation.[28] The ICA found that the 2008 merger created a monopoly on the Linate (Milan)-Fiumicino (Rome) route, which, in the ICA's view, was still the case. In this regard, the ICA held that currently "*Alitalia-CAI* [i.e., the merged entity] *is free of competitive pressures from other airlines*", because of Linate's specific administrative regulations which make it impossible for other companies to acquire slots on this airport. The ICA also found that high-speed rail transport services between Rome and Milan did not constitute a sufficient competitive constraint to Alitalia-CAI services on the Fiumicino-Linate route, as intermodal substitutability in the early morning and late evening slots would still be limited (*i.e.*, the slots preferred by time-sensitive passengers).[29]

Accordingly, the ICA concluded that the Alitalia-CAI monopoly persisted on the Linate-Fiumicino route. As a consequence, the ICA ordered Alitalia-CAI to adopt, within 90 days from the notification of the decision, all the necessary measures aimed at removing the monopoly. Although the ICA did not formally impose any specific remedy on Alitalia-CAI, the decision clearly spells out the ICA's preference for structural remedies, namely the release of time-sensitive slots to a newcomer in the market. According to the ICA, "*the removal of Alitalia-CAI's Linate-Fiumicino market power seems to require the introduction of a competitive restriction that could only be imposed by the presence of another airline that could compete with Alitalia-CAI on the time sensitive slots*", and, "*to offer a credible alternative to the incumbent, a competing airline would need to have access to a number of time slots sufficient to ensure a minimum efficient offer and flight frequencies that could guarantee an adequate supply for the time-sensitive slots*".[30]

Alitalia-CAI appealed the ICA's decision before the Administrative Tribunal of Lazio (*Tribunale Amministrativo per il Lazio, i.e.*, the court having exclusive jurisdiction over the appeals lodged against the ICA's decisions, "TAR Lazio"). On October 10, 2012, the TAR Lazio rejected the appeal in its entirety.[31]

The other key merger reviewed during the Reference Period, and cleared by the ICA subject to an articulated set of remedies, involved the Italian insurance sector. The transaction at stake concerned Unipol's €1.1bn acquisition of Fondiaria Sai ("Fonsai"), through the acquisition of Fonsai's parent company Premafin.[32] Notably, this case is one of the few instances in which the ICA, applying art. 17(1) of the Antitrust Law, ordered the merging parties to suspend the implementation of the transaction pending the expiration of the 45-day term envisaged for the phase II.[33]

The clearance of the transaction was subjected to a twofold set of remedies which can be briefly summarised as follows.[34]

First, Unipol was forced to divest certain assets (consisting of, among other things, companies, brands, insurance portfolios representing a significant amount of premiums, and infrastructures), in a "*short time-frame*" and through the supervision of an ICA-approved advisor, in order to reduce, below 30%, its share in a number of key insurance markets at both the national and provincial level.

Second, strict measures were taken in order to ensure the break of the direct and indirect financial and personal links existing between Unipol and Fonsai on the one hand, and, on the other hand, (i) the Generali group, *i.e.*, the first Italian insurance group, and the merging parties' closest competitor, (ii) Mediobanca, and (ii) the Unicredit group, *i.e.* other important Italian operators active in the Italian financial sector.[35]

It is worth noting that the Italian government has recently enacted new legislation aimed at contrasting the same type of competitive constraints addressed by the ICA in the context of the review of the Unipol/Fonsai merger. Indeed, the ICA has always taken a very strict and critical attitude towards the numerous personal links traditionally characterising the Italian insurance, banking, and financial sectors, as the ICA considers that they contribute to a large extent to the lack of an adequate level of competition in the Italian market. Article 36 of the recently enacted Law No. 214/2011 addresses these concerns by preventing directors, auditors, and top executives of companies active on the banking, insurance and financial sectors from holding similar positions in competing companies.

In particular, in order to contrast the "web" of personal links in the financial sector, Article 36(1) of Law No. 214/2011 set forth new eligibility criteria for corporate governance bodies, providing that "*no member of management boards, supervisory boards and statutory board of auditors, as well no executive officer, of undertaking or group of undertakings which are active on the markets for banking, insurance and finance*" shall, at the same time, serve in "*equivalent*" positions in competing undertakings or groups of undertakings. Article 36(2) clarifies that "*competing undertakings or groups of undertakings*" means undertakings which are "*active on the same product and geographic markets and which have no relationship of control*" (with the undertaking in which a person already serves as an executive) within the meaning of Article 7 of the Italian Antitrust Law.

Pursuant to Article 36(2)-*bis*, failure to comply with the obligation to opt for one of the conflicting offices within 90 days from the appointment to the conflicting office will cause the automatic termination of *both* offices, with the competent corporate bodies formally declaring the respective termination of the relevant office within 30 days from the moment at which it acquires knowledge of the existence of the interlocking directorate. In case of failure to act by the competent corporate body, the sector-specific surveillance authority (*i.e.*, the Bank of Italy of the Italian Insurance Authority) shall declare the termination of the office.

Key policy developments

As of January 1, 2013, Article 5-*bis* of Law Decree No. 1 of January 24, 2012 (the so-called "*Decreto Cresci Italia*"), as converted with modifications by Law No. 27/2012, introduced, *inter alia,* two significant amendments to the Antitrust Law.

First, the two turnover thresholds set forth by Article 16 of the Antitrust Law are no longer alternative, but *cumulative*. Therefore, only mergers meeting both thresholds are reportable to the ICA. This reform will eliminate the merger control administrative burdens and related costs for transactions with little or no impact in Italy. (In fact, a considerable number of mergers will no longer be required to be filed with the ICA.) Predictably, the reform will preclude to the ICA the possibility to carry out the traditional *ex ante* scrutiny of a not negligible number of potentially anticompetitive transactions. This will be the case, for instance, concentrations involving targets with a national turnover up to €47m, and operating exclusively at the local level.

Second, Law No. 27/2012, by amending Article 10-*bis* of the Antitrust Law, has repealed the traditional filing fees system and has introduced a new set of rules for the collection of the funds required to finance the ICA's activities. Particularly, Article 10(7)-*ter* and Article 10(7)-*quater* of the Antitrust Law introduced an annual tax that will be levied on all Italian corporations (S.p.A., S.r.l., S.a.p.a.) which generate a total turnover above €50m.[36] The amount of the contribution is equivalent to the 0.08%[37] of the corporation's overall turnover.[38] Pursuant to Article 10(7)-*ter* of the Antitrust Law and Article 2(2) of the "*Modalità di contribuzione*", such contribution cannot exceed €400,000 which corresponds to 100 times the minimum contribution (€4,000). The contribution for 2013 was due by October 30, 2012, whereas, from 2013 onwards, it shall be paid by July 31.[39]

A number of undertakings have challenged the new contribution system before the Administrative Tribunal of Lazio, alleging: (a) the breach of constitutional principles claiming that the functioning of the ICA and thus the "protection of competition" is a matter of public interest which should not be borne only by large-cap corporations; and (b) the violation of Article 5 of the Directive No. 2008/7/EC,[40] pursuant to which "*Member States shall not subject capital companies to any form of indirect tax whatsoever in respect of the following [...] c) registration or any other formality required before the commencement of business to which a capital company may be subject by reason of its legal form*".

Reform proposals

Three reform proposals presented by the ICA with regard to the rules governing the merger review process are currently under the scrutiny of the Italian Government.[41] The common aim of these proposals is to address and solve, via an amendment of Articles 6(1), 5, and 16(2) of the Antitrust Law, certain divergences between the Italian and the EU merger control regimes.

In particular, the reform proposals concern: (i) the substantive test under Article 6(1) of the Antitrust Law; (ii) the procedural and substantive rules applicable to "cooperative" joint ventures; and (iii) the calculation of the turnover thresholds in case of transactions concerning credit institutions, insurance companies and other financial institutions.

The first reform proposal is directed to align the Italian substantive test with the EU substantive test. According to the latter, an operation of concentration can be cleared if it does not "*significantly impede effective competition... in particular as a result of the creation or the strengthening of a dominant position*" (this is the so-called "Substantial Lessening of Competition Test" – the "SLC" Test – as opposed to the Italian "dominance test").[42] In practice, this means that the EU review process puts greater emphasis on the assessment of the likelihood that the transaction will create "market power" according to an "*effects-based-approach*", as opposed to the current Italian test which – at least formally – still confers the central role of the assessment to the notion of "dominant position".[43] With the aim of bringing the Italian test closer to the EU test, the ICA has also recommended the inclusion in the list of factors to be taken into account for the purpose of assessing concentrations, "*the development of technical and economic progress provided that it is to consumers' advantage and does not form an obstacle to competition*", which is one of the factors expressly mentioned by Article 2(1)(b) of the EU Merger Regulation.

The second reform proposal concerns the so-called "cooperative" joint venture. Article 5 of the Antitrust Law refers to the situation in which two or more undertakings create a new company jointly controlled by the parents. Such transactions may have as their object or effect the coordination of the competitive behaviour of the parents. Where such coordination outweighs the structural effects of the transaction for the undertakings concerned, a joint venture is considered to be "cooperative".[44] In Italy, cooperative joint ventures, even if full-function, are still subject to procedural and substantive rules applicable to restrictive agreements, rather than, as at the EU level, to those applicable to mergers.[45] As a result, the same transaction (namely the creation of a full-function cooperative joint venture) is reviewed under a different procedural and substantive framework depending on whether it falls within the ICA's or the Commission's jurisdiction. The ICA had thus proposed to add to Article 5 of the Antitrust Law an explicit reference to the applicability of merger control rules to full-function "cooperative" joint ventures.

The third reform proposal concerns the method for calculation of turnover of banks and financial institutions. Article 16(2) of the Antitrust Law currently provides that, for banking and financial institutions, *"turnover is considered to be equal to 10 per cent of* [their] *total assets, minus memorandum accounts"*. Based on the ICA's proposal, the new version of Article 16(2) should substantially mirror Article 5(3)(a) of the EU Merger Regulation.

***

Endnotes

1. Article 16(1) of the Antitrust Law provides that a concentration must be notified to the ICA prior to its implementation if, in the last fiscal year: (1) the parties' combined Italian turnover exceeded €474m; or (2) the target's Italian turnover exceeded €47m.
2. According to the ICA, concentrations involving foreign companies which did not achieve any turnover in Italy in the last three financial years (including the year in which the concentration takes place), are not reportable. However, this exemption from the duty to notify does not apply *"when it is likely that, post-transaction, the target company will start achieving turnover in Italy"* (*Notification Form*, Supplement to the Bull. 19/1996, as amended, §3). This latter provision severely restricts the scope of the above-mentioned exemption, since in many cases it is difficult to rule out in advance the possibility that, post-merger, the target company will still not realise turnover in Italy.
3. Article 5-*bis* of Law Decree No. 1 of January 24, 2012, converted with modifications by Law No. 24 of March 24, 2012.
4. Source: ICA's official website (www.agcm.it). Please note that official figures are not yet available, as they will be included in the ICA's 2012 Annual Report, which will be published approximately in March 2013.
5. In one case, the inapplicability decision required a Phase II investigation: Decision No. 22839, Case C1109, *Oviesse/Ramo di Azienda di F.lli Giuliani, Medi & C.*, in Bull. 46/2011.
6. Only *Bolton Group International/Luis Calvo Sanz* (decision No. 23876, Case C11589, in Bull. 36/2012), was cleared without remedies. In the six following cases remedies were imposed: decision No. 22622, Case C11072, *Moby/Toremar-Toscana Regionale Marittima*, in Bull. 29/2011; decision No. 23138, Case C11205, *Elettronica Industriale/Digital Multimedia Technologies*, in Bull. 50/2011; decision No. 23542, Case C11461, *Conad del Tirreno/Nove rami di azienda di Billa*, in Bull. 19/2012; decision No. 23670, Case C11613, *Compagnia Italiana di Navigazione/Ramo di azienda di Tirrenia di Navigazione*, in Bull. 25/2012; decision No. 23678, Case C11524, *Unipol Gruppo Finanziario/Unipol Assicurazioni-Premafin Finanziaria-Fondiaria SAI-Milano Assicurazioni*, in Bull. 25/2012; and decision No. 24102, Case C11799, *Bolton Alimentari/Simmenthal*, in Bull. 49/2012.
7. Decision No. 22590, Case C8027B, *Banca Intesa/Sanpaolo IMI*, in Bull. 28/2011.
8. Out of this total, only one case was closed without a finding of violation (decision No. 22765, Case C11105, *Esselunga-Talvera-Quadrilatero/8 punti vendita (Livorno)*, in Bull. 37/2011). In 13 cases the investigation confirmed the violation and the ICA fined the undertakings concerned (see, *e.g.* decision No. 23796, Case C11354, *Società Italiana Acetilene e Derivati SIAD/Rami di*

azienda di Azienda di Martinelli-I.G.C.-Stella Gas-Zanutto (4 rami di azienda), in Bull. 31/2012, where the ICA imposed an overall fine of €20,000 (for failure to notify four concentrations); decision No. 23797, Case C11355, *Rivoira/Rami di Azienda di Brennero gas-Nicheri-Blugas (3 rami di azienda)*, in Bull. 31/2010, where the ICA imposed an overall fine of €15,000 (for failure to notify three concentrations); and decision No. 23163, Case C11070B, *Finifast/5 aree di servizio "Calaggio Sud"-"Campagnola Est"- Sesia Est"-"Valle Scrivia"-"Arda Est"*, in Bull. 1/2012, where the ICA imposed an overall fine of €30,000 (for failure to notify six concentrations).

9. Decision No. 23496, Case C9812B, *Compagnia Aerea Italiana/Alitalia Linee Aeree-Airone*, in Bull. 15/2012. For a more comprehensive description of this case, see below under 'Approach to remedies'.

10. Law Decree No. 134/2008, concerning "*Urgent measures for the restructuring of large companies in a state of crisis*", converted into Law No. 166/2008.

11. Decision No. 22683, Case C11082, *CVA-Compagnia Valdostana delle Acque/Deval-Vallenergie*, in Bull. 31/2011.

12. Commission Notice on remedies acceptable under the Council Regulation (EC) No 139/2004 and under Commission Regulation (EC) No 802/2004, in OJ C 267, 22.10.2008, p. 1-27.

13. Decision No. 23003, Case C11315, *CVA-Compagnia Valdostana delle Acque/Deval-Vallenergie*, in Bull. 46/2011.

14. Council Regulation (EC) No. 139/2004 of 20 January 2004 *on the control of concentrations between undertakings*, in OJ L 24, 29.1.2004, p. 1–22.

15. Decision No. 23496, Case C9812B, *Monitoraggio Post-Concentrazione Compagnia Aerea Italiana/Alitalia Linee Aeree Italiane–Airone*, in Bull. 15/2012; Decision No. 23739, Case C11608, *Alitalia–Compagnia Aerea Italiana/Ramo di azienda di Wind Jet (NEWCO)*, in Bull. 28/2012.

16. Decision No. 23670, Case C11613, *Compagnia Italiana di Navigazione/Ramo di azienda di Tirrenia di Navigazione*, in Bull. 25/2012; and Decision No. 22622, Case C11072, *Moby/Toremar-Toscana Regionale Marittima*, in Bull. 29/2011.

17. Decision No. 24102, Case C11799, *Bolton Alimentari/Simmenthal*, in Bull. 49/2012.

18. The GUPPI is a revised version of the Upward Pricing Pressure Index (UPPI), introduced by the 2010 U.S. Horizontal Merger Guidelines (see http://www.justice.gov/atr/public/guidelines/hmg-2010.pdf).

19. See, U.S. Horizontal Merger Guidelines, section 6.1, page 21:"[i]*n some cases, where sufficient information is available, the Agencies assess the value of diverted sales, which can serve as an indicator of the upward pricing pressure on the first product resulting from the merger. Diagnosing unilateral price effects based on the value of diverted sales need not rely on market definition or the calculation of market shares and concentration*" (emphasis added).

20. In *Bolton Alimentari/Simmenthal*, the merged-entity market share was extremely high (70-80%, based on volume of sales/80-90%, based on value of sales) and, according to the ICA, the GUPPI analysis confirmed the likelihood of a price increase following the completion of the transaction. The transaction was, thus, cleared but subject to remedies.

21. Decision No. 23739, Case C11608, *Alitalia – Compagnia Aerea Italiana/Ramo di azienda di Wind Jet (NEWCO)*, in Bull. 28/2012.

22. On November 18, 2011, the Chairmen of the Italian Parliament, Camera dei Deputati and Senato della Repubblica jointly appointed Giovanni Pitruzzella as the new chairman of the ICA (effective November 29, 2011). Mr Pitruzzella replaces Antonio Catricalà (in office since March 2005), who in turn has been appointed as a member of the newly-formed Italian Government led by Mario Monti. Moreover, as of December 19, 2011, the ICA has a new Secretary General: Roberto Chieppa. Mr Chieppa replaces Luigi Fiorentino who has also been appointed as a member of the new Italian Government.

23. Case C9812B, *Monitoraggio Post-Concentrazione Compagnia Aerea Italiana/Alitalia Linee Aeree Italiane–Airone*, in Bull. 46/2011.

24. See *supra*, note 11.

25. Decision No. 19248, Case C9812, *Compagnia Aerea Italiana/Alitalia Linee Aeree Italiane–Airone*, in Bull. 46/2008.

26. According to that approach, every combination of point-of-origin and point-of-destination should be considered to be a separate market from the customer's point of view. See, *e.g.*, Commission Decision in Case No IV/JV.0019, *KLM/Alitalia*.

27. The routes concerned are: Rome Fiumicino-Bari, Rome Fiumicino-Brindisi, Rome Fiumicino-

Catania, Rome Fiumicino-Genoa, Rome Fiumicino-Lamezia Terme, Rome Fiumicino-Palermo, Rome Fiumicino-Pisa, Rome Fiumicino-Turin, Rome Fiumicino-Trieste, Rome Fiumicino-Venice, Milan Linate-Bari, Milan Linate-Brindisi, Milan Linate-Lamezia Terme, Milan Linate-Naples, Milan Linate-Palermo, Milan Linate-Rome Fiumicino, Naples-Turin, and Naples-Venice.

28. Decision No. 23496, Case C9812B, *Monitoraggio Post-Concentrazione Compagnia Aerea Italiana/Alitalia Linee Aeree Italiane–Airone*, in Bull. 15/2012.

29. According to the ICA, *"for passengers who tend to prefer these time slots, however, rail still appears to offer a limited degree of substitutability with air so that it is only partially able to constrain the market power of Alitalia-CAI"*.

30. The same approach has been endorsed by the ICA with respect to the clearance of the acquisition of Wind Jet by Alitalia/CAI (Decision No. 23739, Case C11608, *Alitalia–Compagnia Aerea Italiana/Ramo di azienda di Wind Jet (NEWCO)*, in Bull. 28/2012).

31. Judgment No. 4964/2012 of October 10, 2012, *Soc. Alitalia spa–Compagnia Aerea Italiana spa v. Autorità Garante della Concorrenza e del Mercato*. An appeal against the TAR judgment is currently pending before the Supreme Administrative Court (*Consiglio di Stato*).

32. Decision No. 23678, Case C11524, *Unipol Gruppo Finanziario/Unipol Assicurazioni-Premafin Finanziaria-Fondiaria SAI-Milano Assicurazioni*, in Bull. 25/2012.

33. Under the Antitrust Law there is no "standstill" obligation for the notifying parties. The parties are therefore free to implement the transaction at any time after the merger filing without waiting for ICA approval. However, most parties choose not to implement their transactions pending review by the ICA. Pursuant to art. 17(1) of the Antitrust Law, the ICA may adopt a suspension order before opening phase II. This is usually the case where the transaction is particularly complex, it is highly likely to raise competitive concerns and be prohibited by the ICA, which may thus order the restoration of conditions of effective competition, including the divestiture of the acquired business.

34. A comprehensive summary (in English) of the remedies imposed can be found on the ICA's internet website at the following URL: http://www.agcm.it/en/newsroom/press-releases/2001-c11524-conditional-go-ahead-for-ugf-premafin-operation.html.

35. Is currently pending before the TAR Lazio the appeal brought by Unipol against the ICA's clearance decision.

36. See, also decision No. 23787 of July 18, 2012, *Contributo all'onere derivante dal funzionamento dell'Autorità della Concorrenza e del Mercato per l'anno 2013*, with two attached documents ('*Modalità di contribuzione agli oneri di funzionamento dell'Autorità Garante della Concorrenza e del Mercato per l'anno 2013*' and '*Istruzioni relative al versamento del contributo agli oneri di funzionamento dell'Autorità Garante della Concorrenza e del Mercato per l'anno 2013*'), in Bull. 32/2012. In the FAQ section of the ICA website, it is clarified that the annual tax also applies to limited liability cooperative companies notwithstanding the fact that the latter are not "corporations" (i.e., capital companies) under Italian civil law.

37. Under Article 10(7)-*quater*, the ICA may increase such value up to a maximum of 0.5‰.

38. In this respect, reference shall be made to the "item" listed under Letter A1 of Articles 2425(1) and 2425-*bis*(1) of the Italian Civil Code.

39. Parent companies can pay the contribution separately for each of the subsidiaries which fulfill the requirements.

40. Council Directive No. 2008/7/EC of 12 February 2008 concerning indirect taxes on the raising of capital.

41. See, ICA Recommendation No. AS988, *adopted pursuant to Articles 21 and 22 of the Antitrust Law, concerning reform proposals for the 2013 annual competition law*, addressed to the Chairmen of "Senato della Repubblica" and "Camera dei Deputati", to the Prime Minister and to the Minister for the Economic Development, Infrastructure and Transports, available online (in Italian) at the ICA website http://www.agcm.it/segnalazioni/legge-annuale.html.

42. See Article 2(2) and (3) of the EU Merger Regulation.

43. The "Italian test" as spelled out in the wording of Article 6(1) of the Antitrust Law, still mirrors the test applied at the EU level before the entry into force of the EU Merger Regulation, under Council Regulation No. 4064/89 of 21 December 1989 *on the control of concentrations between undertakings*, in OJ L 395, 30.12.1989.

44. To assess the cooperative or concentrative nature of a joint venture, the ICA continues to apply the criteria set forth in the Commission's *notice on the distinction between concentrative and cooperative joint ventures*, in O.J. 1994 O.J. (C 385) 1. At the EU level, the 1994 notice

was replaced in 1998 with the notice on the concept of full-function joint ventures, 1998 O.J. (C 66) 1, which, in its turn, has been replaced by the Jurisdictional Notice (*Commission Consolidated Jurisdictional Notice under Council Regulation (EC) No 139/2004 on the control of concentrations between undertakings*, in O.J. C95 of 16.04.2008).

45. See, Articles 2(4) and (5) of the EU Merger Regulation, pursuant to which: "[t]*o the extent that the creation of a joint venture constituting a concentration pursuant to Article 3 has as its object or effect the coordination of the competitive behaviour of undertakings that remain independent, such coordination shall be appraised in accordance with the criteria of Article 81(1) and (3) of the Treaty, with a view to establishing whether or not the operation is compatible with the common market. In making this appraisal, the Commission shall take into account in particular: – whether two or more parent companies retain, to a significant extent, activities in the same market as the joint venture or in a market which is downstream or upstream from that of the joint venture or in a neighbouring market closely related to this market – whether the coordination which is the direct consequence of the creation of the joint venture affords the undertakings concerned the possibility of eliminating competition in respect of a substantial part of the products or services in question*".

Mario Siragusa
Tel: +39 06 6952 21 / Email: msiragusa@cgsh.com
Mario Siragusa is a partner of Cleary Gottlieb Steen & Hamilton LLP, based in the Rome office. His practice focuses on corporate and commercial matters and he specialises in EU and Italian competition law and complex commercial litigation. He lectures regularly at conferences throughout the United States and Europe and has published numerous Articles in U.S. and European legal journals. He is a professor at the College of Europe in Bruges and lectures at the Catholic University in Milan. He graduated with honours from the Law School of Rome University in 1970 and received a Diploma of High European Studies from the College of Europe in Belgium in 1971. He received an LL.M. degree from Harvard in 1972. Mr. Siragusa is a member of the Commission on Law and Practices Relating to Competition of the International Chamber of Commerce in Paris. He is also a member of the Rome Bar.

Matteo Beretta
Tel: +39 02 7260 8242 / Email: mberetta@cgsh.com
Matteo Beretta is a counsel of Cleary Gottlieb Steen & Hamilton LLP, based in the Milan office. His practice primarily focuses on EU and Italian competition law, a practice area in which he advises numerous major international companies in regards to merger control procedures, and cartel and abuse of dominant position matters. He regularly lectures at the Catholic University in Milan and has published numerous articles in European legal journals. He graduated from the University of Milan in 1991; obtained an LL.M. degree from the Institut d'Etudes Européennes de l'Université Libre de Bruxelles in 1992 and an LL.M. from the New York University School of Law in 1999. He is a member of the Bergamo Bar.

Cleary Gottlieb Steen & Hamilton LLP

Piazza di Spagna, 15, 00187 Rome, Italy
Tel: +39 06 6952 21 / Fax: +39 06 6920 0665 / URL: http://www.clearygottlieb.com

Japan

Koya Uemura
Anderson, Mōri & Tomotsune

Overview of merger control activity during the last 12 months

Over the last 12 months, there were a couple of prominent cases of merger control by the Japan Fair Trade Commission (the "JFTC").

One of those cases concerns a merger between Nippon Steel Corporation, the largest steel company in Japan, and Sumitomo Metal Industries, Ltd., the third-largest steel company in Japan. The combined new company would have become by far the largest steel company in Japan, and would have a substantially high market share in some of the overlapping product markets. Nonetheless, on December 14, 2011, the JFTC cleared this merger with modest conditions with two relatively minor product markets (i.e., non-oriented electrical steel sheets and high-pressure gas pipeline engineering business).

The second case that attracted wide public attention was a merger between Tokyo Stock Exchange Group, Inc. (the operator of Tokyo Stock Exchange) and Osaka Securities Exchange Co., Ltd. (the operator of Osaka Securities Exchange). This was a merger between the largest stock exchange and the second-largest stock exchange in Japan by value of trade. On July 5, 2012, the JFTC cleared the merger only with modest conduct remedies in three relevant service markets: (i) a service for listing stocks in markets for emerging companies; (ii) a service for trading stocks; and (iii) a service for trading Japanese equities index futures.

On the policy side of merger control, the JFTC has been reviewing many cases under the revised Guidelines to the Application of the Antimonopoly Act Concerning Review of Business Combination (the "Revised Merger Guidelines") and the new Policies Concerning Procedures of Review of Business Combination (the "New Procedures Policies"), both of which came into force on July 1, 2011, as further explained below.

New developments in jurisdictional assessment or procedure

The Revised Merger Guidelines, like their predecessor, describe how the JFTC analyses the substantive competitive impact of mergers (in the statutory wording, "substantially restrain competition"). These Guidelines include several important revisions, which are, among others: (i) explicit reference to the definition of geographic markets across the border; (ii) explicit reference to competitive constraint from not only actual but also potential imports; and (iii) a more lenient failing company defence.

1. Defining geographic markets across the border

For a couple of years before the revision of its merger guidelines, the JFTC had been under extreme pressure from Japanese industries and other governmental agencies of Japan. The typical criticism had been that the JFTC was neglecting the reality of international competition surrounding Japanese companies, in that after the burst of the bubble economy in the 1990s, the Japanese economy had not been growing substantially for the last 20 years and was expected to shrink in the longer term, mainly due to the falling birth rate and the ageing population. Further, in spite of a shrinking domestic market, there were too many Japanese companies competing in the Japanese market, but they were too small to compete with larger rivals in the international market: the logical solution to this issue was for

Japanese companies to merge with each other.

On June 18, 2010, the Cabinet adopted a comprehensive economic report named "The New Growth Strategies 2010", and pointed out the necessity for the JFTC to take into account competition in global markets in its merger review.

Against this background, the Revised Merger Guidelines explicitly refer to an example of a geographic market definition in East Asia: "if a major domestic and overseas supplier is selling at a materially equivalent price in the sales areas worldwide (or in East Asia), and if the user is selecting their major supply source from suppliers around the world (or in East Asia), then a world (or East Asia) market will be determined."

The JFTC might comment that the reference to geographic markets across the border simply confirms its current practice and is not intended to change it. However, it appears that this specific reference to the East Asia market is intended to address the public criticism mentioned above. It is therefore expected that the JFTC will define geographic markets across the border in more merger cases.

2. Potential imports

The Revised Merger Guidelines explicitly stipulate that, "regardless of whether imports are currently being conducted or not", the competitive pressure by imports may be considered sufficient to constrain the exercise of market power by the merged company. In other words, potential imports can be considered as sufficient competitive restraint, just as actual imports are. The interesting point about the Revised Merger Guidelines regarding potential imports is that they do not make any distinction between actual imports and potential imports and treat both under the same criteria in determining, in response to the price increase after the merger, whether or not imports of the relevant products would increase within a certain period (generally two years) and thus function as a competitive constraint on the market power that may be exercised by the merged entity.

Some may argue that, even if the same criteria is applied to both actual and potential imports, in reality, potential imports will be far less likely to be an effective constraint than actual imports. They may be right, but since the JFTC generally has a tendency to apply its guidelines relatively strictly, the potential consequence of the explicit recognition of potential imports as a competitive constraint should not be undervalued in practice. Also, this revision is probably intended by the JFTC to address the public criticism that the JFTC has not paid as much attention to the reality of international competition as it should have.

3. Failing company defence

The old Merger Guidelines recognised the failing company defence only in very limited cases, such as when a target (either the entire target company or a targeted business to be acquired) was in net capital deficiency. The Revised Merger Guidelines have slightly extended the defence to cover cases where the target has been "continuously" suffering "significant" operating losses. According to the JFTC's response to the public comments on the draft Revised Merger Guidelines, when the target is considered to have been "continuously" suffering, "significant" operating losses shall be determined from the viewpoint of whether the target is highly likely to exit the market.

This revision is mainly intended to address criticism from Japanese industries of the old Guidelines: that, if an acquirer had to wait until the target became in net capital deficiency, it was often too late to rescue the ailing target. In reality, however, the JFTC had been recognising the failing company defence relatively loosely even by the standards of the old Guidelines (please refer to Xing's acquisition of BMB in 2009). The Revised Merger Guidelines may strengthen the tendency for the JFTC to recognise the failing company defence even more loosely.

4. Shrinking demand

The Revised Merger Guidelines stipulate that, if demand for a product has been "continuously and structurally" falling well under the supply of the product as a result of a decrease in demand, the JFTC may recognise that fact as a competitive constraint on the exercise of market power by the merged company. Because many areas of Japanese industries have been shrinking, there have been a lot of merger cases in which the combined market share was substantially high but the mergers were still cleared by the JFTC, because the exercise of market power by the combined company was highly unlikely. This revision of "shrinking demand" was not included in the original public draft of the Revised Merger Guidelines, and was added in response to public comment. Such incorporation into the JFTC's guidelines of public comment was not common in the past, but was in line with the JFTC's tendency in the last couple of years before the revision of the Guidelines to listen to the public voice more carefully than before.

What "continuously and structurally" exactly means is not explained under the Guidelines, but in light of the JFTC's past practice, this would typically be intended to be applied to cases of product markets where demand has been declining over the years due to a change in market structure, but production capacities have not been easily curtailed because large upfront capital investments were required and a large part of the investment costs were sunk (for example, in the case of certain chemical products). It is theoretically sound and consistent with the JFTC's past precedents to recognise shrinking demand and accompanying excess capacity as a factor to constraint on market power.

5. Neighbouring markets

The Revised Merger Guidelines added another example of competitive constraint from neighbouring markets. They state that, if competing products in neighbouring product markets (i.e., products that are not, in a strict sense, within the properly defined product market under scrutiny but are still considered to be competing with the relevant product) are highly likely to replace demand for the relevant product in the near future, then such a fact may be considered as a factor stimulating competition in the relevant market. This additional example is probably intended to be applied to cases where innovation is very active and currently dominant products are likely to lose the market share. Please refer to the JFTC's decision on the Panasonic/Sanyo merger in 2009, holding that the combined market share of the parties in nickel hydride batteries (almost 100%) was not a problem because lithium-ion batteries would replace nickel hydride batteries in the near future.

New developments in merger review procedure

The New Procedures Policies replaced the JFTC's Policies Dealing with Prior Consultation Regarding Business Combination Plans (the "Old Policies"). Under the Old Policies, the general practice in Japan was that if the parties to a merger thought the JFTC might not clear the merger, to voluntarily consult with the JFTC for its view on the merger well before filing the notification required under the Antimonopoly Act. This was called "prior consultation". Of course, as prior consultation was totally a voluntary procedure, companies were allowed to file a merger notification without it. However, almost all Japanese companies chose to go through prior consultation.

One advantage of the voluntary prior consultation procedure was that, because of its voluntary nature, companies could enjoy procedural flexibilities in various aspects.

On the other hand, prior consultation was infamous for taking too long. Under the Old Policies, the initial 30-day review period (so-called "Phase I") only started, not from the date of the filing of the prior consultation, but from the date when the JFTC admitted that it had received all information it believed was necessary for its merger review. Similarly, the JFTC was supposed to issue a list of questions to the parties within 20 days of the filing of a prior consultation, but since the Old Policies were not legally binding, in reality, the JFTC sometimes issued multiple rounds of questions even after the initial 20 days. On occasion, the JFTC sometimes asked thousands of detailed questions to the parties and, combined with the JFTC's very restrictive position in admitting it had received all necessary information, Phase I did not even start after more than one year. This prolonged Q&A period before Phase I came to be dubbed by some practitioners as "Phase Zero".

Many business people rightfully criticised this practice as unpredictable in terms of the schedule, not transparent enough, and unfair. Some governmental agencies pressured the JFTC to correct it. More fundamentally, the prior consultation was viewed to be a "belt and braces" approach, because after the clearance of the JFTC at the prior consultation, the parties were still required to file a statutory notification under the Antimonopoly Act (although it was certain that the mergers cleared in the prior consultation would be cleared in the statutory review procedure as well).

The New Procedure Policies completely changed the procedure of the JFTC's merger review. Under the New Procedure Policies, the notorious prior consultation was abolished. The main purpose of a new consultation under the New Procedure Policies (now called a "pre-filing consultation") is for the parties to seek JFTC's view on relatively technical issues such as how to fill in statutory notification forms, and the JFTC will not express its review on substantive competitive issues in the pre-filing consultation. That is, JFTC's clearance will be given only through the statutory review procedure.

The biggest advantage of this practice is that the time necessary to obtain the JFTC's clearance has become substantially shorter than under the Old Policies. Now, under the statutory review procedure, the JFTC's review must be done strictly in accordance with the schedule stipulated under the Antimonopoly Act. More specifically, the initial 30-day Phase I review starts from the date of acceptance of the notification by the JFTC, and the JFTC is required to accept the notification as long as the notification form satisfies the formalistic requirements (such as providing information on the domestic turnover of parties' group and market share data in the relevant product and geographic market). In fact, after the introduction of the New Procedure, it has been taking substantially less time to obtain JFTC's merger clearance than before, particularly with respect to competitively challenging cases.

On the other hand, there may be some disadvantages. Since the timeline of the statutory merger review is strictly laid down by the Antimonopoly Act (Phase I review must be completed within 30 days, and Phase II review must be completed within the later of either 90 days from the date of the start of Phase II, or 120 days from the date of the filing of the notification), there is little flexibility in terms of the schedule. Perhaps the most troublesome issue is that under the Antimonopoly Act, the JFTC can issue a cease-and-desist order only before the expiration of the Phase II period. This is so, even when the parties agree on an extension of the review period. In mergers that may raise anticompetitive concerns, parties propose (sometimes in accordance with a suggestion by the JFTC) certain remedies and try to obtain at least conditional clearance. However, due to the strict statutory deadline to issue a cease-and-desist order, the JFTC may not have time to analyse whether the proposed remedies are acceptable, and may flatly block the merger, rather than conditionally approve it. Particularly in cases of mergers subject to multi-jurisdictional notifications, it is important to coordinate the schedule of reviews between different competition authorities, but due to this procedural inflexibility, it could be extremely difficult to make such coordination.

In order to avoid inconvenience caused by such inflexibility of statutory review process, the parties may choose to contact the JFTC well before the filing of a statutory notification. That is, regardless of the abolition of the old prior-consultation under the Old Policies, as a matter of actual practice, the parties may still contact the JFTC in advance to seek JFTC's "unofficial" view on whether the merger may cause substantial restraint of competition. Due to its official position that the prior consultation under the Old Policies was abolished and replaced by the pre-filing consultation under the New Procedure Policies, the JFTC will not officially provide its opinion in response to such an early contact. Nonetheless, in reality, the JFTC generally welcomes an early contact by the parties, and accepts substantial voluntary submissions and evidence from the parties. This process sometimes works like a statutory review under the Antimonopoly Act in some respects (a quasi merger review), but the JFTC does not provide its final opinion (like it did under the Old Policies). However, the JFTC is expected to suggest that it has completed its analysis and the parties be advised to file a statutory notification. This suggestion is usually considered as an "implicit clearance", and the parties can reasonably expect that the JFTC will clear the merger to be reported afterwards without further substantial review. By following this approach, the parties can avoid the inconvenience that may be caused by inflexible statutory review process.

Another approach to avoid procedural inflexibility would be that the parties file a statutory notification without an early contact with the JFTC and its quasi merger review, but that when the review enters into Phase II, the parties intentionally withhold some answers to information requests from the JFTC in order to avoid the 90-day period commencing.

Under the Revised Merger Guidelines, the JFTC will shorten the 30-day waiting period more flexibly than before. Before the revision of the Merger Guidelines, the waiting period was shortened only if: (i) it was clear that there would be no substantial restraint of competition; and (ii) there are reasonable grounds to shorten the waiting period, for example, the target is financially distressed and needs immediate financial assistance and where, in cases of TOB, the payments of the purchase price of tendered shares are scheduled to occur before the expiration of the 30 days. Under the Revised Merger Guidelines, with respect to mergers that clearly will not cause substantial restraint of competition, the 30-day waiting period will be shortened whenever the parties request so in writing, down from around 14 days to around 21 days. This would be good news for companies wanting to close mergers as soon as possible.

Key economic appraisal techniques applied

Unfortunately, economic analysis is not commonly used in the JFTC's merger review. Of course, the Revised Merger Guidelines, like their predecessors, refer to the SSNIP (small but significant and non-transitory increase in price) test (or hypothetical monopoly test) to define a relevant market. In reality, however, the JFTC seems to mainly rely on more traditional evidence such as opinions of customers when it defines relevant markets and assesses possible anticompetitive impacts, rather than sophisticated econometric analysis. In the past, although less so in recent years, in defining the market, the JFTC has sometimes even blindly followed classifications for certain regulatory purposes (which are often completely irrelevant from the viewpoint of competitive analysis). Such practice may lead to market definitions which are easier for laypersons to understand, but tends to lead to rather arbitrary market definitions for the purpose of objective antitrust analysis.

When I represented a party to a merger in a prior consultation before the JFTC, I received a question from the JFTC, essentially asking, "If the price of product XXX increases by a small percentage (for example, from 5% to 10%), will your company switch production from product XXX to product YYY within two years?" Putting aside the fundamental error in this question that if the price of product XXX increases, the company should switch production to product XXX from other products, not the other way around, the question suggests that the JFTC may have been asking a similar simple question to customers (for example, "If the price of XXX increases from 5% to 10% for two years, will you switch from XXX to other products?") and may have been using the answers to such questions for the "SSNIP test". However, how customers will react to a future price increase is, by definition, based on their own forecast and will inevitably depend on various assumptions. Therefore, there could be a serious risk of error in using customers' naked answers to such a simple and straightforward question to define relevant markets, and therefore, questions asking customers' reactions to future price increases must be crafted very carefully.

Furthermore, in 2009 the JFTC flatly rejected a SSNIP-based market definition, replying, "as for the result of economic analysis submitted by the parties, it is suspected that the data on screw-joint reinforcing bars [a product which the parties asserted constituted a relevant product market] used for that analysis is significantly deviated from common assumptions of the SSNIP test", without explaining what "common assumptions of the SSNIP test" meant, and in what sense the data submitted by the parties deviated from them (Kyoei Steel and Tokyo Tekko).

Considering the JFTC's simple and straightforward question and its rejection of economic data submitted by the parties for the SSNIP test, it is very unlikely that the JFTC defines a relevant market by strictly applying the SSNIP test, and even less likely that the JFTC uses econometric data in competition analysis in general. Therefore, few antitrust practitioners take the SSNIP test very seriously in Japan.

On the other hand, when clearing mergers in Phase I, the JFTC tends to heavily rely on the Herfindahl Hirschman Index ("HHI") as a safe harbour. For example, in the case of the merger between Nippon Oil and Nippon Mining Holdings in 2009, the JFTC defined "Asia market" as a geographic market for paraxylene and found no anticompetitive concern with respect to paraxylene, because the post-merger HHI calculated, based on the assumption that the relevant geographic market was Asia, was well below the safe harbour threshold. The JFTC stressed that it quickly cleared the merger in Phase I based on such a broad geographic market and resulting low post-merger HHI, and if the relevant geographic market was defined in Japan, the case would have proceeded to Phase II.

In this sense, how a relevant market is defined is extremely important in Japan, because the JFTC heavily relies on the HHI. This is in clear contrast with US competition authorities, who recently adopted new Horizontal Merger Guidelines which place less importance on market definition.

Key policy developments

As explained so far, Japan's merger control was revised in various important respects both in substantive competitive analysis and procedure. However, there is a further need to reform the merger filing practice.

First of all, the filing requirements should be streamlined. Under the Antimonopoly Act, whether a certain merger must be notified depends on the types of legal structure of the merger, and the filing requirements are similar but different from one structure to another. There are five types of merger structures stipulated under the Antimonopoly Act: (i) share acquisitions (Article 10); (ii) statutory mergers (or amalgamations, Article 15); (iii) company splits (Article 15-2); (iv) statutory joint share transfers (or *kyodo kabushiki iten*, a popular merger structure in which parties jointly establish a new holding company and become a subsidiary of it. Article 15-3); and (v) business transfers (Article 16). These legal structures were originally set forth in the Japanese Companies Act, and therefore, these may not cover all merger structures in foreign jurisdictions. For example, since there is no single provision about reverse triangular mergers in Japan, whether such a structure is required to be filed in Japan must be analysed and dissected in accordance with the five categories above. However, such an approach could be too cumbersome for foreign companies, and trying to make merger structures in foreign jurisdictions fit into Japanese ones may not properly reflect the economic reality underlying the mergers. It is therefore proposed that the Antimonopoly Act should abandon such a structure-based approach and adopt the EU-style which is a more simple and flexible approach that focuses on the transfer of control.

Second of all, the notification forms need to be substantially revised and updated. The current notification forms are slightly different from one structure to another but require similar types of information. They include, among others: (i) descriptions of the parties (such as their name, location of headquarters and main business); (ii) descriptions of the parties' group companies (such as their domestic turnover and amount of gross assets); and (iii) market shares of the parties and competitors in relevant markets. However, the notification forms do not require detailed information on competition in a market at all.

Theoretically speaking, the main purpose of a Phase I review should be for the JFTC to decide whether it is necessary to proceed to more detailed review (i.e., Phase II review). However, the current notification forms are so simple and formalistic that it seems almost unthinkable that the JFTC could decide whether a Phase II review is necessary solely based the notification forms. For example, the notifications do not have to include: (i) the reason why the relevant markets are so defined; (ii) the structure of the relevant market (such as distribution channels and supply chains); and (iii) how easy or hard it is to enter into the market (the cost of entry). On the other hand, the current forms require relatively detailed (and seemingly irrelevant) information on affiliated companies. For example, the notification forms require the name, main business and main business location of companies more than 20% of whose shares are owned by the parties or parties' group companies, as long as those companies have a turnover in Japan of more than 3 billion yen (before the revision of the notification forms on July 1, 2011, things were even worse; the parties were required to report companies [with more than 3 billion yen domestic turnover] more than 10% of whose shares were owned by the parties or the parties' group companies!). However, information about companies in which the parties hold such a minority shareholding does not seem to be relevant for antitrust analysis. Thus, when parties have minority shareholding in many companies, a merger filing in Japan could be unnecessarily cumbersome and time-consuming.

Third of all, under the Antimonopoly Act, who is required to notify the JFTC differs from one structure to another. That is, in cases of share acquisitions, only the acquirer of shares should notify (neither the target nor the seller of the shares need to); in cases of statutory mergers, both parties should notify; in cases of company splits, under the law, the company acquiring the part of business of the other company should notify but the JFTC's practice, interestingly, requires both parties to report;

in cases of statutory joint share transfers, again, both parties shall notify; and in cases of business transfers, only the transferee should notify (not the transferor). However, such distinctions between legal structures do not seem to have strong theoretical basis.

Such distinctions may be problematic, not only theoretically but also practically, because under the Antimonopoly Act, the JFTC has authority to request additional information in Phase I only from the notifying party. Therefore, for example, in cases of business transfers (in which only a transferee is a notifying party), the JFTC cannot request information from the transferor of the business. As explained earlier, before the revision of the merger filing procedure on July 1, 2011, almost all merger reviews were made through a voluntary prior consultation, and since the procedure was of a voluntary nature, the parties voluntarily submitted information requested by the JFTC. However, after the prior consultation was abolished on July 1, 2011, all mergers are reviewed under the statutory review procedure. Therefore, the JFTC being unable to request information from non-notifying parties may cause serious problems. It should be proposed that all parties to any mergers, regardless of their legal structures, should notify the JFTC, and the JFTC should be able to request additional information from all of them.

Fourth of all, it is not very clear when and how the parties can or should agree with the JFTC on the issue of remedies. The language of the Antimonopoly Act does not appear to limit the timing for the parties to propose remedies. In reality, the current notification forms require that the notifying parties propose specific contents of remedies to the JFTC in the notification forms. No company, however, would dare to propose remedies at the time of the notification!

Before the revision on July 1, 2011, this practice was workable because the parties had generally agreed with the JFTC on remedies in a prior consultation (that is, well before the notification). As prior consultation was abolished, making the parties propose remedies in the notification forms does not seem workable.

The New Procedures Policies state that the parties can offer remedies to the JFTC "any time during the reviewing period", but this is immediately followed by the proviso: "provided, however, that the contents of [the remedies] may not be sufficiently reflected in the contents, etc. of the prior notice [of a cease-and-desist order] depending on the time of its submission". Therefore, the parties are likely to be effectively forced to propose remedies in quite early stages of Phase II in order to give the JFTC sufficient time to consider the proposal, but on the other hand, under the Antimonopoly Act, the period of Phase II is strictly limited to within 90 days from the date when the submission of all necessary information is completed, and the parties and the JFTC cannot agree on the extension of the 90 days at all. Such an inflexible schedule may not work very well, and it should be proposed that the parties and the JFTC agree on the extension of the review period.

Ending remarks

Some people may wonder if there will be any change to the JFTC's policy of merger review after the earthquake and tsunami on March 11, 2011. Naturally, if production capacities of competitors were destroyed by the earthquake, it may become more difficult to obtain the JFTC's clearance of a merger in the same industries, because less excess capacity generally means fewer competitive constraints on the merged entity. This general rule may be applicable to the paper industry in Japan, for example. However, setting aside such a general observation, it is highly unlikely that the JFTC will take a protectionist approach (favouring Japanese companies over foreign companies) or will confuse competition policy with industrial policy by giving priority to Japanese companies' competitiveness in the global market in exchange for Japanese consumers' welfare. What the JFTC should do after the earthquake is to further refine its techniques in merger review and keep the review procedure fair, open and predictable, just as before the earthquake.

Koya Uemura
Tel: +81 3 6888 1141 / Email: koya.uemura@amt-law.com

Mr Koya Uemura is a partner working primarily in the field of competition law. His practice includes advising on various areas of Japanese and international competition law, including abuse of dominant position, merger control, and cartels. He has extensive experience of representing his clients (including foreign and domestic electronic manufacturers, natural resource companies, high-tech chemical material companies, medical device manufacturers, and freight forwarders) in investigation of the Japan Fair Trade Commission (JFTC). He also has extensive experience in merger control and has represented clients before the JFTC and obtained its clearance in many cases. He is a member of the Section of Antitrust of the American Bar Association, and an officer of the Antitrust Committee of the International Bar Association. He was selected as one of the "Leaders in their Field (Leading Individuals)" in Chambers Asia 2011 in the area of competition law.

Anderson, Mōri & Tomotsune

Izumi Garden Tower, 6-1, Roppongi 1-chome, Minato-ku, Tokyo, Japan
Tel: +81 3 6888 1141 / Fax: +81 3 6888 3141 / URL: http://www.amt-law.com

Latvia

Ivo Maskalans
BORENIUS

Overview of merger control activity during the last 12 months

During the year 2012, the Competition Council of the Republic of Latvia ("the CC") which is the sole authority responsible for merger review in Latvia, has reviewed only ten merger notifications. The CC has cleared all merger notifications, by imposing behavioural remedies only in two cases. Six out of these notifications were cleared during the first phase of investigation (which according to the Competition Law lasts one month). The number of reviewed notifications is relatively stable as compared to the year 2011 when the CC reviewed only nine notifications (all cleared, only in one case remedies imposed), and the merger activity has not changed much. Such a tendency is rather contrary to the practice of previous years (year 2008 and before) when the CC was overloaded with merger notifications. For example, during the year 2008 the CC reviewed 51 notifications, and the number of reviewed notifications in 2007 was even higher, at 74.

Such dramatic change can be explained by the overall merger activity during the world crisis and the merger notification thresholds which have been changed (increased) several times in recent years.

In general, the CC imposes complete merger prohibitions very rarely (CC has done so only three times since the merger control mechanism was introduced in Latvia), and it is possible to get clearance for a deal even if the market shares of the parties involved are rather high. For example, in a recent (year 2012) merger between *MTG Broadcasting AB and AS Neatkarīgie Nacionālie Mediji*[1], the CC allowed the merger even though, after completion of the merger, the new undertaking acquired a market share of almost 70% of the relevant market (distribution of TV channels in Latvia). In this decision the CC imposed various behavioural remedies on the merger participants, nevertheless some of these remedies consisted only of a more detailed disclosure of the obligations which were imposed by the general prohibition of the abuse of dominant position. This was one of the most important recent merger cases, as it created a significant precedent to be used in similar cases in the future.

New developments in jurisdictional assessment or procedure

While merger activity during the last year in Latvia was not particularly high, the CC has taken a rather formalistic approach with regard to what could qualify as a merger. For example, the CC actively communicated (through the website) its rather new reasoning regarding application of merger control to lease agreements. According to this document, long-term lease of premises where the same economic activity was also preformed previously (for example, a retail shop was present in this premises and the same type of retail shop enters in this premises) is deemed a merger within the meaning of the Competition Law and should be notified to the CC if the thresholds[2] are satisfied.

In these documents the CC has also expressed its opinion regarding calculation of turnover which should be taken into account when assessing whether the thresholds are met. According to the usual practice, the turnover of a market participant is calculated by adding the income from the business activity of the market participant in the previous financial year, sale of goods and supply of services, and deducting from this sum, sales discounts and other discounts, value added tax and other taxes which are directly related to the sale. Likewise the calculation of the turnover in specific cases (in case of insurance or financial institutions) is subject to more complex calculations.

In addition, it should be taken into account that according to the recent practice of the CC in a case on conclusion of a lease agreement regarding premises (which can be deemed a merger), the turnover which must be taken into account is the turnover generated by the particular premises (not an owner or a previous lessee of the premises) to the previous lessee during the previous year (for example, the turnover generated by the particular retail outlet which was located in those premises).

Likewise it has been confirmed by the CC once again that foreign-to-foreign transactions must be notified if the notification thresholds are exceeded, even in the case such transactions have not materially affected the competition in Latvia.

In contrast, the obligation to notify does not apply in case of credit institutions or insurance companies whose main activity includes transactions with securities at their own expense or at the expense of others; have time-limited ownership rights to the securities of the market participants which they have acquired for further sale; if the said credit institutions or insurance companies do not exercise the voting rights created by the said securities in order to influence the competing activity of the relevant market participants; or they exercise the voting rights created by the said securities only in order to prepare investment of the market participant, its shares, assets or the relevant securities, and this investment is made within one year of acquisition of the voting rights. The CC may extend this term upon application of the respective credit institution or insurance company, if it proves that the relevant investment was impossible during the year.

Similarly the obligation to notify does not apply in cases of insolvency or liquidation of the market participant, when the liquidator or administrator obtains decisive influence over an undertaking.

As regards to procedure preliminary meetings and correspondence with the representatives of the CC, such are possible in order to clarify whether in the specific case it is necessary to give notification of the intended merger. It is worth taking into account that, according to the latest amendments to the Administrative Procedure Law (law which regulates the procedure in merger cases as long as the particular issues are not regulated by the Competition Law), electronic communication (including e-mails) can be used in order to exchange binding documents within the procedure.

It is also possible to ask the CC to formulate its opinion regarding the need to notify the merger in written form. However, in order to receive a written answer the CC might ask to present them extensive information regarding the merger and the parties involved, which is almost identical to the amount of information necessary to fill the merger notification.

If the notification is submitted, the CC usually takes approximately one month to adopt the decision with respect to the merger, even if it is clear that the merger cannot raise any substantial competition concerns. Rare exceptions could be made if the adoption of the decision is vital for economic interests of the government (for example, a state owned undertaking sells its shares or assets) or circumstances of the case are so obvious that the likelihood of any competition concerns is very small.

The CC usually takes a careful look at the submitted notification, and if the information which, according to the particular regulation, must be mentioned in the notification is not submitted (even if such information is not material for the review of the merger notification), the CC asks to submit additional information and accepts the notification as "complete" only when all necessary information has been submitted. The CC usually reviews the submitted notification and states whether it can be deemed complete within one or two weeks' time.

The filing of the merger notification must be made prior to completion of the transaction, and there is no mandatory suspension obligation. Therefore, closing before clearance is permissible where the final decision is to permit the merger. If, however, the transaction is finalised after the notification but prior to the decision of the CC, where the decision is to prohibit or permit with binding conditions, the notifying parties would be penalised for an unlawful merger. According to the Competition Law, if a merger of market participants has occurred which is contrary to a decision of the CC, it may adopt a decision regarding the imposition of a fine on the new market participant, or on the acquirer of control of up to LVL 1,000 for each day that the infringement continues, beginning from the day when the illegal activity started. The payment of a fine does not release the market participants from the obligation to comply with the provisions of the Competition Law and with the decisions of the CC. Therefore, the transaction may be finalised before the final decision of the CC, but one must consider the potential risk that the CC might take a negative or conditional decision.

The Competition Law does not require that a binding agreement be executed before the merger notification is submitted. The law requires that a notification should be submitted before the activity which alters the state of the market. Therefore, the merger notification can be submitted on the basis of a letter of intent or memorandum of understanding.

Key industry sectors reviewed and approach adopted to market definition, barriers to entry, nature of international competition etc.

There are no particular industries in which the merger activity in year 2012 or previous years was particularly high. Nevertheless it is worth mentioning that finance, retail and electronic communication sectors, along with several other industries, were on the agenda of the CC during the year 2012. During this period the CC has reviewed a lot of mergers of retail shops, pharmacy outlets and petrol stations, and usually such mergers have not been found problematic.

The CC restricts its analysis to the effect of the merger on Latvia (the CC has indicated it in several recent cases). As regards the definition of the relevant market, the CC usually defines the relevant geographic market within the borders of Latvia. Nevertheless, in several cases at retail level the market has been defined more narrowly. Likewise in several cases where the product in question is traded globally (for example, worldwide commodity exchange for such product exists) the CC has recognised that the relevant geographic market should be defined more broadly than Latvia (for example, in a case with respect to sale of wood pulp).

The CC usually follows the case law adopted by the European Commission with respect to the definition of the relevant market. Nevertheless, local specifics (such as taste and the customs of consumers in Latvia) are taken into account as well.

Key economic appraisal techniques applied e.g. as regards unilateral effects and co-ordinated effects, and the assessment of vertical and conglomerate mergers

According to the principle established by the Competition Law, the CC may prohibit mergers that create or strengthen a dominant position or significantly reduce competition in any relevant market in order to ensure effective competition in Latvia's economy. A 'dominant position' is defined as the economic position of a market participant or several market participants, if such participant or such participants have the capacity to significantly hinder, restrict or distort competition in any relevant market for a sufficient period of time, by acting with full or partial independence from competitors, clients, suppliers or consumers.

When assessing mergers, the CC generally follows the dominant test. Nevertheless in several cases the CC has also taken into account the portfolio effect (i.e. the undertaking will have a competition benefit over its competitors because of the ability to offer a wider range of products as compared to them) of the merger. Likewise the "failing firm defence" (i.e. more favourable treatment of the merger if the acquired target is in financial difficulties) was used as a factor which contributed to adoption of a positive decision regarding mergers.

Vertical mergers are deemed to be less problematic; nevertheless accessibility to the supplies of the product in such cases is the factor to which attention is paid.

Approach to remedies (i) to avoid second stage investigation, and (ii) following second stage investigation

The CC is very open in terms of agreement regarding particular remedies. In the vast majority of cases behavioural remedies have been adopted. In cases where the remedies are adopted, the decision regarding application of remedies is usually taken during the second phase of investigation.

As regards particular remedies, the CC is usually willing to know what remedies the parties of the merger are willing to offer in the particular case, and the offer of the parties is usually taken as the starting point for further negotiations between the authority and the merger participants.

Particular examples of remedies include: (i) the obligation not to bundle two different products; (ii) setting the maximum discount which can be applied in cases where different products are sold together; (iii) restriction to product sale through intermediaries (thus the products must be available from the particular undertaking directly); (iv) imposition of particular contractual terms according to which the product can be sold, for example, terms regarding termination of the agreement; (v) charging the price for launching (instalment) of a service which is consistent with instalment costs; (vi) restrictions on use of a particular trade mark for a certain period of time; (vii) purchase of certain services only via public tender organised according to particular terms (length of the period when the offer could be submitted, obligation to communicate such tender on the website, etc.).

Key policy developments

The cartels and the retail market for consumer goods have been the priorities of the CC during the last few years, and the CC has not prioritised merger control issues. Nevertheless, also with regard to merger control, the CC has followed its overall policy and has examined mergers in the grocery chains industry in more detail than others.

Reform proposals

As for the present, the draft law on amendments to the Competition Law is at a very early stage (the CC is consulting with experts regarding the proposed amendments). One of the proposed amendments foresees that in a case where the market share threshold (40% market share in any relevant market in the territory of Latvia) for the merger notification is triggered in order to benefit from the LVL 1.5m (approximately €2.1m) exemption (no merger notification is needed in the case where the turnover of one of the two merger participants is below LVL 1.5m), the overall turnover of both parties must not exceed LVL 5m (approximately €7.1m).

Besides that, it is planned to introduce a state fee for the review of the merger notification. The exact amount of the fee is still unknown.

It is also planned to increase the fine for non-submission of the merger notification, and implementation of the merger in a manner contrary to the decision of the CC, to 5% of the annual turnover of the new market participant or the acquirer of control (in comparison, the current maximum amount of the fine is LVL 1,000 (€1,430) per day from the day of the illegal merger).

* * *

Endnotes

1. The decision in Latvian is available at: http://www.kp.gov.lv/files/pdf/UNldnCrDP7.pdf
2. The total turnover of the merger participants in the last financial year in the territory of Latvia exceeded LVL 25m and each of the two merger participants has a turnover exceeding LVL 1.5m in the previous financial year in the territory of Latvia. Provided these thresholds are met, the merger filing is mandatory; or the combined market share in the relevant market of the market participants involved in the merger exceeds 40 per cent; and each of the two merger participants has a turnover exceeding LVL 1.5m in the previous financial year in the territory of Latvia.

Ivo Maskalans
Tel: +371 67 201 823 / Email: ivo.maskalans@borenius.lv

Ivo Maskalans has more than eight years of experience in a wide range of complex Competition Law-related matters. With respect to Competition Law matters Ivo has advised such clients as: Coca-Cola, IBM, Maxima (the biggest grocery chain in Latvia), Otis, JTI, Novatours (one of the biggest tourism operators in the region) and others.

Ivo Maskalans has a Master's degree in law awarded by the School of Business Administration "Turiba" (2006) and a postgraduate diploma in EC Competition Law from the University of London King's College (2008).

Before joining BORENIUS, Ivo Maskalans worked as a Deputy Head of the Legal Division for the Competition Council of the Republic of Latvia and practised Competition Law in one of the biggest law firms in the Baltic region.

BORENIUS

Lāčplēša street 20a, Riga, Latvia, LV-1011
Tel: +371 67 201 800 / Fax: +371 67 201 801 / URL: http://www.borenius.lv

Lithuania

Elijus Burgis & Ieva Sodeikaitė
Raidla Lejins & Norcous

Overview of merger control activity during the past 12 months

In 2012, the Competition Council of the Republic of Lithuania ('LCC'), which is a state authority implementing merger control in Lithuania, issued a total of 29 authorisations to implement concentrations. This marked a sharp drop in the number of merger clearances compared to 2011, when 49 authorisations were issued by the LCC. A comparison of the 2012 figures with previous years is shown in the table below:

Dynamics of concentration cases[1]

Year	2007	2008	2009	2010	2011	2012
New notifications received	78	54	42	40	46	Not yet publicly available
New authorisations granted	74	52	47	33	49	29

The number of transactions cleared during the first stage investigation, and transactions cleared during the second stage investigation, is not publicly available. This notwithstanding, it may be stated that the majority of mergers are cleared in the first stage investigation, i.e. within 1 (one) month from filing.

The small number of transactions notified in 2012 is likely to be a reflection of the current M&A landscape in Lithuania. Despite a strong 2011, investors were generally cautious towards the country and the Baltics in general in 2012, and wanted to see how the region would react to the pressure of a weak euro area. M&A activity in 2012 was also impacted by the high number of deals seen in 2011, which meant that many investors needed to reload and were focused on implementing the mergers conducted in the previous year.

The coming years are likely to see smaller numbers of merger filings due to a number of changes to the Lithuanian merger control regime introduced by the new wording of the Lithuanian Law on Competition, which came into effect on 1 May 2012[2]. The main amendments to the merger control regime concern turnover thresholds, non-full-function joint ventures and the concept of a group, amongst others. These amendments are briefly discussed below.

Increased turnover threshold

Pursuant to the Law on Competition, a concentration must be notified to the LCC where, for the financial year preceding the concentration, statutory thresholds are met. The new law has changed one of these thresholds, namely the threshold of the combined aggregate income of all the undertakings concerned, triggering the notification: the threshold has been increased from LTL 30m (*approx* €8.7m) to LTL 50m (*approx* €14.5m). Meanwhile, the threshold of the aggregate income of each of at least two of the undertakings concerned remains the same: more than LTL 5m (*approx* €1.5m). Consequently, from 1 May 2012, the intended concentrations must be notified to the LCC where (*i*) the combined aggregate income of the undertakings concerned exceeds LTL 50m, and (*ii*) the aggregate income of each of at least two undertakings concerned exceeds LTL 5m.

Non-full-function joint ventures no longer notifiable in Lithuania

Until 1 May 2012, the merger control regime in Lithuania applied to both full-function and non-full-function joint ventures. As a result, transactions establishing a joint venture had to be notified to the LCC, regardless of whether the resulting joint venture was 'full-function' or not, once the turnovers of the undertakings participating in the concentration exceeded statutory thresholds.

Pursuant to the amendments to the Law on Competition, the creation of a joint venture which does not perform, on a lasting basis, all the functions of an autonomous economic entity, is not considered to constitute a concentration within the meaning of this law. Accordingly, as of 1 May 2012, the creation of a non-full-function joint venture is no longer notifiable in Lithuania. The said amendment brought the Lithuanian rules into line with the EU rules, which do not require non-full-function joint ventures to be notified.

New concept of a group

When an undertaking participating in the concentration belongs to a group, the Lithuanian Law on Competition requires the undertakings concerned to include fully the turnover of their associated undertakings in order to determine whether the turnover thresholds are met.

The new law has changed the concept of a group of associated undertakings, relevant for calculating the income of the undertakings involved in a concentration. The provisions of the Law on Competition, effective prior to 1 May 2012, required the undertakings participating in a concentration to include, for the purpose of calculating the aggregate income, those economic entities in which their shareholding accounted for 1/4 or more of the authorised capital or assets, or carried 1/4 or more voting rights. Following the entry into force of the new law, only those economic entities in which the shareholding of the undertakings concerned accounts for 1/3 or more of the authorised capital or assets, or carries 1/3 or more voting rights, must be included in the aggregate income.

As a result of the amendments described above, from 1 May 2012, fewer transactions bringing about the change of control are caught by the Lithuanian merger control regime, and are thus notifiable to the LCC. On the one hand, these amendments allowed a more effective use of the LCC's limited resources, by absolving the LCC of the need to assess transactions of little significance to competition. At the same time, the enacted amendments reduced the burden on merging firms.

New developments in jurisdictional assessment or procedure

Intensified control of non-notified concentrations

The Lithuanian Law on Competition establishes a mandatory *ex ante* merger control system requiring the undertakings participating in a concentration to notify the intended concentration to the LCC, and to obtain its prior approval before the concentration may be completed. During the last two years the LCC has intensified its activity, aimed at ensuring that the above requirement is respected.

In 2011, four investigations were initiated in view of suspicion that the undertakings had implemented concentrations without having notified the LCC and without having obtained the authorisations to implement such concentrations. Six investigations were opened in 2012. This marks an increase in the intensity of the LCC's activity regarding non-notified concentrations and is a clear signal that the LCC is determined to take a strict stance on violations of the obligation to notify the intended concentrations where the statutory thresholds are met. In its 2011 Annual Report the LCC stated that, with a view to ensuring an effective implementation of concentration control, all the undertakings participating in concentration or undertakings acquiring control should fulfil the obligation provided for in the Law on Competition, to notify the LCC about the intended concentration and to obtain an authorisation before implementing such concentration. If the concentration is implemented without authorisation, this violates the fundamental principles of concentration control. According to the LCC, regardless of whether the concentration had or did not have any significant adverse effects on the market, it shall assess such infringements strictly and shall impose the sanctions provided for in the Law on Competition, including fines that may amount to 10 per cent of the total annual income of the undertaking having committed an infringement.

The control of non-notified concentrations is likely to remain among the priorities of the LCC in 2013 as well, since, according to the LCC, it allows drawing attention of the entities planning to implement concentrations to the importance of the filing obligation, and deterring them from potential violations of the Law on Competition by failing to submit a notification of a concentration to the LCC.

Self-assessment of ancillary restraints

The provisions of the Law on Competition, effective prior to 1 May 2012, provided that the resolutions of the LCC permitting concentrations shall specify possible restrictions, which are directly related and necessary in order to effect such concentrations. As of 1 May 2012, the aforementioned provision is absent from the Law. This resulted in a change of the LCC's approach towards the assessment of restrictions directly related and necessary to concentrations. In particular, since the end of 2012 the LCC, when assessing notifications of concentrations, does not assess the restrictions on the activity of the parties to the transaction. Such restrictions are deemed to be covered by the LCC's clearance decision to the extent that they constitute ancillary restraints. However, it is now the task of the undertakings concerned to assess whether and to what extent their agreements can be regarded as ancillary to a transaction. The LCC will consider as ancillary restraints those restrictions which are in line with the principles set out by the European Commission[3]. A principle of self-assessment of the restrictions at issue brings Lithuanian practice in line with the EU rules, which do not oblige the Commission to assess and individually address ancillary restraints.

Key industry sectors reviewed and approach adopted to market definition, barriers to entry, nature of international competition etc.

Typically, the LCC adopts short-form clearance decisions that do not elaborate on the LCC's approach adopted to market definition, barriers to entry, etc. Full-form decisions discussing these issues are, as a rule, adopted in cases where objections by third parties to a proposed concentration are received by the LCC, and, as a result, are rather rare.

No full-form decisions were adopted by the LCC in 2012. However, several full-form decisions were adopted in 2011, one of which is discussed in greater detail below.

In 2011, the LCC had an opportunity to review extensively the pharmaceutical sector, since it received three concentration notifications related to undertakings operating on the markets of wholesale and retail trade in pharmaceuticals and other goods. In two instances (when *Central European Pharmaceutical Distribution N.V.* acquired 100 per cent of shares in UAB *Nacionalinė farmacijos grupė* and when UAB *Saulėgrąžų vaistinė* acquired 67 per cent of shares in UAB *Thymus vaistinė*) the LCC issued authorisations to implement concentration. However, the authorisation to implement concentration for UAB *Gintarinė vaistinė,* by acquiring 100 per cent of shares in UAB *Saulėgrąžų vaistinė* and 100 per cent of shares in UAB *Thymus vaistinė,* was issued only after the companies participating in the concentration submitted commitments eliminating the possible adverse effects of concentration.

Resolution No. 1S-208 of 7 October 2011 UAB Gintarinė vaistinė/UAB Saulėgrąžų vaistinė/ UAB Thymus vaistinė: clearance with remedies

By this concentration UAB *Gintarinė vaistinė* aimed at expanding the company by acquiring its competitors UAB *Saulėgrąžų vaistinė* and UAB *Thymus vaistinė*. All of these companies owned large pharmacy chains operating in a number of municipalities of Lithuania.

For the purposes of assessing the concentration at issue, relevant product markets were defined as (i) retail trade in pharmacies in pharmaceuticals and other goods, and (ii) wholesale in pharmaceuticals and other goods. The LCC considered the former to be local in scope, as final consumers usually purchase pharmaceuticals and other goods within a certain local territory (i.e. close to their place of residence or work, or their health care institution), while the geographic market of the latter was considered by the LCC to be national in scope. Only the market for the retail trade in pharmaceuticals and other goods in separate municipalities was affected by the concentration at hand.

When assessing the impact of this transaction on competition, considerable focus was placed by the LCC on those municipalities in which both a pharmacy of UAB *Gintarinė vaistinė* and the pharmacies owned by the acquired companies were operating. It was established in the course of the investigation that as a result of the transaction, UAB *Gintarinė vaistinė* would have acquired significant shares of the market in five municipalities. Furthermore, the market share held in those municipalities by UAB *Gintarinė vaistinė*, together with its closest competitors UAB *Eurovaistinė* and UAB *Nemuno vaistinė*, would have amounted to 79-94 per cent. Therefore, the LCC concluded that the proposed concentration could have caused adverse effects in local markets by significantly restricting possibilities for small market participants to enter or expand in these markets. The adverse effects on competition would have been caused by a decrease in the number of competitors, a considerable market share acquired by UAB *Gintarinė vaistinė* as a result of the concentration, an increased degree of market concentration, and an advantage of big pharmacy chains over a number of other, especially small, market participants only engaged in the retail trade of pharmaceuticals, because the operators of big pharmacy chains were engaged in both the wholesale and retail trade in pharmaceutical goods.

In order to avoid possible adverse effects on competition, the LCC imposed conditions and obligations on UAB *Gintarinė vaistinė*, in particular to divest specific pharmacies in the territories of five municipalities. The divestment of pharmacies had to prevent UAB *Gintarinė vaistinė* from acquiring a significant market share in those municipalities resulting from the concentration, to reduce possible adverse effects on competition and to avoid restrictions on market entry and expansion possibilities for small market participants.

Key economic appraisal techniques applied

The LCC appraises notified concentrations with a view to establishing whether they would create or strengthen a dominant position or would result in a substantial restriction of competition in a relevant market. If this is the case, the concentration will be blocked.

It may be noted that, pursuant to the Law on Competition, dominance is presumed if an undertaking holds a market share of not less than 40 per cent (or 30 per cent in the case of an undertaking engaged in retail trade) in the relevant market. Dominance is also presumed where each of a group of three, or a smaller number, of undertakings with the largest shares of the relevant market jointly hold 70 per cent (or 55 per cent, in the case of undertakings engaged in retail trade) or more of the relevant market.

There is no clear guidance under the national merger control legislation as to how the LCC assesses concentrations. Therefore, we are not aware of particular economic appraisal techniques applied by the LLC. Nor have we recently noticed any change in the way the assessment of concentrations is carried out by the LLC. In our view, when assessing concentrations, the LCC mainly follows the guidance and the decisional practice of the European Commission.

Based on the statements in its 2011 Annual Report, when examining concentrations, the LCC gives particular attention to those concentration cases that involve competing undertakings, since they could have the greatest negative impact on competition.

Approach to remedies

Where a concentration raises competition concerns that it could result in the creation or strengthening of a dominant position or a substantial restriction of competition, the LCC may grant conditional clearance to the merger by imposing certain obligations and conditions on the undertakings participating in a concentration, or on controlling persons. The numbers of mergers cleared with remedies during the period of 2007-2012 are shown in the table below:

Concentrations cleared with remedies[4]

Year	2007	2008	2009	2010	2011	2012
Total authorisations granted	74	52	47	33	49	29
Authorisations subject to terms and conditions	2	4	1	0	1	0

Obligations and conditions imposed by the LCC may be of a behavioural or structural nature (i.e. selling a part of assets or shares, cancelling or changing an agreement etc.). It is for the parties to the concentration to put forward remedy proposals. Such procedure, however, is not explicitly regulated in the Law on Competition or secondary legislation. Then, it is for the LCC to decide on the suitability of the proposed remedies, i.e. whether the remedies adequately eliminate the competition concerns raised by the transaction.

There are no clear guidelines under the national merger control legislation as to the types of remedies that are likely to be preferred or accepted by the LCC. In past decisions, both structural and behavioural remedies were accepted by the LCC. However, when devising remedies, the parties to the concentration could seek guidance from the Commission Notice on remedies[5], as the guidance provided by the Commission is generally followed by the LCC.

Key policy developments

New approach to seriousness of failure to notify concentration

Not only has the year 2012 seen an increased intensity in the LCC's activity as regards non-notified concentrations, but also a radical change in the LCC's approach towards the gravity of the infringement committed by failing to submit a notification of a concentration to the LCC.

In its earlier decisions the LCC considered the implementation of a concentration without a prior authorisation to be a minor breach of the Law on Competition. For example, in *Maxima*[6] and *City Service*[7] decisions, the LCC expressly stated that 'by their nature the infringements of merger control provisions are minor offences'. Accordingly, the LCC imposed a fine of LTL 100,000 (*approx* €28,960) on UAB Maxima LT for implementing 9 (nine) non-notified concentrations, and a fine of LTL 10,000 (*approx* €2,896) on AB City Service for implementing 1 (one) non-notified concentration. Upon completion of an additional investigation by the LCC, the latter fine was further reduced to LTL 8,900 (*approx* €2,577)[8].

However, in its *Corporation of European Pharmaceutical Distributors N.V.* decision,[9] the LCC suddenly changed its approach and noted that the implementation of a concentration without a prior authorisation is, by its nature, a serious infringement. Accordingly, the LCC imposed on Corporation of European Pharmaceutical Distributors N.V. a fine of LTL 110,000 (approx €31,860) for implementing 1 (one) non-notified concentration, such amount being more than 11 times higher than the fines imposed by the LCC for similar infringements in the past.

It should be noted that the aforementioned change in the LCC's approach towards the seriousness of the infringement was not conditioned by changes in legal regulation. Rather this new approach emerged following the decisional practice of the European Commission in its *Electrabel/CNR* decision,[10] where the Commission considered the implementation of a concentration without prior approval to be a serious infringement by its nature, and noted that the infringement at issue breaches the most basic principle of the EU system of merger control, which is *ex ante* control. According to the Commission, the seriousness of the infringement is not diminished by the fact that the transaction does not raise competition concerns. This view is shared by the LCC, which considers implementing a concentration without prior authorisation to be a serious infringement of the Law on Competition, regardless of whether the competition has been restricted or not because of the implementation of the concentration.

The aforementioned development may also have been prompted by the conclusions of the National Audit Office of the Republic of Lithuania ('NAOL') announced in 2011. Having carried out an audit aimed at ensuring a competitive environment in Lithuania, the NAOL concluded in its audit report that the LCC imposes relatively mild fines on entities for violations of competition without assessing damage to the market and consumers; therefore fines do not have a sufficient deterrent effect. According to the NAOL, small fines may have an opposite effect on the objective being pursued: entities may be interested in conducting anticompetitive activities if the benefit received from violation is much higher than the likely fine.

Reform proposals

To the best of our knowledge, no substantial reforms of the Lithuanian merger control regime are currently being considered.

Endnotes

1. Based on the 2011 Annual Report of the Competition Council of the Republic of Lithuania, available at http://kt.gov.lt/en/annual/2011_eng.pdf.
2. Law Amending the Law on Competition of the Republic of Lithuania No. XI-1937, dated 22 March 2012.
3. Commission Notice on restrictions directly related and necessary to concentrations (2005/C 56/03) and decisional practice of the Commission in merger control cases.
4. Based on the 2011 Annual Report of the Competition Council of the Republic of Lithuania, available at http://kt.gov.lt/en/annual/2011_eng.pdf.
5. Commission Notice on remedies acceptable under Council Regulation (EC) No 139/2004 and under Commission Regulation (EC) No 802/2004, OJ C267, 22 October 2008.
6. Competition Council resolution No 2S-21 regarding compliance by MAXIMA LT, UAB with the requirements of part 1, Article 10 and part 2, Article 11 of the Law on Competition of the Republic of Lithuania, dated 16 October 2008.
7. Competition Council resolution No 2S-19 regarding compliance by AB City Service with the requirements of part 1, Article 10 and part 2, Article 11 of the Law on Competition of the Republic of Lithuania, dated 15 July 2010.
8. Competition Council resolution No 2S-13 regarding compliance by AB City Service with the requirements of part 1, Article 10 and part 2, Article 11 of the Law on Competition of the Republic of Lithuania, dated 2 October 2012.
9. Competition Council resolution No. 2S-4 regarding compliance by Corporation of European Pharmaceutical Distributors N. V. with the requirements of part 1, Article 10 and part 2, Article 11 of the Law on Competition of the Republic of Lithuania, dated 29 March 2012.
10. European Commission decision in case M.4994 – Electrabel/Compagnie Nationale du Rhone, dated 10 June 2009.

Elijus Burgis
Tel. +370 5 250 0800 / Email: elijus.burgis@rln.lt
Elijus Burgis is a Partner and Head of Raidla Lejins & Norcous' Vilnius office Corporate Transactions Practice Group. Mr Burgis has more than 13 years' experience in advising on different M&A, privatisation, banking, project finance and competition law matters. International law directories have ranked him among the leading Lithuanian experts in M&A, Banking and Competition law. Elijus Burgis holds a Law degree from Vilnius University, Lithuania and a Master of European Law degree from Stockholm University, Sweden. During the years of his practice Mr Burgis has been an adviser in a number of the largest M&A transactions and financing projects in Lithuania, and has also advised clients on various matters related to corporate, banking and finance, securities and competition law.
Since 2009 Mr Burgis has been a Member of the International Bar Association (IBA); since 2002 Member of the Lithuanian Bar Association; since 2002 Member of the European Young Bar Association, President (2005-2006); since 2000 Member of the Lithuanian Young Bar Association, President (2004-2009).

Ieva Sodeikaitė
Tel. +370 5 250 0800 / Email: ieva.sodeikaite@rln.lt
Ieva Sodeikaitė is an Associate with the EU & Competition Practice at Raidla Lejins & Norcous' Vilnius office. Ms Sodeikaitė advises clients on all aspects of EU and Lithuanian competition law, including merger control, horizontal and vertical restraints, abuse of dominance, competition law compliance, etc. Prior to joining the firm, she practised at another leading Lithuanian law firm and completed an internship within the Merger Network of the Directorate-General for Competition at the European Commission. Ms Sodeikaitė obtained a Master of Laws degree from Mykolas Romeris University, Lithuania. She also holds an LL.M. degree in European Competition Law and Regulation from the University of Amsterdam, the Netherlands, and has been a Member of the Lithuanian Bar since 2010.

Raidla Lejins & Norcous

Lvovo 25, LT-09320 Vilnius, Lithuania
Tel: +370 5 250 0800 / Fax: +370 5 250 0802 / URL: http://www.rln.lt

Netherlands

Kees Schillemans & Emma Besselink
Allen & Overy LLP

Overview of merger control activity during the last 12 months

In 2012, 91 concentrations were notified to the Dutch Competition Authority (*Nederlandse Mededingingsautoriteit*, the 'DCA'), two of which were later withdrawn.

Altogether in 2012 the DCA took 99 first phase decisions and six second phase decisions. Out of the first phase decisions, two decisions concerned cases in which clearance was granted after remedies were offered by the notifying parties. More than two thirds of the DCA's first phase decisions were short form decisions. Six cases were referred to a second phase, which entails that a new filing is made by the parties, in which they apply for a licence to implement the transaction and provide more detailed information. Four of these cases were cleared after remedies were offered by the notifying parties; one case was cleared without remedies; and in one case the licence was refused by the DCA, after it concluded that the remedies offered by the notifying parties were not sufficient to address the competition concerns.

In three cases the DCA granted an exemption from the prohibition to effectuate a concentration before merger control clearance had been granted.[1] The DCA has also published ten informal opinions on questions regarding merger control.

New developments in jurisdictional assessment or procedure

Although there have been no recent decisions relating to warehousing structures, the DCA does not appear to have any fundamental objections to the use of warehousing structures to avoid or delay merger control filings. Particularly in view of the EU judgment in the *Lagardère* case, there seems no ground for such fundamental objections.

The pragmatic approach of the DCA towards mergers which do not raise competition concerns is shown by the fact that almost two thirds of the decisions issued in the past 12 months have been short form decisions. Some of these decisions have been adopted within two weeks of notification.

In its judgment of 13 January 2011, the Court of Rotterdam found that the notification requirement set out in the Dutch Competition Act does not apply to the seller, but only to the acquirer (and the target).[2] Until then, the DCA had on various occasions imposed fines upon both seller and acquirer for failing to notify a concentration. On appeal, the Trade and Industry Appeals Tribunal (*College van Beroep voor het bedrijfsleven*, 'CBb') has now confirmed the judgment of the Court of Rotterdam.[3] In two cases in which the DCA had fined the seller and an administrative appeal was pending, the DCA subsequently withdrew the fine.[4] However, in a separate case in which the seller had not appealed the original fine, but requested that the fine be withdrawn following the CBb judgment, the DCA found that the decision imposing the fine had become final, and that the CBb judgment could not be considered a new fact or a change of circumstances that would allow it to reconsider the fine. The request was therefore denied.[5]

As mentioned above, in three cases in 2012 the DCA granted dispensation from the standstill requirement and allowed parties to effectuate a concentration due to the urgency of the situation. One of these decisions was a short form decision and does not give insight into the reasoning of the DCA.

In both other cases, the target was in financial distress and the DCA came to the conclusion that it was not possible for them to await clearance. In the case *Rabobank-Friesland Bank*,[6] concerning the acquisition by Rabobank of rival bank Friesland Bank, the DCA considered that it was necessary to immediately effectuate the concentration in order to prevent uncertainty among customers and in the financial markets. This view was supported by the Dutch Central Bank. In the *iCentre/i-Am Store* case,[7] the DCA also found that it was not possible for the parties to await merger control clearance. In particular, the tax authority had announced that it was intending to apply for i-Am Store's bankruptcy if payment was further delayed; i-Am Store's bank had already limited its credit facility, and its most important supplier, Apple, had threatened to stop supplying.

Key industry sectors reviewed and approach adopted to market definition, barriers to entry, nature of international competition etc.

As was the case in 2011, in 2012, the DCA examined a large number of mergers in the health care sector. Also, several mergers in the food and retail industry were reviewed by the DCA.

Three notable cases in the health care sector concerned hospital mergers in the areas Southern Limburg,[8] Haarlem[9] and Tilburg.[10] In each of these cases, the DCA concluded after its first phase investigation that a further, second phase investigation would be necessary since the mergers would lead to high market shares in the respective areas, and the possibilities for market entry were limited. Following the second phase investigation, however, the DCA concluded that the respective concentrations would not have a significant adverse effect on competition. The reason for this was, first of all, the fact that health care insurers had means to discipline hospitals in the event they increased their prices. Secondly, the hospitals agreed to a price cap that would apply until at least 1 January 2016. It is unusual for the DCA to accept a price cap as a remedy, and it has been stated in legal commentary that the aforementioned decisions will make it quite difficult for the DCA to oppose future mergers between hospitals.

In the food industry, a notable case was *NPM Capital – Lion Capital – Buitenfood – Ad van Geloven*.[11] Pursuant to the transaction, two large producers of frozen snacks would be transferred into a joint venture between NPM Capital and Lion Capital. The case was initially notified to the European Commission, who approved the non-Dutch part of the transaction and referred the case to the DCA for the assessment of the effects on the Dutch market. In assessing the concentration the DCA found, first of all, that in the upstream market for the production of frozen snacks, private label and branded products should be considered to belong to the same market (both in the retail and in the out-of-home distribution channels). The notifying parties subsequently argued that their private label sales should be attributed to the retailers for the purposes of the competitive analysis, since it was the retailers who determined the price, positioning and marketing of these products. The DCA disagreed, however, stating that not including the private label market share would lead to an underestimation of the parties' market shares, since they were the most important producers of private label snacks. The transaction was cleared, however, upon the condition that the 'Van Dobben' brand for the retail channel would be transferred to a third party, who would have to rebrand the products within the six year licence period.

Key economic appraisal techniques applied e.g. as regards unilateral effects and co-ordinated effects, and the assessment of vertical and conglomerate mergers

The abovementioned *NPM Capital – Lion Capital – Buitenfood – Ad van Geloven* case is the first example of a case in which the DCA has used a 'nested logit model' in order to predict the effects of the notified concentration on prices. The model, that had been previously used by the European Commission in e.g. the *Unilever/Sara Lee*[12] and *Kraft Foods/Cadbury*[13] cases, entails econometrically estimating a nested logit demand system. The nested logit demand system is a particular functional form of demand from which own- and cross-price elasticities are derived. It is based on discrete choice modelling and allocates each product into a particular product category or "nest" to allow for some correlation of consumer tastes across products. A merger simulation is then carried out on the basis of the nested logit demand system in order to predict the impact of the transaction.

Approach to remedies (i) to avoid second stage investigation and (ii) following second stage investigation

In general, the DCA shows a preference for a relatively short first phase without significant delay, and the standard for reaching a second phase is in practice not very high. As a result, in order to avoid a second phase investigation in cases that may lead to competition concerns, notifying parties will generally have to offer remedies in the first phase that clearly remove any competition issues.

An example of this is the *Euretco-Intres* case[14] which concerned the acquisition by Euretco, a retail service organisation, of Intres, which was active in a similar field. Both parties also exploited franchise formulas in the area of sports equipment. On the market for offering sports franchising services, the parties' combined number of franchised shops would have been by far the highest in the Netherlands (70-80%). Even though the DCA agreed with the notifying parties that a larger number of franchisees did not necessarily mean that Euretco and Intres would have more power over the individual franchisees, the DCA considered that Euretco's SPORT 2000 formula and Intres's Intersport formula were very attractive to potential franchisees, given their level of brand recognition. Also, the DCA found that a larger number of franchisees could result in more attractive purchasing conditions, so that the combination would be more attractive to potential franchisees. In light thereof, the DCA considered that there could be potential competition issues in the strong combined position in the market for offering sports franchise services. Following further questions from the DCA on this point, the notifying parties decided to amend the notification in order to exclude from the transaction the sport franchise activities of Euretco. The SPORT 2000 formula would be held separate and sold to a third party. The transaction was subsequently cleared in the first phase.

A notable case concerning remedies in the second phase was *Continental Bakeries – A.A. ter Beek*,[15] in which the DCA refused to grant a licence for the transaction, finding that the remedies offered were not sufficient to address the competition concerns. The case concerned two producers of baked goods. The concentration would lead to overlap and high market shares in the area of the production of rusks. The DCA found that the market was highly concentrated and that the competitive pressure exerted by the remaining market players following the concentration would be limited. The second phase investigation confirmed the DCA's initial concerns. The notifying parties therefore proposed a remedy in the form of the sale of a production line to a third party. Continental Bakeries would place a certain amount of orders for the production of rusks with that third party during a year after the sale. The DCA found this remedy to be insufficient. It stated that, although in exceptional cases a remedy pursuant to which production capacity (rather than part of the undertaking) is sold can be acceptable, the buyer should in that case be in a position to directly operate in the market with the production capacity acquired. According to the DCA, in the case at hand it was uncertain to what extent a new competitor would, as a result of the remedy, actually become permanently active on the market.

In the area of merger remedies, the District Court of Rotterdam issued a judgement partially annulling a fine that had been imposed by the DCA on the Dutch newspaper company *Wegener* for failing to comply with a behavioural merger remedy.[16] The commitments entailed an obligation for *Wegener* to ensure the mutual independence of two of its newspapers (one of which had been acquired as a result of the transaction). The DCA had argued that the commitments meant, *inter alia*, that there could be no commercial coordination between the newspapers. The Court found that in order to be able to impose a fine for breach of commitments, it should be sufficiently clear from the commitments that they prohibit that particular conduct. According to the Court this was not the case in respect of the majority of the conduct for which the DCA had imposed fines. The fine was therefore substantially lowered.

Key policy developments

Following the abovementioned CBb judgment, the DCA will no longer fine the seller in a transaction for failure to notify.

Furthermore, the DCA's decision in the *Saipol S.A.S.*[17] case indicates a change in its fining policy when imposing fines for failure to notify. In the initial fining decision in this case, the DCA had found that the starting amount of the fine should be multiplied by two due to the seriousness of the offence ('the seriousness factor'), since the DCA's 2009 fining guidelines partly had the aim of imposing higher fines. Upon administrative appeal, however, the DCA came to the conclusion that, since there were no specific factors requiring an increase or decrease of the amount of the fine, a seriousness factor of one (1) should have been applied.

Reform proposals

As of 1 April 2013, the current DCA will merge with the Dutch Telecommunications Authority and the Dutch Consumer Authority and form a new market authority, to be called the Authority for Consumer and Markets (*Autoriteit Consument en Markt*, the, 'ACM'). In order to ensure the efficient functioning of the ACM, a draft bill has also been published containing several amendments to the material and procedural rules in the fields in which the ACM will have jurisdiction.

Some of these amendments concern the turnover thresholds under the Dutch merger control rules. First of all, it is intended that the national turnover threshold for insurers be brought in line with the thresholds for other undertakings. The national threshold for insurers is currently €4.5m rather than the €30m thresholds that applies to other undertakings. Secondly, the worldwide turnover threshold will be increased from €113.45m to €150m. It is unclear when the draft bill will be adopted and enter into force.

* * *

Endnotes

1. Decision in case 7149/*Rabobank – Friesland Bank*, 30 March 2012; decision in case 7530/*iCentre – i-Am Store*, 31 October 2012; decision in case 7483/*TBI – Groothuis*, 27 July 2012.
2. District Court of Rotterdam, 13 January 2011, LJN:BP0781.
3. Trade and Industry Appeals Tribunal, 24 February 2012, LJN: BV6874.
4. DCA, press release dated 20 July 2012, *'NMa: geen boete voor verkopende partijen na niet melden concentratie'*.
5. Decision in case 7385/*Driesprong*, 9 May 2012.
6. Decision in case 7149/*Rabobank – Friesland Bank*, 30 March 2012.
7. Decision in case 7530/*iCentre – i-Am Store*, 31 October 2012.
8. Decision in case 7235/*Orbis – Atrium*, 2 November 2012.
9. Decision in case 7332/*Spaarne Ziekenhuis – Kennemer Gasthuis*, 2 November 2012.
10. Decision in case 7295/*TweeSteden Ziekenhuis – St. Elisabeth Ziekenhuis*, 2 November 2012.
11. Decision in case 7313/*NPM Capital – Lion Capital – Buitenfood – Ad van Geloven*, 14 September 2012.
12. Case COMP/M.5658 – *Unilever/Sara Lee Body Care*, 17 November 2010.
13. Case COMP/M.5644 – *Kraft Foods / Cadbury*, 6 January 2010.
14. Decision in case 7316/*Euretco – Intres*, 27 June 2012.
15. Decision in case 7321/*Continental Bakeries – A.A. ter Beek*, 14 December 2012.
16. District Court of Rotterdam, 27 September 2009, LJN:BX8528.
17. Decision in case 6905/*Niet-gemelde concentratie Saipol S.A.S.*, 17 August 2012.

Kees Schillemans
Tel: +31 20 674 1000 / Email: kees.schillemans@allenovery.com
Kees Schillemans is a partner at Allen & Overy LLP. Kees specialises in EU and competition law. He regularly represents clients in proceedings before competition and regulatory authorities and courts. Kees has extensive experience in merger control proceedings before the Dutch Competition Authority and the European Commission. He also advises and litigates on matters of EU law and private enforcement of competition law. Kees regularly publishes on competition law and regulatory matters and is a lecturer in an international LLM programme.

Emma Besselink
Tel: +31 20 674 1000 / Email: emma.besselink@allenovery.com
Emma Besselink is an associate at Allen & Overy LLP. Emma specialises in EU and Dutch competition law and the regulatory aspects of the telecom and postal markets. She both litigates for and advises clients on all competition and regulatory issues related to administrative, tendering and communication law. Emma joined Allen & Overy in 2008 after studying at the University of Leiden.

Allen & Overy LLP

Apollolaan 15, 1077 AB Amsterdam, Netherlands
Tel: +31 20 674 1000 / Fax: +31 20 674 1111 / URL: http://www.allenovery.com

Nigeria

Folasade Olusanya & Adekunle Soyibo
Jackson, Etti & Edu

Overview of merger control activity and procedure

M&A activity has grown remarkably in Nigeria since the first merger in the early 1980s. Today, M&A deals are consummated in virtually all sectors of the economy, culminating in a notable increase in the number of merger notifications being considered for approval. It is, however, noted that the number of merger notifications being assessed annually remains small in comparison with some African jurisdictions like South Africa.

The merger control regime in Nigeria is regulated principally by the Investment and Securities Act No. 29 of 2007 (the "ISA") and the rules and regulations made pursuant to the ISA. There are other sector-specific legislations such as the Insurance Act and the Nigerian Communications Act which regulate mergers, in the insurance and telecommunications sectors of the economy respectively. Regulation of M&As by the respective regulatory authorities in such sectors is subject to the final approval of the Securities and Exchange Commission ("SEC")[1]. SEC is the overall supervising authority for mergers, acquisitions and business combinations in Nigeria. It is empowered by the ISA to act as both a securities regulator and competition regulator for the purposes of merger control.

The merger control provisions of the ISA have been largely influenced by the Competition Act of South Africa. The provisions of Sections 119-127 of the ISA are *in pari materia* with those of Sections 11-15 of the Competition Act of South Africa (Merger Control). Similar to the provisions under the South African Competition Act, mergers have also been categorised as small, intermediate and large[2].

The notification requirements for M&As are mandatory: all mergers, acquisitions and business combinations (whether international or otherwise) are subject to the prior review and approval of SEC[3]. This is with the exception of small mergers[4] or acquisition of shares by a holding company solely for the purpose of investment (but without an attempt to create any restraint of competition)[5]. Small mergers are, however, required to be notified to SEC upon completion of the merger process. SEC may also require that it be notified of a small merger within six months of commencement of implementation, where it is of the opinion that the merger may substantially prevent or lessen competition or cannot be justified on public interest grounds[6]. Upon the notification, the implementation of the merger will be put on hold until it has been considered and approved by SEC.

The merging entities within the intermediate and large merger thresholds are further required to notify registered trade unions representing a substantial number of their employees, or the employees concerned, of the merger by providing them with a copy of the notification provided to SEC[7].

Following the notification to SEC and the employees, a first stage clearance of scheme of merger documentation is carried out by SEC; thereafter, the shareholders of the merging companies will be summoned by way of an order of court[8] to examine and approve the scheme of the merger. Upon obtaining shareholders' approval, a second stage assessment and clearance of the merger will be conducted by SEC before granting its final approval to the scheme of merger. The merging entities will then proceed to court for an order sanctioning the scheme of merger. The court order sanctioning the scheme effects the transfer of the undertaking, property and liabilities of the merging entities to the resultant entity. The procedure for acquisition is, however, different in that it involves one stage of assessment and does not require the sanction of court.

Analysis of M&A notifications between 2011 and 2012

M&A notifications in 2010 increased to 27 from 14 in 2009. There were a total of 42 notifications in 2011. As at the end of the third quarter of 2012, 30 notifications were being considered by SEC. A considerable number of the notifications in 2011 emanated from deals within the financial services, telecommunications and consumer goods sectors. In 2012, the bulk of the notifications occurred in the financial services, oil and gas and consumer goods sectors. Both 2011 and 2012 witnessed a couple of international acquisitions.

The recapitalisation of about five distressed banks, and the policy directive of the Central Bank of Nigeria which discontinued the universal banking model and mandated commercial banks to divest from non-core banking business, were responsible for the significant M&A activity in the financial services sector both in 2011 and 2012. In the consumer goods market, increased foreign direct investment from multinational companies, regional expansion opportunities due to financial crises, recession in the Eurozone countries, and the increased disposable and discretionary income of Nigeria's growing middle class were the driving forces for M&A activity in this sector. Divestment by oil majors of their interests in on-shore assets, and consolidation of operating efficiencies in CDMA telecommunications segments, have been responsible for activity within the oil and gas and telecommunications sectors respectively.

A significant portion of the notifications assessed by SEC will fall within the threshold of large mergers. However, there has not been deliberate effort by SEC to categorise the notifications received along the small, intermediate and large thresholds. Notifications assessed by SEC are usually classified as mergers, acquisitions or restructuring. Below are statistics of the notifications considered by SEC in 2011 and 2012:

M&A STATISTICS FOR 2011

Category	Number of notifications	%
Mergers	5	11.9
Acquisitions	20	47.6
Restructuring	12	28.6
Banking Consolidation	5	11.9
TOTAL	42	100

Source: SEC Annual Report 2011

M&A STATISTICS FOR 2012

Category	Number of notifications	%
Mergers	9	30
Acquisitions	14	46.7
Restructuring	7	23.3
TOTAL	30	100

Source: SEC Quarterly Publication, 3rd Quarter of 2012

New developments in jurisdictional assessment

SEC's approach is to assess every merger, acquisition and business combination. In recent times, SEC has also insisted on its right to be pre-notified even in the face of obvious statutory exemptions. For example, in spite of the statutory exemption from notification for holding companies acquiring shares solely for the purpose of investment, SEC has made it clear that it is required to receive prior notice of such investments by holding companies, and its "No Objection" to the transaction obtained in respect thereof. SEC's rationale is that despite the exemption, such investments should be assessed to determine whether they create any substantial restraints of competition or creation of a monopoly in any line of business.

It is being contemplated, under the proposed amendments to the Rules and Regulations made pursuant to the ISA, that an acquisition will now entail the purchase of at least 30% of shares or equity interests or assets of a target company. Currently, an acquisition is defined as the purchase of sufficient shares in another company to give the acquiring company control. Typically, this will be above 50% of the share capital of the target company. The implication of the proposed amendment is that acquisition of shares of 30% and above of the share capital or assets of a company will be notified to and assessed by SEC. This proposed amendment has been severely criticised, as it will subject the majority of the share acquisitions that are of insignificant value to the scrutiny of SEC.

The proposed amendments to the Rules and Regulations made pursuant to the ISA introduced a new provision for effecting a business combination. It defines a business combination as the coming together of two or more separate companies into a single entity in a manner other than a merger. This process also involves the calling of a shareholders' meeting by way of an order of court to approve the merger, and court sanction for the business combination. The particular difference between the business combination and a merger is not clear from the rules, but indications from SEC are that this will be used for consolidation of related businesses and companies within a group who, for obvious reasons, will not want to go through the rigorous process of a scheme of merger.

Generally, in the event of a failure to notify SEC of a merger, acquisition or business combination, SEC may exercise its powers to investigate the merger and require such company to file the appropriate documents and seek ratification of the transaction. Where the appropriate documents are not filed, SEC would prohibit the transaction. It is also typical for SEC to impose penalties in addition to requesting that new documentation be filed for ratification of the transaction.

Industry sectors reviewed

There were no particular sectors focused upon by SEC in 2012 (or in any other previous years). Typically, M&A deals are assessed by SEC based on the strength of competition in the relevant sector and the probability of the company behaving competitively and co-operatively, taking into account any factor that is relevant to competition within that market. In assessing the strength of competition within the relevant sector, SEC will take into account, amongst others, the actual and potential level of import competition, ease of entry into the market, level and trends of concentration, history of collusion, and degree of countervailing power in the market. Deals with an international flavour will, however, be scrutinised by SEC more closely in order to protect the Nigerian market. Nevertheless, SEC over the years has approved a considerable number of international acquisitions, as shown in the M&A tables above. As earlier indicated above, the bulk of mergers and acquisitions occurred within the financial services, telecommunications, consumer goods and oil and gas sectors. A breakdown of the sectors assessed by SEC in 2011 and 2012 is as follows:

SECTOR ANALYSIS 2011

Sector	No. of applications	%
Automobile	2	4.8
Banking	7	16.7
Beverages & Brewers	5	11.9
Capital Market & Securities	5	11.9
Energy Equipment & Services	1	2.4
Food Products	4	9.5
Hospitality	2	4.8
Information & Communication Technology	4	9.5
Insurance	6	14.3

Sector	No. of applications	%
Manufacturing	3	7.1
Oil & Gas	1	2.3
Other Financial Institutions	2	4.8
TOTAL	**42**	**100**

SECTORS 2011

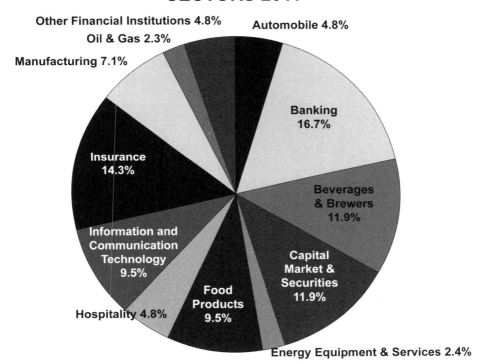

SECTOR ANALYSIS 2012

Sector	No. of applications	%
Automobile	1	3.45
Banking	4	13.8
Beverages and Brewers	2	6.9
Capital Market and Securities	1	3.45
Conglomerate	1	3.45
Engineering and Construction	1	3.45
Food Products	4	13.8
Hospitality	1	3.45
Information & Communication Technology	1	3.45

Sector	No. of applications	%
Insurance	5	20.7
Manufacturing	0	0
Oil & Gas	1	3.45
Other Financial Institutions	6	17.24
Real Estate	1	3.45
TOTAL	**29**	**100**

SECTORS 2012

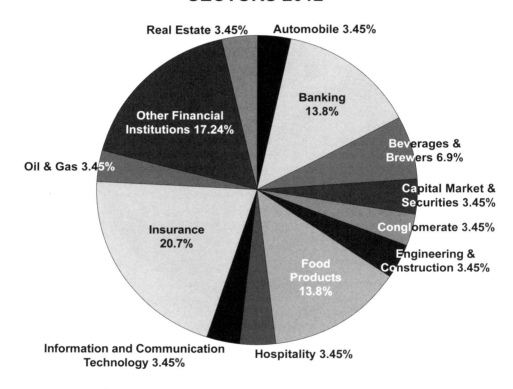

Remedies

Under Section 128 of the ISA, where SEC determines that the business practice of a company substantially prevents or lessens competition, it is empowered to break up the company into separate entities in such a way that its operations do not cause a substantial restraint of competition in its line of business or market. SEC may also prohibit the implementation of a merger, approve a merger subject to conditions, or issue a declaration that a merger is prohibited and impose penalties. SEC may investigate or appoint an inspector to investigate a merger and may designate one or more persons to assist the inspector. These remedies are seldom implemented by SEC; rather, the usual approach by SEC is to require and insist that the relevant parties to the merger provide adequate information, and comply with the requirements of SEC through the issuance of a deficiency letter before proceeding with the assessment.

Reform proposals

A good number of the asset acquisitions concluded within the Nigerian market are not captured by SEC. The ISA contemplates that a merger may be achieved through the purchase of the assets of another company[9]. However, SEC appears to be focused on share acquisition deals. For instance, it appears that none of the acquisition of on-shore assets of oil-majors concluded in 2012 were notified or assessed by SEC, nor are the extant laws clear as to issues to be assessed by SEC in respect of the acquisition or purchase of assets. This capacity of SEC to act as both a securities and competition regulator is often put to question. In most countries, these roles are handled by separate regulatory agencies for efficient supervision of M&A activity. The key reform proposal for Nigeria therefore is a requirement for the enactment of a comprehensive competition law, and the establishment of a competition commission to oversee and set the policy direction for M&A activity in Nigeria.

* * *

Endnotes

1. Section 118 (4) of the Investment and Securities Act No. 29 of 2007.
2. A Small Merger is a merger with a value of combined assets and turnover below N250,000,000.00 (approx. US$1,500,000.00), Intermediate Merger is one with a value above N250,000,000.00 but less than N5,000,000,000.00 (approx. US$31,250,000.00) while the larger merger is with value above N5,000,000,000.00 (approx. US$31,250,000.00). (See Section 120 of the ISA and Rule 232 (B) of the SEC Rules and Regulations.)
3. Section 118 (1) of the Investment and Securities Act No. 29 of 2007.
4. Section 122 (1) of the Investment and Securities Act No. 29 of 2007.
5. Section 118 (3) of the Investment and Securities Act No. 29 of 2007.
6. Section 122 (3) of the Investment and Securities Act No. 29 of 2007.
7. Section 123 (2) of the Investment and Securities Act No. 29 of 2007.
8. The Federal High Court assumes jurisdiction over company matters in Nigeria.
9. Section 19 (2) (a) of the Investment and Securities Act No. 29 of 2007.

Folasade Olusanya
Tel: +234 1 773 6361 / Email: folaolusanya@jacksonettiandedu.com
Folasade Olusanya is a Partner and head of the Corporate/Commercial Department at
Jackson, Etti & Edu. She advises on complex Mergers and Acquisitions and Cross-
Border Acquisitions within Nigeria and the West African sub-region respectively. She
has been consistently ranked in the Chambers and Partners 2008-2012 Editions and was
recently described in the 2012 Edition as "terrific on legal matters" and recommended
for her excellent all-round practice. She is also listed as a leading lawyer in the Mergers
and Acquisitions Category by IFLR 2013. Folasade is an active member of the Mergers
and Acquisitions Committees of the Capital Markets Solicitors Association in Nigeria
and the Section on Business Law of the Nigerian Bar Association. She also advises in
relation to banking and finance and capital markets matters.

Adekunle Soyibo
Tel: +234 1 773 6361 / Email: kunlesoyibo@jacksonettiandedu.com
Adekunle Soyibo is a Senior Associate at Jackson, Etti & Edu and an integral member
of the Merger and Acquisitions Group of the Corporate / Commercial Department. He
has advised on big ticket Mergers and Acquisitions within banking, insurance, oil and
gas and manufacturing sectors. The recent acquisition of Union Bank of Nigeria Plc
by a consortium of private equity firms in which he was involved was described in the
IFLR 2013 as "the largest private equity deal in Sub-Saharan Africa". Adekunle is a
member of the Merger and Acquisitions Committee of the Section on Business Law
of the Nigerian Bar Association and also advises in relation to power, private equity
and tax matters.

Jackson, Etti & Edu

3-5 Sinari Daranijo Street, Off Ajose Adeogun, Victoria Island, Lagos, Nigeria
Tel: +234 1 462 6841 / Fax: +234 1 271 6889 / URL: http://www.jacksonettiandedu.com

Norway

Eivind Vesterkjær & Eivind Sæveraas
Advokatfirmaet Thommessen AS

Overview of merger control activity during the last 12 months

During the period February 2012 to February 2013, the Norwegian Competition Authority ("NCA") received 359 standardised notifications – out of which 344 were cleared after phase I (15 days working period) and 11 during phase II (maximum 125 working days). In effect, the NCA intervened in five cases. Two concentrations were prohibited, whilst three concentrations were approved subject to commitments.[1]

Compared to previous years, the number of notifications seems to have remained stable, albeit there has been a slight increase in the number of intervention decisions in the last year.[2] Statistics show that a complete notification is ordered in roughly 3% of cases.

No cases were referred to the European Commission, but the Commission has referred parts of one case to the Norwegian Competition Authority.[3]

New developments in jurisdictional assessment or procedure

Overview

The Norwegian merger control regime has not undergone significant changes in recent years. A brief recap of some key jurisdictional issues is given below in the section, 'Key jurisdictional issues'.

Among the significant developments are: (i) the issuance by the NCA of a guidance letter confirming that the Norwegian merger control regime only applies to concentrations with effect in the country (see section below, 'Concentrations having an effect within the realms of Norway'); (ii) recent case law from the NCA pertaining to jurisdictional questions including asset transfers and the question of whether or not the assets transferred constitute a business with a market presence, triggering a merger filing obligation (see section below, 'Norgesgruppen case'); and (iii) case law from the NCA pertaining to sanctions against pre-implementation ("gun jumping") (see section below, 'Pre-implementation').

Finally, it should be noted that the Report of the Committee and the proposals submitted to the Ministry in the report of 14 February 2012 are likely to change this. A summary of some of the key proposals is given below.

Brief recall of some key jurisdictional issues

Notification of concentrations which meet the jurisdictional thresholds is compulsory in Norway.

Mergers which qualify for merger review, but raise no concerns, are cleared in the first phase, i.e. after 15 working days. Note that even in these instances, the NCA does not approve concentrations prior to the expiry of the 15 working days period.

The standardised notification can be done by a relatively simple form, in which the parties are required to describe their market activities, any affected markets (i.e. markets in which the parties' activities overlap and they have a combined market share post-concentration of 20% or more – or where there are vertical issues) and name the five most important competitors, customers and suppliers within these affected markets.

Pre-notification contact with the NCA is not mandatory and normally not initiated. If initiated due to the complexity of the concentration, the substantive issues raised or the timing of the transaction, the NCA is nevertheless often positive to pre-notification contact in the form of an informal meeting or briefing memo. However, the NCA will not formally take a position on any substantive issues during such pre-notification contact.

The Norwegian Competition Act only requires merger filings for concentrations that are of a lasting nature. Warehousing is therefore generally not excluded under the NCA if the transfer of the shares (or assets) to the trustee is temporary, but should be carefully assessed on a case-by-case basis. The Norwegian Merger Control regime does not contain a similar clause as the EUMR Article 3 (5) *litraa*. This could entail that the parties have somewhat more discretion as to how the warehousing is organised (for instance, it is not clear whether or not the trustee must be a financial institution).

The Norwegian merger control regime only applies to concentrations having an effect within the realms of Norway

Pursuant to Section 5 of the Norwegian Competition Act, only actions that produce, or are liable to produce, effects in Norway fall within the scope of the Act. The NCA has recently confirmed in a written guidance letter[4] that this general principle also applies with regard to the merger control rules. The effect doctrine has implications both for the obligation to notify concentrations and for the NCA's power to intervene against a concentration or acquisition.

Firstly, concentrations that neither produce nor are liable to produce any effects in Norway do not require notification, even if the jurisdictional thresholds are exceeded. This may be the case, for example, if the geographic market affected by the concentration does not comprise the territory of Norway, but the Norwegian notification thresholds are nevertheless exceeded, as a result of revenues originating from unrelated activities pursued by the undertakings concerned in other product markets. In practice, such concentrations are rarely notified.

The effects criterion is subject to interpretation and in order to eliminate any risk of sanctions, it is usually preferred to draft a cost-effective standardised notification, meeting the minimum information requirements. Such notifications are usually cleared during the 15 working days period without any difficulties.

Secondly, the NCA only has the power to intervene against a concentration if the NCA can substantiate that the concentration will produce, or is liable to produce, effects in Norway (and provided that the concentration creates or strengthens a significant restriction of competition).

The NCA's merger control review of the ICA – Norgesgruppen case: Assignment of lease agreements to premises and transfer via single purpose joint venture – a concentration within the meaning of Norwegian merger control

In August 2012 the NCA ordered a complete notification regarding Norgesgruppen's take-over of the ownership/tenancy rights of Ica Maxi's grocery store premises in 12 locations in Norway. Norgesgruppen ASA ("Norgesgruppen") and ICA Norge AS ("ICA") together, are estimated to have about half of all sales in the groceries market in Norway.

The concentrations raised several difficult jurisdictional issues pertaining to: (i) whether or not transfer of lease agreements constituted a notifiable transaction; (ii) whether the transfer of several lease agreements between the same parties constituted one or several concentrations; (iii) whether the established single purpose joint venture was an undertaking concerned in the concentration, or only the seller and the ultimate buyer were undertakings concerned; and (iv) whose turnover should be decisive for the assessment of the jurisdictional thresholds.

The key facts of the case were as follows:
*   On 26 April 2012 Lagopus Eiendomsutvikling AS (Lagopus) entered into an agreement with the retail chain ICA concerning the takeover of 23 properties – some through ownership takeover and some through leaseholds takeover. The properties were previously utilised by ICA under the chain concept 'ICA Maxi' supermarkets.
*   Prior to the transfer of the properties and the lease contracts, the ICA Maxi supermarkets ceased business. Lagopus did not therefore take over the business of ICA Maxi as such. The

warehouse, furnishing, equipment, chain concept, supply-contracts and local supply agreements were part of the assets transfer deal.

- Lagopus is a consortium of miscellaneous market players within the real estate and retail markets, established to restructure the properties, renegotiate the overtaken lease contracts, locate new tenants and resell the overtaken (and if necessary restructured) properties. The owners are Norgesgruppen (35%), Solist (25%), Profilér (25%) and Guardian Capital (15%).
- During the summer of 2012 Lagopus entered into lease agreements with Norgesgruppen and several other tenants. Norgesgruppen (and the chain concepts Meny, Eurospar and Spar Kjøp) was the biggest tenant, taking over 60/70% of the premises previously operated by ICA Maxi.
- Norgesgruppen committed to rehire at least 750 of the ICA employees.

The NCA ordered Norgesgruppen to notify the acquisition of both the properties and the lease contracts, on the basis that the acquisition of the properties and the lease contracts from ICA (via Lagopus) constituted one single concentration – or alternatively several notifiable concentrations. The NCA was of the opinion that an investigation was necessary, as potential negative effects on the grocery market both nationally and locally were suspected.

The case is still under investigation, however it follows from the letter the NCA sent to the parties on 17 August 2012, ordering the complete notification, that the assignment of tenancy rights was equivalent to a transfer of property within the meaning of the Competition Act, due to the long duration of the leaseholds.

The NCA considered that the physical location (the premises) is the essential asset in the grocery market, since the customers are loyal to the location of the store. The NCA equated the assignment of tenancy rights with an assignment of the grocery business as such. This was due to, amongst other facts, that a buyer of a grocery business which intends to re-establish a grocery business in the same premises, often is a competing grocery chain, therefore already possessing the necessary additional inputs to conduct business (i.e. intellectual property rights, know how, purchase and distribution agreements etc.). Moreover, the majority of the agreements assigned contained a clause which required a complete assortment of groceries.

Based on the NCA's assessment, it should be noted that the transfer of lease agreements may constitute a notifiable concentration even if warehouse, furnishing and equipment, supply-contracts or local supply agreements are not taken over. The NCA found support in this conclusion in the fact that Norgesgruppen – as a majority stakeholder in Lagopus – committed itself to offer an important number of ICA employees work at the affected locations. Norgesgruppen and the other stakeholders were to make sure that at least 2/3 of the ICA employees were offered jobs. It did not alter the assessment of notifiability that the transfer of lease agreements by itself required the landlords' consents.

The NCA did not consider Lagopus an undertaking concerned in the concentration, and the fact that Lagopus had no turnover did not therefore affect the assessment of the merger filing requirement.

As concerns the transfer of the lease agreements from ICA Norge to Lagopus, the NCA does not seem to consider this a separate concentration within the NCA. In any event, this transaction was transitory in nature and therefore did not constitute a lasting change of control.

Pre-implementation ("gun jumping") – sanctioned with fine of approx. €50,000

In 2012 the NCA considered four cases pertaining to pre-implementation of concentrations and violation of the standstill obligation. In doing so, the NCA significantly raised the level of fines from previous cases.

Generally, non-compliance with the obligation to file notifiable concentrations exceeding the jurisdictional thresholds can be sanctioned with imprisonment, criminal fines and administrative fines. In practice, only the latter sanction is effectively applied by the NCA.

The NCA does not sanction violations of the obligation to file as such. Instead it sanctions the resulting violation of the stand-still obligation. Under the current regime there is an automatic standstill obligation after the first 15 days, which can be automatically extended by another 25 days if the NCA decides to investigate the transaction further. Adding to this, the NCA has the ability to impose individual standstill obligations. In its report the Committee has suggested establishing an automatic standstill obligation until the case is closed, however it is emphasised that the parties may apply for an exemption from the standstill obligation[5].

To date, the NCA has only accorded such exemptions in a few cases where at least one of the parties was in financial difficulty[6]. This is in line with the preparatory works, which state that an exemption should only be accorded to prevent serious consequences for the parties or the society as such.

In principle, the maximum fine for violating the standstill obligation may amount to up to 10% of the (group) revenues of the undertaking concerned in the last financial year. In practice the fines for breaching the standstill obligation are significantly lower and have (to date) never been higher than 0.1% of the consolidated turnover of the undertaking concerned. The highest administrative fines imposed to this date amount to NOK 350,000 (approximately US$60,000 or €48,000) (August 2012).

In the four cases dealt with by the NCA in 2012, the fines ranged from NOK 250,000 to NOK 350,000.[7] In all but one case: (i) the infringement was notified to the NCA on the undertaking's own initiative; (ii) acts of implementation were wholly or partly reversible; and (iii) the concentrations did not have any negative effects on competition. It is assumed that the level of the fines would be higher, had these elements not been present.

In the last case the acts of implementation were irreversible (physical integration), but the fine was somewhat reduced due to the incumbent company's assistance in the infringement case, and the long case handling period.[8] The fine was set to NOK 300,000.

Note that the NCA has applied a strict interpretation of the standstill clause and the notion of implementation. Thus, in V2012-15 the implementation consisted in transferring the transaction fee to a settlement agent, while the settlement agent at the same time had registered the share transfer in the shareholder book.

Key industry sectors reviewed and approach adopted to market definition, barriers to entry, nature of international competition etc.

Overview

The mergers considered by the NCA cover a wide range of industry sectors. The geographic focus of the cases dealt with by the NCA is national (and in particular regional or local) competition issues. This is a consequence of the low jurisdictional turnover thresholds and the interplay with the EUMR mechanisms. By its membership of the EFTA and its accession to the EEA-Agreement, Norway is bound by the EUMR jurisdictional mechanisms. This entails that the NCA generally has no competence in cases which have a community dimension and where the European Commission is therefore competent to act, i.e. mergers involving major market players and potentially affecting several EU member states.

If any industry sectors should be highlighted, the NCA appears to have a particular focus on retailing (in particular food-retailing/grocery, but also bookstores, gardening stores etc.), media (local advertising market) and telecommunications/broadband wholesale markets.

Geographically, the NCA has a tendency to focus on local or regional aspects in its merger control, thus being loyal to statements in the preparatory works of the Competition Act. There are several examples of cases where remedies on local markets have been necessary to obtain clearance of transactions that did not give rise to significant concern at the national level. In the past 12 months the NCA has continued this focus on local markets, entailing that local and/or regional markets were defined in four out of the five cases in which the NCA intervened in 2012/2013.

Retailing

The structure of the Norwegian food retailing market has generally benefited four major grocery retailers, which together hold a combined market share of up to 90%: Norgesgruppen is the leader in grocery retailers, followed by Coop Norge Handel, Reitangruppen and ICA Norge. Added to this, the supply industry for several products is also concentrated.

In 2010, the Norwegian government established a group called the Food Chain Evaluation Committee *(Matvarekjedeutvalget),* consisting of representatives from government, grocery, and other interest groups. It conducted an in-depth evaluation about whether the industry structure in 2011 ultimately benefits consumers. In April 2011, the committee presented a number of conclusions and recommendations about how to improve conditions in grocery retailers. One of the conclusions stated that leading grocery retailers engage in non-competitive practices. The conclusions were hotly debated in the industry, and are still under evaluation.

The NCA is currently dealing with several cases pertaining to the food retailing market and the upstream markets.

Firstly, the NCA is currently handling a complete notification as concerns the establishment of a full-function joint venture for a full-range assortment of food, nutrition, direct-distributed diary products and related goods (wholesale) by Tine SA ("Tine") and Servicegrossistene AS ("Servicegrossistene"). Tine is Norway's largest producer, distributor and exporter of dairy products, whilst Servicegrossistene is an independent food retailer (wholesale) to the institutional household markets.

Secondly, the NCA is handling a complete notification as concerns Orkla ASA's acquisition of control of Rieber & Søn ASA (referred from the Commission with regards to the transaction that affects the Norwegian market). Whilst Orkla is a leading branded consumer goods company in the Nordic region, Rieber & Søn is also a focused foods company, with several strong food retail brands in Norway (and other countries).

Thirdly, the NCA is considering several standardised notifications related to the food retailing markets.[9]

Lastly, and as mentioned above, the NCA considered – and cleared – Norgesgruppen's acquisition of the ICA Maxi properties and lease agreements.

The NCA has also considered other retailing markets:

In case V2012-18 Plantasjen/Oddernes Gartneri, the NCA considered a concentration involving two major gardening retailers in the Kristiansand area in the south of Norway. The NCA prohibited the concentration, based on the negative horizontal effects on competition which were identified in the local market. The relevant market was sale of gardening goods to consumers sold by gardening retailers in the Kristiansand area (under 20 minutes' travel time from Oddernes Gartneri). Prior to the concentration, the market was concentrated and characterised by high barriers to entry (few new entries, high investment costs) and limited potential competition. Post-concentration, the market would be characterised by very high market concentration, limited responding possibilities and high barriers to entry. The alleged efficiencies could not sufficiently outweigh the loss of competition. See further discussions regarding this case and the approach taken by the NCA in the section, 'Key economic appraisal techniques'.

In case V2011-5, the NCA intervened against the proposed merger between the Norwegian bookstore chains Norli and Libris and ordered divestiture of several local bookstores. The reason was that several of the local bookstore markets were characterised by high concentration, high barriers to entry and limited potential competition. In the NCA's view the merger would lead to reduced competition in the sale of physical books from general bookstores in Trondheim, Kristiansand, Drammen, Kongsberg, Lillehammer, Haugesund, Levanger and Sarpsborg.

Telecommunication/broadband wholesale markets

In case V2012-8 (Telenor/LOS Bynett) conditional approval was granted of Telenor Norge AS's purchase of Los Bynett AS and Bynytt Privat AS. The concentration concerned the markets for (i) sale of wholesale market for trunk segments of leased lines with capacity above 8 mbit/s, and (ii) sale of internet access to private consumers. Both markets were defined as regional markets confined to the Agder-region and Vestfold region. This was due to the geographic scope of Los Bynett's network infrastructure (substitution possibilities).

Pre-concentration, the wholesale market was, according to the NCA, characterised by high concentration ratio, high barriers to entry and limited potential competition (high investment costs relating to the establishment of own infrastructure, and uncertainty as to the possibility of leasing infrastructure from Telenor), and a moderate degree of buyer power. These characteristics would be further enhanced post-concentration in particular, since the parties were close competitors.

Against this background, the NCA ordered the parties to sell/make available a continuous transport network within the Agder-region, and that Telenor re-let capacity of which Los Bynett disposes in the Vestfold region, and accepts reasonable requests for access pertaining to leased lines to business customers insofar as the Telenor and Los Bynett infrastructure overlaps.

As concerns the retail market, the NCA assessed that this market was also characterised by high market concentration and high barriers to entry, with limited potential competition. Post-transaction, the parties would have close to a monopoly market position, and incentives to raise price. In conclusion, the NCA nevertheless found that the alleged and approved efficiencies outweighed the loss of competition.

In a similar case also involving broadband wholesale markets concerning Startfase 483 AS (EQT) and Ventelo Holding AS, the NCA did on 30 January 2012 also order complete notification. The concentration was ultimately cleared without conditions.

Media/advertising markets

In case V2012-11 A-Pressen/Mecom (Edda Media), the NCA found that the geographic market should be defined as local/regional. The NCA emphasised the degree of substitutability in the local/regional markets, and placed a lot of weight on the use of diversion rates and market surveys. See further discussions regarding this case and the approach taken by the NCA in the section, 'Key economic appraisal techniques'.

Other relevant cases

In case V2013-1 involving Nor Textil AS and Sentralvaskeriene AS, the NCA revealed competition concerns in the regional market for dry-cleaning of flat clothes, and prohibited the concentration. Potential competition from Sweden was not taken into consideration in this case, based on the fact that the Norwegian prices were 10-15% lower than the prices in Sweden, which according to the NCA did not give the potential competition any incentives to enter the Norwegian market.

In case V2012-10 concerning Mekonomen AB's acquisition of sole control in Meca Scandinavia AB, the NCA considered the aftermarkets for spare parts and other automobile-related products. Both parties were independent market players within this aftermarket, supplying spare parts to wholesalers and consumers.

The NCA defined the relevant product market as sale of spare parts, save tyres, vehicle body, rim and car glass, to independent repair shops from independent spare parts wholesalers covering a broad product portfolio. As concerns the relevant geographic market, the NCA made a preliminary conclusion that this was national, although no final conclusion was made, since this was not necessary in order to conclude the competitive analysis. The NCA found that the market was characterised by a high concentration ratio, considerable barriers to entry, limited possibilities to respond to price increases given the intricate distribution networks, and lock-in mechanisms pre-concentration. The parities' combined market share was around 50-60%. The NCA cleared the concentration on condition that the acquirer had to apply non-discriminatory terms towards the repair shops, and reduce the lock-in measures.

Key economic appraisal techniques applied e.g. as regards unilateral effects and co-ordinated effects, and the assessment of vertical and conglomerate mergers

Overview

The NCA has in two recent cases started to implement alternative economic techniques to supplement the definition of the relevant market by estimating diversion ratios through the use of customer surveys. The first case concerned the media market, and involved a proposal from A-pressen AS to purchase Edda Media AS (owned by Mecom Europe AS).[10] The second case concerned the retailing (gardening) market and involved Plantasjen's proposal to purchase Oddernes Gartneri (see 'Key industry sectors: retailing', above).

Illustration: A-pressen's acquisition of Edda Media

The NCA started to consider A-Pressen's proposal to acquire Edda Media in late 2011. Both companies have business activities within several media-related areas and are regarded as the second- and third-largest "media houses" in Norway – Schibsted ASA being the largest.

The main areas of overlap between A-pressen and Edda Media are local and regional newspapers with circulation in the urban and rural areas in the South and South-West parts of Norway.

The NCA concluded that the merger would create a significant restriction of competition in the markets for (i) sale of advertising space in traditional newspapers (advertising market), and (ii) supply of news in traditional newspapers (reader content market). Both markets were defined geographically narrowly, comprising the local/regional market based on the parties' biggest newspapers' distribution areas. The NCA approved the concentration with remedies:

- in the Telemark region, the parties needed to divest either the newspaper Varden ("VA") or Telemarksavisa ("TA"); and
- in Fredrikstad (city), the parties needed to divest of the newspaper Demokraten.

When defining the relevant markets, the NCA focused on substitutability within the regional/ local markets. The NCA started the analysis on the basis of considering the distribution area of the relevant newspapers, and put great emphasis on questionnaires and diversion ratios. The NCA further performed a customer survey of subscribers and local advertisers in six of the merging parties' newspapers which had substantial geographical overlap.

A customer database consisting of subscribers and advertisers was supplied by the parties for each newspaper. A telephone survey was conducted until 25% of the advertisers per newspaper, and a sample of 200 subscribers per newspaper, had answered the questionnaire.

The subscribers/advertisers were asked whether they would have chosen another newspaper if, for example, "Varden" was not available, and if so, which other newspaper. (It could be questioned whether by doing so, the customer survey focused on the average customer instead of the marginal customer, as under the SSNIP-test.)

Based on the advertiser's and customer's stated second choice of newspaper in the survey, the NCA estimated diversion ratios for subscribers and advertisers in the aforementioned newspapers. These results were interpreted and discussed in the context of critical loss analysis to identify the relevant markets.

In conclusion, the NCA found that TA and VA represented a relevant product market as concerns reader content. In the advertising market, the NCA found that all the investigated newspapers with geographical overlap represented relevant product markets.

When assessing the competitive effects in the reader market, the NCA found that there was sufficiently strong competition between TA and VA that the merger was likely to give rise to unilateral effects. After the merger the parties would control the only two regional newspapers TA and VA, as well as the majority of other local newspapers in the county of Telemark. The NCA referred to survey results and information put forward by the parties and third parties, which pointed out that the subscribers considered the two regional newspapers as very close substitutes, and that other newspapers did not exert strong competitive constraints on the two newspapers.

The NCA concluded that network effects, and the availability of substitutes for advertisers which could constrain the potential for the merging parties to raise prices for readers, were not found particularly strong. This was again – in the NCA's view – supported by the diversion ratios.

When the NCA assessed the advertising market in isolation, it found sufficiently strong competition between the parties' newspaper titles so that the merger was likely to give rise to unilateral effects. The parties would, after the merger, control the only two regional newspapers, TA and VA. Survey results pointed out that the advertisers viewed the two regional newspapers as very close substitutes. When taking the two-sidedness of the advertising market into consideration, the NCA did not find any constraining effect stemming from the readers in relation to the potential to exercise market power over advertisers. Hence, the NCA concluded that the indirect network effects did not affect the initial assessment.

The A-pressen/Edda-media case (and the Plantasjen/Oddernes Gartneri case) illustrate that NCA has begun using customer surveys and diversion ratios to define the relevant markets, but also in the competitive analysis.

Approach to remedies

The NCA has a slightly less developed approach to remedies than the European Commission. However, in practice the European Commission's Notice on Remedies will provide guidance that is relevant also in the Norwegian context, and the Commission's Form RM can serve as guidance for the drafting of remedy proposals also in relation to Norwegian merger control.

Case law from the NCA has shown that the NCA has a more frequent tendency to accept behavioural remedies to correct competition concerns than other European Competition Authorities. Furthermore, the NCA also accepts structural remedies, or a combination of structural and behavioural remedies[11].

It should be noted that problems have recently been observed related to the implementation of structural remedies in at least three cases:

Firstly, in the Norli/Libris case (V2012-1) the NCA did reverse its decision regarding the order of divestment of the relevant book shop on the grounds of the lack of interest in the shop. In the other two cases, the potential buyer did not fulfil the criteria laid down by the NCA. In the first case, the buyer was not assessed as independent enough with regard to the parties, due to cross-ownership and cross-management issues[12]. In the other case,[13] the settlement related to the structural remedy proposed was not accepted. The NCA did not accept settlement in shares, but required compensation in terms of money.

As regards timing, remedy proposals can in principle be put forward at any stage of the proceedings. In practice, it may be difficult to have a fruitful discussion with the NCA about remedies early in the process, due to the fact that the NCA has not yet completed its competitive assessment of the concentration. Also, remedy proposals should of course not be presented too late – in such cases the NCA may not have the time to analyse and market-test them.

Key policy developments – the consumer welfare standard approach takes over

In Norway the merger control rules have been based on a total welfare standard[14], meaning that all types of efficiencies (including transaction-related efficiencies) may be taken into consideration to counter the negative effect on competition, regardless of whom the efficiencies will benefit.

It should be noted that in its assessment of the Competition Act in NOU 2012:7, the Committee has suggested moving away from the total welfare standard approach and over to the consumer welfare standard approach, in which consumer harm is a necessary condition for intervention, or with regard to efficiencies.

It has been recommended to insert this change in the preparatory works of the new legislation and not to change the wording of the Norwegian Competition Act as such. Section 1 of the Competition Act, which states the purpose of the Act, already provides that the effect on the consumer shall be especially considered.

Reform proposals in Norwegian merger control

Overview

The purpose of the current Competition Act[15] of 2004, was *inter alia* to align Norwegian merger control rules with the EU Merger Control Regulation. Thus, since 2004 the Norwegian merger control regime has for the most part been harmonised with the EU legislation.

Nevertheless, some differences have persisted. For the purpose of further harmonisation, and in order to achieve more efficient competition rules, the Norwegian merger control regime has – as stated above – recently been evaluated by a governmental Committee.

The Norwegian Competition Act Review Committee ("the Committee"), appointed by the Government in December 2010, has suggested several legislative and regulatory changes to the current merger control regime, amongst others:[16] The key changes are presented below.

The Ministry is expected to make a formal proposal to the Parliament some time in spring 2013, but the amendments are not expected to take effect before 2014.

The new jurisdictional turnover thresholds

As mentioned above, it is suggested to raise the thresholds for merger control review to concentrations so that:

- the parties' combined Norwegian turnover shall exceed NOK 500m (currently NOK 50m); and
- each of at least two of the undertakings concerned shall have a turnover in Norway exceeding NOK 100m (currently NOK 20m).

It is close to certain that there will be adopted changes in the Norwegian turnover thresholds; however, the exact level is yet to be determined. The changes cannot be expected to enter into force before 2014.

Merger control procedure harmonisation

Harmonisation of the rules regarding undertakings concerned and calculations of turnover with the EUMR

The Committee has suggested harmonising the Norwegian rules regarding the definition of "undertakings concerned" and the calculation of turnover to those set forth under the European Merger Control Regulation.

The current Norwegian rules regarding calculation of turnover, and the notion of undertakings concerned, are found in the Norwegian merger control regulation which refers to the Norwegian Accountancy Act. The Norwegian rules are not entirely harmonised with the EU rules, and are criticised by the Committee for being unclear.

Firstly, the Norwegian Merger Control Regulation is not entirely clear as to what constitutes the relevant turnover by merger versus acquisition of control. For mergers, the Regulation only refers to the turnover of the involved undertakings, whilst the EUMR also includes turnover of other companies directly or indirectly controlled by the merging undertakings, *cf.* EUMR, article 5 (4) and EC jurisdictional notice, paragraphs 177 *et seq.*

Secondly, it is not entirely clear what is meant by the terms "control" and "company group" in the Norwegian Merger Control Regulation.

Thirdly, the Norwegian Merger Control Regulation creates confusion with regards to differences between a physical person acquiring control and an undertaking acquiring control. Whilst under the EUMR it would be natural to assume that all turnover to the companies directly or indirectly controlled by the same company or person should be included when assessing the jurisdictional thresholds, this is not clear under the Norwegian Merger Control Regulation.

Harmonisation of the substantial test for clearance with the EUMR

The Committee suggests harmonising the substantive test against which concentrations should be appraised with the similar criterion in the EUMR, so that the decisive criterion is whether the concentration would significantly impede effective competition.

The current relevant test pursuant to Section 16 of the Competition Act is whether or not the concentration would create or strengthen a significant impediment of competition, contrary to the purpose of the Act. In theory, this allows the NCA to intervene against even marginal increases in concentration in highly concentrated markets, without assessing the real impact on competition.[17]

Improvements of notification procedure

The Committee suggests abolishing the current two-legged notification procedure. Instead of the current system with standardised notifications possibly leading to complete notifications, the Committee suggests introducing one common filing form, somewhat more limited in substance than the present complete filing form. For certain transactions, in particular foreign-to-foreign transactions with no or only marginal effects within the Norwegian markets, the Committee nevertheless suggests introducing a simplified notification.

If adopted, the changes would increase the first-stage case handling period from 15 to 25 working days, however, allowing for pre-deadline clearance, so that the NCA at any time of the procedure can state that it will not pursue the case further. Moreover, the case handling period of the second stage is proposed to be reduced from 70 to 55 working days. The maximum total case handling time will amount to 115 days compared to 125 working days under the current regime.

Remedies

The use of remedies in Norwegian merger control procedure is currently reviewed in the reform proposal for the purpose of rendering their use more effective. In its report the Committee aims towards obtaining the proposal of remedies at an earlier stage in the procedure, and to make it clearer that it is up to the parties to suggest remedies to neutralise possible competition concerns.

***

Endnotes

1. V2012-8 Telenor Norge AS/LOS Bynett, V2012-10 Mekonomen/MECA and V-2012-11 A-pressen/Edda Media AB.
2. As mentioned, there have been five intervention decisions from the NCA in the last 12 months, compared to only two in 2011. The number of complete notifications was approximately the same in these two periods.
3. Case M.6753 Orkla/Rieber & Son.
4. Written guidance letter dated 9 November 2011 (case number 2011/586).
5. This is relevant if the concentration does not fall within the scope of the regulation exempting certain types of acquisitions of securities from the prohibition of implementation prior to clearnce (FOR-2009-03-09-292).
6. A2012-15 - Bankruptcy.
7. V2012-13, V2012-12, V2012-15 and V-2012-14.
8. V-2012-14.
9. See standardised notifications regarding: Coop Haugland SA - Ølen Samyrkelag SA (received 21/02/2013), ICA Norge AS - Rimi Sortland (Natland Mat AS) (received 13/02/2013), ICA Norge AS - Rimi Nedre Hagavei (KaRu Mat AS)(received 13/02/2013), Hakon Invest AB - ICA AB (received 11/02/2013), AS Lokalavisene / Media Bergen AS - Bydelsavisene AS (received 08/02/2013) and REMA Industrier AS - Stanges Gårdsprodukter AS (received 05/02/2013).
10. Decision V2012-11.
11. V2012-11 A-Pressen/ Mecom (Edda Media).
12. V2012-16 Lemminkäinen / Mesta.
13. V2012-17 Telenor/LOS Bynett.
14. In case V2005-12 the NCA had taken a consumer welfare approach. The case was brought in appeal before the Ministry of Government Administration, Reform and Church Affairs, which overruled them on this point.
15. Which entered into force on 1 May 2004.
16. Official Norwegian Reports NOU 2012: 7.
17. The European Commission, on the other hand, has previously considered that a small increase in concentration in an already concentrated market does not amount to a creation or strengthening of a dominant position, ref. Case IV/M.289 Pepsico/KAS section 6.5 and case IV/M.430 Proctor & Gamble/Schichedanz point 153, and the Commission's guidelines on the assessment of horizontal mergers, point 25 and 26.

Eivind J. Vesterkjær
Tel: +47 23 11 1123 / Email: eve@thommessen.no
Eivind J Vesterkjær joined Thommessen in 1990, and has been a partner since 1999. In the years 1990-1991 he took his diploma (DEA) in Community Law at Université de Paris II (Panthéon-Assas). Between 1991 and 1993 he worked as a Deputy Judge. He assists clients in a wide range of industries, including consumer goods, construction, energy, telecommunication and transport. Vesterkjær assists clients on various matters related to both competition law and public procurement. His work includes negotiations and contracts, including M&A contracts and procurement contracts, notifications to the authorities, assistance during investigations, dispute resolution and litigation in these areas. He has been responsible for the handling of several high-profile merger cases in recent years.
Vesterkjær has written several publications on public procurement regulations as well as on competition law matters.

Eivind Sæveraas
Tel: +47 23 11 1262 / Email: eis@thommessen.no
Eivind Sæveraas is an associate partner at Thommessen. He has more than 15 years' working experience within the field of competition law. He joined Thommessen in 1998 after having worked for the Competition Authority from 1995. Mr Sæveraas is primarily recognised for his work with abuse cases and several high-profile merger cases, as well as other competition law matters, including cartel cases and litigation. He assists clients in a wide range of industries, including construction, energy, tele-communication, publishing, media, insurance and transport. He is also recognised for his academic skills, he is a frequent speaker and writer on competition law matters and is co-editor and co writer for the commentary to the Norwegian Competition Act that was published in 2009.

Advokatfirmaet Thommessen AS

Haakon VII's gate 10, PO Box 1484 Vika, NO-0116 Oslo, Norway
Tel +47 23 11 1111 / Fax +47 23 11 1010 / URL: http://www.thommessen.no

Pakistan

Mehmood Mandviwalla & Summaiya Zaidi
Mandviwalla & Zafar Advocates and Legal Consultants

Introduction

With the establishment of the Competition Commission of Pakistan (**"CCP"**), the merger control regime in Pakistan has seen some major developments in the last six years, including the introduction of specific legislation regulating and controlling mergers. Under Pakistani law, the Companies Ordinance, 1984, empowers the Securities and Exchange Commission of Pakistan (**"SECP"**) and the High Courts to regulate and sanction the amalgamation and reconstruction of companies. However, over the last few years special laws have been enacted to regulate amalgamations and mergers which include the Competition Ordinance, 2007, which is replaced by the Competition Act, 2010.

As a consequence, the merger control regime in Pakistan may be viewed to be in a nascent stage, since there are a limited number of cases that have been tried under the new legislation. However, the work of CCP and SECP shows that this area of law has been focused upon specially to ensure that mergers do not result in discrimination to the shareholders or other stakeholders.

Overview of merger control activity

Following the establishment of CCP in 2007, mergers have been controlled through the Competition (Merger Control) Regulations, 2007 (**"Regulations"**), the Competition Act, 2010 (**"Act"**) and Guidelines on the Assessment of Horizontal Mergers, 2008 (**"Guidelines"**). These legislative enactments ensure that undertakings conform to international best practices as far as possible and, as a consequence, are under constant review. The latest amendment to the Regulations was introduced on February 21, 2012 wherein a new clause 4A(ia) was inserted to the existing Regulation 4A(i). Now "a transaction in which a holding company (whether incorporated in or outside Pakistan) merges, amalgamates, combines or ventures jointly with its subsidiary or the subsidiaries thereof (whether incorporated in or outside Pakistan) to merge, amalgamate, combine or venture jointly with each other" shall also be exempt from filing a pre-merger notification.

Statistical overview

The summary table below shows the number of acquisitions, mergers, joint ventures and exemptions that have been granted by the CCP from 2008 to 2011.

Table 1

Nature of Transaction	2008-2009	2009-2010	2010-2011
Acquisitions	43	48	67
Mergers	19	13	14
Joint Ventures	2	2	3
Exemptions	91	44	66

Source: Competition Commission of Pakistan

It is interesting to note that while the number of mergers and joint ventures remained relatively the same, the number of acquisitions increased considerably while the number of exemptions have significantly decreased.

The table below demonstrates the number of cases and proceedings that CCP has effectively dealt with in the last few years:

Table 2: Number of cases from 2008-2011

Nature of Case	2008-2009	2009-2010	2010-2011
Abuse of Dominance	5	5	4
Prohibited Agreements	3	4	7
Deceptive Marketing	0	3	4

Source: Competition Commission of Pakistan.

The cases dealing with the abuse of dominance have remained relatively constant, while the other two types of cases have shown increases. The most important development is the increase in matters related to deceptive marketing in the last two years. In 2012, two cases with regard to deception marketing were decided by CCP; the first was a show-cause notice issued to paint manufacturers for the practice of placing redeemable tokens inside paint packets without any disclosure of either their amount or their presence in the packet. The second case was with regard to the conduct of Al-Hilal Industries Private Limited, and its brand called "Fresh Juice" which was allegedly deceiving the consumers by printing incorrect percentages of content on the packet. In both these cases the scope of deceptive marketing was analysed in view of Section 10 of the Act, and both undertakings, in consideration of the CCP's compliance-oriented approach, were reprimanded to ensure responsible behaviour in future with regard to the marketing of their products.

Another recent case before CCP relates to advertisements promoting products manufactured by Reckitt Benckiser Inc., called "Veet". The main argument in that case is whether the slogan adopted by the advertising campaign to promote the product was misleading or was intended to deceive consumers.

It is expected that the number of deceptive marketing cases in Pakistan will increase to ensure that all industry partners follow responsible marketing practices, and the levels of accountability for deceptive advertising are increased. This is in conformance with the CCP's agenda of protecting consumers from misleading or deceptive advertising.

Jurisdictional assessment or procedure

CCP regularly conducts reviews and analyses competition levels in the market through Section 11 of the Act, read with the Regulations, which provide for approval process for mergers through the Mergers and Acquisitions Department. This Department assesses whether an intended merger has the potential to substantially lessen competition by creating or strengthening a dominant position in the relevant market. Under Regulation 6 of the Regulations, CCP must first assess the *"strength of competition in the relevant market, and the probability that the merger parties in the market after merger will behave competitively or co-operatively...".* In order to accomplish this, the same Regulation lists the following as some of the factors that CCP considers:

a)   *"the actual and potential level of import competition in the market;*

b)   *the ease of entry into the market, including tariff and regulatory barriers;*

c)   *the level and trends of concentration, and history of collusion, in the market;*

d)   *the degree of countervailing power in the market;*

e)   *the dynamic characteristics of the market, including growth, innovation, and product differentiation;*

f)   *the nature and extent of vertical integration in the market;*

g)   *whether the business, or part of the business of a merger party or merger, has failed or is likely to fail; and*

h)   *whether the merger situation will result in the removal of an effective competitor."*

In Phase I of the review, CCP determines whether the transaction falls within the meaning of a merger and raises competition concerns. If the intended transaction is declared a merger, which does not reduce competition levels in the market, CCP communicates its approval within 30 working days. However, if CCP declares that the transaction requires a more detailed assessment, then the intended transaction enters into Phase II of review, under Regulation 11 of the Regulations. The decision under Phase II must be communicated to the concerned parties within 90 working days. If CCP determines that the intended merger will result in reduction of competition by creating or strengthening a dominant position and does not fall under exemptions listed in Regulation 14, CCP may adopt the following procedures: (a) prohibit the consummation of the intended merger; (b) approve the intended merger; or (c) conditionally approve the intended merger.

In 2010-2011 most of the mergers under review with CCP were granted No-Objection Certificates ("NOC"), which is the first stage clearance. In 2011, there were 67 NOCs issued to acquisitions, 14 to mergers and 3 to joint ventures as detailed in Table 1. Three acquisitions entered the second phase of review by CCP, namely: Fauji Fertilizer Company Limited's acquisition of 79% of the shareholding of Agritech Limited; VimpleCom Limited's acquisition of Wind Telecom SPA (formerly Weather Investments Sarl); and lastly, Universal Terminal Limited's acquisition of 100% shares of Coastal refinery. Orders for clearance were issued to the first two acquisitions by CCP based on conditions specified. The third acquisition was granted an NOC after a thorough review by CCP upon concluding that the acquisition would not create or strengthen a dominant position in the market.

Statistical data provided by CCP reveals that in the year 2012 the number of NOCs issued totalled 58, while the total number of cases resolved by the CCP was 58 as well. In 2012, only one case proceeded to the Phase II review.

Key industry sectors reviewed and approach adopted to market definition, barriers to entry, and nature of international competition

This part of the chapter first provides a general statistical perspective on the number of cases based on sectoral classification brought before CCP in 2011. Then a sectoral view of the Cooking Oil sector will be analysed.

Table 3: Sectoral classification of cases 2011

Area	Number of Cases
Cement	1
Electronic Goods	1
Shipping	2
Housing	2
Steel	3
Sugar	4
Foods products, Beverages and Distribution	4
Chemical Products, Petrochemicals, Petroleum products, Fertilizer	4
Pharmaceuticals	5
Textiles	6
Power and Energy	12
Financial services, Investment, Modaraba, Banking, Leasing	15
Conglomerates	22

Source: CCP Annual Report 2011

The Competition Assessment Framework applied by CCP also addresses possible barriers to entry and exit and, in the context of the Cooking Oil sector under review, there are three barriers to entry and one exit barrier which have been identified and discussed below:

Natural barriers

A natural barrier for this market would be the monopolistic production of palm oil domestically. But in reality the creation of this barrier does not seem evident *"due to free trade and the availability of substitutes"* (Competition Commission of Pakistan, 2011, p.38).

Capacity utilisation as a strategic barrier

Firms already operating in the market may create obstacles for entry of potential firms *"by building and maintaining excess capacity"*. This allows the existing firm to discourage new firms from entering the market by increasing their production levels, as they have the capacity to produce more than they are producing at a given point in time. Therefore, not producing goods at the maximum level of the capacity of a firm allows it to use this capacity utilisation as a strategic barrier to limit or obstruct a new firm's entry into the same market (Competition Commission of Pakistan, 2011, p.39).

The table below provides a view on specific manufacturers and the percentage capacity utilised by them over a five-year period.

Table 4: Capacity utilisation over several years of respondent firms

No.	Manufacturer	2005	2006	2007	2008	2009
1	A.C.P. Oil Mills (Pvt.) Ltd.	82.18%	94.98%	78.02%	82.19%	25.66%
2	Ahmed Vegetable Oil and Ghee Mills (Pvt.) Ltd.	58.94%	45.11%	58.39%	53.57%	41.17%
3	Chiniot Enterprises (Pvt.) Ltd.	57.25%	67.32%	44.20%	26.47%	38.53%
4	Dalda Foods (Pvt.) Ltd.	50%	58%	88%	100%	95%
5	Habib Oil Mills (Pvt.) Ltd.	46%	63%	55%	54%	35%
6	Hamza Vegetable Oil Refinery and Ghee Mills (Pvt.) Ltd.	N/A	23.38%	24.31%	22.77%	24.28%
7	Mahboob Industries (Pvt.) Ltd.	40%	45%	60%	65%	65%
8	M. H. Oil Mills (Pvt.) Ltd.	73%	84%	84%	117%	61%
9	Punjab Oil Mills (Pvt.) Ltd	83.12%	94.78%	99.82%	96.16%	104.16%
10	Sadiq Sons Ghee and Oil Mills (Pvt.) Ltd.	50%	50%	40%	40.50%	40%
11	United Industries Limited	95%	99%	88%	97.5%	98%
12	Wali Oil Mills Ltd.	31.52%	43.07%	26.73%	38.50%	22.41%

Source: (Competition Commission of Pakistan, 2011, p.41)

Taxes and duties (regulatory barriers)

Currently in Pakistan, the manufacturers of cooking oil pay approximately Pakistan Rupees 30,000/MT in taxes and duties on the import of edible oil. The table below details the amount of taxes payable on the import of Palm Oil and Palm Olien from Malaysia.

Table 5: Taxes on oil and ghee

Description of tax	RBD Palm Oil	RBD Palm Olien
Customs duty/MT	9,180 (under FTA with Malaysia)	7,620 (under FTA with Malaysia)
Special excise duty	1,000	1,000
Sales tax 17%	13,651	13,651
Income tax 3%	2,818	2,818
Total*	**26,649**	**25,089**

*Freight charges from Malaysia to Karachi and then onward destination in Pakistan are not included

Source: (Competition Commission of Pakistan, 2011, p.22)

CCP has analysed the trend of duties payable on import with changes in international prices of imported edible oils. It was revealed that previously when international prices of these products rose, the duties payable were correspondingly reduced so as to avoid over-burdening the consumer. However, the government has not practised this and has failed to *"give relief to common people due to its own financial reasons"* (Competition Commission of Pakistan, 2011, pp.21-22).

Exit barriers

As mentioned earlier, firms in the cooking oil sector are significantly under-utilised in the context of their capacity, but this aspect may be understood if a *"barrier to increase utilization may be the presence of unregistered small players. However, the existence of unregistered and small players, which normally maintain very low administrative costs, should cause at least some firms to close down and exit from the business"*. Interestingly enough, despite serious variations in price, not even one registered firm has exited the market and this may be due to the presence of an exit barrier. *"The creation of a huge production capacity without cognizance of demand, may have become an exit barrier"* (Competition Commission of Pakistan, 2011, pp.41-42).

Key appraisal techniques applied

Though mergers are generally viewed as effective ways of increasing the level of operations of a company, mergers can even threaten the levels of competition within the relevant market. The Guidelines issued under Regulation 28 of the Regulations, explain two major ways in which horizontal mergers may significantly reduce the levels of competition; firstly, *"by eliminating important competitive constraints on one or more undertakings, which consequently would have increased market power, without resorting to coordinated behaviour"*, and secondly, *"by changing the nature of competition in such a way that undertakings that previously were not coordinating their behavior, are now significantly more likely to coordinate and raise prices or otherwise harm effective competition"* (Competition Commission of Pakistan, 2008, p.7). This section focuses on how horizontal mergers are assessed in view of the Guidelines and the key appraisal techniques employed by CCP. The process followed by CCP in assessing mergers generally involves the following:

(a) *"Definition of the relevant product and geographic market;*
(b) *Competitive assessment of the merger"* (Competition Commission of Pakistan, 2008, p.3).

The concentration of market power must be determined by CCP because *"market concentration or saturation typically makes it impossible or highly difficult for new firms to enter the market and present a challenge to the existing undertakings"* (Competition Commission of Pakistan, 2010, p.23).

Concentration levels in a relevant market

To determine the overall concentration levels in the market, CCP often applies the Herfindahl-Hirschman Index (HHI) which reveals the level of competition within the relevant market. This is calculated by "summing the squares of the individual market shares of all the undertakings in the market", and can range from 0 to 10,000. (Competition Commission of Pakistan, 2008, p.5) The formula is as follows:

$$HHI = MS_1^2 + MS_2^2 + MS_3^2 + MS_4^2 \ldots + MS_n^2$$

or

$$HHI = \sum_{i=1}^{n} (MS_i)^2$$

An increase in the HHI demonstrates a decrease in competition and an increase in market power. Large undertakings are awarded greater weight by the HHI, and the following table provides one with a view of how to gauge levels of competition in the relevant market with the help of the HHI.

Table 6: Concentration of market and HHI

HHI	Concentration of Market
0-1,000	Un-concentrated market

HHI	Concentration of Market
1,000-2,000	Moderately concentrated markets
2,000-10,000	Highly concentrated markets

Further, it is important to mention the concept of relevant market in this section, as the concentration of market share is with regard to a kind of product in a specific market. According to the Section 2(k) of the Competition Act, 2010, the relevant market has been defined as follows:

"The market which shall be determined by the Commission with reference to a product market and a geographic market and a product market comprises of all those products or services which are regarded as interchangeable or substitutable by the consumers by reason of the products' characteristics, prices and intended uses. A geographic market comprises the area in which the undertakings concerned are involved in the supply of products or services, and in which the conditions of competition are sufficiently homogeneous and which can be distinguished from neighboring geographic areas because, in particular, the conditions of competition are appreciably different in those areas."

However, there may be difficulties with using the HHI to determine the overall concentration levels in the market. One significant difficulty, for example, is if the market shares of companies A, B, C and D are equal percentages; according to the calculation of the HHI, it would appear that the market is competitive and the industry is not dominated by one company or another. A closer look at the nature of services that the companies provide might reveal that company A provides a service to 70% of the market, which the other three companies do not. While company A may be acting in a monopolistic manner, it would appear according to the HHI that it is not.

Competition Assessment Framework

The Competition Assessment Framework has been formulated to serve as a guide for the identification of barriers to competition in the developing world. It assesses the levels of competition in a particular sector and provides several indicators to determine these competition levels, and the *"analytical framework is structured based on the identification of the relevant market, market structure, barriers to entry, the role of government policies or institutions, consideration of vested interests, and signs of anti-competitive behavior by firms"* (Competition Commission of Pakistan, 2011, pp.1-2). This assessment framework has been discussed in detail earlier in Part IV with regard to the cooking oil sector analysis.

Approach to remedies (to avoid second stage investigation, following second stage investigation)

Compliance to competition law

CCP follows a compliance-oriented approach in terms of the conditions it imposes on the companies or the intended merger, and the remedies it provides them. In the Fauji Fertilizer case, decided early in 2012, the Commission imposed certain conditions in the matter of the acquisition of 79% shares of Agritech Limited by Fauji Fertilizer Company Limited under Regulation 11(5)(b) of the Merger Control Regulations (Fauji Fertilizer Company Limited, 2012, 202). These conditions were imposed to ensure that these "efficiencies would result in lower prices, improved quality, enhanced services or newer products" for the benefit of the consumers (Fauji Fertilizer Company Limited, 2012, 210).

Advice from the Acquisitions & Mergers Facilitation Office

CCP even provides advice to undertakings intending to merge in the future to avoid Phase II investigative procedures, and this is through its Department called the Acquisitions & Mergers Facilitation Office ("AMFO"). This Office informally advises prospective participants in mergers and acquisitions on whether their proposed ventures fall within CCP's requirements and laws regulating such mergers. In 2011, more than 35 undertakings, law firms and consultants were assisted during their concerned merger processes, while in two cases non-binding advice was provided. These two cases concerned the acquisition of shares of Unilever Pakistan Limited by its Parent Company, Unilever Overseas Holdings Limited UK, and the acquisition of 100% shares of Ansaldo Energia SPA by Joint Venture Vehicle Company, comprising Finmeccanica SPA Italy and FR Marinsail Limited (Competition Commission of Pakistan, 2011, p.45). Statistical data provided for by the CCP for the year 2012 reveals that two firms were provided non-binding advice by the AMFO.

Key policy developments

CCP, in pursuance of a level playing field agenda, has developed several strategies and policy frameworks to develop the merger control regime which guarantees high levels of competition in the market. The different areas of focus are as follows:

Compliance policy

CCP introduced a Voluntary Competition Compliance Code in July 2010, the main aim of which is to ensure that *"undertakings achieve the overall purpose of competition law, which is to make markets competitive for the benefit of both undertakings and consumers"*. The Code establishes a formal internal framework for undertakings to ensure compliance with the provisions of the Competition Act, 2010 (Competition Commission of Pakistan, p.4). The essential features of this Code are:
(i)   assessment of the risk of non-compliance with Competition Laws of Pakistan;
(ii) development and enforcement of the Compliance Code and Policy frameworks;
(iii) selection and appointment of an Officer for Compliance;
(iv) training of employees as well as consequences of non-compliance by the same; and
(v)   evaluation on a regular basis of the effectiveness and enforcement of the Code (Competition Commission of Pakistan, pp.10-14).

In furtherance of this compliance agenda, CCP also exercises control of a merger after it has been granted approval under Regulation 21 of the Regulations. This is to ensure that the concerned undertaking complies with the decision of CCP and may be required to submit a monthly compliance statement. In VimpleCom Limited's acquisition of Wind Telecom SPA (formerly Weather Investments Sarl), CCP issued a NOC subject to conditions, one of which included the filing of a compliance report within three months from the date of the closing of the transaction (2011 CLD 1471).

Competition advocacy policy

Realising the challenge that many developing countries face with regard to competition advocacy, CCP has undertaken to inform the industries and businesses of the measures they must undertake to adhere to *"welfare-enhancing pro-competitive solutions"*. In 2011, an advocacy strategy was developed which focused on the following areas:
(i)   *"educating the business and legal community using the platforms of chambers and bar councils;*
(ii)   *raising general public awareness through consumer rights groups;*
(iii) *using print and electronic media as a tool of advocacy; sensitizing media to competition law, briefing journalists on case studies and enforcement orders;*
(iv)   *holding seminars to highlight the key areas of competition law enforcement, i.e. public procurement, cartelization, deceptive marketing and merger filing;*
(v)   *lobbying with regulators; and*
(vi)   *reaching out to business schools and academia to increase awareness of the Competition Act"* (Competition Commission of Pakistan, 2011, p.46).

Leniency policy

CCP is also encouraging competition in circumstances where prohibited agreements under the Act have been entered into by allowing for a policy of leniency in punishment if the said undertaking comes forward of its own volition. In furtherance of this, it has issued Competition (Leniency) Regulations in November, 2007 which empowers CCP, under Regulation 3, to grant an undertaking the benefit of exemption/total immunity from, or reduction in, financial penalties. This remedy is available only to those undertakings that are the first to provide CCP evidence of a prohibited activity, and which refrain from further participation in the alleged activity from the time of its disclosure to CCP.

Competition Consultative Group

This Group regularly holds annual meetings in Pakistan to receive feedback from the relevant stakeholders in the market with regard to the strategies of enforcement and advocacy. A meeting was held in Lahore on June 30, 2011 where CCP members delivered presentations on aviation sector study and deceptive marketing.

In 2012, a total of four meetings were held by this Group in three major cities of Lahore, Karachi and Islamabad, and one meeting has already been held in Karachi in 2013. Four other meetings are scheduled to be held throughout this year, making the total number of meetings of the Group for 2013 five.

Reform proposals

Section 32 and 33 of the Act establishes a parallel judicial system whereby CCP has been given powers that would normally be vested in a civil court under the Code of Civil Procedure, 1908. Similarly, Section 41 of the Act provides that an appeal shall lie to an Appellate Bench of CCP in respect of an order passed by a member or an authorised officer of CCP. Under the Constitution of the Islamic Republic of Pakistan, 1973, establishing a parallel judicial system, can be liable to be struck down by the Superior Courts of Pakistan. Further, under Article 203, read with Article 175 of the Constitution, supervision and control over the subordinate judiciary vests in the High Courts. Hence, any tribunal that is not subject to judicial review and administrative control of the High Court or the Supreme Court may not fit within the judicial framework of the Constitution. This anomaly should be removed by a constitutional amendment in order to ensure that CCP orders are not challenged on this ground and their orders are not held to be *ultra vires* of the Constitution.

The State Bank of Pakistan regulates the banking sector. There may be actions that the banking sector may take under banking laws that may be inconsistent with the Act. Similarly, laws applicable to other sectors may provide protection through a *non-obstante* clause from violation of the Act. It is therefore important that all such laws are harmonised to ensure that there is no inconsistency between the Act and the laws that are regulating other sectors.

CCP should ensure that there is no retrospective enforcement of the Act. The Act came into force in 2010 and all actions prior to the date of enactment should not be brought within the purview of enforcement.

The Act gives unfettered discretion to CCP to arbitrarily impose penalties. Section 38 of the Act dealing with penalties suffers from excessive delegation and hence can be challenged before the Superior Courts. CCP should ensure that the penalties imposed are not disproportionate and have co-relation to the alleged violation.

Mehmood Mandviwalla
Tel: +92 21 3586 7041-3 / Email: mehmood@mandviwallaandzafar.com
Mehmood Mandviwalla is the Senior Partner of the law firm Mandviwalla & Zafar. He completed LLB (Hons) from the London School of Economics and Political Science, and was called to the Bar at Lincolns Inn. He is also the founder of SAARCLAW, an association of the legal communities of South Asian countries.

Mr. Mandviwalla has extensive experience spanning over 30 years in all aspects of commercial and corporate law including, anti-trust, banking, mergers and acquisitions, contract law and negotiations, strategic planning, corporate and financial restructuring, privatisations, Islamic modes of financing; aviation; media; sports law and project finance.

He has drafted various statutory enactments and regulatory frameworks for Pakistan. He is a regular speaker on Competition and other Banking and Corporate Laws. Mr. Mandviwalla serves on various Boards including the State Bank of Pakistan and GlaxoSmithKline Pakistan Limited.

Summaiya Zaidi
Tel: +92 21 3586 7041-3 / Email: summaiya@mandviwallaandzafar.com
Summaiya Zaidi completed her LLM in Law, Development and Governance from the School of Oriental and African Studies. She obtained her BA and LLB from the Lahore University of Management Sciences. She is an Associate with Mandviwalla & Zafar, Advocates and Legal Consultants, and has been dealing with Competition Law; Mergers and Acquisition and Corporate Advisory. She has also worked as a litigation lawyer assisting seniors in the High Court and Supreme Court of Pakistan in Constitutional Law. She has been a visiting lecturer at the Hamdard Law School.

Mandviwalla & Zafar Advocates and Legal Consultants

Mandviwalla Chambers, C-15, Block 2, Clifton, Karachi, Pakistan
Tel: +92 21 3586 7041-3 / Fax: +92 21 3586 0895 / URL: http://www.mandviwallaandzafar.com

Portugal

António Mendonça Raimundo & Miriam Brice
Albuquerque & Associados

Overview of merger control activity during the last 12 months

In Portugal, there are two key factors that have affected merger control numbers. Above all, we would point to the economic and financial crisis that Portugal has faced since 2008. This crisis led to a decrease in transactions and new investments. Also, the enactment of the new Competition Law in 2012 – with the establishment of new thresholds and some innovations as regards additional criteria – could have contributed to a reduction in the number of operations subject to mandatory notification before the Portuguese Competition Authority (*Autoridade da Concorrência*).

The new Portuguese Competition Act – Law nr. 19/2012, of May 8 ("**PCA**") – establishes the new competition legal act concerning mergers, anticompetitive practices and abuses of dominant position and, as regards merger control, establishes new thresholds for merger notifications.

Under the former Portuguese Competition Act – Law nr. 18/2003, of June 11, a concentration affecting the Portuguese market became subject to notification to the Portuguese Competition Authority if one of the following requirements were met:[1]

a) the concentration led to the creation or reinforcement of a market share exceeding 30% in the national market (or in a substantial part of it) for a specific product or service; or

b) the turnover of the participating undertakings in Portugal exceeded €150m in the previous accounting year (net from directly related taxes), provided that the individual turnover in Portugal of at least two of the participating undertakings exceeded €2m.

Those thresholds provided for under the former Competition Law were less demanding, in the sense of the applicability of the mandatory filing, than the ones provided for in the new PCA.

Under the new PCA, currently in force, in case the thresholds for mandatory notification to the European Commission established by Regulation (EC) nr. 139/2004 are not met, a concentration is subject to mandatory notification to the Portuguese Competition Authority if one of the following requirements are met:[2]

a) as a consequence of the concentration, a market share equal to or greater than 50% of the domestic market in a specific product or service, or in a substantial part of it, is acquired, created or reinforced;

b) as a consequence of the concentration, a market share equal to or greater than 30%, but smaller than 50% of the domestic market in a specific product or service, or in a substantial part of it, is acquired, created or reinforced in the case where the individual turnover in Portugal in the previous financial year, by at least two of the undertakings involved in the concentration, is greater than €5m, net of taxes directly related to such a turnover; or

c) the undertakings that are involved in the concentration have reached an aggregate turnover in the previous financial year greater than €100m, net of taxes directly related to such a turnover, as long as the turnover in Portugal of at least two of these undertakings is above €5m.

On one hand, we have moved from a market share threshold of 30% to a market share threshold of 50%, despite some cases where operations that involve the acquisition, creation or reinforcement of market share between 30% and 50% have also been subject to mandatory notification, provided that the additional criteria of the turnover described in b) above is met.

On the other hand, besides moving from a €100m of aggregate turnover to an aggregate turnover of €150m, the single turnover additional criterion moved from €2m to a more demanding €5m now applicable.

In our opinion, those criteria could theoretically lead to fewer mandatory notifications, since they consist in more demanding, but also more effective, criteria, submitting only to the mandatory appraisal of the Portuguese Competition Authority the operations that are more likely to have adverse effects under the competition law perspective.

Despite that fact, the Portuguese Competition Authority was quite active in 2012 as to merger analysis when compared with the previous year. In 2012, 61 operations were submitted to the Portuguese Competition Authority, a number much higher than the 48 operations submitted in 2011, and very close to the 62 operations submitted for the Portuguese Competition Authority's analysis in 2010.

The final outcome of the 61 operations submitted to the Portuguese Competition Authority for analysis in 2012 was as follows:

Second Phase: 2 out of the 61 operations notified entered into second phase, which is called the investigations stage: The Proc. 28/2012 regarding the acquisition by Informa D&B (Serviços de Gestão de Empresas), Soc. Unipessoal, Lda., of exclusive control over the company Coface Serviços Portugal, S.A., through the purchase of its full share capital[3], and the Proc. 38/2012 regarding the acquisition by Arena Atlântida – Gestão de Recintos de Espectáculos, S.A., of exclusive control over the Pavilhão Atlântico and the Atlântico – Pavilhão Multiusos de Lisboa, S.A.[4] In the first case, the Portuguese Competition Authority adopted a decision of extinction of the proceedings under the terms of the Portuguese Administrative Procedural Code, since the notifying party presented a binding request for withdrawal of the proceedings. In the second case, the Portuguese Competition Authority decided to enter the in-depth investigation declaring that, based on the collected elements, the operation raises serious doubts as to its compatibility with an effective competition in the markets of promoting live music events, ticketing services and operation of indoor areas in shows and big size events. The concentration was not yet decided by the Authority.

Decisions in first phase: from the remaining 59 notifications; 4 notifications resulted in a decision of inapplicability, i.e. not subject to mandatory notification under the applicable law; and 54 were already cleared in first phase, without conditions or obligations attached, since they were considered by the Portuguese Competition Authority as not likely to create or reinforce a dominant position as a result of which effective competition would have been significantly impeded.

Proceedings referred to the European Commission: In 2012 there was no proceeding referred to the European Commission.

Compared to the previous years, as mentioned above, the Portuguese Competition Authority was very active in 2012 but, in our opinion, maybe in practical terms, not so demanding in what concerns merger analysis, which is understandable, having in mind the economic and financial crisis of the Country and the specific need of transactions and investment in Portugal.

New developments in jurisdictional assessment or procedure

With the enactment and entering into force of the new PCA, the substantive assessment of merger operations was reviewed in line with EU Law. In accordance with the new law, mergers that may create "significant impediments to effective competition" may now be prohibited,[5] and not only in cases where there is a "creation or reinforcement of a dominant position", as it was stated in the former law. Therefore the control over merger operations was strengthened in order to be more efficient, it now being possible to oppose a concentration avoiding negative consequences for competition without it being necessary for such a concentration to seem capable of strengthening an individual dominant position.

One should also stress the elimination of the reference in law to the contribution of mergers to the international competitiveness of the domestic economy. Such consideration was considered to be out of line with the objectives and position that the Portuguese Competition Authority wants to pursue.

Also, innovatively, in accordance with the new PCA, two or more concentrations between the same natural or legal persons within a period of two years, even when individually considered as not being subject to prior notification, are considered a single concentration subject to prior notification, when the concentrations jointly reach the turnover threshold entailing the mandatory notification to the Portuguese Competition Authority, after the conclusion of the agreement on the last of these operations and before its implementation.

We should also stress that this innovation, connected with the express provision regarding the obligation to report bundles of operations, reduces or even eliminates the possibility of avoiding the mandatory notification in cases of bundles of operations in short periods.

As to the analysis of concentrations by the Portuguese Competition Authority, it is performed on a case-by-case basis, with the main purpose of assessing their possible effects on the market's competition structure, while safeguarding the maintenance and development of effective competition in the national market, taking into consideration the consumers' interests.

Within the abovementioned assessment, the Portuguese Competition Authority takes the following criteria into consideration:

a) The structure of the relevant markets, and the existence or absence of competition from undertakings in these markets or in separate markets.

b) The position of the undertakings concerned in the relevant markets and their economic and financial power, compared with those of their main competitors.

c) The purchaser's market power and its ability to prevent the reinforcement of situations of economic dependence *vis-à-vis* the undertaking that results from the concentration.

d) Potential competition and the existence, in fact or in law, of barriers to entry into the market.

e) The possibility of choice for suppliers, clients and users.

f) The access of various undertakings to sources of supply and markets for their goods.

g) The structure of existing distribution networks.

h) Developments in the supply and demand of the products and services at issue.

i) The existence of special or exclusive rights conferred by law or stemming from the nature of the products being traded or the services supplied.

j) The control of essential facilities by the undertakings concerned and the possibility of access to these facilities provided for competing undertakings.

k) Any technical and economic progress that does not constitute an impediment to competition, provided there are efficiency gains that benefit consumers, stemming directly from the concentration.

Accordingly, the Portuguese Competition Authority will not clear concentrations that create or reinforce a dominant position in the national market or in a substantial part of it, or that may raise relevant obstacles to effective competition in the market.

In accordance with the new PCA, the concentrations subject to mandatory notification to the Portuguese Competition Authority must be notified before the parties have concluded an agreement and prior to its implementation, if this is to be the case, following the date of the preliminary announcement of a public offer of acquisition or exchange, or the announcement of the acquisition of a control shareholding position in an undertaking with shares listed on a regulated stock market or, in the case of a concentration, resulting from a public procurement procedure, after the definitive tender selection and before the public contract is signed off. This is also an innovation of the new PCA since, in the former law, there was a specific deadline to notify the concentrations seven working days after the conclusion of the agreement. Now, the notice of the operations may be given at any time after executing the agreements. However, they still cannot be implemented before they have been subject to a non-opposition decision from the Portuguese Competition Authority.

Notice of these operations may be given at any time after the underlying agreements are executed. However, they may not be implemented before they have been subject to a non-opposition decision.

A proposed concentration can also be subject to a prior appraisal by the Portuguese Competition

Authority. The notification in this case is presented before the execution of the agreement, when it is demonstrated that the parties have a serious intention to conclude it. Such procedure is voluntary, informal and confidential. It is a symptom of the flexibility of the law in order to fulfil the needs of the undertakings as regards internal timings to get an approval from the Portuguese Competition Authority, allowing the procedure to be faster.

The new PCA provides for the approval, by the Portuguese Competition Authority, of a simplified notification form for mergers which, further to a preliminary assessment, prove not to entail significant competition concerns.

The Portuguese Competition Authority approved recently a new Notification Form for Mergers between Undertakings, which is contained in the Regulation 60/2013.[6] Such Regulation includes the procedural rules that have to be complied with when a concentration is notified, and the relevant information to deliver to the Authority. Besides the Regular Form, it includes the above-referred Simplified Notification Form for those mergers that, further to a preliminary assessment, prove not to entail significant competition concerns. In this case the necessary information is reduced and therefore it contributes to a reduction of costs on gathering information by the notifying undertakings.

Key industry sectors reviewed and approach adopted to market definition, barriers to entry, nature of international competition etc.

The Portuguese Competition Authority issued, on December 30, the "Competition Policy Priorities for 2013". This document sets the priorities of the Portuguese Competition Authority for 2013, in accordance with article 7(3) of the new PCA that refers: *"During the last quarter of each year, the Competition Authority shall publish on its Internet site the competition policy priorities for the following year, though making no sectoral reference where its sanctioning powers are concerned."*[7]

In the referred document on the priorities for 2013 for the Portuguese Competition Authority, within the scope of the Portuguese Competition Authority's sanctioning powers, the importance of fighting cartels and abuse of dominant positions were referred as considered to be ones that *"cause the most damage to the economy and to the welfare of consumers"*. Therefore reference was made to the combating of cartels either through *ex officio* initiatives or through wider dissemination of, and recourse to, the leniency regime, and to the fighting of abuses of dominant positions that impact on the competitive capacity of those undertakings that are not in a dominant position, and thus on the market equilibrium.[8]

In the referred document on the priorities for 2013 for the Portuguese Competition Authority, within the scope of the Portuguese Competition Authority's supervisory powers, the importance of better understanding of how relevant sectors of the economy work was made. In this way, it is stated in the referred document that the Portuguese Competition Authority will endeavour to identify behavioural or structural aspects of the economy that are in need of improvement, and to spotlight possible infringements that need to be subject to a sanction. Special reference was made to payment cards[9] and to the sectors of energy, telecommunications and ports. As regards these specific sectors, the Portuguese Competition Authority expressly stated in the referred document that *"those areas where competition comes into play will be analysed and monitored in all due detail"*.[10]

Similarly to what was already established in the former Competition Law, as regards merger proceedings, in accordance with the new PCA, whenever there is a concentration in a market that is subject to sectoral regulation, the Portuguese Competition Authority, prior to taking a final decision, shall request the opinion of the sectoral regulatory authority.[11]

Key economic appraisal techniques applied e.g. as regards unilateral effects and co-ordinated effects, and the assessment of vertical and conglomerate mergers

We shall look in more detail at the recent Public Consultation on the *"Project of Guidelines for the Economical Analysis of Horizontal Mergers"*. Such Guidelines are meant to provide guidance on the evaluation performed by the Competition Authority as regards the impact on the competition of horizontal mergers, aiming to contribute to a more transparent, efficient, faster and legal certainty of the merger procedures.

Such document will be under public consultation until 2 May 2013, and comprises not only the conceptual aspects of the economic merger's analysis but also the ones related to the information and methods of empirical analysis relevant for the assessment of the impact of a merger on the competition.

Approach to remedies (i) to avoid second stage investigation and (ii) following second stage investigation

In accordance with the applicable law and practice, the notifying party may, at all times, undertake commitments with a view to maintaining effective competition. The Portuguese Competition Authority may reject such commitments and/or propose other commitments whenever it is considered that those are insufficient and/or inadequate.

In practical terms, such remedies are to a certain extent "negotiated" between the notifying undertaking and the Portuguese Competition Authority.

Portuguese Competition Authority also issued in 2011 the *"Guidelines on Merger Remedies"*,[12] in line with the EU Law and practice. Such Guidelines are meant to provide guidance regarding the selection, definition, implementation and monitoring of remedies within merger control cases. It includes the following subjects: concept definition; selection of remedies (in accordance with the relevant principles); risk analysis; monitoring trustee; divestiture trustee; types of remedies; structural remedies or remedies related to the future behaviour of the merger entity, their requirements and objectives; procedural aspects; change of remedies and consequences on failure to comply with remedies. Such Guidelines also contain templates on the commitments undertaken before the Portuguese Competition Authority, divestment orders and of monitoring terms.

Key policy developments

Besides all the above-mentioned developments, one should mention the *"Competition Policy Priorities for 2013"* issued by the Portuguese Competition Authority on December 30. In such document it is stated that *"Portugal finds itself in a difficult economic situation, with undertakings facing very adverse market conditions. Such circumstances justify a strengthened competition policy, enabling the markets to function competitively. Strong competition is one of the features essential for the adjustments that are in progress, and will contribute towards generating sustained growth in the economy and bringing a rise in the welfare of consumers."*[13]

Within the express priorities to 2013 for the Portuguese Competition Authority described in the referred document, within the scope of the Portuguese Competition Authority's supervisory powers, the importance of ensuring effective control of concentration operations was referred to, with the priorities described as follows: *"control of concentration operations: if these could lead to significant impediments to effective competition in the domestic market or a substantial part of it, they demand rapid action from the Portuguese Competition Authority with a view to (i) authorising the mergers contingent on appropriate remedies, or (ii) if this is not possible, not authorising them".*[14]

Reform proposals

Besides the new PCA, the new thresholds adopted, different procedure and the different approach as regards the substantive assessment and the recently published new Notification Form, one should underline the recent Public Consultation on the *"Project of Guidelines for the Economical Analysis of Horizontal Mergers"*.

Merger control is in our opinion already pretty swift in most cases, and we have also simplified procedures for the simpler cases that render them less costly. With the new regulations adopted and with the above referred new guidelines under discussion, merger control is expected to become more efficient.

* * *

Endnotes

1. Article 9(1) or the former Portuguese Competition Act – Law nr. 18/2003, of June 11.
2. Article 37(1) of Portuguese Competition Act. – Law nr. 19/2012, of May 8.
3. Case nº CCent 28/2012, *Informa / Coface Serviços*, decided by PCA in November 25, 2012.
4. Case nº CCent 38/2012, *Arena Atlântida / Pavilhão Atlântico* Atlântico, S.A.,* Portuguese Competition Authority decided to enter in-depth investigation on February 11, 2013.
5. Article 41(4) PCA.
6. Regulation nr. 60/2013, published on February 14 in the Official Gazette.
7. "Competition Policy Priorities for 2013", December 30, p.1.
8. "Competition Policy Priorities for 2013", *cit.*, p.2.
9. Being referred that the Portuguese Competition Authority "will keep track of the upcoming regulatory framework, as set out by the European Commission, and, together with the Bank of Portugal (*Banco de Portugal*), will take the necessary action to bring domestic operations in line with the cross-border regulations that the European Commission introduces, with any adjustments deemed to be justified specifically for Portugal".
10. "Competition Policy Priorities for 2013", December 30, p.2.
11. Article 55(1) of PCA.
12. *"Guidelines on Merger Remedies"*, July 28, 2011.
13. "Competition Policy Priorities for 2013", p.2.
14. "Competition Policy Priorities for 2013", *cit*, p.2.

António Mendonça Raimundo
Tel: +351 213 431 570 /Email: amr@albsa.pt
António Mendonça Raimundo joined Albuquerque & Associados in 1987. He heads the Corporate and M&A Department of the Firm, and is specialised in International Contracts and Mergers and Acquisitions, both at a national and international level. He also has significant experience in Competition Law, notably in the field of merger control filings. His practice in that area includes cases before both the European Commission and the Portuguese Competition Authority. He engages in the negotiation of Joint Ventures and strategic international alliances. He has done much work in foreign investment and operations in the telecommunications sector, negotiating foreign investment contracts and working on privatisation and state assets transfer. He has published several works, including *Leasing Law in the European Economic Community*, London, Euromoney Books, (co-author: Financial Leasing Law in Portugal), *Contracts of Agency and Distribution in Portugal,* 1992, Chamber of Trade and Industry, Valencia (Spain), *Telecommunication Law in Europe,* London, Butterworths, 1998, and Tottel Publishing, 2005 (co-author of the Chapter on Portuguese Telecommunications Law), *International Comparative Legal Guide to Competition Litigation 2013*, Global Legal Group, 2012 (co-author of the Portuguese Chapter) and *Telecommunication Laws in Europe,* Ed. Joachim Schrerer, Bloomsbury Professional Limited, 2013, (co-author of the Portuguese Chapter).

Miriam Brice
Tel: +351 213 431 570 / Email: mb@albsa.pt
Miriam Brice joined Albuquerque & Associados in 2007. Admitted to the Portuguese Bar Association in 2006, Miriam has a Post-Graduate qualification in Competition and Regulatory Law from the Institute of Economy, Finance and Tax Law and also a Post-Graduate qualification in Sanctionatory Law of the Regulatory Authorities from the Institute of Criminal Law and Criminal Sciences; both Institutes from the Law Faculty of the Lisbon University. In addition, she concluded her Master Degree in EU Law at the Law Faculty of the Lisbon University with a thesis on Abuse of Dominant Position. Miriam has been involved in several complex merger notifications to the Portuguese Competition Authority and in advising many national and multinational companies on Competition Law issues in the areas of abuse of dominance, restrictive practices, mergers, special and exclusive rights and state aids. Her practice includes cases before both the European Commission and the Portuguese Competition Authority.
Her main practice areas are Competition Law, EU Law, Commercial Law, Corporate Law and Mergers & Acquisitions, International Contracts and Telecommunications.
Miriam has published several works, including: many articles in the E-Competitions Bulletin, www.concurrences.com, *International Comparative Legal Guide to Competition Litigation 2013*, Global Legal Group, 2012 (co-author of the Portuguese Chapter) and *Telecommunication Laws in Europe,* Ed. Joachim Schrerer, Bloomsbury Professional Limited, 2013, (co-author of the Portuguese Chapter).

Albuquerque & Associados

Calçada Bento Rocha Cabral, 1, Lisbon, Portugal
Tel: +351 213 431 570 / Fax: +351 213 431 568 / URL: http://www.albuquerque-associados.com

Romania

Silviu Stoica & Mihaela Ion
Popovici Nitu & Asociatii

Overview of merger control activity during the last 12 months

The Romanian Competition Council (the "RCC") is the Romanian authority that analyses economic concentrations which fall under the main merger control legislation (namely the Competition Act No 21/1996, hereinafter referred to as the "Competition Act") and the secondary legislation.

Statistics show that the last few years brought a downward trend in the RCC's practice concerning economic concentrations. The number of decisions issued by the RCC regarding merger control has decreased only slightly, but their share in the total number of decisions has fallen sharply. Together, the two criteria show that the RCC's activity has significantly enhanced and that, currently, it is focused on anticompetitive practices.

The main reason for this trend is the general economic crisis that determined a lower number of transactions and, as a consequence, a lower number of notifications to the RCC regarding economic concentrations.

If, in 2010, the RCC has issued 46 decisions with respect to economic concentrations, in 2011 the RCC has issued only 38 decisions and, in 2012, the number continued to decrease to 35 decisions.

In terms of the share in the total number of decisions, in the past years almost 80% of the RCC's decisions concerned economic concentrations. By comparison, in 2011 the share dropped severely to 38%, but slightly recovered in 2012 to 42%.

As a general remark, the RCC's decisions were mainly issued in Phase I of the notification procedure.

For example, in 2011, out of a total of 38 decisions, the RCC has issued: (i) 35 non-objection decisions, (i.e. although the notified economic concentration falls within the scope of the Competition Act, no serious doubts about the compatibility with a normal competition environment on the relevant markets were identified); (ii) one decision on the recalculation of the authorisation fee; and (iii) two sanctioning decisions for implementing an economic concentration before the RCC had issued a decision.[1]

In 2012, out of a total of 35 decisions concerning economic concentrations, the RCC issued: (i) 32 non-objection decisions; (ii) two decisions remedying material errors of decisions previously issued in connection with economic concentration; and (iii) one non-breach decision issued as a result of an investigation into an alleged implementation of an economic concentration before the issuance of a clearance decision.[2]

In 2011 and 2012, the economic concentrations notified to the RCC concerned undertakings acting on a variety of relevant markets, but a special interest is still notable in the markets vulnerable to the effects of the economic crisis (e.g. as regards the relevant food market, the RCC reviewed four notified concentrations in 2012 and two in 2011; with respect to the real estate rental market, the RCC reviewed one notified concentration in 2012 and four in 2011).

New developments in jurisdictional assessment or procedure

After the intense reform process carried out in 2010 with respect to the domestic legislation, in 2011 and 2012 only few amendments were implemented. However, these amendments refer only to the secondary legislation.

The main amendments brought to the secondary competition legislation (namely, the RCC's Regulation on economic concentrations[3] – the "Regulation" and the RCC's Guidelines regarding the right to access the RCC file in cases regarding an alleged breach of articles 5, 6 and 9 of the Competition Act or article 101 and 102 of the TFEU or, in cases of economic concentrations,[4] – the "Guidelines") target, in particular:

(a)   The increase of the RCC's power of decision regarding procedural matters. E.g.: (i) the RCC can decide regarding the necessity to organise hearings in the second phase of the assessment; (ii) the RCC can notify other authorities of possible infringements in their area; (iii) the RCC may carry out the simplified assessment procedure even if the parties have submitted the complete form; and (iv) after opening an investigation concerning an economic concentration, in the second-phase investigation, the RCC may take depositions from proxies of the legal person.

(b)   The individualisation of the fines. E.g.: (i) the limits of the fines for the newly established companies with no turnover in the previous year were reduced to half; (ii) the fines for public authorities regarding their obligation to provide relevant information requested by the RCC were reduced; (iii) the recognition procedure was introduced – if one of the parties, concerned by an investigation report issued in Phase II, after its receipt and after exercising its right of access to the investigation file or during the hearings, admits the breach, the procedure triggers the application of a mitigating circumstance.

(c)   The procedure in case of economic concentration that may raise national security risk (these amendments will be detailed in subsection *Specific provisions in case of economic concentration that may raise national security risk* below).

(d)   The access to RCC's file. E.g.: (i) by contrast to the previous provisions that did not determine a term, currently the hearings, if considered necessary in Phase II, shall not take place earlier than 30 days since the date when the investigation report was communicated to the concerned parties; (ii) according to the new provisions, the access to the investigation file shall be granted only once and the parties do not have access to the other parties' observations on the investigation report, while, before the new amendments, the RCC could have derogated from these rules.

(e)   The assessment procedure for multi-jurisdictional mergers.

In light of the European Competition Network's *Best Practices on Cooperation between EU National Competition Authorities in Merger Review*, the amendments introduced a special provision regarding the correspondence between national competition authorities in case of "multi-jurisdictional mergers" (an economic concentration notifiable both in Romania, to the RCC and in at least another Member State of the European Union).

Thus, the parties involved in the concentration are advised to grant the RCC the permission to provide confidential information to other national competition authorities assessing the same merger (the "NCA"). For this purpose, the Regulation provides a form similar to the one annexed to the *Best Practices on Cooperation between EU National Competition Authorities in Merger Review.* If the parties thus agree, the RCC may provide such information to the NCA without notifying the parties. Even so, the RCC is still compelled to use the information provided by the parties in the form only in the assessment of the relevant economic concentration.

Another general amendment to the Regulation provides that in case it is not clear whether the economic concentration is notifiable or not, the interested party should notify it nonetheless to the RCC.

The already existing criteria in the Competition Act concerning the minimum set of conditions that must be met in order for a transaction to be qualified as an economic concentration, which must be notified to the RCC, remained the same. According to the domestic antitrust rules, the transactions resulting in a change of control over a certain company or business must be cleared by the RCC to the extent that they exceed the following legal turnover thresholds: (i) the aggregate turnover of the parties (in the previous year of the transaction) (e.g. the purchaser and the target) and their groups, is above €10m; and (ii) each of at least two of the undertakings involved has obtained a turnover in Romania exceeding €4m and at the same time, the turnover figures are below the *de minimis* thresholds set by EC Merger Regulation No. 139/2004.

Similar to the provisions applicable at the European Commission level and in other national jurisdictions from the EEA, the Romanian legal framework divides the notification procedure initiated by the RCC in case of notified economic concentrations in two phases.

General remarks on the RCC's control procedure

The Regulation on economic concentrations provides two possible procedures to be followed when assessing an economic concentration. Depending on the expected effects on the competitive environment, the assessment may follow the complete or the simplified procedure. The simplified procedure requires less information and less time for assessment. An economic concentration is notified according to the simplified procedure when it is expected, after implementation, to have insignificant effects on the competitive environment. The effect is considered insignificant in the following cases:

(a) two or more undertakings acquire joint control over a target, provided that the joint venture does not carry out significant activities on the Romanian territory (i.e. the turnover of the joint venture, transferred activities or transferred assets do not exceed €4m on Romanian territory);

(b) there is no overlap among the relevant markets (including upstream and downstream markets) on which the parties to an economic concentration carry out their activity;

(c) the cumulated market share, which corresponds to the market in which the parties to the economic concentration overlap, does not exceed: 15%, in case of horizontal relations; and 25%, in case of vertical relations (upstream or downstream markets); or

(d) an undertaking acquires sole control over a company already under its joint control.

During Phase I, the RCC conducts an assessment of the notification, and information and documents received from the notifying party, and it requests additional information in case the notification is incomplete or inaccurate. As regards the last scenario, it should be mentioned that within 20 days after submitting the notification, in case the RCC establishes that the notification is incomplete or the information provided in the notification form is inaccurate, the RCC will send to the notifying party a written request for information and, if this is the case, it will grant the undertaking a 15-day term to provide the answers (with the possibility of extending the term by an additional five-day period).

At the same time, in practice, the RCC requests information from the market, both from the private sector (competing undertakings, suppliers, clients) and from the public sector (regulatory authorities, National Statistics Institute, professional associations of undertakings, etc.).

In most cases, and even in those transactions which raise no competitive issues, the RCC's traditional approach during the assessment of notifications leads to detailed checking and cross-checking of the information gathered from the market, on the one hand, and of those provided by the parties, on the other hand.

In light of the latest amendments of the Regulation on economic concentrations, the RCC can notify the competent public authorities or institutions in case the former identifies possible breaches of national rules (e.g. tax obligations). When doing so, the RCC will communicate only the information concerning the alleged infringement, and it is bound to protect the confidentiality of the information submitted by the parties.

During Phase I, the parties involved do not enjoy the right of access to the RCC file as such fundamental right of defence is granted to the parties in the last stage of the Phase II merger control procedure, if they get there.

Upon completion of the procedure depicted above, the RCC may reach various conclusions based on which a certain decision shall be issued. Thus, in those cases where the RCC reaches the conclusion that in fact the assessed operation does not meet the legal conditions to fall within the scope of the Competition Act, the RCC shall notify, through an address, the parties concerned about such conclusion within 30 days as of the date the notification is deemed as complete.

In case of an economic concentration notified according to the simplified procedure and that falls under the Competition Act, if the conditions are met and no special circumstances occur, within 45 days as of the effectiveness of the notification, the RCC will issue a non-objection decision (i.e. no serious doubts were identified as regards the compatibility with a normal competition environment on the relevant markets). In some cases, the RCC may decide to return to the complete procedure even if the economic concentration was notified using the simplified form and, in other cases, the RCC may carry out the simplified assessment procedure even if the parties have submitted the complete notification form.

In the complete procedure, to the extent the notified operation falls under the Competition Act, based on the RCC conclusions as regards the operation, and within 45 days of the effectiveness of the notification, the RCC has the legal option: (i) to issue a non-objection decision when the RCC establishes that no serious doubts were identified as regards the compatibility with a normal competition environment on the relevant markets or any identified doubts are removed by proposed commitments; or (ii) to initiate Phase II procedure by opening an in-depth investigation if the economic concentration raises serious anticompetitive issues[5].

According to article 10 of the RCC Regulation on economic concentrations, a notification becomes effective at the date when it is submitted to the RCC, except for the cases when the information provided is incomplete and/or inaccurate and/or imprecise.

From the RCC's recent practice (2009-2012), it can been seen that, in fact, the notifications became effective after one to three months as of the date the notification form was submitted to the RCC (depending on the nature of the information that must be provided by the undertakings).

In those cases when the RCC decides to open an investigation and thus to initiate a Phase II procedure, the RCC shall grant at least a 30-day term to the involved undertakings to submit written observations to the investigation report. According to the new amendments of the Regulation, the RCC will organise hearings only if the involved parties demand so, or if the RCC deems it necessary in order to establish the truth. Previous to these amendments, the organisation of a hearing before the RCC's Plenum was compulsory.

In Phase II of an economic concentration assessment, within five months as of the effectiveness of the notification, the RCC has the following legal options: (i) to issue a decision whereby it declares the economic concentration as being incompatible with a normal competitive environment; (ii) to authorise the economic concentration in cases which do not raise serious doubts; or (iii) to authorise the economic concentration subject to certain commitments undertaken by the parties involved in order to ensure the compatibility of the proposed operation with a normal competitive environment.

The RCC may accept commitments from the undertakings involved in an economic concentration[6] proposed in either of the two Phases. The main purpose of such commitments is to eliminate any anticompetitive concern identified by the RCC and thus to clear the economic concentration.

In case the RCC intends to accept the commitments proposed by the parties, the RCC shall publish on its official website a summary of the case, together with the key content of the proposed commitments. Within the term established by the RCC, interested third parties may communicate to the RCC their observations on the published content of the commitments. In case of commitments proposed by the parties during a Phase I procedure, the RCC has no legal obligation to publish on its official website the parties' intention to propose commitments and the content thereof.

Based on the specific issues identified in the context of a notified concentration, the commitments proposed by the parties may have a structural or behavioural nature but there is no restriction for the parties to propose and for the RCC to accept both types of commitments in case of a notified concentration. According to the Competition Act, structural commitments (e.g. a commitment to divest an activity/business) are preferable in most cases as they are more likely to prevent on a lasting basis the anti-competitive effects that would have been generated by the economic concentration.

When accepting the commitments proposed by the parties, the RCC issues an authorisation decision stating that, in light of and subject to full observance of the undertaken commitments, the notified economic concentration is compatible with a normal competitive environment. The commitments form is annexed to the clearance decision and both documents are also published on the official website of the Romanian competition authority.

Considering the relative short period of time since these provisions are in force, there is no consolidated practice regarding the commitments procedure or the RCC position with respect to such commitments.

The RCC accepted commitments in only two cases concerning economic concentrations, notified at the end of 2010, respectively at the beginning of 2011. The commitments accepted by the RCC were attached to the merger control clearances obtained by Fresenius Medical Care group for acquisitions of two suppliers of renal care services: (a) Euromedic (an international acquisition with pan-European merger control implications); and (b) four Renamed companies active on the Romanian dialysis services market.

The RCC assessed both transactions in parallel, as both involved Fresenius group and raised anticompetitive concerns due to their horizontal effects.

The transactions received clearance from the RCC through Decisions nos. 19 and 20, dated June 20, 2011[7], without initiating a Phase II procedure.

In order for such solution to be reached, the commitments proposed by the notifying parties removed all concerns identified by the RCC on the haemodialysis and peritoneal dialysis services markets rendered in the catchment area of the dialysis centre located in Botosani city, and also on the national distribution market of the dialysis products used in haemodialysis treatment.

Following long meetings with the RCC, the parties presented a complex set of commitments consisting of both structural and sophisticated behavioural remedies aimed at removing the concerns raised by the RCC.

In accordance with the undertaken commitments, Fresenius signed recently a transaction to transfer the dialysis centres from Botosani and Oradea, under the condition that the RCC issues a decision approving unconditionally the transaction according to the commitments. Moreover, the transaction was a notifiable economic concentration. The RCC cleared the transaction on both aspects in October 2012[8] and therefore the structural commitments were accomplished.

Court control over the RCC's decision

The RCC's decision may be challenged mainly by the parties to whom it is addressed, before the Bucharest Court of Appeal within 30 days from its communication. The decision of the Court of Appeal may in its turn be reviewed by the High Court of Cassation and Justice of Romania. Even if the competition legislation does not include a special reference, third parties – justifying a legitimate interest (based on general law provisions) – may also challenge the RCC's decision.

The court of law may decide, upon request, to suspend the enforcement of the decision which is to be reviewed. In case of decisions containing obligations to pay fines, the suspension shall be granted only subject to payment of a judicial bail. In light of the recent amendments, the bail can amount to up to 20% of the value of the fine, while, before the amendment of the Regulation, the bail was 30% of the fine.

Until now, parties directly involved, or third parties, have not submitted to the competent courts of law any legal claims against the RCC's decisions for the authorisation of economic concentrations.

Sanctions for failure to notify an economic concentration

Theoretically, the RCC has the means to actively monitor the general compliance with the rules of the notification procedure, by requesting information from the Romanian Trade Register, the Romanian National Securities Commission or other relevant authorities. However, in the absence of any public information in this respect, we cannot confirm that such monitoring is actually performed. Nevertheless, the RCC may become aware of a failure to notify in the course of other proceedings (e.g. notification of another economic concentration).

As per Article 51 of the Competition Act, the undertaking is sanctioned with a fine ranging from 0.5% up to 10% of the total turnover achieved in the previous financial year if, wilfully or negligently, it: (i) fails to notify a concentration falling within the scope of the Competition Act; (ii) implements a concentration prior to obtaining the RCC's authorisation; and/or (iii) implements a concentration declared by the RCC as incompatible with a normal competitive environment. For newly established companies with no turnover in the previous year, the fines are between Ron 15,000 and Ron 2,500,000.

Before the recent amendments, these limits were twice as high.

Moreover, in case the RCC finds that an economic concentration has been implemented and that such concentration was declared as being incompatible with a normal competitive environment, the RCC, by issuing a decision, may request the undertakings involved to dissolve the entity that resulted from the concentration, in order to restore the situation existing prior to the implementation of the economic concentration, or to impose any other adequate measure in order to ensure that the undertakings involved dissolve/reverse the concentration.

In 2011, the RCC issued two sanctioning decisions: (i) one for failure to notify a concentration falling within the scope of the Competition Act[9]; and (ii) one implementing a concentration prior to obtaining the RCC's authorisation[10]. In 2009, the RCC started, based on a complaint, an investigation into an alleged implementation of an economic concentration before the issuance of a clearance decision. The investigation was closed in 2012 without applying any sanctions because no evidence of infringement was discovered.[11]

Specific provisions in case of economic concentration that may raise national security risk

The Competition Act[12] provides that: (a) in those cases when an operation raises national security risks, the Government, based on the proposal made by the Supreme Council of National Defence (the "SCND"), shall issue a decision which prohibits such operation; and (b) the RCC shall inform the SCND in relation to the economic concentration operations notified to the RCC and which are susceptible to appraisal from a national security standpoint.

The latest amendments to the Regulation regarding economic concentrations regulate a special procedure of cooperation between the RCC, the Government and the SCND in these cases.

Furthermore, the Regulation now provides an independent definition for "operations that may raise national security risks". Thus, "operations that may raise national security risks" means the acquisition by a person of decisive influence on the basis of rights, contracts or any other means, over undertakings or assets of interest to national security, which can function independently and have economic utility.

The analysis from a national security risk standpoint will occur regardless of whether the acquisition of control is also an economic concentration within the meaning of the Competition Act. The following are considered domains of national security[13]:
*   citizen and community safety;
*   safety of the borders;
*   energy safety;
*   safety of information and communication systems;
*   financial, tax, banking and insurance safety;
*   safety of production and circulation of weapons, ammunition, explosives, toxic substances;
*   industrial safety;
*   protection against disasters;
*   agriculture and environment protection; and
*   protection regarding privatisation of state-owned companies or their management.

The new provisions require the RCC, when receiving an economic concentration notification, to notify the SCND about it, providing at the same time the following information about the transaction: description of the nature of the economic concentration (e.g. merger, acquisition); the involved parties and their identification data; field of activity of the involved parties; manner of performing the operation; and the transaction's object (i.e. a company or assets).

According to the Regulation on economic concentration, the SCND shall inform the RCC within 30 days whether the economic concentration should be analysed also from a national security point of view. If the analysis is considered necessary, the involved parties shall be immediately informed about this, and the correspondence from that moment on shall take place between the SCND and the parties.

The analysis regarding the national security risks shall be finalised in a maximum of 45 days as from the date when all the necessary information and documents were made available by the parties. In case, following the analyses, the SCND intends to propose that the Government issue a decision whereby the operation will be prohibited, the SCND will inform both the parties and the Government about its intention within five days.

Nevertheless, SCND's Decision no. 73 dated September 27, 2012 ("SNCD's Decision") imposes an obligation on the RCC to adapt, within 30 days, the terms provided by the Regulation to the responsibilities and functioning mode of SCND. As the Regulation has not been amended following SCND's Decision, it is safe to say that, at this time, the above terms remain in force.

In addition, in case of an economic concentration that does not exceed the turnover thresholds to fall under the Competition Act and, consequently, the notification to the RCC is not compulsory, the party or parties acquiring control must send directly to the SCND the necessary information about the transaction for it to be analysed from a national security standpoint.

SCND's Decision also provides that any notification received directly from the parties will be diverted to the RCC within a 15-day term.

Key industry sectors reviewed and approach adopted to market definition, barriers to entry, nature of international competition etc.

In line with the RCC's aim to have clear overviews on the markets, it should be mentioned that, in general, the RCC's approach is to analyse in detail even those notifications which do not raise significant or particular issues on the market.

Even in those economic sectors where the prices/tariffs are regulated by the state, the RCC further analyses the existence of the possibility of the parties to influence (for example, following the notified economic concentration) the prices/tariffs of the respective products or services. However, it should be mentioned that, in fact, the RCC seems to be more relaxed in case of operations in which the parties involved (especially the target company) were assessed in the past by the RCC. In the case of these operations, the RCC focuses on the new elements of the market, the market trend, the evolution of prices, the entry of new competitors, development of new production capacities etc.

As regards the key sectors analysed by the RCC, in 2011 and 2012, the RCC's decisions focused on the food market, real estate rental market, insurance market and medical services market. Some of the noteworthy economic concentrations are: (a) in the food market, Profi Rom Food acquired sole control over Al Comsib[14]; (b) in the real estate rental market, Carrefour Nederland BV and NE Property Cooperatief UA acquired joint control over Just Development[15] and Nepi Bucharest Three[16]; (c) in the medical services market, Fresenius Medical Care acquired sole control over Nefromed[17] companies and Renamed[18] companies; and Sensiblu acquired sole control over 90 pharmacies owned by News Quality Pharma[19]; and (d) in the insurance market, Alico Insurance Romania acquired sole control over Aviva Life Insurance and Aviva Private Pensions[20].

As regards the definition of the relevant market in certain cases, the RCC relies on past decisions issued by the RCC itself or by the European Commission, using also, for information or demonstration purposes, decisions issued by non-EU competition authorities (e.g. the Federal Trade Commission and even the competition authority from Singapore – Case Fresenius/Einstein, Fresenius/Renamed).

Even if, as regards the products market, the RCC is more open to rely on and use the decisions issued by other competition authorities, when defining the geographical market, the RCC's approach changes, particularly when the parties invoke arguments which support defining a market that exceeds the national territory.

In order to define the relevant market of an economic concentration, the RCC leans to a national or even local market. For example, in assessing Fresenius Medical Care's acquisitions of two suppliers of renal care services, Euromedic (an international acquisition with pan-European merger control implications) and Renamed (most important local competitor of Fresenius), the RCC defined the catchment area of renal care services (the relevant market) as a 50km radius around the dialysis centres[21].

Similarly, the RCC defined the geographical dimension of the pharmacies market as the area around the pharmacy in question, with a radius not exceeding 1.6-3.2km. The RCC defined the market in

2011 as such, while assessing Sensiblu's acquisition of sole control over 24 pharmacies owned by Farmaplanet Group,[22] and relied on it in assessing the economic concentration in which Sensiblu acquired sole control over 90 pharmacies owned by News Quality Pharma[23].

Also, in operations concerning retail markets, the RCC considers the geographical relevant market to be local by drawing a circle around the store which has a radius corresponding to the distance that consumers can travel by car in 10-30 minutes (depending on several factors such as household size and preferences, income levels, store accessibility, store size, transport network).

In reviewing specific markets, with a strict regulation, the RCC's policy is to request information necessary for defining the markets from public regulatory authorities (e.g. Ministry of Health, Romanian National Health Insurance House, ANCOM, etc.). The RCC takes into account the information and opinions provided by such authorities in assessing the specific markets.

In considering the impact of the operation on the relevant market, the RCC uses, in particular, the Herfindahl-Hirschman Index ("HHI"). The higher the HHI is, the more information the undertakings have to provide to the RCC. Even if the concentration of the market should be indicative in assessing the operation, for the RCC the HHI seems to become an essential tool for conducting the competitive assessment, in many cases being the determining factor.

When defining the relevant markets, and during the assessment of economic concentrations, an important role is attributable to the investigations initiated by the RCC *ex officio* on certain markets. The RCC's policy is to review periodically various sectors of industries and markets, and to prepare reports regarding these investigations.

For example, in the second semester of 2011, the RCC issued a report regarding the automotive aftermarkets[24]. The main findings of the report result in: (a) weak concentration of the market; (b) proposals for legislative amendments in order to open the competition of the market of visible parts; (c) the need to increase the level of control, both legislative control and actual control, over counterfeit products and refurbished parts; (d) proposals to simplify some administrative procedures in order to remove the administrative barriers; and (e) the notification of the National Consumer Protection Agency with respect to the abuse of car dealers regarding guarantees.

The RCC also issued, at the end of 2011, a report regarding the sectoral investigation in the market of production, transport, distribution and supply of thermal energy in Bucharest[25]. The conclusions deriving from the report were mainly the following: (a) the technical and administrative configuration of the market cannot ensure a normal competition since the market is monopolistic and extensively regulated; and (b) because tariffs and prices are regulated by specific public authorities, no proposals can, at this time, individually, enhance the competition on the market. The report proposes that in the future the market should be designed as a competitive market with no need for a monopoly or a dominant company in order to increase the economic efficiency of production, transport, distribution and supply of thermal energy.

Key economic appraisal techniques applied

The RCC uses the Significant Impediment to Effective Competition Test (SIEC). In order to declare an economic concentration compatible with a normal competition environment, the RCC takes into account the risk of creating and consolidating a dominant position on the market corroborated with other additional factors, such as:

- the necessity of protection, preservation and further development of effective competition;
- market structure;
- actual and potential competition;
- the parties' market share and economic and financial power;
- alternatives available to suppliers and users;
- suppliers' and users' access to supply sources or markets, and any legal or other barriers to entry relevant markets by other undertakings;
- supply and demand trends for the goods and/or relevant services;
- intermediary and final consumers' interests; and

- technical and economic development, provided that it is to consumers' advantage and does not form an obstacle to competition.

As a result, using the SIEC Test provides a profound and rigorous analysis, similar to the one used in the Community-specific practice.

Approach to remedies (i) to avoid second stage investigation and (ii) following second stage investigation

(i) Avoidance of second stage investigation

In order to avoid reaching Phase II in an economic concentration, communication with the competition authority is essential. Therefore, it is recommended that a communication channel is established from the beginning, i.e. from the moment the notification form is submitted with the RCC.

By communicating with the RCC's representatives, the parties are able to anticipate the potential issues that the RCC might raise regarding the envisaged economic concentration. When this is the case, the parties may: (i) argue why the aspects that concern the RCC from a competition perspective are consistent with a normal competitive environment; or (ii) propose commitments in order to eliminate, before or after the authorisation of the economic concentration, the matters that raise significant impediments to competition.

In the preliminary stage of the notification, the undertakings are recommended to collect information from the market, client declaration, and expert opinions obtained from the parties, or from third parties that confirm that the notification is compliant with a normal competition environment.

As mentioned above, the only example of the commitment's procedure applied so far is the merger control clearances issued by the RCC with respect to the economic concentrations between Fresenius Medical Care Beteiligungsgesellschaft and Euromedic and Fresenius Nephrocare Romania and four Renamed companies[26].

(ii) Following second stage investigation

After entering a Phase II investigation, the RCC has to decide within five months on the economic concentration. In this stage, the RCC may: (i) give a decision to declare the economic concentration as incompatible with a normal competition environment; (ii) authorise the economic concentration because no serious doubts were identified about the compatibility with a normal competition environment on the relevant markets; or (iii) authorise the economic concentration under some commitments in order to comply with a normal competition environment.

According to the public information registered in the RCC's Annual Reports, in our jurisdiction, no economic concentration has reached Phase II after the 2010 reform process.

Key policy developments and reform proposals

The main novelty brought by the latest amendments of the Romanian competition legislation is the development of specific provisions in case of economic concentration that may raise national security risk.

The implications of these amendments in the long term may be significant, but for now they bring to the attention of undertakings intending to enter in a transaction a new concern: their transaction must be notified either to the RCC (in case of notifiable transaction) or to the SCND (in case of non-notifiable transaction) and the decision of one or both of these bodies may interfere or prohibit the implementation of their transaction.

Regarding new expected developments, as mentioned above, SCND's Decision imposes on the RCC the obligation to adapt, within 30 days starting September 27, 2012, the terms provided by the Regulation regarding the responsibilities and functioning mode of SCND. As the Regulation was not amended following SCND's Decision, it should be expected that further amendments to the Regulation will be made.

Separately, so far the RCC has not made public any project to review or update the Competition Act or secondary competition legislation in the merger control area. However, the Action Plan published by the RCC in July 2012 shows RCC's intention to implement in more cases the simplified procedure of assessing economic concentrations. So far, the RCC has issued, in 2011, only three decisions following the simplified procedure and, in 2012, only one.

* * *

Endnotes

1. According to the RCC's 2011 Annual Report.
2. According to the decisions published on the RCC's official website www.competition.ro.
3. Enforced by Order no. 385/2010.
4. Enforced by Order no. 421/2011.
5. Articles 21 and 22 from RCC's Order no. 385 dated August 5, 2010 for approval regarding the economic concentration.
6. RCC's Order no. 688 dated December 9, 2010 for approving the guidelines regarding the commitments implementation on economic concentrations.
7. RCC's Decisions nos. 19 and 20 dated June 20, 2011 and the Commitments attached, published on RCC's official website www.competition.ro.
8. RCC's Decision no. 54 dated October 3, 2012.
9. RCC's Decision no. 14 dated April 27, 2011 for sanctioning SC Asesoft Distribution SRL for the breach of article 15(6) of the Competition Act.
10. RCC's Decision no. 28 dated September, 2011 for sanctioning SC Labormed Pharma SA for the breach of article 15(6) of the Competition Act.
11. RCC's Decision no. 30 dated June 22, 2012.
12. Article 46(9) of the Competition Act.
13. SCND's Decision no. 73 dated September 27, 2012.
14. RCC's Decision no. 7 dated February 21, 2012.
15. RCC's Decision no. 66 dated November 2, 2012.
16. RCC's Decision no. 45 dated September 29, 2011.
17. RCC's Decision no. 20 dated June 20, 2011.
18. RCC's Decision no. 19 dated June 20, 2011.
19. RCC's Decision no. 17 dated April 24, 2012.
20. RCC's Decision no. 20 dated June 6, 2012.
21. RCC's Decisions no. 19 and 20 dated June 20, 2011.
22. RCC's Decision no. 10 dated March 30, 2011.
23. RCC's Decision no. 17 dated April 24, 2012.
24. RCC's report regarding the automotive aftermarkets http://www.consiliulconcurentei.ro/uploads/docs/items/id7387/raport_final.pdf
25. RCC's report regarding the sectorial investigation on the market of production, transport, distribution and supply of thermal energy in Bucharest http://www.consiliulconcurentei.ro/uploads/docs/items/id6530/raport_energie.pdf
26. RCC's Decisions nos. 19 and 20 dated June 20, 2011 and the Commitments attached.

Silviu Stoica
Tel: +40 21 317 79 19 / Email: silviu.stoica@pnpartners.ro
Silviu Stoica is a partner with Popovici Nitu & Asociatii and head of the competition practice group. His practice focuses on a broad range of contentious and non-contentious competition matters, with an emphasis on cartel investigations and industry inquiries, abuses of dominant position and antitrust disputes.

Mr Stoica has been commended in Chambers Europe as "very client-oriented" and "focused on solutions". Established clients of Silviu Stoica include ArcelorMittal, Cargill, Innova Capital, Oresa Ventures and Philip Morris, on a whole array of competition matters and investment issues.

Mr Stoica has been with the firm since its inception, pursuing all carrier stages from associate to senior associate and head of practice group. Silviu Stoica holds a degree in law from the University of Bucharest Faculty of Law and is a member of the Bucharest Bar Association. Mr Stoica attended US Legal Methods – Introduction to US Law Institute for US Law in Washington, DC, and the International Development Law Organization Development Lawyers Course (DLC-20E) in Rome.

Mihaela Ion
Tel: +40 21 317 79 19 / Email: mihaela.ion@pnpartners.ro
Mihaela Ion is a managing associate within the competition practice group of Popovici Nitu & Asociatii. Her area of expertise covers in particular antitrust litigation, unfair trade practices, consumer law, merger control proceedings and state aid. She also assists clients in structuring and implementing compliance programmes, providing regular training as external legal counsel on all relevant aspects of competition law.

Chambers Europe reported Ms Ion as being appreciated for her focus on clients' need and proactive approach.

Ms Ion holds a degree in law from "Lucian Blaga" University of Sibiu and is a member of the Romanian Bar Association. Mihaela Ion holds also a Masters Degree in Competition from Bucharest Academy for Economic Studies and a Masters Degree in International Relation and European Integration from Romanian Diplomatic Institute. She is a PhD Candidate in International Trade Law with Bucharest Academy for Economic Studies, Institute for Doctoral Studies.

Popovici Nitu & Asociatii

239 Calea Dorobanti, 6th floor, Bucharest, 1st District, Postal Code 010567, Romania
Tel: +40 21 317 79 19 / Fax: +40 21 317 85 00 / URL: http://www.pnpartners.ro/

Russia

Evgeny Voevodin, Mikhail Voronin & Svetlana Mosendz
Anti-Monopoly Law Office LLC

Overview of merger control activity during the last 12 months

In June 2012, the Federal Antimonopoly Service of Russia ("the FAS") published its annual report for 2011. In 2011, the FAS reviewed 3,282 prior applications and 5,462 post notifications, of which 2,914 applications were accepted; 60 applications were rejected, and 308 applications were satisfied, together with the issue of special conditions. The number of applications reviewed in 2011 decreased almost by half compared with 2007, and the number of notifications decreased almost three times compared with 2007.

If a transaction could negatively influence competition, the FAS either rejects it or prescribes a set of conditions or actions for the applicant in order to secure competition in the relevant market. The main reason for the rejection of applications was not providing information on the ultimate beneficiary of the acquisition (the persons who actually control the acquirer).

In any analysis of the influence of state control over economic concentration, the changing of the conditions of such control must be considered. The determining influence on the decreased number of applications and notifications considered by the FAS is an increase in the merger control thresholds.

The requirement of prior approval of the FAS for the reorganisation of commercial (including financial) organisations (in the form of mergers and acquisitions) or the creation of commercial (including financial) organisations ceases to apply to cases when such activity is conducted by members of the same group of persons, on conditions provided by Paragraph 1 of Part 1 of Article 9 of the Federal Law No. 135-FZ dated 26 July 2006 On Protection of Competition ("the Competition Law"). Such conditions provide that the acquirer and the target-company constitute members of the same group of persons on the grounds of possession of more than 50% of shares (such companies are under control of the same shareholder). A similar exemption was extended to the case of transactions with shares, assets of commercial organisations (including financial), and rights of control regarding commercial organisations (including financial).

The official report regarding 2012 is not published yet, but in February 2013 the FAS published on its website the presentation of the Head of the FAS, I.Y. Artemyev, "Key results for 2012", where it is established that during 2012, the FAS reviewed 2,494 prior applications and 1,943 post notifications.

The number of applications considered by the FAS in 2012 has decreased, however the number of applications satisfied, together with the issue of special conditions, has slightly increased.

New developments in jurisdictional assessment or procedure

On 6 and 7 January 2012, the Federal Law No 401-FZ, "On Introducing Amendments to the Federal Law On Protection of Competition", entered into force, together with, "Some Legislative Acts of the Russian Federation", and the Federal Law No 404-FZ, "On Introducing Amendments to the Code of the Russian Federation on Administrative Violations", which constitute the so-called "third antimonopoly package".

The "third antimonopoly package" proposed amendments to several groups of antitrust matters, *inter alia* some significant developments in procedure of merger control. The merger control amendments are aimed at decreasing the number of deals which have to obtain FAS advanced approval.

Extraterritoriality. The third antimonopoly package reduces the number of transactions performed outside the Russian Federation which required prior approval from the FAS. Before the third antimonopoly package entered into force, the antimonopoly law was applicable to agreements reached between Russian and foreign persons or companies outside Russia, as well as to actions performed by them, if such agreements are reached and actions are performed involving the fixed assets or intangible assets located in Russia, or otherwise affecting the state of competition in Russia. As a result, approval from the FAS was required for the acquisition of shares or rights in respect of foreign entities with a minimal presence in Russia. The wording given in the Law was completely unclear, so there have been cases where a company does not have any subsidiaries or assets in Russia, but has turnover appearing to be outside the regulations. In such circumstances, some companies choose to apply to the FAS to get confirmation of whether clearance is required or not.

Following the entry into force of the amendments, approval of the FAS is, as previously, required for transactions performed outside the Russian Federation, if the result of the transaction is the acquisition of rights to determine the terms of commercial activity of an entity incorporated in the Russian Federation.

Additionally, approval of the FAS is now also required for transactions in respect of acquisition of foreign entities, if such foreign entity supplied goods to the Russian Federation for a value exceeding 1 billion rubles over the year preceding the date of the transaction.

Threshold values. As mentioned above, an increase in the merger control thresholds is the main reason for the decreasing number of applications filed every year. The third antimonopoly package reduces the number of transactions requiring prior approval of the antimonopoly authorities by raising certain thresholds and changing the way some of them are calculated.

Prior clearance is required for entities operating in commodity markets if:

a) The book value of the acquirer's worldwide assets, the assets of the commercial entities belonging to the acquirer's group worldwide, and the worldwide assets of the target and of commercial entities belonging to its group worldwide, exceed 7 billion rubles; or

b) The aggregate worldwide income of the entities listed above from the sale of commodities during the last calendar year exceeds 10 billion rubles. This threshold should be applied only if the above-mentioned threshold is not met; and

- the aggregate worldwide value of the assets of the target, and of the commercial entities belonging to the target's group, exceed 250 million rubles. This threshold should be applied together with each of the above thresholds; or
- enrolment of the acquirer (or its group) or the target (or its group) in the register of commercial entities, with a market share in excess of 35 per cent maintained by the FAS. This threshold is applied only to Russian legal entities.

The third antimonopoly package has changed the way that assets are calculated for the purposes of applying the threshold values to the acquisitions. For the calculation of the threshold based on the balance sheet value of assets, the companies should not calculate the seller-company's assets.

Procedure. The third antimonopoly package established the changes to the requirements for information, and documents that should be filed to the FAS with the application for approval or notification of transactions.

Particularly, the amendments have reduced the scope of disclosure of the applicant's and target-company's groups of persons. The third antimonopoly package limits it to entities and persons that control and are controlled by the applicant or target-company, and entities and persons that form one group of persons with them and conduct operations on the same commodities markets on which the applicant and target-company operates, and entities and persons under their control. Also, in some cases it is possible to exclude individuals from a group of persons.

Credit institutions. As already noted, the Competition Law provides different thresholds depending on whether the entities involved operate in commodity markets or financial markets. Also, there are separate thresholds for credit institutions.

On 6 December 2012, the Government of the Russian Federation adopted decree № 1263, "On amendments to some acts of the Governments of the Russian Federation". The decree changed the value of assets of microfinance organisations, defined by the Decree of the Government of the Russian Federation of 30.05.2007 № 334, "On establishing the value of assets of financial organisations (except credit organisations) to implement the antimonopoly control". So, the notification of the FAS of the merger and acquisition transactions is required if the value of assets of the microfinance organisation exceeds 1 billion rubles, and 2.2 billion rubles for credit organisations.

Changes have also concerned a Decree of the Government of the Russian Federation of 30.05.2007 № 335, "On establishing the value of assets in order to implement antimonopoly control". Obtaining the prior approval of the FAS for merger transactions is now necessary, if the value of assets of the credit organisation exceeds 24 billion rubles.

Key industry sectors reviewed, and approach adopted, to market definition, barrier to entry, nature of competition, etc.

The Competition Law is pertinent to all industry sectors. There is no public information regarding the number of applications submitted in each sector. But the FAS representatives have often highlighted the sectors of oil, mining, retail, telecommunication and media. The major transactions in each of these sectors are discussed below.

Oil. Among the major transactions of the year, the FAS has authorised the application of OJSC Oil Company "Rosneft" for the acquisition of 100 per cent of "TNK-BP Limited" and 100 per cent of "TNK-BP INDUSTRIAL HOLDINGS LIMITED", and has issued conditions in order to secure the oil market. Both "TNK-BP Limited" and OJSC Oil Company "Rosneft" resumed a dominant position on the market of oil products; their combined share on the market of gasoline and diesel fuel sales exceed 50 per cent. As a result of this transaction, OJSC Oil Company "Rosneft" will become the biggest oil company in the world. The FAS obliges OJSC Oil Company "Rosneft" to comply with the following conditions:
- one-for-all counterparties' pricing system;
- publicity and accessibility of information on the procedure for pricing; and
- unacceptable economic and (or) technological unjustified refusal to enter into contracts with counterparties.

Mining. The FAS has cleared the acquisition of OJSC "Raspadskaya", the owner of one of the biggest coal mines in Russia, by "Evraz PLC" and has issued conditions and obligations. As a result, this transaction will significantly increase the level of concentration on the market of crozzling (half-burnt) coal concentrate, which may create the conditions for the restriction of competition on the market. And in order to prevent monopolistic activities, the FAS obliged OJSC "Raspadskaya", *inter alia,* to provide the trade marketing policy for approval and publication.

Retail. The FAS has also approved the acquisition of 50 per cent of "Evroset Holding N.V.", the biggest Russian mobile retailer, by the company "LEFBORD INVESTMENTS LIMITED" and has issued conditions and obligations. "LEFBORD INVESTMENTS LIMITED" is a company controlled by the second largest Russian mobile network operator – OJSC "MegaFon" – and the other 50 per cent of "Evroset Holding N.V." is possessed by the company "ARARIMA ENTERPRISES LIMITED", which is under control by the OJSC "VimpelCom" – the third largest Russian mobile network operator. The conditions obliged "LEFBORD INVESTMENTS LIMITED" and "ARARIMA ENTERPRISES LIMITED", *inter alia,* not to create discriminatory conditions to the counterparties, including mobile operators, and also to negotiate a Corporate Governance Agreement in relation to "Evroset Holding N.V.".

Telecommunications. The FAS approved the acquisition of 50% plus one share of OJSC "MegaFon" by "AF Telecom Holding Limited", the company that is under the control of Alisher Usmanov. AF Telecom became a main owner of "Garsdale Services Limited" with a share of 82 per cent. As a result "MegaFon" and "Scartel" LLC merged into a single holding, which received 100 per cent of "Skartel" and 50% plus one share of "MegaFon", but with the FAS' condition – non-discriminatory access for other mobile network operators to the LTE networks. "MegaFon" received the maximum frequencies band for the construction of new generation LTE networks of all operators.

Media. The FAS has authorised the application of "JCDecaux", the number one outdoor advertising company worldwide, on the acquisition of 25% of "Russ Outdoor", the largest outdoor advertising company in Russia: in 2011 the profit of "Russ Outdoor" was approximately $300m. As a result "JCDecaux" consolidated its assets with the assets of "BigBoard" (Russian operator of outdoor advertising). In future "JCDecaux" may increase its share in the share capital of "Russ Outdoor". Having examined the transaction, the FAS has found that it will not influence competition on the market of outdoor advertising.

Key economic appraisal techniques applied

Currently, there are not any guidelines concerning economic techniques that the FAS use within the investigation. The FAS approves transactions that will not result in a monopoly in the affected market, and will not restrict competition in the affected market or part of it.

If the company has a market share in excess of 35 per cent, they are automatically entering the register of commercial entities with a market share in excess of 35 per cent maintained by the FAS. Enrolment in the register imposes limitations to such entities and generally the Phase II of investigation is initiated. In this case the approvals are usually satisfied, together with an issue of special conditions (nearly all applications will be satisfied only on condition that such applicant carry out actions aimed at securing competition, or the transaction will be refused).

The substantive test for antimonopoly clearance is whether the concentration will damage competition in Russia. The FAS evaluation of the competitive environment in the commodity market includes consideration of:
(a) the time interval of investigation of the commodity markets;
(b) the product-based borders of the commodity markets;
(c) the geographic borders of the commodity markets;
(d) the make-up of economic entities operating within the commodity market;
(e) the scope of the commodity market and shares of economic entities therein;
(f) the level of concentration of the commodity market;
(g) barriers to entry into the commodity market; and
(h) the state of the competitive environment in the commodity market.

In assessing the competitive effects of a merger, the FAS attempts to determine the existing parameters and dynamics of competition on the affected market, and predicts the effect of a given transaction on that market. The FAS compares the competitive conditions that would follow the merger with those that would prevail in its absence, and endeavours to determine whether the merging entities will face sufficient residual competition to make it unprofitable to increase prices or decrease output.

The FAS generally estimates the level of competition based on the market shares held by the entities:
(1) when the entity has market share that does not exceed 35% – the level of competition is strong and the application probably will be satisfied in Phase I and unconditionally;
(2) when the entity has market share that exceeds 35% but does not exceed 50% – the level of competition is weak and generally the Phase II of investigation will be initiated. The application probably will be satisfied but with an issue of special conditions;
(3) when the entity has market share that exceeds 50% but does not exceed 75% – the level of competition is extremely weak and most definitely the Phase II will be initiated. The application will be hardly satisfied, but only with an issue of special conditions;
(4) when the entity has market share that exceeds 75% – there is practically no competition. The approval of the application will be most definitely refused.

The prohibited transaction may be approved if the parties can prove that the positive effect of the transaction for public interest and for technology development is much greater than its negative consequences.

Approach to remedies (i) to avoid second stage investigation and (ii) following second stage investigation

Under the Federal Law No. 135-FZ dated 26 July 2006, On Protection of Competition (with amendments), the FAS has 30 calendar days to review the application within the Phase I. Such period starts from the day after the FAS receives the application with all the documents and data required to be sent with it. After reviewing the application due to the Phase I, the FAS shall make one of the following motivated decisions:
a)   to approve the application;
b)   to refuse the application;
c)   to extend the time limit for considering the application – to initiate the Phase II.

The time limit for the FAS to review the application under Phase II may be extended up to, but no more than, two months to satisfy any need for further review, and also any need to receive further information from the applicant, should it be established that the transaction may entail restriction of competition, including as a result of the emergence or strengthening of the dominant position of the person of the applicant (group of persons).

If the FAS decides to prolong its consideration of an application, it publishes on its official website data on the transaction declared in the application. Third persons concerned may submit to the antimonopoly body data on the impact of such transactions on the state of competition. There is no other third-party access to the file and no possibilities for third parties to challenge a merger.

The Russian Federation legislation does not provide any remedies that can help to avoid the Phase II of investigation. Also there are not any guidelines or approach followed by the FAS concerning such remedies. So the only way to try to avoid the Phase II is to submit to the FAS additional documents and information that can help the FAS in considering the application, together with all the documents and data required to be sent with the application.

If the Phase II will be initiated because of an FAS ruling that the actions stated in the application will or may entail restriction of competition, there is, however, the possibility to discuss with FAS representatives under which circumstances (i.e. changes to a transaction) it would grant a clearance decision. If a "remedy" is found, the FAS can approve the application while concurrently prescribing that the applicant must carry out actions aimed at securing competition, if it effects the transaction stated in the application. After meeting the conditions specified by the FAS prescription, the applicant must submit to the FAS documents that prove that it did so. It is important to note that the number of FAS clearance decisions made after applicants' changes in transaction is slightly increasing.

Key policy developments

In February 2013, the Head of the FAS Russia presented a Strategy for Developing Antimonopoly Regulation in 2013-2024.

Over and above its protective function and transition to system-wide measures of a macroeconomic nature, the main purpose of the Strategy is to form a pro-competitive legal and institutional regime in the Russian economy.

The main aims of the Strategy are the following: to exclude notification control over economic concentration, and to frame the Administrative Code of the Customs Union in order to create a system such as exists in the EU.

As part of reducing the number of transactions subject to the notification, the Organisation for Economic Cooperation recommends to the FAS Russia to cancel the notification control, cancel prior control in accordance with the Law Concerning Natural Monopolies, and to liberalise the use of Register of Business Entities whose shares of particular commodity markets exceed 35%.

Reform proposals

At the present time a Bill abolishing the post-notification procedures of the transactions of mergers and acquisitions is being passed by the State Duma (Lower Chamber of the Russian Parliament). The

Bill proposes to abolish the post-notification control of a number of transactions.

Currently, the Federal Law "On Protection of Competition" provides that the company must notify the FAS about establishing a new company in a merger or acquisition transactions, if the value of their assets or total annual revenues of the organisations involved in the transaction, is more than 400 million rubles. The Bill abolishes the rule.

The Bill also abolishes post-notification control for acquisitions of shares, rights or tangible assets, if the aggregate value of the assets on the last balance sheet, or the aggregate revenues from the sale of goods of the acquirer's group of persons and the target-company's group of persons, is more than 400 million rubles, while the total value of assets at the last balance sheet of the target-company's group of persons exceeds 60 million rubles.

These amendments to the Competition Law also abolish post-notification control of establishing a new financial organisation in a merger or acquisition transactions and acquisition of shares, rights or tangible assets of the financial organisations.

Therefore the post-notification merger control will remain only in cases if the thresholds established for prior approval are met, but the transaction is intra-group.

Evgeny Voevodin
Tel: +7 495 626 02 26 / Email: yav@antitrust.msk.ru

Evgeny Voevodin started out in 1998 working in international law firm Coudert Brothers (USA). In 2005 Evgeny joined the Moscow office of international law firm CMS Cameron McKenna (the UK), gathering a team of specialists 100% committed to practising Competition Law. Launched in 2008, the Competition Practice headed by Evgeny Voevodin has been recognised as a leading one.

In 2007, in collaboration with the leading Russian experts in the field of antitrust and competition, Evgeny Voevodin established the Competition Support Association, a non-profit partnership. Currently Evgeny is a managing partner of the Anti-Monopoly Law Office LLC, a legal firm specialising in antitrust regulatory matters. Evgeny's team successfully represents Russian companies in competition authorities of the CIS states, and in the European Union Competition Commission in collaboration with antitrust and competition specialists from respective jurisdictions.

Mikhail Voronin
Tel: +7 495 626 02 26 / Email: vmm@antitrust.msk.ru

Mikhail Voronin graduated from Moscow State University in 2009. Mikhail has extensive experience in advising on issues of Russian antimonopoly legislation. He specialises in corporate structuring of business, dealer and distribution agreements, anticompetitive agreements and abuse of dominance, he also represents clients at the FAS and advises clients on the competition-restricting agreements and coordination of economic activity. Mikhail has worked on a number of projects involving mergers and acquisitions, including the analysis and structuring of transactions under competition law and the law on foreign investments.

Svetlana Mosendz
Tel: +7 495 626 02 26 / Email: msv@antitrust.msk.ru

Svetlana Mosendz graduated from Moscow State Linguistic University in 2010. Svetlana has worked on a number of mergers, obtained clearances (strategic, foreign investments) and represented clients at the FAS in antimonopoly and administrative cases. Since 2013 Svetlana has held the office of secretary at the Competition Support Association.

Anti-Monopoly Law Office LLC

21/5, Kuznetsky most St., Office № 2009, 107996 Moscow, Russia
Tel: +7 495 626 02 26 / Fax: +7 495 626 01 26

Singapore

Kala Anandarajah & Dominique Lombardi*
Rajah & Tann LLP

Overview of merger control activity during the last 12 months

<u>Quick overview</u>

Mergers that have resulted, or may be expected to result, in a substantial lessening of competition ('SLC') within any market in Singapore for goods or services, are prohibited.[1] Acquisitions of direct or indirect control,[2] or the creation of fully functioning joint ventures,[3] are also considered mergers. The relevant regulator for merger reviews is the Competition Commission of Singapore ('CCS').

In the last 12 months, the CCS reviewed eight (8) mergers, all of which were cleared after a Phase I review. Significantly, one of the notified mergers, Case CCS 400/004/12 – Proposed acquisition by United Parcel Service, Inc. of TNT Express – was cleared by the CCS, although it was blocked by the European Commission.

The small number of merger notifications in Singapore is likely due to the voluntary regime in Singapore. The onus is on the merging parties to undertake a self-assessment of their transaction and determine whether the transaction ought to be notified to the CCS or otherwise. In assessing whether to notify or otherwise, the following indicative market share thresholds provided by the CCS can be used as a guide:

(a) when the merged entity will have a post-merger market share of 40%; or
(b) when the merged entity will have a post-merger market share of between 20% and 40%, and the post-merger combined market share of the three largest firms ('CR3') is 70% or more.[4]

In the 2012 revised Merger Guidelines issued by the CCS, the CCS introduced a 'safe harbour' for mergers where the turnover in Singapore of each of the parties, for the financial year preceding the transaction, is below S$5m and where the combined worldwide turnover of all of the parties, in the financial year preceding the transaction, is below S$50m.

The thresholds in (a) and (b) above take into account the market share of the merged entity in the relevant geographic market and not just in Singapore. Hence, the CCS will consider the indicative thresholds crossed if the merged entity has a share of 40% or more in a market that is wider than Singapore. A further point to highlight is that Singapore uses a market share test rather than a turnover test, which is the more common test in multiple jurisdictions.

Although the notification in Singapore is not compulsory, the CCS has indicated that if mergers which potentially result in an SLC are not notified, it will investigate the merger. Investigations by the CCS are not time-barred, i.e. the CCS can challenge a merger months or years after it has been implemented. Hence, notification provides the parties with critical legal certainty.

Note that if the CCS concludes an investigation into a merger with a finding that the transaction results in a SLC in Singapore, it has the power under the Competition Act to prohibit the transaction and/or require the parties to unwind the merger if completed. In addition, the CCS may impose monetary penalties (up to 10% of the merger parties' turnover up to three years). Whilst this has not happened yet, the CCS has since July 2012 made clear that it will step up enforcement in relation to non-notified mergers that may, in CCS' views, result in a SLC.

* Foreign lawyer

Transactions reviewed

The eight (8) mergers reviewed over the last 12 months all involved a transfer of shares. There was no notification involving a transfer of assets or the set-up of a joint venture, although such transactions are also covered by Singapore's merger provisions and have been notified to, and reviewed by, the CCS in previous years.

The transactions notified were, in their vast majority, acquisitions of sole control by one undertaking over another. One transaction involved a shift from joint control to sole control (Case CCS 400/005/12 – Proposed acquisition by Heineken International BV of Asia Pacific Breweries Limited). It is important to highlight that in Singapore, as in the EU, a shift from joint control to sole control amounts to a merger under the Competition Act. In other words, the selling of its shares by a joint-venture partner to another partner in the joint venture may require notification to the CCS.

Amendments to notified transactions

In Case CCS 400/010/11 – Proposed merger between Nippon Steel Corporation ('NSC') and Sumitomo Metal Industries Ltd ('SMI') – the transaction initially notified involved an acquisition, with SMI being absorbed by NSC. However, after the CCS had issued its decision approving the merger, the parties altered the structure of their transaction; the merger was eventually effected through a two-step procedure consisting of a share exchange followed by an absorption-type merger.

Whilst the CCS will not challenge a merger that has been notified and cleared by it, this is nevertheless subject to the information provided by the parties being and remaining accurate. Given this, and the fact that the transaction had effectively taken a different form, NSC and SMI informed the CCS of the changes in the structure of the transaction. Following a further review, the CCS issued an addendum to the initial decision. This avoided any (remote) risk of the transaction being challenged by the CCS in the future.

Pre-closing notifications

Whilst, as a direct consequence of the notification regime being voluntary, there is no standstill period in Singapore and, therefore, completed mergers can be notified, the transactions notified to the CCS lately have all been 'proposed' acquisitions. With such notifications, the decisions issued by the CCS are only valid for a limited period of time, one year after the date of the decision being the norm. In practice, this means that the notified transaction must be completed within this one-year period, failing which the CCS clearance decision is not valid, and potentially a fresh application will have to be made.

Significant decision

It is interesting to note that the CCS cleared the proposed acquisition by United Parcel Service, Inc. of TNT Express after a Phase I review, with no commitments, whilst the merger was prohibited by the European Commission. The primary reason for this lies in the scope of TNT's activities, which are mainly carried out in Europe. Based on the parties' market share estimates post-merger, the indicative CCS thresholds were crossed in the market for the supply of international small packet services. Nevertheless, in view of the bargaining powers of the parties' customers, the ability of competitors to meet increased demand, together with the strength of those competitors and the non-transparent nature of the market, the CCS took the view that the risk of coordinated and non-coordinated effects resulting from the merger was low. In the other relevant markets reviewed (i.e. contract logistics, freight forwarding and cargo transport), the CCS did not identify any risk of SLC either, taking into account the small market share of the merged entity. Given this, the CCS cleared the merger on 21 August 2012.

New developments in jurisdictional assessment or procedure

In February 2012, the CCS launched a public consultation on various proposed amendments to the CCS Guidelines on Merger Procedures. After completing the public consultation process, the revised Guidelines on Merger Procedures came into force on 1st July 2012 ('Revised Guidelines').

The key changes introduced by the Revised Guidelines include the following:

Confidential opinion by the CCS

The Revised Guidelines introduce a new process by which parties, who have genuine uncertainty as to whether their merger may infringe the Competition Act, may confidentially receive feedback from the CCS on whether notification is appropriate or otherwise. The CCS has stated that it will endeavour to revert to the parties promptly, i.e. within 14 working days of receiving all necessary information from the parties.

The ability to obtain a confidential advice from the CCS is certainly useful and must be welcomed. Whilst the CCS provides indicative thresholds above which notification of a transaction is strongly encouraged, these thresholds are market-share based, i.e. often difficult to evaluate. Parties have often complained that the market share thresholds were an inconvenient tool to assess SLC. For instance, the merger parties may cross the indicative market share thresholds in Singapore, but fall well below the thresholds if the relevant geographic market is wider than Singapore. Being able to obtain a confidential advice by the CCS in such instances definitely will help the parties in deciding whether to notify their merger in Singapore or otherwise. Additionally, there are cases where the high market share of the merged entity will not, in any event, result in a SLC, due to various countervailing factors. Here again, getting a confidential advice by the CCS is helpful in avoiding unnecessary notifications.

It is important to note that the confidential advice is not binding on the CCS, and the CCS may subsequently decide to investigate a merger that has not been notified, even if the confidential advice had suggested that no notification was necessary, but the facts had changed, or where the merger parties had chosen to ignore a recommendation by the CCS to notify the merger.

This new process of being able to consult with the CCS confidentially is different from, and in addition to, the current process of having Pre-Notification Discussion ('PND') with the CCS. PNDs are a useful tool, as they permit merger parties to ascertain the scope of the information that will be required by the CCS when it formally reviews the transaction. Such discussions serve to expedite the process, as they help to limit/avoid CCS' requests for further additional information during the merger review process. This also helps the parties to start thinking early of the best way to address potential competition concerns, including commitments that could be proposed to the CCS for the merger to go through.

Safe harbour for SMEs

The Revised Guidelines introduce at first sight what appears to be a safe harbour for mergers involving 'small companies'. The CCS is unlikely to investigate mergers between companies where the turnover in Singapore of each of the parties, for the financial year preceding the transaction, is below S$5m and the combined worldwide turnover of all of the parties, in the financial year preceding the transaction, is below S$50m. In practice this serves as a new threshold below which a transaction may not be notified. However, this is not a 'bright line' test, and even a transaction that falls below this threshold may be investigated by the CCS, depending on the market share of the merged entity post-acquisition.

The merger parties, therefore, should still undertake a genuine self-assessment to determine if their transaction is likely to result in SLC, using the indicative market share thresholds as a guide. In the case of conflicting results, it is recommended to seek confidential advice from the CCS.

Treatment of confidential information

When parties notify their merger to the CCS, one of the critical concerns raised regards the effective protection of the respective parties' confidential information from each other and, importantly, from the public as well.

Whilst the Competition Act contains specific provisions in relation to managing confidential information, arguably this has not been sufficiently detailed. In any event, as a general rule, the CCS does not entertain blanket claims of confidentiality, and the parties must identify precisely the information they see as confidential and their reasons thereof.

To assist with such difficulties, the CCS has, in the Revised Guidelines, set out the type of information that will unlikely be viewed as confidential. This includes, *inter alia*, 'information that reflects the merger parties' views of how the competitive effects of the merger could be analysed', or 'information that is of general knowledge within the industry, or is likely to be readily ascertainable by any reasonably diligent market participant or trade analyst'. However, arguably, truly business-sensitive information such as business plans, rationale for the transaction, documents put to the Board of the undertakings for approval of the merger, as well as detailed information in relation to the parties' customers and suppliers, will be viewed as being confidential.

Key industry sectors reviewed and approach adopted to market definition, barriers to entry, nature of international competition etc.

In the last 12 months, the CCS has reviewed merger applications from a diverse range of industries including, amongst others, the sale of beer, steel products such as steel pipes and steel coils and sheets, software for the distribution, management and operations of consumer packaged goods, fuel oil storage products as well as renal dialysis services.

Market definition is a critical part of the merger review process. This is specifically so in a regime where market shares are used as an indicator of a SLC.

The approach adopted by the CCS in relation to market definition is largely consistent with that used in other jurisdictions. The CCS uses the SSNIP (small but significant non-transitory increase in price) test, or the Hypothetical Monopolist test to delineate the relevant product market and the geographic scope of the market. The CCS generally uses an increase of about 10% above the competitive price when applying the SSNIP test.

The CCS recognises, however, that 'defining a market in strict accordance with the test's assumptions is rarely possible' and, therefore, that, '[I]n practice, defining a market requires an assessment of the various types of evidence and the exercise of judgment. It may not be necessary to define the market uniquely, where there is strong evidence that the relevant market is one of a few plausible market definitions, and the assessment on competitive impact is shown to be largely unaffected whichever market definition is adopted'.

In defining the relevant market(s), the CCS typically has regard to case law in various jurisdictions, including the EU, although the market definition adopted by such other jurisdictions is not decisive. Importantly, the CCS conducts its own assessment, based on the views of the merger parties, their customers, their competitors as well as views of other interested parties or stakeholders.

There are two important points to note in relation to the CCS' approach to market definition.

First, the CCS systematically takes into account both demand-side and supply-side substitution. In its decision on the UPS/TNT merger, for instance, the CCS stated clearly that 'in assessing the relevant product market, CCS needs to consider the demand-side and supply-side constraints'. In this case, the CCS considered whether small package services should be segmented based on the speed of delivery. Whilst this was arguable from a demand-side perspective, the CCS noted that, on the supply-side, 'the same players supply express and standard/deferred services and would generally need the same infrastructure to provide express and standard/deferred services'. Given this, the CCS concluded that it was 'not necessary to evaluate express and standard services separately'. Note that in reviewing the merger, the European Commission concluded that intra-EEA express and deferred services were in separate markets.

Second, a definition once arrived at will not necessarily always be applied as is. The CCS recognises that the conditions of competition change over time. As a consequence, the fact that a market has been accepted by the CCS in a previous decision does not mean that the CCS will simply skip the market definition exercise and adopt, *mutatis mutandis*, the same market. To illustrate, in Case CCS 400/008/12 – Proposed acquisition by Asia Renal Care (SEA) Pte Ltd of Orthe Pte Ltd – the parties were both providers of haemodialysis (HD) services to patients in Singapore. In 2010, the CCS had had to review the provision of dialysis services in Singapore, when reviewing the acquisition of Asia Renal Care (SEA) Pte Ltd by Fresenius Medical Care. At that time, the CCS noted that 'while it is arguable that haemodialysis (HD) and peritoneal dialysis (PD) treatments may be substitutes for each other and that the relevant product market is kidney dialysis services, CCS has, in any event, proceeded to consider the effect of the merger on both the (i) HD treatment and (ii) HD and PD treatment markets for kidney dialysis services separately'. In its review in 2012, however, the CCS took the view that HD and PD treatments were not substitutes, and reviewed the markets separately. Further, in 2012, the CCS took the view that dialysis centres operated by Voluntary Welfare Organisations ('VWO') were likely in a separate market than those operated by private operators or restructured hospitals, whereas such distinction had not been drawn by the CCS in its 2010 decision.

Key economic appraisal techniques applied e.g. as regards unilateral effects and co-ordinated effects, and the assessment of vertical and conglomerate mergers

The CCS assesses the likely effects of a merger by reviewing what would be the state of competition in the relevant markets with and without the merger. Whilst in most cases the counterfactual would be the prevailing competitive situation at the time of the merger, the CCS will take into account imminent changes likely to occur, e.g. the failing of one of the parties to the merger. In Case 400/009/12 – Proposed acquisition by Micron Technology Inc. of Elpida Memory Inc. – for instance, the CCS assessed the merger taking into account the fact that Elpida had filed for bankruptcy and was, therefore, likely to exit the market in any event, with or without the merger.

In assessing the likelihood of a SLC, CCS reviews both the co-ordinated effects and non-coordinated effects that would result from the merger. In this assessment, the CCS takes into account a number of factors in addition to the market share of the merged entity. These include, *inter alia*, the structure of the market and the strength of the parties, the existence of barriers to entry and the likelihood of new entrants, the ability for existing competitors to expand in the market, as well as countervailing buyer power. For coordinated effects, the CCS will also look into the level of transparency in the market and whether market conditions are overall conducive to collusion. In Case 400/007/12 – Acquisition by Oiltanking GmbH of Chemoil Storage Limited – the CCS thus noted, based on customers' responses, that competition was not just on prices but also on factors such as location, terminal capability, berth facilities, reputation and tank configuration and concluded, therefore, that such differentiation increased the difficulty for competitors to coordinate.

For vertical mergers, the CCS will focus its review on the ability of the merged entity to significantly foreclose competition in a downstream or upstream market. In Case CCS 400/008/12 – Proposed acquisition by Asia Renal Care (SEA) Pte Ltd of Orthe Pte Ltd – for instance, the CCS considered whether suppliers of HD products would be foreclosed from the market and/or whether competing dialysis centres would find it more difficult to obtain the products needed to carry on their business. In both instances, the CCS found that no such foreclosure effects resulted from the merger.

Approach to remedies (i) to avoid second stage investigation and (ii) following second stage investigation

The merger review in Singapore may be completed during a Phase I or a Phase II review. For mergers that do not raise substantive competition issues, the CCS will issue a favourable decision at the end of Phase I. Conversely, mergers that appear to pose significant competition concerns will move to a Phase II review, requiring a more intensive assessment of the concerns. The Revised Guidelines now provide that, where the CCS envisages moving the merger review to a Phase II, it will set out the specific concerns raised by the transaction in an Issues Letter.

If there is a risk of a merger proceeding to a Phase II, or even of potentially not being approved at Phase I, the CCS will engage the parties to consider how best various issues can be addressed. At times, this is a question of requiring additional and specific information. At other times, the parties may be encouraged to consider and offer commitments to remedy the identified competition concerns as soon as possible in the process. On this, under the Competition Act, the CCS may accept commitments at any time during the merger review, e.g. during Phase I, Phase II or so long as the commitments are submitted before a final decision on the transaction is made.

Although commitments provided in other jurisdictions may be accepted by the CCS as alleviating competition concerns in Singapore, this may not always be the case. The CCS will review the notified transaction from a Singapore perspective, and the issue of whether it raises concerns, and whether the proposed commitments are adequate to remove those concerns, will also be dealt with using a Singapore-centric approach.

Key policy developments

In addition to the changes highlighted in the 'New developments' section above, the Revised Guidelines also reflect a change in the enforcement priorities of the CCS. In this regard, a key policy statement coming out of the revised Merger Guidelines involves a greater emphasis placed on enforcement. In particular, the revised Merger Guidelines bring to the fore the enforcement powers of the CCS, as well as the tools the CCS has at its disposal to review mergers that have been implemented without being notified to the CCS, where such mergers could potentially have an effect in Singapore. Where the CCS identifies transactions that it considers could potentially raise concerns under the Competition Act, it will approach the merger parties to gather further information about the transaction and its effect on competition. The CCS may also approach third parties such as customers, suppliers and/or competitors in this regard. If the CCS takes the view that the merger may result or has resulted in a SLC, it will not hesitate to start an investigation. Apart from specifically highlighting its enforcement powers in the Revised Guidelines, the CCS has also publicly come out to warn businesses that mergers that are not notified to the CCS will indeed attract investigation.

As the risk of not notifying is the possibility of the CCS ordering the dissolution of the merger and the imposition of financial penalties, parties are strongly encouraged to always proceed to a self-assessment of their merger in Singapore, and notify their merger to the CCS when the indicative thresholds are crossed.

The second key policy development is the reminder issued by the CCS that, as mergers result in an exchange of confidential information, the parties have to be extremely mindful of ensuring that information exchange is kept to a minimum for a number of reasons.

This is not least because exchanges of commercially sensitive information (such as prices and customer details) between the merger parties before the merger is completed may amount to an anti-competitive agreement, in violation of Section 34 of the Competition Act. This is particularly the case where the transaction is a horizontal merger, i.e. between competitors or potential competitors on the market. Seeing the strong stance taken by a number of competition authorities around the world *vis-à-vis* exchange of commercially sensitive information, and the 2012 decision by the CCS in the Ferry Operators case, this warning in the Revised Guidelines must not be under-estimated.

Other considerations

Where the Commission proposes to make an unfavourable decision, the merging parties may apply to the Minister for Trade and Industry within 14 days of the date of notice for the merger to be exempted on grounds of public interest considerations. The Revised Guidelines clarify that the term 'public interest consideration' refer to 'national or public security, defence and such other considerations as the Minister may, by order published in the Gazette, prescribe'. To date, no exemption has been granted by the Minister.

Reform proposals

Given that the CCS has only recently completed its review of the Guidelines on Merger Procedures, no further reforms are expected at this time.

* * *

Endnotes

1. Section 54(1) of the Competition Act.
2. Section 54(2) of the Competition Act.
3. Section 54(5) of the Competition Act.
4. Paragraph 5.15 of 'CCS Guidelines on the Substantive Assessment of Mergers'.

Kala Anandarajah
Tel: +65 6232 0111 / Email: kala.anandarajah@rajahtann.com
Kala, who has 23 years of experience, heads a Tier 1 Competition and Antitrust practice. She has been involved in every major cartel/dominance investigation, and several merger and other voluntary notifications and leniency applications. She also drafted the Airport Competition Code, and is currently drafting the Brunei Telco-Media Converged Competition Code. She is consistently cited as a leading lawyer in her areas of practice by peer reviewed international agencies such as Global Competition Review, Euromoney *World's Leading Lawyers*, and *International Who's Who of Leading Lawyers.* The Asia Pacific Legal 500 notes that 'Anandarajah … is a leading authority in corporate governance, compliance and competition issues …'. Her recent accolades include citation in the Best of the Best – Women in Business Law in 2010 and again in 2012, and nomination for the Asia Women in Business Law Award (Antitrust) in 2011 and again in 2012, the only person in Singapore to have been nominated for this twice. Separately, Kala sits and assists on a number of not-for-profit and statutory boards. Kala is very widely written, including the first books on Competition & Antitrust laws in Singapore, with many of her books referred to as authorities. She is co-General Editor of *ASEAN Competition Laws,* a looseleaf covering 10 countries.

Dominique Lombardi (Foreign Lawyer)
Tel: +65 6232 0104 / Email: dominique.lombardi@rajahtann.com
Dominique joined Rajah & Tann LLP from France in 2006, bringing and contributing to the Competition & Antitrust practice group, her extensive experience in European competition and antitrust laws and regulatory issues. After she was called to the Paris bar in 1992, she started her career as a competition lawyer in France in a private law firm for several years, before joining the legal department of a leading energy company, where she carried on her work in competition and antitrust laws. Her expertise extends to anti-competitive practices, restrictive practices, merger control, and deregulation law. She is especially knowledgeable in the energy industry, having spent a substantial amount of time on competition law work in that industry.
Dominique is cited as a leading lawyer in the Euromoney *Expert's Guide to the World's Leading Competition & Antitrust Lawyers* 2011 and 2012.
Dominique is an Adjunct Lecturer at Sorbonne Assas International Law School – Asia, where she lectures on European Competition Law.

Rajah & Tann LLP

9 Battery Road #25-01, Straits Trading Building, Singapore 049910
Tel: +65 6232 0111 / Fax: +65 6225 7725 / URL: http://www.rajahtann.com

Spain

Jaime Folguera Crespo & Borja Martínez Corral
Uría Menéndez

Overview of merger control activity during the last 12 months

In the last 12 months, the activity of the Spanish Competition Commission (**"CNC"**) in the field of merger control has followed the declining trend initiated in the previous years. The total number of filings has been lower in relation to 2011 and 2010 figures.

According to the CNC public records, since 1 January 2012 there have been 68 filings (ranging from Case No. 419/12 to Case No. 482/12), of which 53 decisions have been published as of 19 December 2012. It is worth noting that a significant number of transactions have resulted in simplified filings (21 cases, representing roughly one third of the total).

Only two cases resulted in the opening of second phase proceedings: Case C/0432/12, *Antena 3/La Sexta* and Case C/0468/12, *DISA/Shell/SAE/JV* (still ongoing). There was also one case involving first phase commitments in the elevator sector (Case C/469/12, *Otis/Enor*). The year has also witnessed the first case where the Spanish Council of Ministers has ever used its powers. The most relevant elements of these cases are analysed in more detail in the following sections.

New developments in jurisdictional assessment or procedure

From a procedural and jurisdictional standpoint, in 2012 there have been some relevant developments:

(i) Intervention of the Council of Ministers in merger control cases

Without doubt, the main procedural development in 2012 in the field of merger control has been the first intervention of the Council of Ministers in a merger control case since the entry into force of the Competition Act in 2007.

In principle, under Spanish law, the CNC is the competent body for ruling on merger control cases. However, Article 60 of the Competition Act stipulates that the Council of Ministers may exceptionally intervene in merger control procedures on grounds of general interest. This intervention is aimed either at authorising merger operations that have been prohibited by the CNC, or at modifying the conditions imposed by the CNC. This exceptional power provides the Government with a route to avoid frustration of transactions of a general interest from the perspective of the national economy by the imposition of burdensome conditions (or even by the prohibition of the transaction) by the CNC. This provision, widely criticised at the time of the approval of the Competition Act, was never used until August 2012, in a case involving the merger of two free-to-air broadcast stations (Antena 3 and La Sexta).

To understand the background of this decision, it is useful to provide a quick insight on the evolution of the process of consolidation undergone by the audiovisual sector in Spain in the last few years. This process started with a merger between the free-to-air television channels Telecinco and Cuatro in 2010 (Case C/0230/10, *Telecinco/Cuatro*). That transaction was authorised by the CNC subject to certain undertakings mainly related to the commercialisation of advertising spaces by the resulting entity.

While analysing the merger between Antena 3 and La Sexta, the CNC argued that the analysis of this transaction should consider the changes produced in the market as a result of the merger between Telecinco and Cuatro and, therefore, the second transaction would have a greater impact on competition in the market. In particular, the CNC considered that the transaction not only strengthened Antena 3's position in the market, significantly increasing its market share and removing an operator that acted as a "maverick competitor" (i.e., La Sexta), but also resulted in the creation of a *de facto* duopoly in the TV advertising market in Spain. In the opinion of the CNC, these facts and the transparency of the markets were an incentive for the groups formed by Telecinco/Cuatro and Antena 3/La Sexta to align their behaviour in the market to the detriment of advertisers. The CNC decided to clear the transaction subject to compliance with certain conditions which were stricter than those imposed on the merger between Telecinco and Cuatro.

The Council of Ministers decided to intervene and modify the position of the CNC. In particular, it accepted some of the arguments of the notifying party in finding that the conditions imposed by the CNC positioned the resulting entity at a disadvantage in relation to its main competitor and reduced the efficiencies of the merger in such a way that they would not be feasible. The decision of the Council of Ministers expressly mentioned as a ground which justified the change in the conditions the fact that a symmetry between market operators was required in order to implement the reforms required at EU level in audiovisual markets. Consequently, the Council of Ministers' agreement set the conditions of this merger at the same level as the conditions imposed on the merger between Telecinco and Cuatro.

It is remarkable that the agreement mentions the current market contraction as one of the grounds for changing the conditions of the merger authorisation, as well as the budgetary restrictions on advertising. Now that the door is open to government intervention in competition matters, the question may be raised whether the current crisis might lead the Council of Ministers to be more inclined to carry out interventions. This would be particularly relevant if it leads to the authorisation of merger transactions that, while raising competition concerns, may be beneficial for the national economy, such as the creation of "national champions".

(ii) Judicial decisions on ancillary restraints

On 15 October 2012, the *Audiencia Nacional* (i.e., the Spanish high court that decides on appeals lodged against decisions from the CNC) published a judgment on a cartel case in the sanitary waste sector. However, part of the original decision was related to a non-compete obligation agreed in the context of an economic concentration.

In this regard, the CNC had considered that, in view that the non-compete clause did not seem to be covered by the limits of the EU Commission's notice on ancillary restraints, it should be considered restrictive by object and, therefore, null and void. Additionally, the CNC imposed on the party trying to enforce the clause a significant fine (see case S/0014/07, *Sanitary Waste*).

The *Audiencia Nacional* annulled the CNC decision in this point, declaring that the non-compete clause should not be considered as restrictive by object. The court found that, in view of the fact that the restrictive clause was closely related to the value transferred to a buyer in the context of an economic concentration, it would only be restrictive if it had an effect on competition. As the administrative file showed that the party affected by the clause had been able to successfully compete, the court declared that the fine was not justified. This is the first time that a Spanish court has found that a non-compete clause in a merger case falling outside the boundaries of the ancillary notice should be considered restrictive by its effects, and not by its object. This decision is being appealed by the CNC before the Supreme Court.

(iii) Increase of enforcement activity in merger cases

As a general trend in its antitrust enforcement policy, in 2012 the CNC has focused a significant effort in monitoring the compliance of the companies with its decisions. In merger control this new priority (which has even resulted in a new division within the Investigation Directorate for these purposes) has resulted, also for the first time, in the opening of proceedings for potential infringements of conditions imposed by the CNC in two merger control decisions (Cases SNC/0025/12, *Redsys*, and SNC/0024/12, *Mediaset*). In both cases the CNC conducted a previous investigation on the degree of fulfillment of the conditions and declared the infringement. The CNC has already ruled on the responsibility of the company in the first of these cases, imposing a €819,000 fine, and is expected to rule on the second in the near future. In view of the low number of conditioned decisions in Spain, the fact that two proceedings have been opened in a short period of time evidences the will of the authority of seriously pursue this monitoring activity.

These enforcement activities in merger control have also resulted in three gun-jumping decisions, where the CNC has imposed fines to companies that were found to have neglected a filing obligation (Cases SNC/0015/11, *Gestamp*, SNC/0017/12, *Isolux* and SNC/0022/12, *Verifone*). Fines in these cases ranged from €286,000 to €89,700.

Another significant development in merger control procedure refers to the value of the formal consultation process. In view that the Spanish merger control rules provide for a market share threshold to identify notifiable transactions, it is common that companies in a merger face a certain degree of uncertainty as to the market definition and the resulting market shares. To help companies to overcome these doubts, the Competition Act foresees a formal consultation process. This process, however, is seldom used due to the lack of proper regulation and clear time deadlines. In the past, the CNC has considered that the existence of this formal consultation process prevented the companies from avoiding responsibility for a gun-jumping infringement by claiming that they had considered different market definitions than the ones finally established by the authority on a *bona fide* basis.

The *Audiencia Nacional*, in a Judgment of 28 September 2008, *Bergé*, has expressly condemned this argument. In that case, the CNC had fined a company for not notifying a transaction in the sector of harbor infrastructure in the North of Spain (Case SNC/0006/10, *Bergé*). In fact, the CNC had initially asked for information on the transaction and had closed it investigation. However, following a third-party claim, it reopened the case and, at the end of its investigation, found out that the market should be narrower. As a result, the transaction entailed an acquisition of a market share higher than 30% triggering the notification threshold. The company indicated that, in view of the precedents from the European Commission and the CNC, it was reasonable to foresee a wide market definition, and that the attitude of the CNC had confirmed this issue.

The court supported the views of the appellant and annulled the decision, considering that in view of the existing precedents, it was acceptable that the company had reached a reasonable conclusion in relation to the market definition. This reasonability was enough to discard any administrative liability (i.e., fines). In this regard, the court expressly stated that it was not possible to hold that the lack of use of the formal consultation process may be construed as an evidence of the infringement.

Key industry sectors reviewed and approach adopted to market definition, barriers to entry, nature of international competition etc.

In the last 12 months, the CNC has assessed a number of sectors, although it has not developed a special interest in any of them. The activity of the CNC in relation to merger control is limited to the filings submitted to it. The CNC usually adopts a case-by-case approach, although when several transactions are notified in one sector in a brief period of time, it normally relies on its previous decisions as a roadmap.

As indicated above, the last months have witnessed a significant number of transactions in the field of the financial and insurance sector, health industry (including medical devices, drugs, etc.), energy (especially in relation to the sale of distribution assets) and supermarkets:

- As already indicated, the leading role of the financial sector in the assessment of the CNC is a consequence of the restructuring phase of the Spanish banking markets, especially in relation to savings banks. As banks normally have a significant turnover, almost any transaction in the sector is caught by the merger control thresholds.
- In the case of health industries, the market share threshold in Spain is normally met, as the market definition tend to be narrow, either in relation to product market (pharmaceutical products) or the geographic markets (hospital services).
- In the case of energy, the size of the companies and, in the case of the distribution assets, the market share (100%) can also explain this fact.
- Finally, a narrow geographic market definition (local markets) is also responsible for a number of mergers in this sector.

With the possible exception of the pharmaceutical products, where the market is always defined on a case-by-case basis, for the rest of these sectors (financial, insurance, energy and supermarkets) the CNC has a well established practice on defining the markets and identifying the competitive drivers. Knowing this practice in advance may save a lot of time and effort in the filing and clearance process, as it allows the parties an early identification of any potential concern.

Key economic appraisal techniques applied e.g. as regards unilateral effects and co-ordinated effects, and the assessment of vertical and conglomerate mergers

Article 10 of the Competition Act expressly sets out the criteria that the CNC must consider in its substantive assessment. These criteria include (a) the structure of all the relevant markets, (b) the market, economic, and financial position of the undertakings concerned, (c) the actual or potential competition, (d) the alternatives available to suppliers and consumers, (e) barriers to entry, (f) evolution in the supply and demand trends, (g) bargaining power of the customers or suppliers, and (h) possible economic efficiencies.

In practice, the CNC closely assesses these criteria following the advice provided by the European Commission in its decisions and notices. As a result, the practice of the authority does not normally differ from that of the European Commission.

The CNC normally starts its assessment of a transaction taking into account the structure of the market, studying the evolution and level of market shares as a first element. In this regard, it is highly unlikely that the CNC poses competition concerns where the parties do not have a significant market share. It is also common that even in case of high market shares, the CNC does not find competition concerns when the parties provide evidence of the contestability of the market (i.e. exposure to competitors). Thus in the assessment of the CNC, robust international or potential competition, the inexistence of barriers to entry or similar factors may compensate a high market share.

Another factor considered by the Spanish competition authorities in merger assessment has been the appraisal of the options available for the different suppliers, distributors, consumers and users. The size of competitors, the historical evolution of supply and demand, the existence of foreign competition, the existence of coordinated effects, and the degree of vertical integration between the parties or the structure of the market have been closely examined by the Spanish competition authorities.

It is not common that the CNC performs an in-depth assessment of coordinated effects. Aside from the second-phase cases referred to below, a good example of how the CNC confronts these concerns is Case C/0353/11, *Ebro/SOS Assets*. In this case, the CNC performed a close assessment of the possible coordinated effects in the context of the concentration of the two main rice brands in Spain. In particular, the CNC was concerned about the possibility that the transaction may create coordination between distribution brands in the downstream markets. The transaction entailed that in Spain there would be a single operator offering rice for "white labels" or distribution brands and, therefore, the authorities identified a potential risk of the resulting company influencing the price of the distribution brands. The case was cleared in first phase with commitments.

Approach to remedies (i) to avoid second-stage investigation and (ii) following second-stage investigation

As indicated in "Overview of merger control activity" above, in the last 12 months there have been only two clearance decisions that were subject to compliance with certain commitments from the parties; one in a second-phase decision and the other in a first-phase case.

As to remedies, the CNC tends to favour structural commitments and conditions, although it also studies and accepts behavioural solutions to competition concerns raised in merger cases. In relation to the practice of the CNC in the last year, the CNC has accepted a majority of behavioural commitments.

When the parties identify the risk of a potential competition concern arising from a reportable transaction, it is extremely important that they start analysing possible remedies as soon as possible in order to submit the commitments in the first phase and avoid the opening of the second phase (see Case C/469/12, *Otis/Enor*). The proposal of commitments usually involves some discussion with the CNC officials.

Under the Competition Act, the CNC can accept commitments submitted by the parties if they remove the competition concerns, but it may also impose conditions *ex officio* in the case that the parties do not submit any commitment or the proposed commitments are deemed to be insufficient.

The cases involving commitments imposed by the CNC in the last year are the following:

a) Case C/0432/12, *Antena 3/La Sexta*: We have already referred to this case in describing the intervention of the Council of Ministers. However, it is still interesting to review the conditions imposed by the CNC as a reference to its latest practice. The concerns of the CNC in that case were that the transaction may affect several audiovisual markets in Spain, especially the television advertising market. This impact was a consequence of (i) the disappearance of La Sexta (considered almost as a maverick) as an independent operator, (ii) the market share of the resulting entity, and (iii) the creation of a virtual duopoly in the media sector in Spain, with a clear risk of coordination. The conditions imposed by the CNC to address these issues were very stringent and included, among others, the ones identified in the following paragraphs.

- In relation to the TV advertising market (where most of the concerns were raised), the CNC tried to ensure that the resulting entity would not use the control of Antena 3 and La Sexta combined advertising time would not restrict competition. Therefore, the CNC imposed (i) the termination of any agreement between the parties for the joint management of advertising on free-to-air digital terrestrial television channels owned by third parties, and (ii) the prohibition from entering into similar new agreements. The CNC also imposed the obligation of the resulting entity of marketing the advertising time of the resulting entity through different companies. Bundling of the advertising between the two channels was also forbidden. The resulting entity was also compelled to publicise its product offer every three months. Finally, the CNC imposed on the resulting entity an obligation that conducting negotiations with advertisers and media agencies should be transparent, objective and foreseeable.

- In relation to the free-to-air television market, the CNC imposed some conditions such as prohibiting the resulting entity from expanding its range of free-to-air channels by leasing terrestrial digital channels from third-party operators.

- Finally, as to the market for audiovisual content, the CNC was forced to limit the term of its agreements for the exclusive acquisition of content to three years, excluding pre-emptive acquisition rights and extensions.

b) Case C/469/12, *Otis/Enor:* This case entailed the acquisition by Otis of a regional operator active in the installation and maintenance of elevators and escalators (among other related markets). The local nature of some markets (maintenance of elevators) gave rise to some horizontal concerns in some provinces, with significant overlaps. As not enough countervailing factors were identified, the CNC cleared the transaction in first phase, accepting the commitments proposed by the parties, which included granting to the clients of the resulting entity the faculty of terminating the exclusivity agreements in force, make available to its competitors information on the termination of existing contracts (enabling competitors to compete for these clients), and a non-solicitation obligation in relation to clients that decide to switch to another operator for a limited period of time.

Key policy developments

In general terms, there have not been significant policy developments in the field of merger control in Spain in the last 12 months. It is worth noting, however, that the enforcement of merger control faces a major challenge in 2013, as the Government plans to merge in a single body a number of sector regulators, including the CNC among others.

The proposal has been formally submitted to the Parliament that is discussing it as this book went to print. According to the plans made public by the Government, the new body is expected to be active within the first half of 2013.

The fact that the current CNC is going to be a part of a wider agency, with different priorities and shared resources, poses a serious challenge to the future developments of competition law in Spain, and in merger control in particular. Although no procedural changes have been announced, it is likely that the birth of the new agency (or super-regulator, as it has been labelled in the press) disrupts the normal operation of the body. For example, there is no clarification as to cases where a report from a sector body is legally required. As most sector regulators would be part of the same organism as the CNC, it is not clear if the report is still necessary. This decision is very relevant, as the need for a report deprives the parties of an eventual right to submit a simplified filing (and a simplified filing fee).

Reform proposals

The Spanish merger control regime keeps working with reasonable efficiency. The CNC normally takes its decisions in short deadlines and maintains a certain degree of flexibility and a fluent communication with the parties.

However, in the regulatory field, there are grounds for improvement. Our main criticism of the Spanish merger control system is the maintenance of the market share threshold for notifications. As advanced in "New developments", above, the market share threshold is still a source of legal uncertainty for companies, particularly in sectors where no precedents exist. It requires a sound economic assessment which, in a large number of cases, is inconclusive or which the parties do not have enough information to perform. Even with the current standard of reasonableness of the assessment that is required by the *Audiencia Nacional*, this part remains a complex part of merger control assessment in Spain.

In addition to this major proposal, we believe that the Spanish merger control procedure could be further improved by the adoption of certain measures:

- First of all, access to the administrative file by the notifying party should be generally acknowledged from the moment of the filing (currently it is only limited to second phase cases). Although Spanish law guarantees free access of the parties to an administrative procedure to the administrative file, the CNC systematically denies this access in first-phase procedures. This denial is significant in cases where the CNC sends information requests to third parties, launches market investigations or requests the intervention of a sector regulator, as the result of these actions could affect the outcome of the case. Therefore, we hold that the CNC must recognise the right of the notifying parties to have access to the file at any moment, in order to identify the existence of potential elements that may influence the assessment of the CNC.
- Secondly, the Spanish merger control procedure could also be improved by clarifying the criteria and procedure in case of referral of cases to the European Commission under Article 22 of Council Regulation (EC) No 139/2004 of 20 January 2004 on the control of concentrations between undertakings.
- Thirdly, as transactions where a report from a sector regulator is required cannot qualify for a simplified filing, it would greatly increase the legal certainty of the parties that the CNC would make public a list of sectors that would fall within this case. Indeed, the CNC has not always maintained the same line. For example, in 2012, it decided that the insurance sector would be subject to this provision and started requiring reports from the insurance regulator. In this line, it would also be extremely helpful to clarify that in the future, no report is required. It is somehow unnecessary that the decision body of an agency that must take a decision on merger control has to adopt first a technical report on the transaction.
- Finally, the CNC should also relax the stringent criteria set for granting an exemption to the suspension obligation. This year the CNC has made clear the difficulty of obtaining an exemption that, in our view, amounts to a tacit acknowledgment that these exemptions are not going to be granted by the CNC (Case C/0432/12, *Antena 3/La Sexta*).

In view of the fact that the great majority of the transactions submitted to the CNC are cleared in first-phase without any objection or commitment (see "Overview of Merger control activity", above), the CNC should take into account that the risk for competition of implementing most of the notified transactions is absolutely remote (at least for simplified decisions). On the contrary, the delay in the implementation of some transactions has become a heavy burden to the notifying parties, that have to bear the financial costs of the delay and that can lose commercial opportunities arising from the transaction.

Jaime Folguera Crespo
Tel: +34 91 58 60 657 / Email: jaime.folguera@uria.com
Jaime Folguera is based in Uría Menéndez's Madrid office. He joined the firm as a partner in 1993, having been an EU legal affairs advisor to several Spanish government agencies. He currently heads the Competition Law Practice Area.

His practice focuses on EU and Spanish competition law, and is regularly asked to advise on EU and Spanish mergers in various sectors, such as banking and insurance, energy, telecommunications, pharmaceuticals and basic industries.

He is often consulted on cases related to horizontal agreements, distribution, individual or collective abuse, and State aid. He is frequently involved in proceedings before the European Commission, the Spanish Competition Authority and other regulatory agencies, as well as before the European Union and Spanish courts.

Borja Martínez Corral
Tel: +34 91 58 60 657 / Email: borja.martinez@uria.com
Borja Martínez is a Principal Associate based in Uría Menéndez's Madrid office. He joined the firm in 2002, having worked both in the Brussels and Madrid offices.

He has worked on a wide variety of national and international antitrust infringement cases before the Spanish and EU authorities, and is regularly asked to advise on mergers, analyse agreements and strategic alliances and state aid issues.

He regularly advises companies in a variety of sectors, among others: banking; telecommunications; media; building materials; pharmaceuticals and energy.

Uría Menéndez

Príncipe de Vergara, 187, Plaza de Rodrigo Uría, 28002 Madrid, Spain
Tel: +34 91 58 60 657 / Fax: +34 91 58 60 753 / URL: http://www.uria.com

Sweden

Peter Forsberg & Liana Thorkildsen
Hannes Snellman Attorneys Ltd

Overview of merger control activity during the last 12 months

Although the number of notifications has decreased in Sweden as a result of new, and higher, merger notification thresholds introduced in 2008, there are still around 50 notifications to the Swedish Competition Authority ("SCA") each year.

In fact, since 2009, the number of notifications has been steadily increasing until a drop in 2012, which possibly may be explained by the economic slowdown and, hence, decreased merger activity in Sweden.

In 2012, 36 concentrations were notified to the SCA. This number is significantly lower than in 2011 (63 notifications), 2010 (57 notifications) and 2009 (43 notifications). During the period between 2009 and 2012, the vast majority of the notified concentrations were unconditionally cleared during the SCA's preliminary investigation period (Phase I), i.e. within 25 working days. In-depth investigations (Phase II) were initiated in two cases in 2012, four in 2011, one in 2010 and two in 2009. It should be noted that the number of in-depth investigations in Sweden has increased during the last two years. Only one clearance decision during this period was subject to commitments (2011).

In contrast to e.g. the European Commission, the SCA is not empowered to block concentrations. If the SCA considers that the concentration would significantly impede effective competition and ought to be prohibited, the authority must file an application for summons with the Stockholm District Court ("District Court") requesting the prohibition of the concentration. On several occasions, the parties have abandoned a concentration and withdrawn the notification in cases where the SCA has filed a summons application, due to the rather long court proceedings which risk hampering the deal. During the period between 2009 and 2012, the SCA filed a summons application in two cases: the *Åhlens/Departments Store* case (2009) and *ComHem/Canal Digital* case (2011). In the Eniro 118 118/Teleinfo (118 800) case (2012), the parties withdrew the notification after they received the draft summons application from the SCA (i.e. the statement of objections). None of the cases have been ultimately subject to a final judgement by the District Court, as the parties withdrew their notifications.

The SCA is not obliged to motivate its clearance decisions and, in cases without any competition concerns, the authority generally only clears the transaction without any reasons. The SCA has recently stated its ambition to increase the transparency of its decision-making process, including an aim to motivate its decisions even in less complicated cases. In 2012, the SCA made only three motivated clearance decisions, in comparison with nine decisions in 2011.

New developments in jurisdictional assessment or procedure

Pursuant to the Swedish Competition Act ("Competition Act"), a concentration is subject to a mandatory notification requirement to the SCA only if both of the following thresholds are met: (i) the combined aggregate turnover in Sweden of all the undertakings concerned in the preceding fiscal year exceeds SEK 1bn (approx. €115m) ("combined turnover threshold"), and (ii) each of at least two of the undertakings concerned have a turnover exceeding SEK 200m in Sweden (approx. €23m) ("individual turnover threshold"). However, if only the combined turnover threshold is met (but not the individual turnover threshold), the SCA may order the submission of a notification if there are particular reasons. Historically, the SCA has almost never used this facility to order the submission of a notification, although this option existed already, pursuant to the previous competition act (from 1993). However, in recent years, the SCA has increasingly used this facility and ordered the parties to submit notifications. Only during the last three years the SCA ordered the submission of a notification in three cases: one in 2012 and two in 2010. In addition, the SCA ordered the submission of a notification in one case at the beginning of 2013.

As stated above, the submission of a notification of a concentration which is not subject to a mandatory notification requirement may be ordered where the combined turnover threshold is met (but not the individual turnover threshold) if there are particular reasons. There are no clear guidelines in respect of what constitutes particular reasons. The preparatory works of the Competition Act clearly state that orders to submit a notification should be used only in exceptional situations. However, the practice of the SCA seems to indicate that the authority gives the concept of particular reasons a rather wide interpretation, and can request notifications as soon as there is a mere risk of effective competition being impeded. The SCA's increasing number of orders to submit notifications of concentrations that are not subject to a mandatory notification requirement indicates that the authority is prepared to use its powers to investigate concentrations to an increasing extent.

In light of such a development, acquiring party/-ies should keep in mind that even in cases where the transaction is not subject to a mandatory notification requirement, a consideration shall be made as to the possible risks of the SCA ordering a notification and, once the combined turnover threshold is met, the parties may always voluntarily submit a notification to the SCA.

Although the SCA has on several occasions demonstrated its preparedness to use its powers to investigate concentrations, the authority seems simultaneously to take an increasingly pragmatic approach in its decision-making. The SCA's practice shows that the authority generally does not use its full review period of 25 working days, and clears concentrations within shorter periods of time, especially in cases where it is obvious that there are no competition concerns. In recent years, a number of concentrations have been cleared by the SCA within one week from filing the notification. As an example, in the *Carnegie Investment Bank/HQ Bank* case, the parties requested the SCA to grant an exemption from the stand-still obligation based on the fact that the target company, HQ Bank, was under liquidation. Although the SCA refused to grant the exemption from the stand-still obligation, the SCA issued its clearance decision within one week from the submission of the notification.

In 2010, the SCA adopted new *Regulations on the notification of concentrations between undertakings under the Swedish Competition Act* ("Regulations"), which entered into force on 15 November 2010. The main change following the Regulations is that the SCA does not issue any acknowledgement of receipt confirming that the notification is complete, and that time of the review period has commenced. Such amendment entails a certain uncertainty for the parties, in respect of when the notification is considered to be complete. The SCA, however, aims to promptly notify the parties to the concentration, in case any information required is missing. Such a change resulted in an increased amount of pre-notification contacts with the authority. It should be noted that the SCA encourages pre-notification contacts, and they are subject to absolute confidentiality. During the pre-notification contacts it is possible to obtain informal guidance in respect of, *inter alia*, market definitions, market data to be provided and possible waivers. Although guidance provided by the SCA is not binding for the authority, such contacts are very helpful, particularly in order to identify the information required for the notification to be considered complete from the day of the submission of the notification. Out of 36 notifications in 2012, pre-notification contacts were held in 26 cases, in comparison to 34 cases out of 63 notifications in 2011, and 24 out of 57 in 2010.

Key industry sectors reviewed and approach adopted to market definition, barriers to entry, nature of international competition etc.

The SCA does not have any predefined key sectors or key policy areas in merger control. In its assessment of notified concentrations, the SCA generally focuses on national and regional competition. The authority generally seeks guidance from EU case law, taking into account the national specifics of the market. In respect of the geographic market, the SCA typically defines markets as national or regional.

During the past three years, the SCA has reviewed three concentrations which concerned the publishing industry.

In 2010, the SCA ordered Bonnierförlagen, a company which is a part of a larger international media group, active in publishing and distribution of books, newspapers, magazines, television, radio and music, to submit a notification when the company acquired Pocket Grossisten in Sweden AB, a distributor of paperbacks (*Bonnierförlagen/Pocket Grossisten* case). The acquisition was not subject to a mandatory notification requirement; however, the SCA requested the submission of the notification on the basis of particular grounds. There was a vertical overlap between the activities of Bonnierförlagen and Pocket Grossisten with regard to the sale of paperbacks. The acquisition of Pocket Grossisten was unconditionally cleared in Phase II. Two years later, in 2012, the SCA ordered Bonnierförlagen to submit a notification when the company acquired Pocket Shop AB, a bookstore chain in Sweden (*Bonnierförlagen/Pocket Shop* case). Both Bonnierförlagen and Pocket Shop are active within retail of paperbacks, and Bonnierförlagen is also a major purchaser of publication rights for paperbacks as well as a wholesaler of paperbacks. Thus, there were both vertical and horizontal overlaps between the activities of the parties. The case is particularly interesting as the transaction was not subject to a mandatory merger notification requirement, however, the SCA ordered Bonnierförlagen to submit the notification on the basis of particular grounds, despite the fact that the authority recently had reviewed the publishing market in the *Bonnierförlagen/Pocket Grossisten* case. The SCA feared that due to the horizontal and vertical overlaps between the activities of the companies, it could not be excluded that the proposed acquisition could significantly impede the existence or development of effective competition in Sweden. The SCA went one step further and conducted a Phase II in-depth investigation, during which the concentration was unconditionally cleared.

Further, in 2012, the SCA reviewed another concentration which concerned the publishing industry in the *Bokia/Akademibokhandeln* case, which related to the acquisition of joint control over Akademibokhandelsgruppen and Bokia by KF Media and Stiftelsen Natur & Kultur and Killbergs Bokhandel. KF Media included two publishing houses, an online bookstore, and Akademibokhandelsgruppen, which operated Akademibokhandeln, the leading bookstore chain in Sweden with 66 stores nationwide. Bokia was one of the largest bookstore chains in Sweden with 22 own-retail stores, 48 franchise stores and online store. Even in the present case, there was a horizontal overlap between Akademibokhandeln's and Bokia's activities with regards to the retail and online sale of books. The central question in the case was whether the online sale of books, and sale of books in groceries and departments stores, belong to the same relevant product market as traditional physical bookstores. The transaction was subsequently cleared in Phase II.

Key economic appraisal techniques applied e.g. as regards unilateral effects and co-ordinated effects, and the assessment of vertical and conglomerate mergers

Pursuant to the Competition Act, a concentration is prohibited if it would significantly impede the existence or development of effective competition in Sweden as a whole, or in a substantial part, particularly as a result of the creation or strengthening of a dominant position. When assessing a notified concentration, the SCA, thus, applies the "Significant Impediment of Effective Competition Test" ("SIEC test") in line with the SIEC test applied by the European Commission.

As stated above, the prohibition may only be imposed by the District Court or, if the District Court's decision is appealed, by the Market Court, on the SCA's request to prohibit the concentration. However, the concentration will not be prohibited if this would affect national interests or security. There is no case law on this exception, and the general view is that it should be interpreted narrowly.

Although the creation or strengthening of a dominant position is not decisive under the SIEC test, a dominant position seems to remain an important, but not decisive, indicator for the probability of a concentration impeding effective competition. However, there has been a clear trend towards increased use of formal economic theory and quantitative methods in recent merger case analysis in Sweden, particularly the use of the upward pricing pressure method ("UPP"), where there is a shift away from concentrating the competition analysis on market definition and market shares, towards considering the degree of rivalry between the companies, including identifying the closest competitors. The UPP method focuses on the assessment of the parties' incentive to increase or decrease prices after the concentration, with emphasis on the following variables: diversion ratios (i.e. how close competitors the merging parties are), gross margins and efficiencies.

The UPP test has explicitly been applied by the SCA in a number of recent cases, in the *Office Depot/ Svanströms* (2011), *Arla/Milko* (2011), *Cloetta/Leaf* (2012) and *Eniro 118 118/Teleinfo (118 800)* (2012) cases. The *Office Depot/Svanströms* and *Cloetta/Leaf* were cleared in Phase I, whereas the *Arla/Milko* case was cleared in Phase II subject to commitments. In the *Eniro 118 118/Teleinfo* case, the parties withdrew their notification due to SCA's intention to prohibit the concentration.

The *Office Depot/Svanströms* case concerned the acquisition of Svanströms & Co AB by Office Depot Sweden AB, both active in the office supply market. The SCA stated that although the parties were differentiated from each other and competed with other players on the market, the companies were each other's closest competitors. However, the fact that the parties faced competition from specialised competitors offering exclusively office supplies as well as from competitors, not purely office suppliers, decreased the risk of upward price pressure. Ultimately the SCA concluded that even if Office Depot, after the acquisition of Svanströms, were likely to increase its market power in channels of distribution previously used by Office Depot, this increase in power would be counterbalanced by the vast number of competitors exercising pressure on Office Depot in each distribution channel.

The *Cloetta/Leaf* case concerned acquisition of Leaf Holland B.V. ("Leaf") by Cloetta AB, both active in the confectionery industry. The activities of the parties overlapped in several markets. In the sugar confectionery market and in the refreshment market, particularly the throat lozenge market, the parties' most important products did not compete closely with one another. In addition, a significant overlap was identified in the bagged chocolate and sugar confectionery segment, within which both parties had very strong brands. However, the SCA concluded that the parties' products were highly substitutable with those of competing manufacturers, both within and outside of this segment. The confectionery market was described by the SCA as highly competitive and driven by innovation, with high potential for new entry and expansion. The SCA concluded that the merged entity would not have an incentive to increase prices, as other confectionery manufacturers would continue to exert substantial competitive pressure.

In the *Eniro 118 118/Teleinfo* case, the question of merger efficiencies played a more central role. The case involved an acquisition by Eniro 118 118, Sweden's largest directory enquiry service provider, of a maverick competitor, Teleinfo, which focused solely on directory services via telephone and sms. The parties' business overlapped horizontally with respect to their operations within the voice segment: Eniro had a market share about 60-75% in 2010, whereas Teleinfo's market share was about 5-20%. There was only one more provider of voice, of significance. The SCA obtained data on diversion in that segment from second-choice questions posed in a survey commissioned by the authority, and obtained margins from the parties themselves. The parties to the concentration claimed efficiencies; however, such efficiencies were presented at a late stage in Phase II. Generally, in its assessment of efficiencies, the SCA applies the EU's horizontal merger guidelines, meaning that in order to take efficiencies into account they need to benefit consumers, be merger-specific and be verifiable. The first criterion, benefiting consumers, is integrated with the consumer welfare standard of the UPP-approach, so the same method that is used to evaluate costs in the UPP analysis can be used to evaluate the efficiency gains. The second and third criteria – specificity and verifiability – are much more difficult to evaluate in a short amount of time. In the *Eniro118 118/Teleinfo* case, the detailed efficiency calculations were presented at a very late stage of the SCA's investigation, and they were not backed up by internal documents. This implied that the SCA had to evaluate the calculations without access to underlying source evidence. As a result, the SCA concluded that the criteria of merger-specificity and verifiability had not been met, and announced its intention to file an application for summons, requesting prohibition of the concentration. The parties withdrew the notification.

In the *Arla Foods/Milko* case, the concentration concerned the acquisition of Milko dairy cooperative, Sweden's third-largest dairy group, by Arla Foods, the largest player in the dairy market in Sweden. Arla Foods and Milko were each other's main competitors in substantial parts of Sweden in a number of markets, such as milk for consumption. The SCA undertook a full Phase II investigation and performed detailed counterfactual analysis, including the UPP-method. The SCA found that prior to the merger, Milko acted as the principal competitive constraint on Arla in certain parts of Sweden, and that the merger would remove that constraint. The case is notable, as the parties claimed the "failing firm defence", due to Milko's difficult financial situation. The parties argued that in the absence of the merger, Milko would become insolvent and exit the market. Although not all the requirements of the failing firm defence, as defined in the practice of the European Commission, were met, the SCA cleared the concentration subject to commitments. This is only the second time the failing firm defence has been applied in Sweden, with the first case having occurred over ten years ago. The SCA found that it was likely that, given Milko's difficult financial situation, the company would become insolvent. As a result, Milko's members would need to switch to supplying another dairy company. The SCA concluded that while some of Milko's assets would be unlikely to find a purchaser in such circumstances, some of Milko's other assets, in particular its largest dairy and some associated trademarks, would find one or more purchasers. In light of this, the SCA cleared the transaction, subject to a commitment by Arla to divest Milko's largest dairy and associated trademarks to an independent third party. The SCA found that the transaction, as amended, would lead to the same situation as that which would likely apply in the absence of the merger.

Approach to remedies (i) to avoid second stage investigation and (ii) following second stage investigation

Undertakings can offer remedies to address competition concerns and avoid the prohibition of the concentration. The remedies will be accepted if the SCA considers them sufficient to eliminate the adverse effects on competition. Remedies can be offered at any stage in the notification process, during Phase I investigation in order to avoid a Phase II investigation, or later (once a Phase II investigation has been initiated). Generally, remedies are offered at the end of Phase II investigation after the notifying undertakings have received the SCA's draft summons application (i.e. statement of objections).

Although both structural and behavioural remedies may be considered and accepted, structural remedies, particularly divestments, are often considered to be more appropriate and effective than behavioural remedies. For remedies to be accepted during Phase I, the adverse effects on competition, and the way to address those effects, must be sufficiently clear-cut. Therefore, to be accepted in Phase I, it is advisable to offer remedies as early as possible in the Phase I period.

Generally, remedies are accepted by the SCA subject to fines for non-compliance. In 2011, the SCA in the *Arla Foods/Milko* case accepted Arla Foods', the leading dairy producer in Sweden, commitments to sell a dairy facility and a number of trademarks, and cleared the acquisition of Milko, third-largest dairy producer in Sweden. The clearance decision was subject to a fine of SEK 100m.

Since 2008, the SCA has cleared two concentrations subject to commitments: in the *OneMed/Simonsen Material* case in 2008, and, as mentioned above, *Arla Foods/Milko* case in 2011. Both cases concerned structural remedies.

Compliance with remedies is monitored by the SCA and is largely based on the principles of the European Commission notice on remedies acceptable. A monitoring or divestiture trustee may be appointed to oversee the parties' compliance with the remedies.

Key policy developments

There have been no key policy developments in Sweden in recent years.

Reform proposals

In April 2012, the Swedish Government appointed a committee to investigate certain measures in order to ascertain effective competition law enforcement. As regards merger control, the committee will consider whether there is a need to introduce new rules giving the SCA powers to suspend the time limits in merger investigations (similar to the European Commission's powers under Article 10.4 in the EU Merger Regulation).

The results of the inquiry are expected to be presented in March 2013. The enquiry may result in a proposal for legislative changes.

Peter Forsberg
Tel: +46 7 60 000 080 / Email: peter.forsberg@hannessnellman.com

Peter Forsberg is a partner and a head of the Competition & Procurement practice group at Hannes Snellman in Stockholm. He advises Swedish and international companies on competition law and public procurement law issues. In particular, he has solid experience of domestic and international merger control, competition law disputes and compliance work. He regularly represents clients in proceedings before national competition authorities as well as before the European Commission. He has recently been involved in matters in the following sectors: energy, financial services, food and consumer products, forest products, pharmaceuticals and telecommunications.

Liana Thorkildsen
Tel: +46 7 60 000 056 / Email: liana.thorkildsen@hannessnellman.com

Liana is an associate at Hannes Snellman in Stockholm. She is specialised in EU and Swedish competition law and advises on all aspects of competition law. In particular, she provides advice in respect of cross-border and domestic merger clearance cases, cartel investigations and cartel appeal proceedings.

Hannes Snellman Attorneys Ltd

Kungsträdgårdsgatan 20, Box 7801, SE-103 96, Stockholm, Sweden
Tel: +46 7 60 000 000 / Fax: +46 8 679 8511 / URL: http://www.hannessnellman.com

Turkey

Gönenç Gürkaynak & K. Korhan Yıldırım
ELIG Attorneys at Law

Overview of merger control activity during the last 12 months

The Turkish merger control regime is primarily regulated by the Law on Protection of Competition No. 4054 (the Competition Act) dated 13 December 1994 and Communiqué No. 2010/4 on Mergers and Acquisitions Requiring the Approval of the Competition Board (the new Merger Communiqué) published on 7 October 2010. The new Merger Communiqué entered into force as of 1 January 2011.

In the first year of the new Merger Communiqué's application, the Competition Authority reviewed more than 230 merger cases (239 to be precise, including mergers, acquisitions and joint ventures) and 14 privatisation cases. Figures and statistics for 2012 were not available at the time of writing.

The number of concentrations notified to the Competition Authority in 2011 (239) is higher than the number for 2010 (210). Although the new Merger Communiqué has brought significant changes by abolishing the market share threshold and replacing it by two alternative turnover thresholds, the number of notified concentrations has slightly increased. The Competition Authority seems inclined to interpret this increase to be the result of the "still relatively low" jurisdictional thresholds. For more information, please see the next section.

The Competition Board granted unconditional clearances for the vast majority of transactions notified to it in 2011. Very few transactions fell to Phase II reviews (i.e. where the Competition Board takes the merger case/transaction to a second stage, which then becomes a fully-fledged investigation), and only three transactions received conditional clearances. There has not been any transaction prohibited in the last 12 months.

The Competition Board reviewed a total of 239 merger cases in 2011, which included 186 cases that received unconditional clearance, 50 cases that were found to be not notifiable (i.e. a decision that the notified concentration does not exceed the applicable jurisdictional thresholds) or that fell outside of the merger control regime (i.e. a decision that the notified transaction falls outside of the scope of applicability of merger control rules for not bringing about a change of control). 168 of the 239 cases were about acquisitions, whereas three of the remaining were about mergers and 68 were about joint ventures. The high number of joint venture notifications is a result of the exception for joint ventures from the affected market threshold. For more information concerning this exception, please see the next section.

New developments in jurisdictional assessment or procedure

With the introduction of the new Merger Communiqué, two measures were thought to be sufficient to decrease the number of merger notifications: increasing the jurisdictional turnover thresholds, and putting in place an additional condition that seeks the existence of an affected market for notifiability. However, these measures have turned out to be insufficient to net the extra amount of worldwide mergers, particularly the worldwide turnover threshold (worldwide turnover of one of the transaction parties exceeds TRY 500m, and at least one of the remaining transaction parties has a turnover in Turkey exceeding TRY 5m). Indeed, only 16% of the transactions notified to the Competition Authority in the first 8 months of 2011 were between Turkish parties, and 41% of them were between non-Turkish parties.

The introduction of the new guideline on Undertakings Concerned, Turnover and Ancillary Restrictions in Mergers and Acquisitions ("Merger Guidelines") has also reversed the trend for dealing with fewer merger control notifications because the guideline finds the existence of one or more overlaps at the global level sufficient to trigger a notification requirement, provided that one of the transaction parties has activities in Turkey in at least one of such overlap areas. On the other hand, the Merger Guidelines define the overlapping markets extremely broadly and as a result of this definition, the affected market threshold remains less helpful for decreasing the merger control notifications.

While fewer notifications were expected with the new Merger Communiqué, the past 12 months witnessed an increase in the number of notified concentrations. This increase led the Competition Board to significantly shorten the reasoned decisions with respect to mergers, acquisitions and joint ventures. The Competition Board's reasoned decisions on merger cases rarely exceed three pages now.

After the reactions, the Competition Authority opened the "Discussion Paper on the Thresholds Included in the Communiqué Concerning the Mergers and Acquisitions" to public opinion in August 2012. The Discussion Paper aims to abolish the global threshold in an effort to lighten the Competition Authority's workload. For more information concerning the Discussion Paper, please see the section on key policy developments.

Following a public consultation process, the Turkish Competition Authority has also introduced another guideline on the remedies that would be accepted by the Competition Authority in mergers and acquisitions. The guideline provides detailed explanations in relation to different forms of remedies such as divestiture, ownership unbundling, compulsory licensing, compulsory granting access to facilities, etc. The guideline also lays down procedures for the operation of trustees. The principles and procedures adopted by the guideline are very similar to, if not the same as, the EU system.

Key industry sectors, barriers to entry, nature of international competition

As a traditional trend, the Turkish Competition Authority typically pays special attention to those transactions that take place in sectors where infringements of competition are frequently observed and the concentration level is high. Concentrations that concern strategic sectors that are important to the country's economy (such as automotive, telecommunications, energy, etc.) attract the Turkish Competition Authority's special scrutiny as well. The Turkish Competition Authority's case handlers are always extremely eager to issue information requests (thereby cutting the review period) in transactions relating to these sectors, where even transactions that raise low-level competition law concerns are looked at very carefully. In some sectors, the Turkish Competition Authority is also statutorily required to seek the written opinion of other Turkish governmental bodies (such as the Turkish Information Technologies and Communication Authority pursuant to Section 7/2 of Law on Electronic Communication No. 5809). In such cases, the statutory opinion usually becomes a hold-up item that slows down the review process of the notified transaction.

The consolidated statistics regarding merger cases indicate that transactions in the industry for chemicals and chemical products took the lead by 28 notifications. The sectors for food products, machinery and defence industry and medical instruments followed the chemicals industry with over 20 transactions per each. The most significant decrease has been noted for transactions in the energy sector. Statistics for 2012 have not been released yet.

2011 and 2012 witnessed the Competition Board taking some of the very important decisions in the history of the Turkish merger control regime:

In AFM/Mars (11-57/1473-539), transaction parties requested authorisation on the merger of AFM and Mars, which are the two largest movie theatre operators in Turkey. AFM operates in nine provinces of Turkey with 182 movie theatres, whereas Mars operates in 14 provinces of Turkey with 239 movie theatres. In defining the relevant geographical market, the Competition Board divided the overlapping provinces in which both undertakings operate. It concluded that consumers would prefer movie theatres within a 20-minute driving distance. Given that AFM and Mars have a significant combined market share in these submarkets, the transaction would have a significant impact on the effective competition. The transaction parties proposed several remedies to the Competition Board. These remedies include divestitures concerning 12 movie theatres. In this transaction, the Competition Board granted conditional clearance, reserving that clearance would be revoked in case of a failure to transfer the 12 movie theatres to third parties. The Competition Board requested the parties to regularly supply information on annual average ticket prices and changes thereto for the next five years.

In Total/Aygaz (11-41/873-274), the Competition Board decided that Aygaz's acquisition of Total's LPG dealer contracts and a part of its LPG distribution business assets would not lead to a significant lessening of competition. The Competition Board stated that Aygaz is Turkey's leading bottled LPG distributor and acquiring Total's assets would increase its current market share by 4.51%. The Competition Board addressed the HHI Index by indicating highly concentrated market structure, homogeneity of the product and the resulting potential to create a dominant position in favour of Aygaz. However, the Competition Board took into consideration other factors in the market such as the low switching costs for customers, several parts of the Turkish market which will not be affected, shrinking capacity and vertical integration. Finally the Competition Board cleared the transaction unconditionally by stating that the transaction would not create or strengthen a dominant position.

In Diageo Plc/Mey Icki (11-45/1043-356), the Competition Board found that Mey Icki was in the dominant position in the gin market, while it was not in the markets for vodka and liquor. The Competition Board indicated that the proposed transaction would give rise to competition problems in the markets for gin and liquor but not in the market for vodka. It launched a Phase II review into the transaction. Diageo Plc unsuccessfully proposed several remedies, which the Competition Board did not find to be acceptable. Subsequently, Diageo Plc proposed more complex and radical solutions, including the transfer of "Maestro Assets" in the gin market and "Hare Assets" in the liquor market, together with the "Bilecik Production Facilities" to third parties. The Competition Board accepted these new remedies. It cleared the transaction but conditioned the clearance upon the fulfilment of the remedies within a certain period of time. Six months after the conditional clearance decision, Diageo Plc transferred the said assets to Antalya Alkollu Ickiler and the Competition Board approved this transfer as fulfilling Diageo's obligation.

In Dardanel (12-04/151-42), the Competition Board cleared the transaction for the acquisition by Yildiz Holding of Dardanel. The transaction concerned the market for canned fish and received unconditional clearance. Prior to the transaction, Yildiz Holding already owned Kerevitas in the same market and thus the Competition Board assessed whether the proposed transaction would create or strengthen a dominant position in the relevant market. The Competition Board cleared the transaction by majority. It took into account factors such as the increasingly-successful private label products. Three of the seven members of the Competition Board objected to the decision by stating that the transaction should have been taken to a Phase II review.

In Sok Markets (11-45/1044-357), the Competition Board granted clearance to the acquisition of Sok Markets, a retail market chain, by Ulker Group. Ulker Group is a market leader in several FMCG food products in Turkey and it has a 4.94% shareholding in BIM Markets, Turkey's leading retail market chain in 2010 controlled by the Topbas Group. Both Sok Markets and BIM Markets are regarded as discount retail markets which represent a sub-segment of retail markets. Ulker committed to not gain control over BIM Markets by increasing its shareholdings percentage or placing its employees on the boards of BIM Markets. The Competition Board placed strong emphasis on the resulting vertical integration and the relations between the two groups. It concluded that the two retail market chains would act with separate economic interest, have diverse decision-making mechanisms, not be economically dependent to each other and consequently would remain in competition with each other. As a result, the Competition Board cleared the transaction by accepting Ulker's commitment.

Key economic appraisal techniques applied

The Turkish Competition Act regime currently utilises a 'dominance test' in the evaluation of concentrations. Pursuant to article 13/II of the new Merger Communiqué, mergers and acquisitions which do not create or strengthen a sole or joint dominant position and do not significantly impede effective competition in a relevant product market within the whole or part of Turkey, shall be cleared by the Competition Board. Article 3 of the Competition Act defines dominant position as "any position enjoyed in a certain market by one or more undertakings by virtue of which those undertakings have the power to act independently from their competitors and purchasers in determining economic parameters such as the amount of production, distribution, price and supply". There is no market share threshold above which a firm would be presumed to be dominant. Having said that, market shares of about 40 per cent and higher are generally considered, along with other factors such as vertical foreclosure or barriers to entry, as an indicator of a dominant position in a relevant market. However, a merger or acquisition can only be blocked when the concentration not only creates or strengthens a dominant position but also significantly impedes the competition in the whole territory of Turkey or in a substantial part of it, pursuant to article 7 of the Competition Act.

That said, there is a current proposal of a new law which could result in a shift to the 'substantial lessening of competition' test. The timing of enactment is not clear.

On the other hand, there were a couple of exceptional cases where the Competition Board discussed the coordinated effects under a 'joint dominance test', and rejected some transactions on those grounds. For instance, transactions for the sale of certain cement factories by the Savings Deposit Insurance Fund were rejected on that ground. The Competition Board evaluated the coordinated effects of the mergers under a joint dominance test and blocked the transactions on the ground that the transactions would lead to joint dominance in the relevant market. The Board took note of factors such as "structural links between the undertakings in the market" and "past coordinative behaviour", in addition to "entry barriers", "transparency of the market", and the "structure of demand". It concluded that certain factory sales would result in the creation of joint dominance by certain players in the market whereby competition would be significantly impeded. Nonetheless, the High State Court has overturned this decision of the Competition Board and decided that 'dominance test' does not cover 'joint dominance'. This has been a very controversial topic ever since, because the Competition Board has never prohibited any transaction on the grounds of joint dominance after the decision of the High State Court.

The new affected market condition for notifiability requires the existence of one or more overlaps at the global level sufficient to trigger a notification requirement, provided that one of the transaction parties has activities in Turkey in at least one of such overlap areas. This requirement does not necessitate conglomerate mergers or acquisitions to be notified to the Competition Authority for lack of overlapping markets. Nevertheless, there is an exception for joint venture cases to this requirement. As per the article 7 (2) of the new Merger Communiqué, authorisation of the Competition Board shall be required for joint venture transactions even without any affected market.

In general, the Competition Board evaluates joint-venture notifications according to three criteria: existence of joint control in the joint venture; the joint venture not having as its object or effect the restriction of competition among the parties or between the parties and the joint venture itself; and the joint venture being an independent economic entity (i.e., having adequate capital, labour and an indefinite duration). In recent years, the Competition Board has consistently applied the test of 'full-functioning' while determining whether the joint venture is an independent economic entity. If the transaction is a full-function JV after considering the three criteria above, the standard dominance test is applied.

On the other hand, economic analyses and econometric modelling has been seen more often in the year of 2012. For instance, in the AFM/Mars Cinema case, the Competition Board used the OLS and 2SLS estimation models in order to define price increases that are expected from the transaction. It also employed the Breusch/Pagan, Breusch-Pagan/Godfrey/Cook-Weisberg, White/Koenker NR2 tests and the Arellano-Bond test on the simulation model. Such economic analyses are rare but increasing in practice.

Approach to remedies to avoid second stage investigation

Pursuant to article 10 of the Competition Act, once the formal notification has been made, the Turkish Competition Board, upon its preliminary review (Phase 1) of the notification, will decide either to approve, or to investigate the transaction further (Phase 2). It notifies the parties of the outcome within 30 calendar days following a complete filing. Regarding the procedure and steps of a Phase 2 review, the Competition Act makes reference to the relevant articles which govern the investigation procedures for cartel and abuse of dominance cases.

The Competition Board may grant conditional clearances to concentrations. In the case of a conditional clearance, the parties comply with certain obligations such as presenting some additional divestment, licensing or behavioural commitments to help overcome potential competition issues. The Competition Board recently enacted Guidelines on Remedies that are Acceptable by the Turkish Competition Authority in Merger/Acquisition Transactions in order to provide guidance to remedies. The parties can complete the transaction after the clearance but before the remedies have been complied with however, the transaction gains legal validity after the full compliance. Cases with commitments are increasing in practice, for instance Diageo Plc/Mey Icki and AFM/Mars Cinema have been concluded in the last year.

The new Merger Communiqué enables the parties to provide commitments to remedy substantive competition law issues that may result from a concentration. The parties may submit to the Competition Board proposals for possible remedies either during the preliminary review (Phase I) or the investigation period (Phase II). If the parties decide to submit the commitment during the preliminary review period (Phase I), the notification is deemed filed only on the date of the submission of the commitment. The commitment can be also served together with the notification form. In such a case, a signed version of the commitment that contains detailed information on the context of the commitment should be attached to the notification form.

The Competition Authority does not have a policy of having clear preferences for particular types of remedies. The assessments are made on a case-by-case basis in view of specific circumstances surrounding the merger. Nevertheless, divestitures are the most common procedures either the Competition Board required or the parties proposed, due to its legal certainty feature.

Key policy developments

In 2011 and 2012, the entry into force and enforcement of the new Merger Communiqué was surely the most significant development in the Turkish merger control regime. In addition to this Communiqué, the Competition Board also released a comprehensive guideline on Undertakings Concerned, Turnover and Ancillary Restraints in Mergers and Acquisitions published on 3 May 2011 and Guideline on Remedies Acceptable to the Competition Authority in Mergers and Acquisitions, 16 June 2011.

The Turkish Competition Authority made an announcement on applications made to the Turkish Competition Authority which fall outside the scope of the Competition Act (such as applications relating to unfair competition, protection of the consumer, and regulated industries). This step in clarifying the boundaries of the Turkish Competition Authority's ambits might indicate the overwhelming number of irrelevant submissions that the Authority has had to process and evaluate in the past. In a similar vein, the Turkish Competition Authority released Communiqué No. 2012/2 on the Application Procedure for Competition Infringements in August 2012. Communiqué No. 2012/2's main purpose is to lay down the procedure and principles relating to the evaluation of applications that are to be made to the Turkish Competition Authority with respect to the alleged violations of Articles 4, 6 and 7 of the Competition Act.

The Turkish Competition Authority also opened the efficiency of the current global and local turnover threshold system to discussion. On 31 August 2012, a discussion paper ("Discussion Paper") was published on the Turkish Competition Authority's official website. The Discussion Paper analyses statistics on the Turkish Competition Board's decisions in 2010 and 2011 to draw conclusions as to whether the current turnover thresholds are adequate or are in need of an amendment.

According to the current threshold system, the Board's approval is required for transactions where:
- Total turnovers of the transaction parties in Turkey exceed TRY 100m, and turnovers of at least two of the transaction parties in Turkey each exceed TRY 30m; or
- Global turnover of one of the transaction parties exceeds TRY 500m, and at least one of the remaining transaction parties has a turnover in Turkey exceeding TRY 5m.

According to the Discussion Paper, (i) 60% of the notified transactions exceeded the global turnover thresholds only, and (ii) only 17% of the same exceeded the local turnover threshold in 2011. In 25% of the transactions that exceeded only the global turnover, either the acquirer or the target did not have local turnover in Turkey.

In the light of this data, the Discussion Paper finds the global turnover aspect to be the main reason for the high numbers of merger control filings and the resulting heavy workload of the Turkish Competition Authority. Consequently, the Turkish Competition Authority signals that it may gear up for an amendment to the turnover thresholds after the public consultation on the Discussion Paper.

The new Merger Communiqué also extended the notification form and introduced a new and much more complex notification form, which is similar to the Form CO of the European Commission, in order to receive more information in detail from the parties at once and to reach a decision expeditiously. There is an increase in the economic and legal information requested, including data with respect to supply and demand structure, imports, potential competition, expected efficiencies and synergies, etc. Some additional documents such as the executed or current copies, and sworn Turkish translations of the document(s) that bring(s) about the notified transaction, annual reports including balance sheets of the parties, and, if available, market research reports for the relevant market, are also required. With an amendment to the new Merger Communiqué by Communiqué No. 2011/2 in order to keep up with the technological developments, the Notification Form and attached documents shall be prepared also in electronic form.

The new notification form no longer insists on "signed copies of the agreement leading to the notified concentration". This is a much welcome change allowing the parties to file before the transaction document is signed. This will save very valuable time and certainly constitute an improvement over the currently applicable regime.

With the recent changes observed in Turkish merger control legislation, the Competition Board has geared up for a merger control regime focusing much more on deterrents. As part of that trend, monetary fines have increased significantly for not filing or closing a transaction without the Competition Board's approval. It is now even more advisable for the transaction parties to observe the notification and suspension requirements and avoid potential violations. This is particularly important when transaction parties intend to put in place carve-out or hold-separate measures to override the operation of the notification and suspension requirements in foreign-to-foreign mergers. The Competition Board is currently rather dismissive of carve-out and hold-separate arrangements, though the wording of the new regulation allows some room to speculate that carve-out or hold-separate arrangements are now allowed. Because the position that the Competition Authority will take in interpreting this provision is not clear as yet, such arrangements cannot be considered as safe early-closing mechanisms recognised by the Competition Board. Under Article 10 of the new Merger Communiqué, a transaction is deemed to be 'realised' (i.e., closed) on the date when the change in control occurs. It remains to be seen if this provision will be interpreted by the Competition Authority in a way that provides the parties to a notification to carve out the Turkish jurisdiction with a hold-separate agreement. This has consistently been rejected by the Turkish Competition Board so far, arguing that a closing is sufficient for the suspension violation fine to be imposed, and that a further analysis of whether a change in control actually took effect in Turkey is unwarranted.

Another important change in the Turkish merger control regime is brought about with Article 13 of the new Merger Communiqué. The Competition Board's approval decision will be deemed to also cover only the directly related and necessary extent of restraints in competition brought by the concentration (e.g. non-compete, non-solicitation, confidentiality, etc.). This now allows the parties to engage in self-assessment, and the Board will not have to devote a separate part of its decision to the ancillary status of all restraints brought with the transaction anymore.

Another talking point is the incorrect or incomplete filings. If the information requested in the notification form is incorrect or incomplete, the notification is deemed filed only on the date when such information is completed upon the Competition Board's subsequent request for further data. In addition, the Competition Authority may impose a turnover-based monetary fine of 0.1 per cent of the turnover generated in the financial year preceding the date of the fining decision (if this is not calculable, the turnover generated in the financial year nearest to the date of the fining decision will be taken into account) on the parties in cases where incorrect or misleading information is provided.

The Competition Authority now publishes the notified transactions on its official website with only the names of the parties, and their areas of commercial activity. To that end, once notified to the

Turkish Competition Authority, the "existence" of a transaction will no longer be a confidential matter.

Finally, the Competition Authority has released two new draft guidelines for public opinion, one about horizontal mergers and the other about non-horizontal mergers, just one day prior to the time of writing (4 December 2012).

Reform proposals

A current proposal to change the entire Competition Act legislation is pending before Turkey's Grand National Assembly. If enacted, the proposal will bring about significant amendments to the Competition Act, such as the SIEC Test as the substantive test for merger appraisals and the introduction of *de minimis* exceptions. It is still uncertain, however, when the relevant proposal will be on the Grand National Assembly's agenda. President of the Competition Board Prof. Dr. Nurettin Kaldirimci writes in his message for 2012 that "our greatest wish is the enactment, in the current legislative year, of the Draft Law concerning Amendments to the Act No. 4054, which was prepared within the framework of the 15-year experience of the Competition Board, presented to the Turkish Grand National Assembly as a draft law in the preceding legislative year and which, we believe, will significantly improve organisational efficiency". However there is no solid sign that the draft will be enacted soon.

Gönenç Gürkaynak
Tel: +90 212 327 17 24 / Email: gonenc.gurkaynak@elig.com
Gönenç Gürkaynak holds an LLM degree from Harvard Law School, and he is qualified in Istanbul, New York, and England & Wales (currently non-practising solicitor). He has unparalleled experience in all matters of Turkish Competition Act counselling with over 15 years' experience, starting with the establishment of the Turkish Competition Authority. Prior to joining ELIG as a partner more than seven years ago, Gönenç worked as an attorney at the Istanbul, New York, Brussels and again in the Istanbul offices of a global law firm for more than eight years. He also holds a teaching position at undergraduate and graduate levels at the Bilkent University Law School in the fields of Competition Act and law and economics. Gönenç heads the competition and regulatory department of ELIG. He has had tens of international and local articles published in English and in Turkish, and a book published by the Turkish Competition Authority.

K. Korhan Yıldırım
Tel: +90 212 327 17 24 / Email: korhan.yildirim@elig.com
K. Korhan Yıldırım holds an LLB degree from Galatasaray University Law School, and he is qualified to practise in Istanbul. Korhan is a senior associate at the competition and regulatory department of ELIG. He has been assisting Gönenç Gürkaynak with a vast number of complex matters of Turkish Competition Act counselling, and also in numerous other fields of Turkish law, for more than seven years. Korhan has also published many articles in collaboration with Mr Gürkaynak, and he is particularly experienced in merger control matters and cartel cases.

ELIG Attorneys at Law

Çitlenbik Sokak No: 12, Yıldız Mahallesi, Beşiktaş, 34349 Istanbul, Turkey
Tel: +90 212 327 17 24 / Fax: +90 212 327 17 25 / URL: http://www.elig.com

Ukraine

Mariya Nizhnik & Sergey Denisenko
Vasil Kisil & Partners

Overview of merger control activity during the last 12 months

The number of concentrations filed with the Antimonopoly Committee of Ukraine (the "AMC") in 2011 was a bit higher than in 2010, but still significantly lower than in 2008 and 2007.

The below statistics clearly evidence that almost all transactions filed with the AMC were successfully cleared, except for a few transactions that involved market players holding dominant positions in Ukraine, and transactions that might substantially restrict the competition in Ukraine.

In 2011, 52 transactions out of 756 were cleared after a deeper investigation had been initiated by the AMC with respect to the transaction. In practice, the AMC generally initiates deeper investigation if the transaction concerned may potentially negatively affect competition in Ukraine, e.g. when the parties to the concentration have relatively high market shares in Ukrainian markets (e.g. exceeding 15%).

In 171 cases the applications filed with the AMC for a concentration in 2011 were either returned by the authority or withdrawn by the applicants for their own reasons.

According to the applicable legislation, a transaction prohibited by the AMC may be approved by the Cabinet of Ministers of Ukraine if the parties concerned can prove that the positive effect of the transaction on the public interest is much greater than its negative consequences. However, there were no transactions prohibited either by the AMC or by the Cabinet of Ministers of Ukraine in 2011.

AMC official statistics: merger clearance applications[1]

Year	Applications filed with AMC	Approved transactions (unconditional clearances)	Approved transactions (conditional clearances)	Prohibited transactions
2011	756	585	0	0
2010	697	559	0	0
2009	599	476	4	1
2008	1,021	814	1	0
2007	911	715	4	4

New developments in jurisdictional assessment or procedure

Filing requirements. A great number of global transactions with no effect on the competition environment in Ukraine still trigger local merger control thresholds, and there are no actual factors evidencing any forthcoming changes in the near future. Based on the recent statements of AMC officials, the latter are interested in simplification of Ukrainian merger clearance procedure – which, in certain cases, should provide some efficiency gains and in turn, increase the amount of transactions that are voluntarily cleared with the AMC, and as a result benefit competition as a whole.

Under applicable merger clearance regulations,[2] both parties are responsible for merger clearance in Ukraine. Based on the existing practice, the parties concerned file a joint application with the AMC.

No *de minimis* rule is still applicable in Ukraine, therefore there is no exclusion in case of absence of the substantive overlap[3]. The applicable merger control rules require a substantive amount of information to be included in AMC filing forms. In particular, the notification must include detailed information on the transaction parties, taking into account their control relations, including registration data, contact details, officers, amount of shareholdings/votes, and the Ukrainian turnover of each entity of the entire target and acquirer groups.

Despite the broad definition of the target group (extended to the sellers), the AMC, considering the international practice, has recently adopted a position allowing the parties to limit the definition of, and respectively the information on, a target group to companies that are subject to direct/indirect acquisition. Such limitation is only applicable if the seller loses any control over the target as of the date of closing, and the parties provide sufficient information and documents confirming termination of such control. However, such position is not applicable for the purpose of calculation of triggering thresholds; i.e. in order to find out whether the transaction requires Ukrainian merger clearance or not (whether the thresholds envisaged by law are met), the entire seller group shall be considered.

Furthermore, the notification shall necessarily include the definition of the relevant product and geographical markets, the contact information of the Ukrainian competitors, customers and suppliers, and the volume of sales/gains in respect of each customer/supplier. Having said that, notably, such information shall be filed with the AMC in respect of each company of the target/acquirer group generating Ukrainian turnover, regardless of the markets concerned. In other words, even in the absence of the overlapping markets, the parties are bound to file detailed information about their activities in Ukraine.

Strengthening of the information exemption rules. The applicable rules allow parties to request from the AMC to be exempted from filing certain information, if the latter does not affect the decision to be adopted by the AMC. However, in practice, the information regarding the parties' activities in Ukraine (including the above information regarding customers, competitors and suppliers) is treated by AMC officials as mandatory and, even in the absence of substantial overlaps, to receive any exemption in respect of such information is scarcely possible. Moreover, recent trends in 2012 show that the number of exemptions granted by the AMC to parties' requests on information limitation has significantly decreased, while the number of applications returned by the AMC without consideration, due to incompleteness of documents/information, has increased.

Global closing. Producing respective information at an early stage of a transaction often requires substantial time and costs that, in turn, score in favour of the parties' choice to close the transaction, especially a global one, without Ukrainian merger clearance. At the same time, recently, market players more often use the scenario for allowing the avoidance of any delay regarding the closing of a transaction globally that has minimal Ukrainian "negative consequences".

The applicable provisions do not allow the parties to close a foreign-to-foreign transaction globally prior to obtaining AMC approval (where required), even if the parties commit to refrain from any actions in respect of Ukrainian markets (subsidiaries). The scenario involving closing of the foreign-to-foreign transaction before a Ukrainian clearance and obtaining post-closing approval shortly after the closing (providing the AMC with a reasonable justification for the failure to pre-notify) moderates the above strict rule. Given the technical failure to receive merger clearance before closing, the AMC usually (i) issues post-closing clearance (unless there are legal grounds to reject the transaction); and (ii) imposes a fine as envisaged by law. However in such a case, the parties are usually considered by the AMC as acting in "good faith", and the amount of fine to be imposed is rather technical in nature and not material.

Consideration procedure. Based on the Economic Competition Act[4], the Ukrainian merger clearance procedure (Phase I) takes up to 45 (forty-five) calendar days. If a deeper investigation or expertise is required with respect to the transaction, the AMC may initiate a case on concentration (Phase II), which commences upon providing the AMC with a full set of information/documents additionally requested, and shall not exceed 3 (three) months after the AMC has obtained all additionally requested documents/information.

Given its recent practice within Phase II, the AMC (among other actions) generally requests certain information from the following third parties in order to confirm the existence of strong competition and the lack of a negative effect on the:

1. territorial (regional) departments of the AMC;
2. independent external experts specialising in dairy markets (in practice, these are non-commercial associations of dairy sector companies);
3. major consumers of the parties involved in the concentration; and/or
4. major competitors of the parties involved in the concentration.

In addition, within Phase II, the AMC generally requests from the parties:

1. a business plan for a medium-term period (2–3 years) regarding the markets affected by the transaction (including respective calculations); and
2. an estimation of any negative impact of restriction of competition, and the positive effect for the public achieved by means of:

    *   improvement of production, purchase or sale of products;
    *   technical and technological, as well as economic, development;
    *   optimisation of the export or import of products;
    *   development that unifies the technical conditions or standards of products; and/or
    *   rationalisation of production, etc.

Recently the AMC has changed its approach to applications' consideration with respect to foreign-to-foreign transactions. Previously foreign-to-foreign transactions raising no competition concerns were in practice cleared by the AMC before expiration of the statutory consideration period (i.e. earlier than 45 days). Currently the AMC tends to formally wait for expiration of a 45-day period before the authority issues its clearance.

Sanctions for failure to notify. If the parties' failure to notify (when required) is detected by the AMC, the following negative consequences are to be considered:

*   Fine of up to 5% of the total worldwide turnover of the parties in the year preceding enforcement of the fine (the limitation period for such fines in Ukraine is five years). This is a common AMC practice.
*   Invalidation of the transaction by the court (if the AMC proves that the respective transaction has harmed competition in Ukraine). This is a rather theoretical risk.
*   Recovery of double damages (if any) incurred by any third party as a result of the unauthorised transaction. This rarely happens.
*   Export/import ban (if the imposed fine is not duly paid by the defaulting party). This happens extremely rarely; it is a rather theoretical risk.
*   Publication of the information on the defaulting parties on the AMC's official website. This is a common AMC practice.

The applicable merger clearance regulations do not provide for any mechanism or rules applicable for the determination of the amount of a fine; it depends on the impact of the transaction on the competition situation in Ukraine. As a matter of practice, the AMC applies its internal guidelines to determine a specific amount of fine on a case-by-case basis. However, even if the party in breach is subject to a fine in the amount of 5% of the worldwide turnover as of the last financial year, such a fine would arguably still remain in line with the applicable Ukrainian legislation.

There are certain cases when fines were imposed on parties to foreign-to-foreign transactions when the said transaction did not raise any material competition issues in Ukraine. The amounts of the fine in such cases generally did not exceed €20,000. However, one can observe the apparent and progressive tendency to increase fines applied by the AMC. Such amounts are significantly higher if defaulting parties refuse to cooperate with the AMC.

Detection risks

The AMC representatives regularly announce that one of the AMC's key tasks is the identification of breaches of competition legislation in historical M&A transactions, i.e. the review of historical structuring of target groups of companies for the purpose of checking compliance with the domestic competition legislation.

The risk of detection of foreign-to-foreign mergers where there are some purchaser group revenues in Ukraine mostly depends on the following: a) whether the parties are recorded on the AMC's database (this database contains snapshots of parties to mergers at the time of each transaction they are involved with. If the parties make subsequent transactions requiring filing in Ukraine, the AMC will ask questions, e.g. when did each portfolio company join the group, and was AMC approval required); and b) sensitivity of the relevant market. If the AMC detects violation, the risk of fine imposition is high, especially in cases where either party has any assets in Ukraine.

Therefore, in cases where the group of companies already has certain filing history in Ukraine and its group structure is available in the AMC's database, the detection risk (whether immediate or during any future substantive/unavoidable Ukrainian filing involving such group) is much higher.

Based on the applicable law, both parties (i.e. buyer and seller) are responsible for merger clearance. Therefore, the below risks are applicable to the seller as well. However, the AMC will usually only fine the seller where it is more convenient for the authority to do so (e.g. where only the seller has a subsidiary in Ukraine). The AMC is technically unable to enforce fines outside Ukraine in case of foreign-to-foreign mergers. The risk of enforcement therefore depends on whether the parties have subsidiaries in Ukraine (if they do, the risk of enforcement will be higher).

Moreover, we are aware of certain situations where the AMC initiated cases on violation of competition legislation for failure to notify the AMC following the monitoring of the public announcements of M&A transactions through the internet. During 2011 the AMC identified 86 failures to notify the reportable transaction, which is 19% higher than in 2010.

Advance ruling. There is no commonly-established practice to have a pre-notification meeting with the competition authority to discuss the proposed transaction. Indeed, the possibility to receive informal guidance in respect of a particular transaction without any filings is very limited.

The applicable legislation provides for the possibility to receive preliminary rulings (formal guidance) from the AMC in respect of the contemplated transaction, i.e. a preliminary ruling from the AMC which determines whether prior approval is required, and whether it is likely to approve the contemplated transaction. However, given that the preliminary ruling procedure: i) takes up to one month; ii) requires submitting with the AMC almost the same information as for the actual filing; and iii) legally does not relieve the parties of the need to receive the approval itself, when required, (which takes up to an additional 45 days (Phase I) as described above); such procedure is not commonly used in practice.

Key economic appraisal techniques applied e.g. as regards unilateral effects and co-ordinated effects

As of the current date, no guidelines on the approach to substantial merger assessment have been issued. The AMC grants its approval as long as the transaction will not result in the emergence of a monopoly in the affected market, and will not materially restrict competition in the affected market or in its substantial part. In the case of overlapping market(s), the emergence of a monopoly is tested through the expected aggregated market share(s) (an entity holding a 35% share of the market may be considered as having a monopoly position in the market).

Given the lack of accepted substantial merger assessment tests, the AMC usually applies market share assessment to also identify the effect on competition, i.e. the ability to substantially restrict competition.

Please note that under internal "unpublished" AMC guidelines, the AMC generally estimates the level of competition (and respectively adopts its decision to approve or to prohibit the transaction) based on the market shares held by the parties, presuming that:

1. there is strong competition when neither entity has a market share exceeding 5%;

2. there is sufficient competition when neither entity has a market share exceeding 15%;

3. there is weak competition when one or more entities have a market share exceeding 15% but less than 35%; and

4.   there is extremely weak or no competition when one or more entities have a market share exceeding 35%.

In case of strong competition, the merger clearance procedure is rather technical; in case of weak competition, generally Phase II is initiated, but approval is commonly unconditional; and if competition is extremely weak, the approval is conditional, or the transaction is prohibited.

Based on Article 12 of the Economic Competition Act, the AMC presumes the existence of collective dominance on the respective market if:

1.   no more than three business entities jointly hold the market share in the amount of at least 50%; and/or

2.   no more than five business entities jointly hold the market share in the amount of at least 70%.

Should the collective dominance be presumed, the parties to the transaction shall prove to the AMC that there is a strong competition between the major market players that are active on the respective market.

Generally, the main positions to be proved in respect of collective dominance and to be accepted by the AMC are the following: i) lack of any relations of control between the major players; ii) lack of any cooperation, including contractual arrangements between the major players; and iii) strong pricing competition, etc.

The transaction prohibited by the AMC may be approved by the Cabinet of Ministers of Ukraine if the parties concerned can prove that the positive effect of the transaction for public interest is much greater than its negative consequences. In the last five years, only one concentration prohibited by the AMC was approved by the Cabinet of Ministers of Ukraine.

Approach to remedies (i) to avoid second stage investigation and (ii) following second stage investigation

The "remedies" to be imposed in the case of competition issues are not provided under the relevant Ukrainian legislation. Moreover, there is no guideline or unified approach followed by the AMC with regards to the terms and conditions of divestment implementation. The law provides that any divestment remedy should eliminate or mitigate the negative consequences of a merger for the competition, and can be applied only within a Phase II procedure. The remedies may provide for the limitation of rights to manage, use or dispose of any assets, as well as for the forced disposition of the assets concerned. However, such conditions are rather uncommon for AMC practice.

Whenever the participant holds the monopolistic (dominant) position in the market, the AMC is entitled to decide on a compulsory split of such monopolist. At the same time, the split is not applicable under the circumstances when: (i) there is no possibility to separate the company or its organisational units due to certain organisational or territorial reasons; and (ii) a close technological connection within the company or between its organisational units exists (e.g. if the company utilises more than 30% of the products produced by itself or its organisational unit).

Furthermore, the company that is subject to the split may, at its discretion, decide on a transformation instead of a split, provided that its monopolistic (dominant) position would be eliminated.

At the same time, the applicable law provides no specific requirement to have the divestment remedy complied in full before the merger is completed. However, the AMC is entitled to reconsider its decision on granting the concentration whenever the divestment remedy is not complied with by the applicant / parties to the concentration.

The AMC is entitled, simultaneously with the granting of its permit, to oblige the parties to the allowed transaction to take certain actions that eliminate or extenuate a negative impact of the transaction on competition in Ukraine. Such conditions are often imposed by the AMC and generally include prohibition of the following actions: establishment of barriers for the competitors; fixing unreasonably high or law prices; and division of territories, etc. In addition, in order to control the parties' compliance with such conditions, the AMC obliges the respective parties to regularly report on the status of compliance. However, no guidelines in this respect have been issued.

United Kingdom

Nigel Parr & Mat Hughes
Ashurst LLP

Overview of merger control activity during the last 12 months

Number of Office of Fair Trading ("OFT") merger decisions

The UK's first stage merger authority, the OFT, reports official merger statistics on the basis of the financial year 1 April – 31 March. In the year ending 31 March 2012, the OFT reported that it had published a total of 100 merger decisions (excluding one mandatory water merger reference decision). This is over a third more decisions than in each of the two preceding years (73 decisions in 2010/11 and 72 decisions in 2009/10). However, it is still less than half the level of merger decisions published by the OFT in the peak year of 2005/6 (210 decisions).

As at the end of 2012, the number of merger decisions published so far in the year 2012/13 was 71, which suggests the OFT is on track to publish around 90-100 decisions for the full financial year.

First stage outcomes

Of the 100 cases decided by the OFT in the year 2011/12, 21 mergers were found not to qualify for investigation (21%) and 62 mergers were cleared unconditionally (62%). As regards the remainder, nine mergers were referred to the Competition Commission ("CC") (9%) for a second stage merger review; five were cleared by the OFT subject to undertakings in lieu of reference (5%); and three were potentially problematic but were cleared unconditionally by the OFT using the *de minimis* exception (3%).

Taking a longer-term view, a similar picture emerges when looking at the three years ending 31 March 2012. Over that period, 18% of mergers were found by the OFT not to qualify for investigation and 60% of mergers were cleared unconditionally without relying on any exceptions to the OFT's duty to make references. As regards the remainder, 9% were referred to the CC, 6% were cleared subject to undertakings in lieu of reference, and 6% were cleared by applying the *de minimis* exception. Since 2007 (when it was first applied), the *de minimis* exception has been applied 22 times.

However, it is worth noting that as at the end of 2012 the OFT has so far referred more mergers to the CC in the year 2012/13 than in any of the previous 5 years (11 mergers referred, 16%), with 3 months of the financial year still left to run. The number of mergers cleared unconditionally in 2012/13 is currently down at 52% (37 of 71 cases), and the use of undertakings in lieu is slightly up on previous years so far, at 8% of cases (6 of 71 cases). Whilst the number of cases referred for second stage investigation in any given year will of course vary, these figures support our view that the OFT is adopting an increasingly cautious approach at the first stage of the merger review process. It is notable that the majority of transactions referred by the OFT are ultimately unconditionally cleared following in-depth review by the CC (see further below).

OFT case review meetings

The OFT holds case review meetings ("CRMs") in relation to cases which might warrant reference to the CC, with the OFT inviting the parties to an Issues Meeting to respond to the issues the OFT has previously identified in writing. In a high proportion of these cases, the merger has subsequently either been referred to the CC for a second stage investigation, or undertakings in lieu have been accepted by the OFT (or the *de minimis* exception has been applied).

Considering the three years ending 31 March 2012, only 22% of cases considered at a CRM were subsequently cleared unconditionally by the OFT without the *de minimis* exception being applied. This figure varies year-on-year, and the OFT's latest statistics for the year 2012/13 show that as at the end of December 2012, only 18% of cases considered at a CRM were cleared unconditionally without the *de minimis* exception being applied. In short, an invitation to an Issues Meeting appears to offer a strong indication that the transaction in question is unlikely to be cleared unconditionally at the first stage (absent the possible application of the *de minimis* exception), and merging parties would be well advised to seek to persuade the OFT that an Issues Meeting is not warranted if at all possible. In practice, the best way to achieve this is likely to be to engage in pre-notification discussions with the OFT and seek to address any potential competition concerns well in advance of when an Issues Meeting would need to be scheduled.

Mergers found not to qualify for investigation by the OFT

As noted in the 1st edition of *Global Legal Insights: Merger Control ("GLI: Merger Control")*, and illustrated by the statistics cited above, the OFT concludes relatively frequently that a merger does not qualify for investigation, despite the UK merger control regime being a voluntary one under which parties are free to decide whether to notify their transactions. These cases are probably explained in part by the UK jurisdictional thresholds (particularly the share of supply threshold – see further Chapter 56 of *The International Comparative Legal Guide to: Merger Control 2013 ("The ICLG to: Merger Control 2013")*) not being "bright line" thresholds which are simple to apply, and partly by the caution of some parties (or their advisers) in desiring the legal certainty of the OFT's conclusion on a case. The number of precautionary notifications made to the OFT may well fall in future as a result of the substantial increase in UK merger filing fees from 1 October 2012 – see further below.

Second stage outcomes

Looking at the CC's second stage decisions over the three years ending 31 March 2012, it is notable that a relatively high percentage of transactions have been abandoned following the OFT's reference decision (7 of 24 cases, or 29%). One explanation for this is that a CC investigation inevitably involves considerable further expense and delay, which the parties may not be willing to accept. This is particularly likely to be the case if the transaction is a relatively small one, which is often the case with mergers falling within the scope of the UK merger control regime, as larger mergers tend to fall for consideration by the European Commission under the EU Merger Regulation ("EUMR", see further Chapter 19 of *The ICLG to: Merger Control 2013*). It is also possible that, at least in some cases, the abandoned transactions were considered by the parties (and their advisers) to be unlikely to be cleared by the CC, so the decision to abandon was taken at a relatively early stage in the CC process (obviously this is not an option in the case of completed mergers).

The CC reached adverse findings in only 4 of the 17 cases on which it reported (i.e. 24% of the merger references which were not abandoned) over the three years ending 31 March 2012: one in 2009/10, none in 2010/11, and three in 2011/12. In each of these cases divestment remedies were imposed (see further below).

As at the end of 2012, of the 11 cases referred to the CC so far in the year 2012/13, one transaction has been prohibited (*Akzo Nobel/Metlac Holding* (December 2012)), three have been cleared, two have been abandoned following reference to the CC, and five are ongoing (with provisional adverse findings recently being announced in *Rank/Gala*).

New developments in jurisdictional assessment or procedure

New CC merger procedural guidelines

On 31 October 2012 the CC published new merger procedural guidelines, following a consultation process launched in April 2011. These guidelines describe the main stages of a (second stage) merger inquiry, including indicative timescales, and outline the key interactions between the CC, the merging parties and their advisers during the course of a typical merger inquiry. The new guidelines do not, in themselves, represent any significant change in policy, but they do provide a useful step-by-step summary of the approach adopted by the CC, which highlights in particular the resource-intensive and public nature of the process: merging parties can expect to receive extensive information requests, as well as a site visit, and the majority of documents relating to the inquiry, including the parties' response to the CC's Issues Statement, will be published on the CC's website. The guidelines also confirm that there is no scope for early closure of a merger inquiry at the CC stage (in contrast to the EUMR process – see Chapter 19 of *The ICLG to: Merger Control 2013*): even if the CC concludes at a relatively early stage that the merger does not result in a substantial lessening of competition, or the parties would prefer to secure early termination of the proceedings by offering a remedy, the CC is still required to publish Provisional Findings followed by a Final Report.

It is worth noting that, unlike the draft version of the CC merger procedural guidelines published for consultation, the final version of the guidelines does not deal with the publication of working papers and disclosure of information by the CC in any detail: this is being dealt with separately in revised guidance on disclosure in merger inquiries and market investigations, which is the subject of a separate ongoing consultation process. The disclosure of CC working papers (which set out the CC's thinking on a particular issue prior to the publication of Provisional Findings), and in particular the extent of any redactions, can be a controversial issue, and indeed has been the subject of an appeal to the CAT (*Sports Direct v CC* – ultimately the CAT did not rule on the merits of Sports Direct's application as the CC simply withdrew its paper following the CAT's ruling that Sports Direct's challenge was not premature). The revised disclosure guidance should offer further guidance and clarity on this issue, although the CC is likely to try to retain some flexibility.

Increasing time taken for the OFT to reach a first stage decision

The amount of time taken by the OFT to reach a first stage decision has been increasing in recent years, as has the amount of information required by the OFT. Where a transaction is notified using an informal submission (as opposed to a statutory Merger Notice – see Chapter 56 of *The ICLG to: Merger Control 2013*), or an investigation is launched on the OFT's own initiative, there is no statutory deadline unless the merger is completed, and whilst the OFT aims to reach a decision within a 40-day "administrative timetable" (i.e. approximately two months) of receipt of a complete submission, this can be extended for various reasons and is not binding in any event. For example, of the 14 mergers which the OFT referred to the CC or proposed clearing subject to undertakings in lieu of a reference in 2012, the OFT took under three months to reach its decision in only five cases (36% of cases, with this including the *Global Radio/GMG Radio* case where a fast track reference was requested), with its decision being reached in between just over three months to over six months in the remaining cases.

A drawn-out first stage process can be very resource-intensive and costly. On the one hand, the OFT will wish to manage cases efficiently and the parties will wish to progress mergers for normal commercial reasons (perhaps particularly in respect of completed mergers, which are frequently effectively put "on hold" pending the OFT's decision as a consequence of hold separate undertakings preventing the integration of businesses). On the other, the OFT and the parties may wish to avoid unnecessary merger references or undertakings in lieu of reference being over-wide, particularly given that there is currently no scope for the CC to terminate references early. In particular, where the parties wish to commission customer surveys in order to assess the competitive effects of a merger (which is a common issue as regards retailing mergers), this is bound to add to the timetable due to the time required to design the survey questions, agree them with the OFT, carry out the fieldwork, and analyse the results.

The first phase merger review process will need to change following the introduction of a new 40 working day statutory deadline for all first stage merger reviews as part of the reforms contained in the Enterprise and Regulatory Reform Bill (the "ERR Bill") which is currently going through Parliament (see further below).

Very limited use of "fast track" reference procedure

As discussed in the 1st edition of *GLI: Merger Control*, the OFT introduced a new "fast track" reference procedure in 2009 for transactions which the parties accept will inevitably require an in-depth second stage review by the CC, in response to criticisms that the OFT's first stage procedure was too detailed and onerous for such cases. However, despite the new process being widely welcomed at the time of its introduction, as at the end of 2012 only two applications had been made.

The first of these, made in February 2011 in respect of a proposed merger between two major UK travel agency businesses *(Thomas Cook/Co-operative Group/Midlands Co-operative JV)*, was discussed in the 1st edition of *GLI: Merger Control*. More recently, a second application was made in July 2012 in respect of the *Global Radio/GMG Radio* case. It was not possible for the OFT to make a formal fast-track reference to the CC in this case due to an intervention notice subsequently issued by the Secretary of State on public interest grounds. However, the Secretary of State accepted that the extent and nature of the OFT's report on the competition issues raised by the proposed transaction reflected the fast track reference request and, following the Secretary of State's decision not to make a public interest reference, the OFT decided that it was appropriate for it to act swiftly in referring the merger to the CC in accordance with the parties' original request. However, the reference was ultimately not made until October 2012, two-and-a-half months after the parties' original fast track request. This delay was obviously not a particularly satisfactory outcome from the parties' perspective, and not the sort of timescale envisaged for cases involving a fast track application.

Completed mergers

Whilst there is no general requirement under UK merger control rules to seek, or to have obtained, merger clearance prior to completing a merger which qualifies for investigation, the OFT has the power to seek interim undertakings and adopt orders preventing *"pre-emptive action"* in relation to completed mergers which it decides to investigate (either on its own initiative or in response to complaints). The OFT routinely seeks such interim undertakings in connection with completed mergers *"where there are preliminary indications that the merger raises or is likely to raise competition concerns"* and *"it is appropriate to prevent pre-emptive action"*. For example, the OFT obtained interim undertakings in 25 completed mergers in 2011/12.

A more recent development is that since June 2012 the OFT has imposed directions in four cases requiring the appointment of a monitoring trustee to secure and monitor compliance with interim undertakings *(Global Radio/GMG Radio, Rexel/Wilts, Nakano/Premier Foods,* and *Vue/Apollo)*. Accordingly, the OFT's practice has become more aligned with the CC's, with the CC's Merger Procedural Guidelines of October 2012 indicating that: *"Given the risks of pre-emptive action in a completed merger, the CC usually requires the appointment of a monitoring trustee."*

Exercise of the OFT's discretion not to refer a merger

As illustrated by the statistics set out above, the OFT continues to exercise its discretion not to refer a merger which has met the test for reference to the CC where the parties are able to offer first stage remedies (known as "undertakings in lieu of reference") which remove the competition concerns in a clear-cut manner, or where the markets under consideration are too small to warrant reference (the *"de minimis"* exception – subject to an upper threshold of £10m and a case-by-case evaluation of whether the application of the exception is appropriate).

With regard to undertakings in lieu of a reference, where divestment of certain assets or parts of the acquired business is proposed to avoid a reference to the CC, the OFT is increasingly requiring that a suitable "upfront" purchaser must be identified by the parties and approved by the OFT before the undertakings in lieu will be accepted. Indeed, over the last 12 months, a suitable upfront purchaser requirement has been imposed in 75% of cases in which the OFT has accepted undertakings in lieu of reference (6 out of 8 cases). In the two cases in which no upfront purchaser was required *(Jewson/Build Center* and *Midcounties Co-operative/Tuffin Investments)*, the OFT considered that the risk profile did not merit such a requirement, due to the number of suitable and potentially willing purchasers for the businesses/assets to be divested. However, in the majority of cases, the OFT is likely to require the additional comfort offered by an upfront purchaser requirement.

The OFT may also exercise its discretion not to refer a merger to the CC where either the merger is not sufficiently advanced or is insufficiently likely to occur, or relevant customer benefits (or "efficiencies") generated by the merger can be shown to outweigh the adverse competitive effects of the transaction. However, as at the end of 2012, no merger had not been referred to the CC on the ground that the merger was not sufficiently advanced or was insufficiently likely to occur. In addition, only one merger *(Global Radio/GCap Media)* was not referred to the CC on the ground that relevant customer benefits/efficiencies generated by the merger outweighed the adverse competitive effects of the transaction. However, such benefits have occasionally been referred to in concluding that a merger should not be referred on *de minimis* grounds. For example, in *Ordnance Survey/Local Government Improvement and Development* (2011) the OFT took into account the available evidence that the transaction would result in significant customer benefits: *"Although the OFT did not have sufficiently compelling evidence that the existence of RCBs* [relevant customer benefits] *arising from the Transaction was such as to outweigh the substantial lessening of competition and any adverse effect resulting from it (such as to apply the RCB exception), the OFT nevertheless considers it appropriate to have regard to such benefits – to the extent that they have been substantiated – in assessing the net adverse effect on customers that will be expected to arise as a result of any substantial lessening of competition when considering the potential application of the 'de minimis' exception"*. In addition, the OFT has taken account of benefits which may enhance rivalry in concluding that there is no substantial lessening of competition, notably in *DPG/Zoopla* (2012), see further below.

Key industry sectors reviewed, and approach adopted, to market definition

As noted in the 1st edition of *GLI: Merger Control*, the general approach to the assessment of the competitive effects of mergers in the UK at both the first and second stages of the merger control regime is set out in the joint Merger Assessment Guidelines published in September 2010 by the OFT and CC (the "UK Guidelines") (OFT1254 / CC2). An analysis of the UK Guidelines, including comparison with the similar US and EU guidelines, is contained in Mat Hughes' and David Wirth's paper *"The Economics of Horizontal Mergers – recent lessons in avoiding surprises"* (see Chapter 1 of *The ICLG to: Merger Control 2011)*.

The mergers considered by the OFT and those referred to the CC cover a wide range of industry sectors, with a primary geographical focus on mergers which raise national, regional or local competition issues (due to the combination of the UK jurisdictional thresholds, which are based on UK business activity, and the interplay with the EUMR jurisdictional mechanisms). In recent years particular attention has been given to mergers with local competitive effects, including in particular retailing mergers.

Retailing mergers

As discussed in the 1st edition of *GLI: Merger Control*, both the OFT and CC have considered a number of mergers in the retail/wholesaling sector, with retailing in this context being defined broadly to include both retailers and wholesalers selling goods (e.g. supermarkets, plumbing and heating suppliers, electrical equipment wholesalers, petrol stations, and sports goods retailers) and outlets providing services (e.g. betting shops, funeral parlours, cinemas, sports clubs, and private hospitals). Retailing mergers have remained a sector of particular focus, with useful guidance being set out in the joint CC and OFT "Commentary on retail mergers" of March 2011 ("the Commentary") (OFT 1305 / CC 2 com 2).

The effects of retailing mergers on local competition were considered in detail in the 1st edition of *GLI: Merger Control*, and that discussion is not repeated here. It is, however, worth noting the recent case of *Edmundson Electrical/Electric Center* (2012), in which the OFT argued that the guidance in the Commentary that retail mergers that reduce the number of competitors from five to four are not usually of concern *"only tend[s] to apply in cases where it can be confident, at the first phase, that the relevant market is the narrowest possible market"*, and the OFT could not discount the possibility that concerns might arise in *"areas where the parties are particularly close competitors"*. As illustrated by another recent case, *Rexel/Wilts,* this latter point can be addressed by considering, for example, whether the parties are the only local competitors within a, say, five-minute catchment area even if the OFT considers that the relevant market is generally based on, say, a ten-minute catchment area. In particular, if a merger creates a monopoly in a smaller geographical area, the OFT may wish to confirm that in this location the merged undertaking would not have incentives to increase prices significantly or otherwise worsen some other element of competition.

In *Edmundson Electrical/Electric Center* the OFT concluded, after surveys had been commissioned of all of the potentially problematic areas provisionally identified by the OFT, that certain competitors should be excluded for filtering purposes on the basis that the OFT considered that wholesalers with a turnover of under £10m may not be able to compete with the parties on prices (notwithstanding the existence of buyer groups), and that certain competitors did not actively and strongly compete with the parties due to the nature of their retail outlets (with the OFT emphasising that the survey evidence suggested that few customers would switch to these outlets in the event of one of the parties' branches closing).

Ultimately, in *Edmundson Electrical/Electric Center* the OFT concluded that competition concerns would not arise in localities where the number of competing fascias would fall from five to four post-merger. This conclusion was reached on the basis that:

- in three of the four "five to four" areas which were surveyed, the results of the survey did not indicate that Edmundson would have an incentive to increase prices. In the one locality where the survey results indicated that this might be the case, the OFT agreed that this result was driven by the answer given by one respondent, and other data from branch managers suggested that competition from other suppliers would remain effective; and
- in only two of the nine "four to three" areas did the OFT identify local competition concerns, which suggested that competition concerns should not arise where more than three competitors remained post-merger.

National/regional competitive effects in addition to local effects

In addition to local competitive effects, mergers may also have regional or national competitive effects. Whilst local competitive effects may be capable of being addressed by divesting outlets in those localities where competition concerns arise, remedying regional or national competition concerns may be considerably more difficult since this may require the creation of a new regional or national competitor. Accordingly, even if retailers/wholesalers compete locally, it may also be important to consider whether anti-competitive effects arise at a regional or national level.

As discussed in the 1st edition of *GLI: Merger Control,* national competitive effects may arise even if all firms' customers are purely local to their stores, as firms may set some aspects of their competitive offering nationally and other elements locally (which may be the case, for example, as regards grocery retailing by large supermarkets). In this scenario, those competitive elements which are determined nationally may depend on the aggregated degree of local competition faced by a firm across all of the local markets in which it operates.

For example, in *Sports Direct/JJB Sports* (2010), the CC dismissed any local competition concerns, despite the merger creating local monopolies, after a detailed analysis indicating that price, quality, range and service ("PQRS") were not varied by Sports Direct in response to the extent of local competition. The CC went on to carry out a critical loss analysis as to whether increasing prices at the national level would become profitable, but concluded that this was unlikely. This case and the application of critical loss analysis more generally is considered further in Chapter 1 of *The ICLG to: Merger Control 2013.*

Another scenario in which national/regional competitive effects may arise is if it is appropriate to segment the market into different customer groups according to whether they purchase nationally, regionally or locally. For example, in *Edmundson Electrical/Electric Center* the OFT assessed the competitive effects of the merger of the two electrical wholesalers on a national and regional basis, as well as considering its local competitive effects.

At the national level, the OFT found that large national customers should be considered separately, with Edmundson and another competitor, Rexel, being the main suppliers to such customers due to their requirements as regards price, range availability, national deliveries etc. Whilst Electric Center and another competitor, CEF, also had national branch networks (albeit Electric Center's branch network was much smaller), their businesses focused on smaller customers. This view was supported by internal documents and the bulk of large customers' responses. Accordingly, the OFT concluded that concerns did not arise as regards large national customers.

The OFT also considered the position separately as regards multi-local/regional customers which required supplies in a number of localities or in a region, but not across the UK or primarily in one locality. The OFT considered this position both generally and in the three specific regions where competition concerns, if they existed, were most likely to arise based on the regional overlaps in the parties' branches. In reaching the conclusion that competition concerns did not arise in relation to these customers the OFT took account of:

- the presence of other sizeable wholesalers in these regions, including national wholesalers (both Rexel, the largest competitor to Edmundson, and also CEF) and large independents; and
- survey evidence by region commissioned by Edmundson showing that these customers purchased from large independent wholesalers, CEF and Rexel (and not particularly Electric Center), together with various internal documents indicating the extent of such rivalry.

OFT decision in DPG/Zoopla: clearance of a three to two merger

In April 2012, the OFT cleared the proposed merger between the Digital Property Group Ltd ("DPG") and Zoopla Ltd ("Zoopla"), despite the fact that it led to a reduction in the number of main competitors from three to two. Both DPG and Zoopla were active in the provision of online property advertising through property portals, which are used by consumers looking for properties to buy or rent as well as by estate agents wishing to advertise properties. The market leader was Rightmove and although there were other property portals within the UK, the OFT concluded that they were too small to constrain DPG, Zoopla and Rightmove. The OFT estimated that the merged entity would have a 20-30% combined share of revenue from all property advertising, a 30% share of visits and a 14% share of page views. Rightmove's shares were 45-55% of revenue, 47% of visits and 74% of page views.

Notwithstanding the effective creation of a duopolistic market structure, the OFT cleared the merger. It concluded that the parties were not particularly close competitors as reflected in the fact that their offerings were differentiated, with their services appealing to different groups (estate agents were generally prepared to pay more for DPG's services than for Zoopla's services, suggesting that competition between the two was limited). Moreover, the parties and almost all third party respondents considered that Rightmove was a "must have" for estate agents as there was no other portal with comparable reach, which led the OFT to conclude that Rightmove would continue to provide a significant competitive constraint on the parties post-merger. In addition, the OFT considered that the merger increased the merged firm's ability to match Rightmove in terms of house-hunter use statistics, such as page views and other service offerings. The OFT therefore concluded that the merger was likely to have a pro-competitive impact by creating a portal that could rival Rightmove. The OFT found that prior to the merger estate agents had little choice but to list on Rightmove, allowing it to increase prices significantly in recent years, and that the merged portal would significantly reduce the difference in quality between the parties and Rightmove, which would be likely to lead to a stronger constraint on Rightmove's pricing.

The OFT briefly considered whether there was a realistic prospect that the merger would lead to coordination between the merged firm and Rightmove. The OFT considered that such coordination would only be possible if, along with other conditions, Rightmove and the merged entity would be able to monitor the terms of any coordination. The OFT concluded that there was no realistic prospect of price coordination because the prices charged to individual estate agents are not transparent. The OFT did not consider that there was a realistic prospect that the merger could lead to any other forms of coordination.

Coordinated effects

In *Anglo American/Lafarge* (2012) the CC concluded that a proposed JV which would reduce the number of national bulk cement producers from four to three (with the JV having a market share of 40-50%) would be expected to give rise to a substantial lessening of competition in the bulk cement market through coordinated effects. This is the first CC merger decision since the Enterprise Act came into force in June 2003 where the CC has reached an adverse finding on the basis of coordinated effects.

There were a number of significant complexities which the CC needed to address as part of its detailed investigation, including whether there was pre-existing coordination (it did not formally conclude on this matter, although it did state that the evidence *"indicated that the market was already susceptible to coordination before the proposed JV"*) and precisely how the JV would contribute to any coordinated effects.

As regards whether coordination was occurring, the CC considered a variety of information, including:
- trends in market shares (noting that market share stability may suggest a lack of competition, but there had been some changes in shares/switching and there is no obvious benchmark as to what coordination looks like);
- evidence from the CC price concentration analysis ("PCA") (which suggested that the presence of a nearby Hanson or Cemex plant did not have a statistically significant effect on Lafarge's prices, which might reflect either a lack of rivalry or effective competition, although the CC preferred the former explanation given other evidence); and
- customer switching data and evidence from customers on the behaviour of UK cement producers (both of which the CC found inconclusive).

Arguably the most difficult issue for the parties to address was the increases in the variable profits per tonne of cement over the period 2007 to 2010, which the CC argued appeared inconsistent with cement producers competing for customers in a market with falling demand and excess capacity.

In line with the UK Guidelines (which themselves follow the criteria set out by the European Court in *Airtours*), the CC emphasised that all three of the following conditions must be satisfied for coordination to be possible:
- Condition 1: *"firms need to be able to reach and monitor the terms of coordination"*.
The CC emphasised that the bulk cement market is very concentrated and cement is a relatively homogeneous product. However, the CC did not consider that coordination on prices was most likely, with realised prices not being very transparent (although prices announcements could facilitate a common understanding as to price changes). Instead, the CC considered that coordination would be most likely to occur as regards shares of production or customer win/losses (each producer would know its own share of UK production with a month lag from published trade association data, and would know its own wins and losses).
- Condition 2: *"coordination needs to be internally sustainable among the coordinating group, i.e. firms have to find it in their individual interests to adhere to the coordinated outcome"*.
The standard problem which may destabilise coordination between firms is that firms which deviate from the coordinated outcome (which is commonly referred to as "cheating"), for example, by competing for rivals' customers, may be able to increase their sales and profits for a period of time until the affected rivals respond and their profits then fall. Accordingly, it is relevant to consider the gains from coordination, and whether deviation may be deterred by an expectation that the gains in sales and profits achieved from deviation will be small, as rivals would respond quickly to "punish" such competition.
The CC considered that the gains from coordination were potentially large, as cement is relatively homogeneous and capital-intensive. The CC considered that rivals could respond by targeting the deviator's customers, thereby reducing their sales and profits (the CC noted that long-term contracts were not a feature of the market), and that this would not be particularly costly as price cuts to some customers should not lower prices overall, due to the limited transparency of realised prices and the large number of local markets for ready-mix concrete ("RMX", which is produced by mixing together cement, aggregates and water). The CC also considered that cement producers could punish by taking back in-house cement purchased from other producers (referred to as "repatriation") or through targeted reductions in the price of RMX sold by integrated RMX-cement producers.
- Condition 3: "coordination needs to be externally sustainable, in that there is little likelihood of coordination being undermined by competition from outside the coordinating group".
The CC considered that competition from imports was an insufficient constraint, there were high barriers to entry into the production of cement in the UK, and no evidence of countervailing buyer power. Anglo American's (which owned Tarmac) incentives to expand are considered further below.

Whilst the above analysis is clearly highly relevant, it was insufficient in the sense that the CC also needed to consider how the proposed JV would facilitate and or strengthen any coordination. The CC addressed this by considering how the JV would affect each of the three conditions outlined above, both in circumstances where there was pre-existing coordination and where there was not. The CC concluded that each of three conditions would be satisfied to a greater extent as a consequence of the proposed JV.

Rather than cataloguing all of the discussion under the headings of the three conditions and considering the position with and without pre-existing coordination, it is perhaps most helpful to highlight a small number of points:

- A particular complexity for the CC was considering how Tarmac's (Anglo American) competitive position affected the analysis. On the one hand, the CC found that Tarmac was capacity constrained, such that the JV would not substantially alter the ability of the coordinating group to reach a coordinated outcome. On the other, Tarmac could use its existing planning permission to increase its capacity (it having expanded its capacity materially on two separate occasions in the past ten years), and this consideration would also point to the JV reducing external competitive constraints. After the proposed JV, the threat that the JV entity might expand its capacity further would be lower, as the JV entity would already benefit from Lafarge's excess capacity.

- In any event, it is easier to monitor wins-losses if there are only three large cement producers than if there are four. The JV's incentives to deviate from the coordinated outcome would also be reduced as its share of overall profits from coordination would be larger. In addition, more information from the RMX market would be available to the JV than Lafarge pre-merger, and the JV's vertical integration would be more similar to that of competitors (with various effects, including an increased ability to repatriate sales post-JV).

Key economic appraisal techniques applied

De-emphasising market definition

As a general point, previously discussed in the 1st edition of *GLI: Merger Control*, there has been a shift away from concentrating the competition analysis on market definition and market shares, towards more directly considering the degree of rivalry between firms, including identifying which businesses are the closest competitors. This is particularly an issue in "differentiated" markets, where there is an increasing tendency for market definition questions to be re-focused on whether a merger between rivals creates upward pricing pressure or reduces rivalry in other dimensions (see further the 1st edition of *GLI: Merger Control*).

Theoretical measures of upward pricing pressure

A good overview of the range of economic techniques applied by the OFT and the CC is set out in the UK Guidelines. The various theoretical measures of upward pricing pressure, including Upward Pricing Pressure ("UPP"), the Gross Upward Pricing Pressure Index ("GUPPI"), and estimations of Illustrative Price Rises ("IPR"), and their application by the UK authorities in cases such as *Somerfield/Morrisons* (2005) and *Zipcar/Streetcar* (2010), were also discussed in the 1st edition of *GLI: Merger Control*, and in Chapter 1 of *The ICLG to: Merger Control 2011* and Chapter 1 of *The ICLG to: Merger Control 2013*.

Rather than repeating those discussions, we focus below on some of the key recent developments in this area over the last year or so.

Key drivers of the results and measurement

As discussed in the 1st edition of *GLI: Merger Control*, one of the issues raised by UPP and IPR is that under both of these methodologies, mergers may be found to lead to anti-competitive unilateral effects even where the parties may not be close rivals and the businesses have relatively low gross margins. This naturally leads to questions of measurement.

The UK authorities' use of surveys and studies into the impact of market entry and exit to derive diversion ratios, and the potential difficulties regarding the reliability of such surveys, were discussed in the 1st edition of *GLI: Merger Control*. In terms of key developments over the last year or so in this area, the following points should be noted:

- The OFT is increasingly using "confidence intervals" around estimated diversion ratios to address concerns about the reliability of survey responses (particularly where a survey involves a relatively small number of people). As explained in the 1st edition of *GLI: Merger Control*, a confidence interval can be calculated around any point estimate, indicating that the researcher can be 95% confident that the actual answer lies within a certain range. Two good recent illustrations of the use of confidence intervals around estimated diversion ratios by the OFT are *Rexel/Wilts* (2012) and *Midcounties Co-operative/Tuffin Investments* (2012). It should be noted that confidence intervals will be wide if survey sample sizes are small, particularly as revenue-weighting respondents' answers may give substantial weight to the responses of a small number of high-spending customers.

- Uncertainties as to the right level of margins, and in particular the extent to which costs would fall if there were to be a deterioration in PQRS, have previously led the CC to consider a range of estimates of gross margins (as seen in the *Zipcar/Streetcar* case, discussed in more detail in the 1st edition of *GLI: Merger Control*). As a first phase regulator, the OFT may also wish to take a cautious view as to gross margins (i.e. considering that gross margins are higher by treating a smaller proportion of costs as variable), with this being a noteworthy feature of a number of the OFT's recent decisions where it has applied upward pricing pressure tests (see, for example, *Rexel/Wilts* and *Edmundson Electrical/Electric Center*).

Whilst it is appropriate to consider any uncertainties in the measurement of upward pricing pressure due to imprecision in the estimates of diversion ratios and gross margins, adopting a cautious approach to both these measures risks the OFT making ultra-cautious decisions when identifying potential competition concerns. This is particularly the case as the OFT also takes a cautious approach to the assessment of efficiencies.

Broader issues: breadth of application/incompleteness and empirical support

UPP has been subject to substantial discussion by economists, with one key issue being whether it provides a reliable indicator of mergers which are likely to have appreciable anti-competitive effects (as discussed in the 1st edition of *GLI: Merger Control*).

However, anti-competitive effects may not arise due to normal competitive dynamics such as the entry and expansion of competitors, or the repositioning of their products so that they become closer competitors to the parties, or the exercise of countervailing buyer power. In this regard, it should also be noted that the merger itself might change competitive dynamics by encouraging customers to seek alternative sources of supply and smaller/new suppliers to grow their business. For example, in concluding that there would not be a substantial lessening of competition in the supply of frozen ready meals (FRM) in *Kerry/Headland* (2011), the CC emphasised that:

> *"Whilst before the merger, levels of imports from the Continent were small and customers were not sufficiently familiar with the possible overseas suppliers to know to whom they could turn (we noted that while Kerry provided us with a list of 38 actual or potential importers, customers were able to name very few of these), in our view the merger has created the incentive for customers actively to research their import options, and for potential importers actively to make themselves known to UK customers; in this respect we are aware of some customers who have not switched who are currently looking at overseas alternatives."*

However, UPP raises a broader and more fundamental point about competitive effects analysis. Doane *et al* (2010) have commented that: *"Any model used to predict the effects of a merger must fit the facts of the industry in the sense that the model explains past market outcomes reasonably well."*

This comment correctly warns that caution should be applied in relying on theoretical measures of anti-competitive effects without having close regard to evidence as to how the market in question operates in practice.

In this regard, it is very striking that the CC reached unconditional clearance decisions in *Sports Direct/JJB* (2010) (relating to sports and leisure clothing and footwear) and *NBYT/Julian Graves* (2009) (relating to the retailing of nuts, seeds and dried fruit). As discussed in the 1st edition of *GLI: Merger Control*, in both these cases the CC attached considerable weight to empirical analysis of actual factual observations about outlets' PQRS in competitive and monopoly local markets, rather than theoretical modelling.

Approach to remedies (i) to avoid second stage investigation and (ii) following second stage investigation

As explained in the 1st edition of *GLI: Merger Control*, the OFT takes a fairly strict approach to first stage remedies offered to avoid second stage investigation, in line with many other jurisdictions. The OFT requires such undertakings in lieu of reference to be "clear cut" solutions to the competition concerns it has identified: in practice this typically means a structural remedy, usually a divestment of one of the overlapping businesses which has generated the competition concerns. As discussed above, the OFT has increasingly required a suitable upfront purchaser to be approved by the OFT before accepting divestment undertakings.

As regards second stage remedies, in recent years the CC has only reached adverse findings in a small proportion of merger references (as detailed above in the overview of merger control activity). Whilst the CC in theory has more scope to be creative in terms of the remedies it can impose, including behavioural remedies or a combination of structural and behavioural remedies, in practice it has invariably sought divestment remedies in recent cases. The extent of the divestments required by the CC can be very great, as illustrated by, for example, *VPS/SitexOrbis* (where VPS was required to divest all of the assets and business of SitexOrbis in Great Britain except for a carve-out of the Northern Ireland operations) and *Stagecoach/Preston Bus* (where Stagecoach was required to divest a reconfigured Preston Bus, including a depot, staff, route registrations and vehicles). The extent of divestiture required may even amount to the entirety of the acquired business, as seen in *Stericycle/ Ecowaste Southwest* (in which the remedy imposed by the CC was unsuccessfully appealed to the CAT by Stericycle), or, in the case of an anticipated merger, prohibition of the transaction, as recently seen in *Akzo Nobel/Metlac Holdings* (December 2012). More details of the process of offering remedies to the UK authorities are set out in Chapter 56 of *The ICLG to: Merger Control 2013*.

As discussed in the 1st edition of *GLI: Merger Control*, there is also a well developed process in the UK for the review of remedies at a later point in time if they have become inappropriate. By way of recent example, in April 2012 the CC published a notice confirming it had accepted variations to the undertakings given by FirstGroup plc in 2004 as a condition of the approval of its acquisition of the Scottish Passenger Rail franchise, so as to give FirstGroup plc flexibility in relation to the operation of routes covered by the undertakings which were facing disruption due to significant roadworks in Edinburgh. A detailed discussion of a range of other examples is set out in the 1st edition of *GLI: Merger Control*.

Reform proposals

In early 2011, the UK government published a major consultation document setting out proposals for major reforms to many aspects of the UK competition regime. In March 2012, it published its response to comments received during the consultation process, and its decisions on the various proposals raised. Primary legislation to implement the reforms was introduced into Parliament in May 2012, in the form of the Enterprise and Regulatory Reform Bill ("ERR Bill"). As at the end of December 2012, this Bill is being debated in the House of Lords, and is expected to become law by May 2013, with the reforms entering into force during the course of 2013/2014.

From a merger control perspective, one of the most significant reforms is the merger of the OFT and the CC into a single body, to be known as the Competition and Markets Authority ("CMA"). The current institutional separation of first stage merger reviews (undertaken by the OFT) and more detailed second stage investigations (undertaken by the CC) is seen as promoting robustness and high-quality decisions, and reducing the risk of "confirmation bias" (i.e. the tendency of people unconsciously to favour information which confirms their own beliefs or hypotheses). It is welcome that a two-stage review process is likely to be retained, with first stage decisions being taken by the CMA Board, and second stage decisions being taken by independent panels of experts (equivalent to the current CC members) to ensure a "fresh pair of eyes" at that stage. However, the precise structure of the new body and its decision-making processes is still not entirely clear, and has been the subject of considerable debate.

Assuming that the ERR Bill proceeds through the Parliamentary process as expected, it is anticipated that the CMA will be created by October 2013, and will be fully operational by April 2014. The current OFT and CC merger guidelines will be re-issued by the CMA, with amendments to reflect the new CMA structure and decision-making processes.

The government consulted on the possibility of introducing a mandatory (or hybrid mandatory-voluntary) merger regime. As discussed in more detail in the 1st edition of *GLI: Merger Control*, a key reason for considering a mandatory notification regime was the CC's experience of trying to implement remedies in relation to completed mergers where integration of the two businesses had already commenced. Introducing a mandatory notification and clearance regime would also have brought the UK regime into line with the approach adopted by the vast majority of EU regimes and the EUMR. However, the proposal was opposed by most respondents to the consultation, and the government subsequently confirmed in its response that a voluntary regime would be retained. The relevant thresholds and the substantive assessment test will also remain the same.

There will nonetheless be some important changes to certain aspects of UK merger control procedure, intended to strengthen the voluntary regime. Based on the current draft of the ERR Bill being debated in the House of Lords, these include:

- the introduction of a 40-working-day statutory timescale for all first stage merger decisions, accompanied by stronger information-gathering powers;
- giving the new CMA the discretion to trigger a power to suspend all integration steps in completed and anticipated mergers, and formally setting out in the legislation the type and range of measures that the CMA can take to prevent pre-emptive action at both the first and second stage of a merger investigation, including powers to take steps to reverse action that has already taken place;
- the introduction of new financial penalties (up to a maximum of 5% of aggregate group worldwide turnover) for integration measures taken in breach of CMA orders;
- amending the process for negotiating undertakings in lieu following the first stage decision, including introducing new deadlines for the offer, negotiation, and acceptance of such undertakings; and
- the introduction of a new 12-week statutory time limit (extendable by up to six weeks by the CMA) for the negotiation of remedies at the second stage, which will apply from the date of publication of the CMA's final report.

Finally, the government's consultation also included a suggestion that the UK competition enforcement regime should be self-financing. Despite strong opposition to any increase in merger fees, the government concluded that merger fees should be increased to achieve approximately 60% cost recovery. These increases have already been implemented, through secondary legislation which entered into force on 1 October 2012. Fees now range from £40,000 (where the UK turnover of the target is £20m or less) to £160,000 (where the UK turnover of the target is £120m or more).

Nigel Parr
Tel: +44 20 7638 1111 / Email: nigel.parr@ashurst.com
Nigel Parr is a partner and head of Ashurst's pan-European EU & Competition law department. He has been a partner since 1994. He specialises in all aspects of EU and competition law, particularly merger control, abuse of dominance and cartel investigations, together with the effect of competition law on intellectual property rights. He has extensive experience in dealing with the European Commission, the UK Office of Fair Trading, Competition Commission and Competition Appeal Tribunal, and anti-trust authorities in other jurisdictions. He has acted in relation to more than 40 second stage Competition Commission inquiries in relation to both mergers and wider market investigations. He is co-author of Parr, Finbow and Hughes, "UK Merger Control: Law and Practice", which is the leading practitioners' text book on UK merger control.

Mat Hughes
Tel: +44 20 7638 1111 / Email: mat.hughes@ashurst.com
Mat Hughes is Chief Economist in Ashurst's EU & Competition law department. He is an industrial economist, and formerly worked as an economist at the UK Office of Fair Trading. Mat advises on the economic analysis of regulatory risk under UK and EU competition law and specialist utility regulation; defences in relation to clients' mergers and acquisitions and allegations of anti-competitive practices and agreements; making submissions and complaints to regulators; and the design/development of competition law compliance programmes.

He is co-author, with Nigel Parr and Roger Finbow, of the second edition of "UK Merger Control: Law and Practice". He was co-author with David Wirth and Emily Clark of the "Analysis of economic models for the calculation of damages", which formed part of the "Study on the conditions of claims for damages in case of infringement of EC competition rules", a major review of the extent of private enforcement of competition law across the European Union, which Ashurst prepared for the European Commission.

Ashurst LLP

Broadwalk House, 5 Appold Street, London EC2A 2HA, United Kingdom
Tel: +44 20 7638 1111 / Fax: +44 20 7638 1112 / URL: http://www.ashurst.com

USA

Joshua H. Soven
Gibson, Dunn & Crutcher LLP

Overview of merger control 2011-2012

Over the past two years, the US antitrust enforcement authorities have aggressively scrutinised mergers across all sectors of the economy. The most significant developments have occurred in the technology sector, where the antitrust enforcement authorities have closely reviewed how transactions can affect parties' incentives to license standard essential patents, and in the healthcare sector, where the Federal Trade Commission (the "FTC" or "Commission") has produced a series of victories in challenges to hospital mergers. In addition, both the U.S. Department of Justice, Antitrust Division (the "DOJ") and the FTC (collectively, the "antitrust agencies") have enhanced their litigation capabilities, a development that has improved their ability to challenge transactions in court and arguably given them more leverage when negotiating settlements.

In 2013, the DOJ and FTC will have new leadership but we do not expect the personnel changes to reduce the antitrust agencies' level of enforcement. Indeed, the DOJ may increase its enforcement efforts if the new DOJ Assistant Attorney General, William Baer, is less willing than his immediate predecessors to agree to settlements with complex behavioural components. Over the past several years, these types of remedies have enabled the DOJ to resolve challenges to several substantial vertical mergers without litigation.

US merger enforcement agencies

The DOJ and FTC have largely overlapping jurisdiction to review mergers. To avoid duplicate investigations, the agencies have developed a "clearance" process, which assigns a transaction to a single agency for review. Clearance is resolved quickly in most cases because, for many sectors, the antitrust agencies agree about which agency has greater expertise. For example, the DOJ always reviews mergers that involve the electricity, financial services, and telecommunications sectors, while the FTC handles all transactions in the oil and gas production, and pharmaceutical industries. However, there are a small number of deals (in a variety of sectors) where disagreements between the antitrust agencies can delay clearance by several weeks.

The antitrust agencies bring virtually all challenges to mergers and acquisitions under Section 7 of the Clayton Act, which prohibits any transaction "where in any line of commerce or in any activity affecting commerce in any section of the country, the effect of such acquisition may be substantially to lessen competition, or to tend to create a monopoly".[1] As a practical matter, the antitrust agencies only tend to challenge transactions where there is strong evidence that a transaction is likely to result in price increases, or where the transaction would result in a substantial increase in concentration in an already concentrated market.

State Attorneys General can also challenge mergers in the United States. In most instances, Attorneys General conduct joint investigations with the DOJ and the FTC in merger investigations. In some instances, State Attorneys General seek remedies beyond those sought by the antitrust agencies, which can present challenging issues for parties when negotiating resolutions to merger challenges. During an investigation, counsel should carefully assess the interests of the participating State Attorneys General.

Private parties may also challenge a merger under the Clayton Act. Such lawsuits are unlikely to stop a merger, but they continue to rise in frequency and can impose significant litigation costs on transacting parties. The standard of proof is the same for private litigants as it is for the antitrust agencies, except that private litigants must show "antitrust injury," which means harm to the plaintiffs caused by a reduction in competition produced by the transaction.

Leadership changes

In December 2012, the US Senate confirmed William Baer as the new Assistant Attorney General for the Antitrust Division. Since Christine Varney resigned from the position in August 2011, Sharis Pozen, Joseph Wayland and Renata Hesse have served as Acting Assistant Attorney General. In March 2013, the President appointed FTC Commissioner Edith Ramirez as the new Chairman of the Commission, succeeding Jon Leibowitz, who had held the position since 2009. Ramirez joined the FTC in 2010. As noted, we expect Baer and Ramirez to maintain comparable levels of merger enforcement as their predecessors.

Merger filings and enforcement

Summary of DOJ and FTC merger activity (2011/2012)

Year	Transactions Reported	Combined DOJ/FTC Second Requests Issued	Percentage of DOJ/ FTC Second Requests Issued*	FTC Challenged** Transactions	DOJ Challenged** Transactions
2012	1,445 (est.)	Not available	Not available	25	12
2011	1,450	58	4.1%	17	20
2010	1,166	46	4.1%	22	19

* Percentage listed is of the total number of "Adjusted Transactions In Which A Second Request Could Have Been Issued", as reported and defined in Appendix A of the Hart-Scott-Rodino Annual Report, Fiscal Year 2011, available at http://ftc.gov/os/2012/06/2011hsrreport.pdf.

** Challenged transactions include challenges to reportable transactions and non-reportable transactions.

In fiscal year 2011 (covering October 1, 2010 through September 30, 2011), 1,450 transactions were reported under the HSR Act, representing approximately a 24% increase from the 1,166 transactions reported in fiscal year 2010. Fiscal year 2012 HSR data was not available at the time this article was published. However, the total number of transactions reported in fiscal year 2012 is expected to be very close to the total number reported for fiscal year 2011.

The antitrust agencies challenged 37 transactions in 2011 (compared with 41 in 2010). The DOJ challenged 20 transactions, leading to one permanent injunction against a merger, 11 consent decrees, and eight abandoned or restructured transactions.[2] The FTC challenged 17 transactions, leading to nine consent orders, three administrative complaints, and six abandoned transactions.[3]

The antitrust agencies also challenged 37 transactions in 2012. The DOJ challenged 12 transactions, leading to ten consent decrees or restructured transactions and two abandoned transactions.[4] The FTC challenged 25 transactions, leading to 15 consent orders, three administrative complaints, and seven transactions that were abandoned after the parties learned of the Commission's concerns.[5]

Hart-Scott-Rodino Act and its operation

The Hart-Scott-Rodino Act requires parties to mergers or acquisitions that satisfy certain thresholds to notify the antitrust agencies before consummating the transactions. These thresholds are indexed for inflation on an annual basis. For calendar year 2013, a transaction must be reported under the HSR Act if:

a)   the Acquiring Person will hold, as a result of the transaction, an aggregate total amount of voting securities, assets and/or interests in non-corporate entities of the Acquired Person valued at in excess of **$70.9m;** and

b)   the Acquiring Person or the Acquired Person has annual net sales or total assets of **$141.8m** or more, and the other person has annual net sales or total assets of **$14.2m** or more; or

c)   **regardless of the "size" of the Acquiring and Acquired Persons,** as a result of the transaction, the Acquiring Person will hold, as a result of the transaction, an aggregate total amount of voting securities, assets and/or interests in non-corporate entities of the Acquired Person valued at in excess of **$283.6m.**

The application of the HSR rules can be technical, and parties should consult with counsel when they decide whether they must report a transaction under the HSR Act. Failure to submit an HSR filing when required to do so, or failure to include all of the required information, can produce substantial delays in the parties' ability to close a transaction and result in significant monetary penalties.

For reportable transactions, the parties must wait 30 days (15 days in the case of a cash tender offer or a bankruptcy sale), before they may complete the transaction. During this "initial waiting period", either the DOJ or the FTC may decide to open what is termed a "preliminary investigation" into the transaction. Before either agency opens an investigation, it must receive clearance from the other agency. If the reviewing agency decides further investigation is warranted at the end of the initial 30-day period, it will serve the transacting parties with a request for additional information or "Second Request". A Second Request requires the transacting parties to produce a large volume of documents and data. The typical Second Request is very broad – asking for millions of pages of documents – but the reviewing agency will almost always agree to narrow the scope of the request.[6] The parties may not close the transaction until 30 days after they "substantially comply" with the Second Request, a process that can take a number of months. It is common for the parties to negotiate a timing agreement with the reviewing agency that: (i) specifies when the parties will substantially comply; (ii) provides for a staggered production of responsive materials to assist the efficiency of the agency's review of the materials; and (iii) guarantees that the parties will not close the transaction until a specified number of days after they substantially comply with the Second Request – often more than the 30 days provided for in the HSR statute.

Transacting parties can potentially save millions of dollars (and months of compliance time) through a proactive strategy to narrow the scope of the Second Request. The most effective strategy for saving costs and time is to persuade the reviewing agency to limit the number of official files the company is required to search. Typically, this requires demonstrating through credible information that most, if not all, of the relevant documents are located in the files of senior executives. It is also important to reach agreement with the reviewing agency about the type of data the transacting parties must produce. It is far more common for disagreements about whether the parties have produced sufficient data, as opposed to documents, to delay the parties' ability to substantially comply with a Second Request.

Neither the DOJ nor the FTC can block a transaction on its own; they must seek a preliminary and then a permanent injunction, although in most cases the parties will abandon a transaction if the agency obtains a preliminary injunction ("PI"). For the DOJ to enjoin a transaction, it must file a lawsuit in federal court. The FTC must sue in federal court to obtain a PI, but may obtain a permanent injunction in either federal court or through the Commission's administrative adjudication procedures.

Because Section 15 of the Clayton Act, pursuant to which the DOJ seeks injunctions, does not specify a standard for obtaining preliminary relief, the courts have applied various versions of the traditional equity test, including that the DOJ must show a reasonable probability that it will prevail on the merits.[7] In contrast, the FTC proceeds under Section 13(b) of the FTC Act,[8] which calls for an injunction to be granted, "[u]pon a proper showing that, weighing the equities and considering the Commission's likelihood of ultimate success, such action would be in the *public interest*."[9] For many years, it was unclear whether the courts applied the same PI standard to the DOJ and the FTC. However, in recent cases, including the FTC's *Whole Foods/Wild Oats* merger challenge,[10] the FTC has successfully argued that Section 13(b) does in fact impose a lower evidentiary hurdle than the common law equity standard. These decisions could potentially make it easier for the FTC to obtain a PI, and give the agency greater leverage when negotiating merger remedies.

Mergers involving standard essential patents

The antitrust agencies have prioritised review of transactions that involve the transfer of patents for which the owners had made commitments to standard-setting organisations ("SSOs").[11] This prioritisation is part of the antitrust agencies' decade-long focus on how the US intellectual property system affects competition, and in response to the growing amount of high-profile private litigation over standard essential patents (SEPs).

In February 2012, the DOJ closed its long-running investigations into (i) Google's acquisition of patents owned by Motorola; (ii) acquisitions by Apple, Microsoft, and Research in Motion of certain Nortel patents; and (iii) Apple's acquisition of patents formerly owned by Novell. The investigations focused on whether the acquiring firms would have the incentive to exploit ambiguities in the sellers' Fair Reasonable and Non-Discriminatory ("F/RAND") licensing commitments to SSOs to "hold up" rivals.[12] The DOJ conducted intensive buyer-specific analyses for each acquirer and concluded that each of the transactions was unlikely to alter the status quo with respect to the F/RAND commitments. Because RIM and Microsoft had low market shares in mobile platforms, the DOJ concluded that they were unlikely to pursue an unprofitable patent hold-up strategy. In contrast, Apple's and Google's substantial share of mobile platforms made it more likely that, as the owners of additional SEPs, they would hold up rivals. But with regard to Google's acquisition of the Motorola patents, the DOJ explained that "Motorola Mobility has had a long and aggressive history of seeking to capitalise on its intellectual property, and has been engaged in extended disputes with Apple, Microsoft and others... [and] that transferring ownership of the patents would not substantially alter current market dynamics."[13] With respect to Apple, the DOJ relied heavily on "Apple's commitment to honor Novell's [prior] licensing commitments".[14]

The FTC has also closely scrutinised the potential effects of mergers on the parties' licensing commitments. Late in 2012, the FTC resolved its investigation of Robert Bosch GmbH's acquisition of SPX Service Solutions with a settlement agreement that, among its provisions, included requirements that Bosch not pursue any actions for injunctive relief on certain of SPX's patents, and to make them available on a royalty-free basis to implementers of the relevant standards.[15]

Accordingly, acquirers of patents that involve SSOs or F/RAND commitments should plan to provide the reviewing antitrust agency with significant fact-based analyses as to why the transaction is not likely to affect the seller's licensing commitments. Moreover, if the agencies find that a transaction involving SEPs would likely result in the ability of the acquiring firm to raise the costs of its rivals, it appears likely that the agencies will at least strongly consider seeking some form of relief.

These cases are significant because the DOJ and the FTC are effectively asserting that the sale of a SEP to a buyer that may have different incentives than the current owner may be unlawful, regardless of whether the buyer owns assets that compete with, or are close substitutes for, the SEP. Indeed, the underlying rationale of these matters is that the sale is potentially anticompetitive precisely because there may be no close substitutes for the SEP. The validity of this position has not yet been tested in court. Notably, Commissioner Ohlhausen dissented from accepting the Bosch consent agreement in part because, in her view, the Commission had failed to identify "any meaningful limiting principles [for] the enforcement policy laid out in these cases".[16]

Health care/pharmaceuticals

Both antitrust agencies continued to devote substantial resources to enforcement in the health care sector. This reflects that US health care expenditures exceed 17% of gross domestic product, and the prices for significant portions of health care services are set by market forces rather than government regulation.

The FTC reviews most hospital mergers, and consolidations of health care facilities and physician groups. During the past 18 months, the Commission has had a string of litigation victories in the sector. Last year, the FTC successfully challenged OSF Healthcare System's proposed acquisition of Rockford Health System, alleging that the transaction would reduce the number of hospital systems in the region from three to two, and give the combined system 64% of general acute-care inpatient services in the Rockford, Illinois, area. In April 2012, the presiding district court granted the FTC's request for a preliminary injunction, and the parties then abandoned the transaction.

The FTC scored another significant victory in February 2013 when the Supreme Court ruled that the "state action" doctrine did not immunise from antitrust challenge the merger of Phoebe Putney Memorial Hospital ("Memorial") and Palmyra Medical Center ("Palmyra"), which combined account for 86% of the market for acute-care hospital services in the Albany, Georgia, region.[17] Even though it was undisputed that the transaction would create a dominant hospital in the region, the district court and the Court of Appeals both rejected the FTC's challenge, ruling that the state action doctrine protected the transaction. In reversing the Court of Appeals, the Supreme Court held that Georgia's grant of general corporate power to Memorial's parent "hospital authority" did not constitute the clearly articulated and affirmatively expressed policy to displace competition required for state action immunity to apply. The Supreme Court's ruling means that a number of hospitals that might have obtained state action protection for mergers will no longer be able to do so.

The *OSF* and *Phoebe Putney* wins, along with the FTC's successful hospital challenge in the *Promedica* case,[18] clearly signal that: (a) the Commission will continue to closely scrutinise hospital consolidations, and hospitals contemplating mergers should carefully analyse the antitrust risks; and (b) the FTC's decade-long refinement of its doctrinal and litigation strategies for litigating hospital merger cases are producing results. In particular, the Commission appears to be focusing on transactions where it is relatively straightforward to establish the relevant geographic market – which has been a significant obstacle in past challenges to hospital mergers. Second, the FTC's economists and their testifying experts are successfully convincing the courts of the soundness of their "willingness to pay" models, which focus more on competitive effects rather than market definition. Last, the FTC has brought cases that the Attorney General in the State at issue supports, which is often an important litigation advantage, given that judges frequently view hospital mergers as involving local interests.

The FTC also continued to aggressively investigate transactions in the pharmaceutical sector, requiring the parties in the Watson Pharmaceuticals/Actavis Group and Novartis/Fougera transactions to give up the rights to market certain products as a condition for clearing the deals. These actions were on top of six other pharmaceutical and medical device transactions for which the Commission required remedies in 2011 and 2012.[19]

The DOJ has responsibility for reviewing health insurance mergers. In 2012, the DOJ required Humana to divest certain Medicare Advantage plans to proceed with its acquisition of Arcadian Management Services.[20] The DOJ also closed its investigation into Wellpoint's acquisition of Amerigroup after the parties agreed to sell its Medicaid managed care plans in Virginia.[21] These matters reflect that the DOJ's attention is not limited to mergers of commercial health insurance plans, but also competition among government-sponsored managed care plans. The size and level of consolidation among these government plans is expected to grow as more of the Affordable Care Act's provisions take effect in 2013 and 2014.

Behavioural remedies

The Obama administration's aggressive litigation strategies have garnered the most attention, but arguably the most significant change from the prior administration is the degree to which the antitrust agencies, particularly the DOJ, have entered into remedies with complex "conduct" and "behavioural" components. This development provides significant opportunities for parties to accomplish strategic transactions without litigation and, potentially, divestitures, but also for third parties to gain significant benefits by influencing the substance of the antitrust agencies' behavioural remedies. For example, if persuasively framed as mechanisms to prevent the merged firm from engaging in anticompetitive foreclosure, third-parties may be able to persuade the antitrust agencies to include provisions that facilitate third-party competitors' ability to market their products.

As reported in our last edition, in 2011, Assistant Attorney General Varney updated the Antitrust Division's Policy Guide to Merger Remedies to place less emphasis on structural remedies, stating in the accompanying press release that "effective merger remedies typically include structural or conduct provisions... which the [DOJ] has found that in many vertical transactions... can prevent competitive harm while allowing the merger's efficiencies to be realised."[22]   Shortly thereafter, the DOJ agreed to remedies in the NBC/Comcast transaction that imposed significant licensing requirements on the merged firm.[23]

In August 2012, the DOJ resolved a challenge to a set of co-marketing agreements between Verizon and a group of the largest cable companies in the United States. Among other behavioural requirements, the settlement forbids Verizon from selling cable company products in certain areas where Verizon's FIOS competes with the cable companies' offerings, and bars Verizon after four years from reselling the cable companies' services to customers in areas where Verizon only offers DSL internet services.[24]

The FTC has also entered into merger agreements with significant conduct components. The FTC's remedy, in its investigation of Bosch's acquisition of SPX, required Bosch to discontinue certain SPX-exclusive dealing arrangements with wholesale distributors and independent service technicians.[25]

It remains to be seen whether the new DOJ and FTC leadership will continue to aggressively use conduct remedies. The DOJ recently rejected a proposed vertical solution when it challenged Anheuser-Busch InBev's efforts to purchase full control of Grupo Modelo. Because this transaction is largely horizontal in nature, it may not signal a departure from the DOJ's willingness to agree to conduct remedies to resolve concerns about vertical transactions.

Litigation

As discussed above, the antitrust agencies must litigate (usually in federal court) to enjoin a transaction. Between 2001 to 2007, the antitrust agencies lost four high-profile merger cases in court – *Arch Coal, Oracle, Sungard,* and *Western Refining.*[26] These defeats caused some to suggest that the antitrust agencies needed to refine their litigation strategies and courtroom skills. Since then, both agencies have prioritised enhancing their litigation capabilities. Former Assistant Attorney General Christine Varney created a litigating Deputy Assistant Attorney General position, initially filled by William Cavanaugh and later by Joseph Wayland. In addition, the DOJ appointed its first career Director of Litigation, Mark Ryan. The FTC also has a component dedicated to litigation, headed by experienced private litigators, currently headed by Edward Hassi.

Notably, both antitrust agencies have had a successful litigation record over the past two years. In 2011, a DOJ trial team headed by Wayland successfully challenged in court the *H&R Block/TaxAct* merger, where the DOJ sued to block H&R Block's proposed acquisition of TaxAct, both providers of do-it-yourself tax preparation software.[27] This was the DOJ's first courtroom victory in a merger case since 2003. In a subsequent speech, Wayland emphasised that the DOJ's strategy is to make its case by cross-examining the parties' senior executives, and he put firms on notice that the DOJ would continue to use this technique in subsequent merger challenges.[28]

The DOJ has also demonstrated that it will bring in additional high-profile litigators from private practice. In its successful challenge to the $39bn *AT&T/T-Mobile* transaction, in addition to heavy involvement from Wayland, the DOJ hired two experienced litigators to try the case. The parties abandoned the transaction prior to trial.[29] As discussed, in the last two years, the FTC has also had two significant courtroom victories in challenges to hospital merger cases for which the Commission's litigation strategy has generated substantial praise.[30]

The antitrust agencies' recent string of courtroom victories makes it more likely than ever that they will aggressively challenge in court transactions that they believe are anticompetitive, and that they are unlikely to accept "weak" remedies to avoid litigation. As noted, during the first several weeks of his tenure, Baer challenged Anheuser-Busch InBev's efforts to purchase full control of Grupo Modelo,[31] rejecting the parties' proposed vertical remedy. Parties to transactions that are likely to raise significant antitrust issues should account for this dynamic by developing a litigation strategy well before the reviewing agency makes a final enforcement decision. The antitrust agencies quickly try to assess whether transacting parties are willing to take the matter to court. If they sense that the parties are adverse to litigation, it can give the reviewing agency additional flexibility and leverage in negotiating remedies.

2010 Horizontal Merger Guidelines and unilateral effects analysis

When the antitrust agencies issued the 2010 version of the *Horizontal Merger Guidelines*, there was considerable uncertainty as to whether it would "lower the bar" for the agencies to challenge transactions or otherwise alter the antitrust agencies' methods for analysing mergers. Three years later, the antitrust agencies' enforcement record is consistent with their statements at the time they issued the new *Guidelines,* in that they reflect the methodologies that the agencies have used for years, and are not a material departure from past practices. In particular, merger policy over the last several years shows that 2010 *Guidelines* accurately explain that the agencies do not always start with market definition or structural analyses, but instead often begin with an effects-centered investigation, in which market definition is one of a number of analytical tools.

Arguably, the antitrust agencies' most significant affirmative use of the 2010 *Guidelines* was the DOJ's successful attempt to persuade the district court in the *H&R Block/TaxACT* case to adopt several core components of the antitrust agencies' approach to unilateral effects analysis.[32] Notably, the district court held that companies did not need to be "closest competitor[s]" for the merger to produce unilateral effects, and rejected the holding in *United States v. Oracle Corp.* that "'[t]o prevail on a differentiated products unilateral effects claim, a plaintiff must prove a relevant market in which the merging parties would have essentially a monopoly or dominant position."[33] Instead, the district court "decline[d] the defendants' invitation, in reliance on *Oracle,* to impose a market share threshold for proving a unilateral effects claim."[34] The antitrust agencies will no doubt actively rely on the *H&R Block/TaxACT* decision in future unilateral effects cases.

International agreements and coordination

From 2011-2012, the DOJ and FTC entered into four bilateral agreements with other competition authorities. These agreements reflect the increasing number of transactions for which the parties are required to file in multiple competition authorities, and the desire to increase the efficiency of multi-jurisdictional reviews.

India: In September 2012, the DOJ, FTC, and Competition Commission of India executed a memorandum of understanding ("MOU") that creates a general framework for cooperation on enforcement and policy matters.[35] The agreement provides that the signatories may request advice from one another to the extent permitted by the laws of each jurisdiction. Because the Competition Commission of India is a relatively new agency and the agreement contains no firm requirements, it is uncertain whether the MOU will result in material inter-agency cooperation.

European Union: In October 2011, the DOJ, FTC, and Competition Director-General of the European Commission ("EC") updated their "Best Practices on Cooperation in Merger Investigations."[36] The revised best practices provide a relatively detailed "advisory framework for interagency cooperation". They state that the reviewing agencies in the United States and the EU should: (a) contact one another upon learning of a merger that may require review in both jurisdictions; (b) keep one another informed of important developments, and when warranted, coordinate their investigations; (c) when warranted, ask the parties for information-sharing waivers; and (d) coordinate remedies discussions. The MOU also suggests that the parties plan the timing of their filings and information productions to allow the reviewing agencies to communicate and cooperate at key decision-making stages of their respective investigations. While it is uncertain whether the revised best practices will lead to more convergence in the agencies' results, they clearly reflect the agencies' strong desire for transacting parties to help the two jurisdictions coordinate merger investigations.

China: In July 2011, the DOJ and FTC signed a MOU with China's three antitrust agencies, the Ministry of Commerce, the National Development and Reform Commission, and the State Administration for Industry and Commerce.[37] The MOU provides that, if permitted by the agencies' domestic laws, the agencies will: (a) inform each other of significant competition policy and enforcement developments; (b) enhance each agency's capabilities through training programmes and workshops; and (c) comment on proposed changes to each country's competition laws, regulations, and guidelines. The MOU comes in the wake of a growing number of transactions involving US companies for which notification in China is required.

Chile: In March 2011, the DOJ, FTC, and Fiscalía Nacional Económica of Chile ("FNE") executed a cooperation agreement which provides that when the US antitrust agencies and the FNE both pursue enforcement activities with regard to related matters, they "shall consider coordination of their enforcement activities" and, when permitted by domestic law, seek to conduct their enforcement activities in a manner that is consistent with the other's enforcement objectives.[38]

Adhering to the spirit of these agreements, the US antitrust agencies in 2011 and 2012 coordinated with other competition agencies throughout the world on substantial merger investigations. For example, the DOJ cooperated with the EC on the investigation of Google's acquisition of Motorola's patent portfolio. Emphasising the agencies' close cooperation on the matter, the DOJ and the EC announced their decisions to clear the transaction on the same day, based largely on the same substantive analysis. The DOJ also coordinated its investigation with competition agencies in Australia, Canada, Israel, and South Korea.[39]

Similarly, the DOJ synchronised its remedy for the United Technologies/Goodrich transaction with the EC and the Canadian Competition Bureau. The DOJ determined that the transaction would have reduced competition for certain aircraft components, and the three agencies announced their decisions on the same day. The DOJ and EC required the parties to make similar divestitures as a condition for clearing the transaction,[40] and the Canadian Competition Bureau stated that it would take no action regarding the merger because the United States and EC remedies were likely to be sufficient to alleviate the transaction's anticompetitive effects.

In addition to these high-profile examples of coordination, the DOJ and FTC staff and political leadership frequently contact their counterparts about transactions if there is even a small possibility that they will have effects in multiple jurisdictions. Parties should assume in most cases (even if they do not provide information-sharing waivers) that there is a material possibility that the agencies will keep each other informed to the extent permissible, and parties should develop their advocacy strategies accordingly.

Proposed changes to HSR rules

The FTC's Premerger Notification Office ("PNO"), which administers the HSR filing process, informally permits an acquiring person voluntarily to withdraw a pending HSR filing and resubmit it within two business days without paying an additional fee. Pulling and re-filing an HSR filing can be an effective strategy for parties to avoid a second request, because it gives the reviewing agency a second 30-day period to determine whether a transaction warrants an extensive investigation. However, deciding whether to pull and re-file requires a careful assessment about whether the reviewing agency is in fact likely to close the investigation during the second 30-day period, because if it does not, the re-filing may prolong the investigation by delaying the issuance of a second request.

In February 2013, the FTC issued a notice seeking public comment on a set of proposed changes to the HSR regulations that codified the pull and re-file procedure.[41] The proposed rule also provides that the FTC will consider an acquiring or an acquired person's notification to have withdrawn its HSR filing if the parties make any filing that publicly announces the expiration, termination or withdrawal of a tender offer, or the termination of a merger agreement, with the U.S. Securities and Exchange Commission ("SEC"). The purpose of this change, in the case of a tender offer, is to prevent the reviewing agency from having to decide whether to conduct an investigation into a deal that is not likely to occur. The FTC is accepting comments on the proposed amendments until April 15, 2013.

* * *

Endnotes

1. 15 U.S.C. § 18.
2. *See* Hart-Scott-Rodino Annual Report, Fiscal Year 2011, *available at* http://ftc.gov/os/2012/06/2011hsrreport.pdf.
3. *Id.*

4.   *See* United States Department of Justice 2012 and 2011 Press Releases, *available at* http://www. justice.gov/atr/public/press_releases/2012/index.html.
5.   *See* FTC Competition Enforcement Database, *available at* http://ftc.gov/bc/caselist/merger/index. shtml.
6.   A Second Request also contains a number of wide-ranging questions in writing (interrogatories), which typically require lengthy responses.
7.   *See* 1 ANTITRUST LAW DEVELOPMENTS 414 (Seventh) (2012).
8.   15 U.S.C. § 53(b).
9.   *Id.* (emphasis added).
10. *FTC v. Whole Foods Mkt., Inc.*, 548 F.3d 1028, 1035 (Brown, J.), 1041-42 (Tatel, J.) (D.C. Cir. 2008).
11. *See* Joseph F. Wayland, Assistant Attorney Gen., U.S. Dep't of Justice, Antitrust Policy in the Information Age: Protecting Innovation and Competition (Sept. 21, 2012) ("In reviewing... patent acquisitions, the division has had concern that the hold-up potential of the RAND-encumbered standard-essential patents in these portfolios could be asserted against other members of the industry"), *available at* http://www.justice.gov/atr/public/speeches/287215.pdf.
12. Press Release, U.S. Dep't of Justice, Statement of the Department of Justice's Antitrust Division on its Decision to Close its Investigations of Google Inc.'s Acquisition of Motorola Mobility Holdings Inc. and the Acquisitions of Certain Patents by Apple Inc., Microsoft Corp. and Research and Motion Ltd. (Feb. 13, 2012), *available at* http://www.justice.gov/atr/public/press_ releases/2012/280190.htm.
13. *Id.* In its January 2013 enforcement action against Google, while the FTC did not seek to block or otherwise remedy the Google/Motorola merger, its complaint against Google alleged that Motorola Mobility, prior to being acquired by Google, reneged on a FRAND commitment made to several standard-setting bodies to license its SEPs relating to smartphones, tablet computers, and video game systems by seeking injunctions against firms purportedly willing to accept licenses on FRAND terms. Google continued to seek this injunctive relief after its acquisition of Motorola, and the FTC claimed that this conduct constituted a violation of Section 5 of the FTC Act because it impaired competition in the market for these electronic devices. The FTC's settlement with Google bars Google from seeking injunctions against a willing licensee, either in federal court or at the ITC, to block the use of any SEPs that the company has previously committed to license on FRAND terms. See Press Release, Federal Trade Commission, Google Agrees to Change Its Business Practices to Resolve FTC Competition Concerns In the Markets for Devices Like Smart Phones, Games and Tablets, and in Online Search (Jan. 3, 2013), *available at* http://www.ftc.gov/ opa/2013/01/google.shtm.
14. *Id.*
15. Decision and Order, Federal Trade Commission, In the Matter of Robert Bosch GmbH, Docket No. C-4357 (Nov. 26, 2012), *available at* http://www.ftc.gov/os/caselist/1210081/121126boschdo.pdf.
16. Statement of Commissioner Maureen K. Oklhausen, In the Matter of Robert Bosch GmbH, Docket No. C-4377 (Nov. 26, 2012), *available at* http://www.ftc.gov/os/caselist/1210081/121126boschohl hausenstatement.pdf.
17. *FTC v. Phoebe Putney Health Sys., Inc.*, No. 11-160 (Feb. 19, 2013).
18. Press Release, Federal Trade Commission, Citing Likely Anticompetitive Effects, FTC Requires ProMedica Health System to Divest St. Luke's Hospital in Toledo, Ohio, Area (Feb. 28, 2012), *available at* http://www.ftc.gov/opa/2012/03/promedica.shtm. In addition, in November 2012, the FTC voted to block Reading Health System's proposed acquisition of Surgical Institute of Reading L.P., in Pennsylvania, alleging that the combination of the two health care facilities would lead to reduced quality and higher health care costs for the area's employers and residents. Press Release, Federal Trade Commission, FTC and Pennsylvania Attorney General Challenge Reading Health System's Proposed Acquisition of Surgical Institute of Reading (Nov. 16, 2012), available at http:// www.ftc.gov/opa/2012/11/reading.shtm. The parties abandoned the transaction.
19. Decision and Order, Federal Trade Commission, In the Matter of Teva Pharmaceutical Industries Ltd., and Cephalon, Inc. Docket No. C-4335 (July 3, 2012), *available at* http://www.ftc.gov/os/ca selist/1110166/120703tevacephalondo.pdf; Decision and Order, Federal Trade Commission, In the Matter of Perrigo Company and Paddock Laboratories, Inc. Docket No. C-4329 (July 26, 2012), *available at* http://www.ftc.gov/os/caselist/1110083/110626perrigodo.pdf; Decision and Order, Federal Trade Commission, In the Matter of Valeant Pharmaceuticals International, Inc., Docket No. C-4343 (Feb. 22, 2012), *available at* http://ftc.gov/os/caselist/1110215/120222valeantsanofido. pdf; Decision and Order, Federal Trade Commission, In the Matter of *Grifols*, S.A. and Talecris

Biotherapeutics Holdings Corp., Docket No. C-4322 (Jul 22, 2011), *available at* http://www.ftc. gov/os/caselist/1010153/110722grifolsdo.pdf; Decision and Order, Federal Trade Commission, In the Matter of Hikma Pharmaceuticals PLC, Docket No. C-4320 (June 7, 2011), *available at* http:// www.ftc.gov/os/caselist/1110051/110607hikmabaxterdo.pdf.

20. Press Release, U.S. Dep't of Justice, Justice Department Requires Divestitures in Humana Inc.'s Acquisition of Arcadian Management Services Inc. (Mar. 27, 2012), *available at* http://www. justice.gov/opa/pr/2012/March/12-at-377.html.

21. Press Release, U.S. Dep't of Justice, Amerigroup Corp.'s Divestiture of Its Virginia Operations Addresses Department of Justice's Concerns with Wellpoint Inc.'s Proposed Acquisition of Amerigroup (Nov. 28, 2012), *available at* http://www.justice.gov/opa/pr/2012/November/12-at-1416.html.

22. *See* Press Release, U.S. Dep't of Justice, Antitrust Division Issues Updated Merger Remedies Guide: Updated Guide Recognizes Change in Merger Landscape (June 17, 2011), *available at* http://www.justice.gov/atr/public/press_releases/2011/272365.htm.

23. Final Judgment, United States v. Comcast, No. 1:11-cv-00106 (D.D.C. Sept. 1, 2011), *available at* http://www.justice.gov/atr/cases/f274700/274713.pdf.

24. Final Judgment, United States v. Verizon, No. 1:12-cv-01354 (D.D.C. Aug. 16, 2012), *available at* http://www.justice.gov/atr/cases/f286100/286102.pdf.

25. Decision and Order, Federal Trade Commission, In the Matter of Robert Bosch GmbH, Docket No. C-4357 (Nov. 26, 2012), *available at* http://www.ftc.gov/os/caselist/1210081/121126boschdo.pdf.

26. *FTC* v. Paul L. Foster, Western Ref., Inc., & Giant Indus., Inc., No. CIV 070-352 (D.N.M. May 29, 2007); *United States v. Oracle*, 331 F. Supp. 1098 (N.D. Cal. 2004); *FTC v. Arch Coal, Inc.,* 329 F. Supp. 2d 109 (D.D.C. 2004); *United States v. Sungard Data Sys., Inc.* 173 F. Supp. 2d 20 (D.D.C. 2001).

27. *United States v. H&R Block, Inc.,* 789 F. Supp. 2d 74 (D.D.C. 2011).

28. Joseph F. Wayland, Assistant Attorney Gen., U.S. Dep't of Justice, Litigation in the Antitrust Division (Sept. 19, 2012), *available at* http://www.justice.gov/atr/public/speeches/287117.pdf. *See also* J. Thomas Rosch, Commissioner, Federal Trade Commission, Changing the Way We Try Merger Cases (Oct. 25, 2012), *available at* http://www.ftc.gov/speeches/rosch/121025sedonamergertrial. pdf.

29. Press Release, U.S. Dep't of Justice, Statements Regarding AT&T Inc.'s Abandonment of its Proposed Acquisition of T-Mobile USA, Inc. (Dec. 19, 2011), *available at* http://www.justice.gov/ atr/public/press_releases/2011/278406.htm.

30. *FTC v. OSF Healthcare Sys.,* 852 F. Supp. 2d 1069 (2012); *FTC v. ProMedica Health Sys., Inc.,* No. 3:11-cv-00047, 2011 U.S. Dist. LEXIS 33434, at *45– 46 (N.D. Ohio Mar. 29, 2011); *see FTC v. CCC Holdings Inc.,* 605 F. Supp. 2d 26 (D.D.C. 2009).

31. Complaint, *United States v. Anheuser-Busch InBev SA/NA,* No. 1:13-cv-00127 (D.D.C. Jan. 31, 2013), *available at* http://www.justice.gov/atr/cases/f292100/292100.pdf.

32. *United States v. H&R Block, Inc.,* 833 F. Supp. 2d 36 (D.D.C. 2011).

33. 331 F. Supp. 2d 1098, 1123 (N.D. Cal. 2004).

34. *H&R Block*, 833 F. Supp. 2d at 83-84. The district court also relied on the DOJ/FTC *Commentary on the Horizontal Merger Guidelines* (2006), *available at* http://www.justice.gov/atr/public/ guidelines/215247.htm.

35. *Available at* http://www.ftc.gov/oia/agreements/1209indiamou.pdf.

36. *Available at* http://www.ftc.gov/os/2011/10/111014eumerger.pdf.

37. *Available at* http://www.ftc.gov/os/2011/07/110726mou-english.pdf.

38. *Available at* http://www.ftc.gov/os/2011/03/110331us-chile-agree.pdf.

39. *See* Press Release, U.S. Dep't of Justice, Statement of the Department of Justice's Antitrust Division on its Decision to Close its Investigations of Google Inc.'s Acquisition of Motorola Mobility Holdings Inc. and the Acquisitions of Certain Patents by Apple Inc., Microsoft Corp. and Research in Motion Ltd. (Feb. 13, 2012), *available at* http://www.justice.gov/atr/public/press_ releases/2012/280190.pdf; Press Release, European Commission, Mergers: Commission Approves Acquisition of Motorola Mobility by Google (Feb. 13, 2012), *available at* http://europa.eu/rapid/ pressReleasesAction.do?reference=IP/12/129.

40. *See* Press Release, U.S. Dep't of Justice, Justice Department Requires Divestitures in Order for United Technologies Corporation to Proceed with its Acquisition of Goodrich Corporation (July 26, 2012), *available at* http://www.justice.gov/atr/public/press_releases/2012/285420.pdf.

41. *Available at* http://www.ftc.gov/os/fedreg/2013/02/130214premergerfrn.pdf.

Joshua H. Soven
Tel: +1 202 955 8503 / Email: JSoven@gibsondunn.com
Joshua H. Soven is an antitrust partner in the Washington, D.C. office of Gibson, Dunn
& Crutcher. Mr Soven's practice focuses on government antitrust investigations, antitrust litigation, and counselling on competition issues. He has served in high-level
positions at both U.S. antitrust agencies. From 2007-2012, Mr Soven was Chief of the
Litigation I Section of the Antitrust Division of the Department of Justice, where he
directed investigations and litigation challenges in the insurance, consumer products,
packaging, and dairy sectors, including the reviews of the InBev/Anheuser-Busch, International Paper/Temple-Inland, Grupo Bimbo/Sara Lee, and Unilever/Alberto Cul-
ver transactions. From 2004 to 2007, Mr Soven was an Attorney Advisor to Federal
Trade Commission Chairman Deborah Platt Majoras, where he advised the Chairman
on antitrust investigations in the pharmaceuticals, media, energy, and semiconductors
sectors. From 1998 to 2004, Mr Soven served as a Trial Attorney in the Networks and
Technology Enforcement Section of the Antitrust Division of the Justice Department
where he led investigations in the software, electronic payment system, and financial
services sectors, including *United States v. First Data* (D.D.C. 2003). Mr Soven is a
Senior Editor of the *Antitrust Law Journal* and has served as a Lecturer at the Kellogg
School of Management at Northwestern University.

Gibson, Dunn & Crutcher LLP

1050 Connecticut Avenue, N.W., Washington, DC 20036-5306, USA
Tel: +1 202 955 8503 / Fax: +1 202 530 9518 / URL: http://www.gibsondunn.com